"This book is a major work from a unique ph
Wakefield traces Freud's reasoning and theore
theory of the Oedipus complex. He demonstra
Freud's formulations of infantile sexuality and O
to rescue the core proposition of the sexual theo.,
failure of the seduction theory. Wakefield's analysis of the logic and pattern of
Freud's thinking and reasoning is unmatched by anything I have read in the area
of Freud scholarship. It is as if the reader has occupied Freud's mind and is privy
to the sequence and pattern of his thoughts. An additional virtue of the book is
that even if that is not its intention, it speaks to a long-standing barrier between
clinicians, on the one hand, and theorists and researchers, on the other. Wakefield's analysis of Freud's reasoning and use of clinical data is unmatched in its
lucidity and cogency. It serves as a model for a meaningful discussion of the
use of clinical data in theory building. For anyone interested in bridging the
gap between clinical practice and theory in psychoanalysis, this book is a
must-read."

Morris Eagle *is professor emeritus at the Derner Institute for Advanced*
Psychological Studies, Adelphi University, and author of Toward a Unified
Psychoanalytic Theory: Foundation in a Revised and Expanded
Ego Psychology

Freud's Argument for the Oedipus Complex

In this close reading of Freudian theory, Jerome C. Wakefield reconstructs Freud's argument for the Oedipal theory of the psychoneuroses, placing the case of Little Hans into a philosophy-of-science context and critically rethinking the epistemological foundations of psychoanalysis.

Wakefield logically evaluates four central Freudian arguments: the "undirected anxiety" argument which contends that Hans suffered from anxiety before he developed his horse phobia; the "day the horse fell down" argument where, engaging in some scholarly detective work, Wakefield resolves a century-old dispute between behaviorists and psychoanalysts about when Hans witnessed a frightening horse accident; the "N=1 sexual repression" argument that the trajectory of Hans's sexual desires matches the Oedipal theory's predictions; and lastly, the "detailed symptom characteristics" argument that the Oedipal theory is needed to understand otherwise inexplicable details of Hans's symptoms. Wakefield demonstrates that, although Freud's arguments are brilliantly conceived, he misread the facts of the Hans case and failed to support the Oedipal theory as judged by his own stated evidential standards. However, this failure creates an opportunity for renewed consideration of psychoanalysis's distinctive contribution: the understanding of an individual's unique meaning system and confrontation with meanings outside of focal awareness in order to reshape an individual's fate.

This book will be of interest to psychoanalysts and psychotherapists alike, and will prove essential for scholars working in the fields of psychoanalysis, philosophy of science, and the history of psychiatry.

Jerome C. Wakefield is university professor, professor of social work, affiliate professor of philosophy, professor of the conceptual foundations of psychiatry in the Department of Psychiatry (2007–2019), associate faculty in the Center for Bioethics in the School of Global Public Health, and honorary faculty in the Psychoanalytic Association of New York Affiliated with NYU Grossman School of Medicine, at New York University.

PSYCHOLOGICAL ISSUES

The basic mission of *Psychological Issues* is to contribute to the further development of psychoanalysis as a science, as a respected scholarly enterprise, as a theory of human behavior, and as a therapeutic method.

Over the past 50 years, the series has focused on fundamental aspects and foundations of psychoanalytic theory and clinical practice, as well as on work in related disciplines relevant to psychoanalysis. *Psychological Issues* does not aim to represent or promote a particular point of view. The contributions cover broad and integrative topics of vital interest to all psychoanalysts as well as to colleagues in related disciplines. They cut across particular schools of thought and tackle key issues, such as the philosophical underpinnings of psychoanalysis, psychoanalytic theories of motivation, conceptions of therapeutic action, the nature of unconscious mental functioning, psychoanalysis and social issues, and reports of original empirical research relevant to psychoanalysis. The authors often take a critical stance toward theories and offer a careful theoretical analysis and conceptual clarification of the complexities of theories and their clinical implications, drawing upon relevant empirical findings from psychoanalytic research as well as from research in related fields.

Series Editor David L. Wolitzky and the Editorial Board continue to invite contributions from social/behavioral sciences such as anthropology and sociology, from biological sciences such as physiology and the various brain sciences, and from scholarly humanistic disciplines such as philosophy, law, and ethics. Volumes 1–64 in this series were published by International Universities Press. Volumes 65–69 were published by Jason Aronson. For a full list of the titles published by Routledge in this series, please visit the Routledge website: https://www.routledge.com/Psychological-Issues/book-series/PSYCHISSUES

Freud's Argument for the Oedipus Complex

A Philosophy of Science Analysis of the Case of Little Hans

Jerome C. Wakefield

Routledge
Taylor & Francis Group

NEW YORK AND LONDON

Cover image: *The Counterattack of Michelotto da Cotignola at the Battle of San Romano*; Paulo Uccello (1397–1475). Louvre, Paris, France; Mondadori Portfolio/Electa/Antonio Quattrone/Bridgeman Images.

First published 2023
by Routledge
605 Third Avenue, New York, NY 10158

and by Routledge
4 Park Square, Milton Park, Abingdon, Oxon OX14 4RN

Routledge is an imprint of the Taylor & Francis Group, an informa business

© 2023 Jerome C. Wakefield

Library of Congress Cataloging-in-Publication Data
Names: Wakefield, Jerome C., author.
Title: Freud's argument for the Oedipus complex : a philosophy of science analysis of the case of Little Hans / Jerome C. Wakefield, PhD, DSW.
Description: New York, NY : Routledge, 2023. | Includes bibliographical references and index. |
Identifiers: LCCN 2022010966 (print) | LCCN 2022010967 (ebook) | ISBN 9781032224053 (hardback) | ISBN 9781032224084 (paperback) | ISBN 9781003272472 (ebook)
Subjects: LCSH: Oedipus complex. | Graf, Herbert, 1903 or 1904-1973--Psychology. | Psychoanalysis.
Classification: LCC BF175.5.O33 W35 2023 (print) | LCC BF175.5.O33 (ebook) | DDC 150.19/52--dc23/20220518
LC record available at https://lccn.loc.gov/2022010966
LC ebook record available at https://lccn.loc.gov/2022010967

ISBN: 978-1-03222-405-3 (hbk)
ISBN: 978-1-03222-408-4 (pbk)
ISBN: 978-1-00327-247-2 (ebk)

DOI: 10.4324/9781003272472

Typeset in Times New Roman
by Taylor & Francis Books

Contents

Acknowledgments

Like the parallel volume, *Attachment, Sexuality, Power*, that is being published simultaneously with this one, this book has been in preparation for a very long time. Regrettably, I cannot thank everyone who has helped along the way, there are simply too many. My gratitude goes first and foremost to my wife Lisa Peters and my sons Joshua and Zachary Wakefield for their support, encouragement, and love, and their tolerance of the time away from them that my seemingly endless efforts on this book required. They make it all worthwhile. Lisa also provided helpful editorial feedback on some chapters.

I owe my gratitude to my teachers and colleagues in the field of philosophy of science, especially Neil Thomason, who tried so valiantly to bring my understanding up to date, and Morris Eagle, whose unequalled command of both psychoanalysis and philosophy of science made him an invaluable interlocutor in discussing the issues addressed in this work. More distantly, I owe my thanks to philosophers of psychoanalysis by whom I was inspired, including Frank Cioffi and Adolf Grunbaum, and philosophers of science by whom I was influenced in my training, including Michael Scriven, Carl Hempel, and Paul Feyerabend. As well, the manuscript was improved as a result of discussions of psychoanalytic theory with the editor of this distinguished series, David Wolitzky, and I thank him for his patience and support. I am also once again enormously grateful to my indefatigable and knowledgeable research assistant and colleague, formerly known as Jordan Conrad but now happily known as Dr. Jordan Conrad, PhD, for help with the manuscript, valuable feedback on every chapter, and many enjoyable conversations. As well, Jordan worked intensively with me as a coauthor of Chapter 4, summarizing Freud's view of the Hans case.

Finally, I thank the superb and patient team at Routledge—current and past—for seeing me through the long process that has finally yielded this book and the opportunity to share my investigations with interested readers. These include especially the senior editor and senior publisher, Kate Hawes, and wonderfully supportive editorial assistant Georgina Clutterbuck, but thanks also go to earlier editorial assistants Hannah Wright and Charles Bath, as well as the long-ago associate editor, Kristopher Spring, who initially encouraged this project.

Chapter 1

Introduction

Freud's Lakatosian Moment, or, Why Freud's Case of Little Hans is the Most Important Clinical Theory Paper Freud Ever Wrote

In this book, I provide a novel analysis and critical evaluation of Freud's argument for his construct of the Oedipus complex and for his central clinical-theoretic hypothesis, the Oedipal theory of the etiology of the psychoneuroses, that dominated psychoanalysis for a century. Despite its centrality to Freud's influence on psychology as well as our broader culture, I believe that Freud's argument for his Oedipal theory has not been adequately reconstructed and evaluated previously. I also rethink Freud's epistemological defense of his psychoanalytic methodology against the potent "suggestion objection" (as I call it) that Freud was merely suggesting the right answers to his patients rather than uncovering veridical Oedipal memories. Along the way, I solve a century-old mystery at the heart of a dispute between Freudians and behaviorists about when a certain horse accident occurred.

My examination of Freud's argument proceeds by a close analysis of Freud's case history, "Analysis of a Phobia in a Five-Year-Old Boy" (1909a), more commonly known as the case of "Little Hans" after the pseudonym Freud gave the boy. This is the case in which Freud presented his most explicit defense of the Oedipal theory, yet scholars have generally paid it less attention than Freud's other case histories. My reasons for focusing on the Hans case go well beyond its explicit concern with Hans's Oedipus complex. They include a new appreciation of the case's crucial role in Freud's overall defense of his clinical theory against the most prominent rival theory—the "fright theory", as I will call it—and against the suggestion objection. The evaluation of Freud's clinical theory has often proceeded as if the Hans case, being a child case and one not treated first-hand by Freud, is thereby of lesser interest than his other cases and clinical theory papers, but I will argue that it is uniquely important in evaluating Freud's Oedipal theory from an epistemological philosophy of science perspective, and that Freud understood it as such.

After some introductory material, I explain why this case is uniquely important to Freud's clinical project when understood from a philosophy of science perspective. I use the insights and terminology of the philosopher of science Imre Lakatos to clarify Freud's scientific theoretical development and the situation he faced at the time of the Hans case report. As I intend the

DOI: 10.4324/9781003272472-1

phrase, a philosophy of science analysis includes logical reconstruction of arguments, concepts, and methodological assumptions, and once clarity is achieved, a comparative evaluation of the evidential support and explanatory power of the given theory in comparison with available rival theories, taking into account both confirmatory and disconfirmatory evidence. The characteristics of what I am calling a philosophy of science analysis are quite different from a clinical-interpretive approach in which a presupposed theory is used to understand and interpret a patient's associations. Such clinical approaches may seem "confirmed" by the ability to apply them to find what appear to be illuminating hidden meanings in the patient's statements. However, as we know, many different mutually contradictory theories can be confirmed in this way because the ability to find illuminating meanings hidden within a patient's associations is not necessarily an indicator of the truth of the presupposed theory but can be instead the result of the cleverness and degrees of interpretive freedom of the interpreter. This is true of science in general, for there are generally many different theories of a given domain of data and partisans of a given theory can always find confirmatory aspects that are consistent with the theory. Science progresses instead by proposing empirical tests that will differentiate between theories, by assessing the strengths of rival theories in accounting for existing data, by considering evidence that disconfirms rather than only evidence that corroborates, and by evaluating the comparative evidential support and explanatory and predictive power among available rival theories.

Background to the Hans Case and the Oedipal Theory

The boy in question in the Little Hans case was Herbert Graf, who was treated for a horse phobia, a serious matter in 1908 Vienna, which boasted roughly 70,000 horses at the time. The phobia started in early January 1908 when Herbert was four-and-three-quarters years old and was resolved in May, shortly after his fifth birthday in April. Herbert was analyzed by his father, Max Graf, an eminent music critic who at that time was an avid follower of Freud's and a member of his inner psychoanalytic circle. He analyzed Herbert with Freud's frequent guidance and in one instance his personal intervention. Herbert Graf went on to a distinguished career as an opera stage director and served for many years in this capacity at the Metropolitan Opera in New York City before returning to Europe to be the general manager of the Grand Theatre in Geneva. (For details on Herbert's family's history, see Wakefield, 2022.) For consistency with quoted text, from here on I will generally refer to Herbert as "Hans."

The Hans case is distinctive in many ways. It is the first recorded instance of child analysis, the clearest account of Freud's theory of phobias as displaced anxiety, and the first depiction of psychoanalytic supervision, with Freud guiding Hans's father in performing the analysis. But above all, the Hans case is the original and most direct clinical evidence Freud provided for his Oedipal theory of child psychosexual development and his sexual theory of neurosogenesis—Freud's theory that all neuroses originate etiologically in specifically sexual difficulties. Freud claimed that the results of the Hans case validated the results of his adult analyses, and he repeatedly cited this point in his subsequent writings (see Chapter 3). For these reasons, the case is still required reading in most psychoanalytic training institutions. During the period of Freud's cultural ascendancy, the case was widely read by undergraduate college students in psychology and humanities courses. It even appeared as a historical example of a phobia in the DSM-IV-TR Casebook (Spitzer et al., 2002).

After Freud published his controversial theories concerning early childhood sexual development in his *Three Essays on the Theory of Sexuality* (1905b), he asked his followers to keep diaries of their children's development that might be used to support his theories. Hans's parents proceeded to do so, periodically sending notes to Freud, and Freud published some papers based on these diaries of Hans's normal development to support his theory of child sexuality. However, at a certain point Hans developed a horse phobia and the diary and the submission of notes to Freud continued as a clinical case record of Hans's psychoanalysis by his father with Freud's guidance, forming the basis for the publication of the Hans case history.

There are many attempts to analyze the Hans case. I limit myself here to an examination of Freud's 1909 account, with occasional reference to some altered views he expressed later as his theory of anxiety evolved. As noted, I also consider two rival theories. One is the "suggestion objection," that the insights that Freud's patients reported were not veridical memories but resulted instead from Freud subtly—and, as we shall see, sometimes not-so-subtly—suggesting to the patients what he wanted them to report (see Chapters 2 and 3). The other is the "fright theory," that nonsexual emotions such as fear can cause neuroses (see Chapter 5). For a few of the many other accounts, from Bowlby to family therapy, see Midgley's (2006) review and Wakefield (2022).

Hans developed a horse phobia after witnessing a horse accident in which a horse pulling a bus-wagon fell down in the streets of Vienna. Freud interpreted the boy's subsequent intense fear of horses as resulting not from the accident itself but from how the horse accident symbolized Hans's unconscious desires and conflicts. These consisted specifically of his sexual desire for his mother and jealous anger toward, and fear of revenge from, his father. This is the set of interrelated mental contents that Freud called the "Oedipus complex," after Sophocles's play in which Oedipus kills his father and marries his mother. The Oedipal theory hypothesized a universal developmental stage of male psychosexual development at about the ages of two to five years old in which a son experiences intense sexual desire for his mother. This inchoate but specifically sexual desire—potentially involving bodily premonitions of copulatory movement—is accompanied by angry jealousy of the boy's father for possessing his mother and a resultant desire to get rid of or kill the father. The boy's sexual and aggressive fantasies cause a fear of vengeful retribution by his father in the form of castration (actually, penectomy), a form of punishment that would remove the organ that is the origin of the pleasurable feelings that create the offending desire. However, the son also loves and needs the father, so he is conflicted about his jealous and murderous feelings. Freud's central clinical-theoretic claim is that all psychoneuroses originate from a failure to resolve the Oedipus complex and are thus ultimately always generated by sexual issues.

Here, for example, is how Freud described the Oedipus complex in an encyclopedia article:

> In the very earliest years of childhood (approximately between the ages of two and five) a convergence of the sexual impulses occurs of which, in the case of boys, the object is the mother. This choice of an object, in conjunction with a corresponding attitude of rivalry and hostility towards the father, provides the content of what is known as the Oedipus complex, which in every human being is of the greatest importance in determining the final shape of his erotic life. It has been found to be characteristic of a normal individual that he learns to master his Oedipus complex, whereas the neurotic subject remains involved in it.
>
> (1923, pp. 245–246)

Freud thus claimed that the underlying source of Hans's anxieties was that he was "a little Oedipus who wanted to have his father 'out of the way', to get rid of him, so that he might be alone with his beautiful mother and sleep with her" (1909a, p. 111). Freud claimed that because Hans's desires could not be satisfied and were suppressed, they emerged in anxiety symptoms triggered by unconscious associations to the horse accident. (A full description of Freud's account of Hans's phobia is provided in Chapter 4.)

Note that unlike commentators who attempt to soften Freud's blunt Oedipal formulations regarding incestuous sexuality and murderous rage by interpreting Freud's talk of sex and aggression as elliptical for broader sensual feelings or feelings related to cultural gender norms and so on, I take Freud's assertions as he clearly intended them, as statements about a child's literal sexual and murderous feelings. The Oedipal theory builds on many partial truths about triangular family relationships that are short of claims about universal psychosexual developmental stages, but that was not what Freud had in mind. Nor did he have in mind an occasional form of pathology, as some other theorists have interpreted the Oedipus complex. Rather, according to Freud, the Oedipus complex is a normal and essential universal stage of psychological development, and the resolution of the Oedipus complex propels the boy's psychological development forward in multiple ways. As Morris Eagle (2018) observes, "how the individual resolves oedipal conflicts plays a determinative role in psychological development, including sexual identity, superego formation, and the capacity to integrate love and desire" (pp. 95–96). And, Freud holds, all psychoneuroses are caused by something going wrong in the child's resolution of this stage of psychosexual development.

Freud reaffirmed the theory and its centrality throughout his work, from the earliest statements in *The Interpretation of Dreams* ("Being in love with the one parent and hating the other are among the essential constituents ... determining the symptoms of the later neurosis" [Freud, 1900, p. 261]) to his last works published posthumously ("I venture to say that if psycho-analysis could boast of no other achievement than the discovery of the repressed Oedipus complex, that alone would give it a claim to be included among the precious new acquisitions of mankind" [Freud, 1940, pp. 192–193]). Indeed, he insisted that acceptance of the Oedipal theory "has become the shibboleth that distinguishes the adherents of psycho-analysis from its opponents" and that "every new arrival on this planet is faced by the task of mastering the Oedipus complex" (Freud, 1905b, p. 226, n.1 [footnote added 1920]). As philosopher Patricia Kitcher says: "Nothing was more central or more original in psychoanalysis than the postulation of the Oedipus complex" (1992, p. 107).

The Oedipal theory remained at the heart of Freud's clinical theory for much of a century, guiding psychoanalytic interpretations and shaping patients' views of themselves and their relationships to their family members. Moreover, the Oedipal theory captured the minds of a wider audience of intellectuals and laypersons, exerting a strong influence on the arts, literature, the humanities, and the popular culture of the educated lay public. More than any other specific hypothesis, the Oedipus complex constituted the core of what Freud's theory became for our culture. Although psychoanalysis has been moving past the dominance of the Oedipal theory over the past few decades, a clear understanding of the argument for and scientific status of the Oedipal theory can still be of use in helping psychoanalysis to construct a fruitful future.

Why Select the Hans Case Versus One of Freud's Other Case Histories for Evaluation of His Oedipal Argument?

The Hans case is one of only five full-length case analyses that Freud published. The other four are the cases of Dora (1905a), the "Rat Man" (1909b), the "Wolf Man" (1918), and Schreber (1911). (The case of Anna O. is sometimes mentioned but was authored by Freud's colleague, Josef Breuer [1895].) However, the importance of these cases in evaluating the scientific status of Freud's mature clinical theory varies greatly.

Freud's study of Schreber consists of an analysis of Schreber's (1903/2000) published memoir detailing his psychotic illness. Freud never saw or treated Schreber. Moreover, in attempting to extend his theory of the neuroses to the psychoses, Freud arrived at a dubious analysis of paranoid schizophrenia as a projection of repressed homosexuality.

"Dora" was an eighteen-year-old girl when Freud saw her in October 1900 for symptoms such as mutism and a chronic cough that Freud diagnosed as hysteria. The case, as Freud acknowledges, was a failure because Dora fled therapy after eleven weeks, likely due to Freud's heavy-handed and questionable sexual interpretations according to which Dora was in love with her father, sexually desirous of her father's friend, Herr K., who had attempted to seduce her, and also in love with Herr K.'s wife, who Dora knew was having an affair with Dora's father.

Although the Dora case was published earlier than the Hans case, it is not a good target for evaluation of Freud's argument for his shift to the Oedipal theory for three reasons. First, Freud was still transitioning from the seduction theory to the Oedipal theory and the case has a confusing theoretical muddiness to the point that there are debates as to what Freud actually believed or was willing to say at the time. Freud seems to be waffling as he works his way toward a clear acknowledgment of the changes in his theory in 1906. Second, unlike the Hans case, Freud does not present the detailed back-and-forth between patient and analyst in the Dora report that is required for understanding the evidence that led him to specific conclusions, and is provided in the Hans case. In fact, he declares at the outset that he will not explain how he inferred his various conclusions:

> There is another kind of incompleteness which I myself have intentionally introduced. I have as a rule not reproduced the process of interpretation to which the patient's associations and communications had to be subjected, but only the results of that process. Apart from the dreams, therefore, the technique of the analytic work has been revealed in only a very few places.
>
> (1905a, pp. 12–13)

The reason for this—and the third problem—is that, whereas the Hans case is explicitly aimed at the goal of providing more direct evidence for the Oedipal theory, the Dora case, which actually occurred in 1900, shortly after the publication of Freud's *Interpretation of Dreams*, is "intended to show the way in which the interpretation of dreams plays a part in the work of analysis" (p. 15). Freud thus organized the case presentation around the analysis of two dreams and described it as "a continuation of the dream book" (p. 4).

Consequently, the Hans case is one of only three credible full-length psychoanalytic case histories in which Freud applied his mature Oedipal theory. It is the earliest of these (although not by much—the Rat Man case appeared in the next issue of the same journal), thus potentially the most illuminating of Freud's recent theoretical shift. Yet, relative to the Rat Man and Wolf Man cases, the Hans case has tended to be downplayed or dismissed. This may be because Hans's father, not Freud himself, performed Hans's analysis. Moreover, a child's analysis is less complex than an adult's, and Hans's fear of horses can be dismissed as less serious than the severe problems afflicting the Rat Man and Wolf Man. However, for Freud's purposes, this relative straightforwardness of the Hans case is precisely the case's value. In the two adult analyses, childhood events are speculatively reconstructed long after the fact and through many layers of accumulated meaning. Such retrospective reconstruction is precisely what Freud wanted to minimize in the Hans case in order to maximize the directness and persuasiveness of the evidence and make the Hans case a unique epistemological document.

Regarding the Hans case's relative simplicity and superficiality compared to Freud's full-blown adult analyses, Freud comments in the Wolf Man case that the Hans case is relatively simple because children have not yet built up years of additional psychical structures on top of their original early memories, and also because of the relative directness of expression of child desires and fantasies. Such a case is "more trustworthy, but it cannot be very rich in material" (1918, p. 8). From an epistemological perspective, it is evidential trustworthiness rather than richness of material that you are looking for. The simplicity is an advantage because the case provides more direct access to evidence for or against the most basic Freudian hypotheses, even if it fails to manifest some of the more complex and clinically challenging epicycles that emerge in adult analyses. Of course, if you are already a convinced Oedipal theorist or clinician, then it will be of more interest to explore the nuances and complexities of an adult analysis. However, if you are interested in whether the Oedipal theory is scientifically valid and in assessing Freud's argument for the theory's basic hypotheses, the simpler situation has its advantages.

The Epistemological Advantages of the Transcribed Evidence in the Hans Case

There is a further important reason why, for those interested in evaluating the scientific status of Freud's interpretations of clinical data, the Hans case is underappreciated as an epistemologically unique record. Hans's father, Max, who performed the analysis, transcribed his discussions with Hans in shorthand during or shortly after each session and regularly sent the record of his conversations with Hans to Freud (Freud at one point indicates that he received his "Weekly Report from Hans's Father" [1909a, p. 32]). Indeed, in the original German publication, Freud indicates that the case is merely "communicated by" him rather than written by him. It is the father's record of the analysis, not Freud's version of it, that is presented in the published case history, along with Freud's added running commentary and discussion section. As Freud explains in his introduction, he is reproducing verbatim Hans's father's diary of the analysis as it was given to him:

> The case history is not, strictly speaking, derived from my own observation ... the treatment itself was carried out by the child's father, and it is

to him that I owe my sincerest thanks for allowing me to publish his notes upon the case ... I shall now proceed to reproduce his father's records of little Hans just as I received them.

(pp. 5–6)

Moreover, we know that Max retained a copy of the published case history because, in a later interview, Hans reports that he eventually became aware of his being Little Hans years later when, packing his father's books for a move, he discovered a copy of the publication on his father's bookshelf. Although of an agreeable personality sometimes to a fault, Max was not hesitant about assertively challenging Freud (Wakefield, 2007), and it is unlikely that Freud would have tampered with Max's case notes knowing the book would be seen by him.

We can be confident that the father was, indeed, taking notes during the treatment because the note-taking and the sending of the notes to "the Professor" (as Hans and his father referred to Freud) become topics of conversation within the analysis. For example, when Hans tells his father about a dream he had about two giraffes, the father observes that Hans "noticed that I was taking everything down, and asked: 'Why are you writing that down?'" (1909a, p. 38). When the father informs Hans that "I shall send it to a Professor," Hans, apparently thinking back to another instance of such note-taking when he reported a fantasy, says, "Oho! So you've written down as well that Mummy took off her chemise, and you'll give that to the Professor too," to which his father answers "Yes" (p. 38). Again, when his father accuses Hans of thinking about masturbating, Hans objects that "it is good all the same, because you can write it to the Professor" (p. 72). Hans even approaches his father and expresses his readiness to engage in analysis with the opening comment: "D'you know what? Let's write something down for the Professor" (p. 97). The recording of the analysis was an integral part of the analytic process.

The importance of this feature of the Hans case for an analysis of Freud's reasoning is underscored by issues with regard to the accuracy of Freud's other case histories. Historians of psychoanalysis have discovered Freud's original notes written out each night for about the first third of the Rat Man's treatment and compared them to the published case history. Significant discrepancies have been identified, with alterations even of such basic information as how long the case lasted in ways that strengthened the plausibility of Freud's account (Mahony, 1986). Even Freud's defenders acknowledged the distortions, while attempting to minimize them, as in Peter Gay's (1988) comment that the publication followed the process notes "apart from a handful of interesting deviations" (p. 262). Given that the persuasiveness of Freud's interpretations often depends on subtle points in the therapeutic interaction, the fact that these "interesting deviations" occur in the only known fragment of Freud's notes leads to a natural suspicion that the details of other published cases may not be entirely reliable as well. Indeed, similar worries have been raised about the reliability of the Dora case record. Rather than taking daily notes, Freud wrote up the case from memory after it ended, and some dates mentioned by Freud that could be independently checked have been found to be grossly in error, encouraging concern about more subjective potential lapses. As we shall see, even in the Hans case itself, in his commentary, Freud errs in important ways on factual matters relevant to the plausibility of his interpretations, despite the case record being before him. However, due to the case record, these errors can be immediately corrected and his interpretations reassessed.

When Freud's interpretations in various case histories are criticized, analysts often reply—and Freud himself said—that the problem is that in a case history the narrative does not include a full account of the back-and-forth providing the context for the intervention. Due to Max's transcription, the Hans case is unique in being close to a full transcript of the case. There were interactions between Max and Freud outside of the analytic sessions between Max and Hans, but where such interactions impacted Max's treatment, the case record indicates that Freud suggested that Max adopt a certain strategy or offer a certain explanation to Hans. The one actual interaction between Freud and Hans is recorded in the case record in detail. Consequently, the case data and Freud's inferences from the case data in reaching his conclusions can be separated and their relationship assessed with some confidence. In this crucial respect, the Hans case is unique among the case histories as a basis for assessing Freud's theoretical inferences from case data.

Lakatos on Empirically Progressive Versus Ad Hoc Degenerative Reactions to Theory Falsification

I now turn to a more profound reason for focusing on the Hans case: simply put, the Hans case is the most important clinical theory paper Freud ever wrote—at least from a philosophy of science perspective, for the purpose of assessing the scientific status of his Oedipal-theoretic claims. The reason is that the Hans case is where Freud sought to save his Oedipal theory from the potentially fatal accusation that it was an ad hoc hypothesis with no independent motivation for acceptance other than that it saved his cherished sexual theory of the neuroses from falsification. (There is also a second overlapping reason for the Hans case's special importance—namely, that the Hans case is Freud's only data-based attempt to respond to the suggestion objection, which is considered in Chapter 3.) To understand the challenge to which Freud was responding, in the sections following this one I review the nature of Freud's shift from his earlier "seduction theory" of hysteria to the Oedipal theory. But first, in this section I present some basic philosophy of science concepts needed to understand the scientific situation Freud confronted at the time he put forward the Oedipal theory.

For a philosophy of science perspective useful for understanding Freud's situation, I will rely on some of the terminology and concepts that philosopher of science Imre Lakatos (1968; 1970) devised to describe the nature of scientific progress, and especially to explain how science often progresses after a theory is falsified. In referring to Lakatos's views, I am neither endorsing his account as a general account of scientific progress or scientific methodology nor embracing all of the ways he himself understood these phenomena. I am rather borrowing some basic aspects of his account that prove useful for understanding Freud's particular theoretical development— and tweaking those a bit to adapt them to Freud's situation. Lakatos's concepts and terms are useful in this context because he attempts to understand precisely the kind of scientifically challenging position in which, I will argue, Freud found himself at the time of the Hans case, and offers commonsense guidelines that most scientists and philosophers of science would likely accept.

In trying to understand how scientific progress occurs, Lakatos is particularly concerned with a specific and frequent phenomenon in science in which a theory that has previously exhibited promising explanatory power and evidential support encounters a potentially falsifying empirical result. Whereas it would be easy to understand such a situation as demanding the abandonment of the theory and a discontinuous leap to a new theory, Lakatos sees these situations as yielding opportunities for the core part of the original theory to extend itself continuously in order to meet the challenges raised. Lakatos does not see typical scientific theories as univocal isolated entities that confront the world in an all-or-nothing manner. Instead, specific theories are parts of larger research programs that encompass a sequence of theories in a continuous theoretical effort to develop a core idea. Each individual theory in the research program is composed of many different claims and hypotheses that are often somewhat independent of each other, so that there are generally ways of adjusting some of a theory's assertions or assumptions while keeping other, more central components constant.

Lakatos argues that theorists and researchers do not consider all the statements in the theory to be equal. Among the many hypotheses that make up a theory, theorists are generally committed to some core idea of the theory that they consider to be the theory's primary insight or most distinctive contribution. Other auxiliary hypotheses, assumptions, parameter settings, and further less-critical details of the overall theory may be considered the "periphery" of the theory relative to the highly valued core. Note that one need not embrace an inflated notion of the core as something fixed and absolute; it may vary over time, have gradations so that some claims have more "coreness" than others, and depend on what specific theorists think is central at a given point in time. Nonetheless, members of a research community will often struggle to hold onto a core insight even when the overall theory has experienced a falsification, and they will attempt to do so by adjusting the periphery of the falsified theory in a way that eliminates the falsification but preserves the core insight and the explanatory power that the theory has already achieved. In sum, according to Lakatos, the core idea of a research program may be preserved despite falsification of a specific theory by making changes to peripheral features of that theory that eliminate the falsification. The new theory ideally retains the power to explain everything that the old theory explained, so there is no loss in explanatory power.

Multiple research programs with rival core ideas about a given phenomenon will often be competing in a field to offer the most explanatory power and achieve the most evidential support. Lakatos suggests that in the event of theory falsification, a research program follows a "positive heuristic" of what to do—namely, change the peripheral auxiliary hypotheses to evade the falsification—and a "negative heuristic" of what not to do—namely, do not alter the core. The peripheral aspects of a theory can thus be thought of as a "protective belt" of assumptions that can be altered to protect the core.

However, following the positive and negative heuristics and thereby saving the core of one's research program from falsification raises a serious problem. Thus far, there is no reason to think that the adjustments represent advancement toward the truth. Given the degrees of freedom open to a theorist in adjusting a theory and the cleverness of theorists, presumably almost any theory can be adjusted again and again to evade apparent disconfirmations while retaining core doctrines. This tactic, in which one creates an amendment to a theory in order to defend one's most cherished ideas against falsification, but where that is the only virtue of the altered theory, is pejoratively labeled an "ad hoc hypothesis" or "ad hoc revision." That is a pejorative in science because a purely ad hoc revision offers no new evidence in return for the new beliefs one is adopting. Indeed, it is precisely the persistent creation of such ad hoc explanations to preserve a beloved doctrine that characterizes pseudoscience and dogma and protects them against contrary evidence. So, the question is why anyone should take the revised theory seriously as a scientific hypothesis when the motivation for its construction is to evade falsification, whereas openness to falsification by data is an essential property of science.

The answer Lakatos offers is that there is a crucial difference between empirically fruitful versus *purely* ad hoc adjustments to a theory, yielding a distinction between what he called "progressive" versus "degenerating" research programs. Ad hoc adjustments that merely evade falsification and preserve the core of a theory without successfully predicting anything new in return for the new peripheral hypotheses imply that the research program is degenerating and cannot be taken seriously as a scientific—as opposed to dogmatic or pseudoscientific —proposal. What makes for legitimate science is when the adjustment to the theory is progressive—that is, when the altered theory not only explains everything the old version of the theory explained but also predicts something new, and preferably something the prediction of which is unexpected, bold, novel, and risky, offering persuasive evidence. Revised theories may be looked at with some suspicion and skepticism until the new prediction can be successfully tested, but if the test is successful, then the theory is likely to be taken seriously as possible scientific progress rather than a pseudoscientific defense of a dogma.

Thus, if we think of a "Lakatosian moment" in science as the moment on which Lakatos focuses at which a theorist confronts a clear falsification of their theory, the response that is required according to Lakatos involves two essential components, if the larger research program is to continue to be considered progressive and to be taken seriously as science, not pseudoscience. First, the theory's peripheral hypotheses must be adjusted in a way that saves the research program's core hypothesis and continues to explain all that the theory formerly explained. Second, the adjusted peripheral hypotheses must be shown to have new and persuasive predictive powers and are not purely ad hoc devices for avoiding falsification of the core.

This is the apt schema Lakatos provides for understanding how scientists attempt to preserve a core hypothesis and retain its explanatory power when the theory in which it appears has been falsified, and at the same time attempt to avoid descending into ad hoc pseudoscience so that the altered theory is taken seriously. To achieve this, they must show that the altered theory has more to recommend it than just saving the theorist's core hypothesis. It must produce some new and bold empirical knowledge, thus expanding the theory's explanatory power. This requirement seems to express scientific common sense that transcends the details of Lakatos's or any other particular philosophy of science system.

I will use Lakatos's schema as a framework for understanding Freud's specific situation when he confronted the falsification of his seduction theory (discussed below). Freud saved his core sexual theory of the neuroses from that falsification by proposing the Oedipal theory. But, as we shall see, Freud then finds himself in the position of needing a bold, novel prediction to avoid the accusation that the Oedipal theory is a purely ad hoc hypothesis. The Hans case was his solution.

Freud's Lakatosian Moment

To explain Freud's Lakatosian moment, I must briefly recount the history of theoretical developments that got Freud to that point. Freud's theory of the sexual etiology of the neuroses started out as a theory of what he variously referred to as the "simple," "common," or "actual" neuroses. This included neurasthenia proper, a kind of nervous depletion often attributed to the demands of modern civilization, and anxiety neurosis, originally a subtype of neurasthenia which Freud split off into a separate category. Freud theorized that the actual neuroses had exclusively somatic sexual etiologies; neurasthenia proper was caused by excessive sexual discharge due to masturbation or persistent emissions and anxiety neurosis was caused by inadequate discharge due to unconsummated excitement or coitus interruptus.

At the same time, Freud was working with Joseph Breuer to develop psychological treatment for the psychoneuroses, primarily hysterical neuroses that had a variety of physical symptoms with no discoverable physiological basis, and obsessional neuroses. It was well-known that hysterical symptoms were sometimes triggered by physical traumas or emotional traumas such as extreme fright, and Breuer and Freud theorized that behind other hysterical neuroses in which no such obvious physical or emotional trauma was known to have taken place there were in fact unremembered psychological traumas that caused, maintained, and were symbolically expressed in the symptoms. They attempted to recover these unconscious traumatic memories, initially using hypnosis. Although they emphasized sexual traumas as a cause of hysteria, given the frequent triggering of hysterical neurosis by emotions such as fright, Breuer was explicitly opposed to the idea of a universal sexual explanation of the psychoneuroses, and Freud initially accepted this approach:

> At the time at which I was attributing to sexuality this important part in the production of the *simple* neuroses, I was still faithful to a purely psychological theory in regard to the *psychoneuroses*—a theory in which the sexual factor was regarded as no more significant than any other emotional source of feeling.
>
> (1906, p. 272)

Nonetheless, given the frequent comorbidity and similar symptoms of the two types of neuroses—for example, anxiety often accompanied hysterical symptoms—Freud eventually put forward a unified sexual theory of the actual and psychoneuroses: "in view of the close connections between the psychoneuroses and the simple neuroses ... it could not be long before the knowledge arrived at in the one field was extended to the other" (pp. 272–273).

Freud supported his sexual theory of the psychoneuroses with the results of his psychoanalyses of hysterical patients in which he pushed his explorations for memories related to the patient's symptoms ever earlier in search of repressed traumas that would adequately explain the patient's symptoms. At first, he arrived at sexual incidents around puberty. However, the pubertal memories were often either too trivial or too lacking in suitable details to serve as adequate traumatic explanations of the hysterical symptoms. So, Freud continued his explorations further back into childhood:

> Luckily for our explanation, some of these sexual experiences at puberty exhibit a further inadequacy, which is calculated to stimulate us into continuing our analytic work. For it sometimes happens that they, too, lack suitability as determinants ... [W]e must look for the determinants of these symptoms ... in experiences which went still further back ... In doing so, to be sure, we arrive at the period of earliest childhood.
>
> (1896, p. 201)

In his patients' repressed memories from earliest childhood, Freud claimed to find the sexual traumas that he sought:

If we have the perseverance to press on with the analysis into early childhood, as far back as a human memory is capable of reaching, we invariably bring the patient to reproduce experiences which, on account both of their peculiar features and of their relations to the symptoms of his later illness, must be regarded as the aetiology of his neurosis for which we have been looking. These *infantile* experiences are once more *sexual* in content, but they are of a far more uniform kind than the scenes at puberty that had been discovered earlier. It is now no longer a question of sexual topics having been aroused by some sense impression or other, but of sexual experiences affecting the subject's own body—of *sexual intercourse* (in the wider sense). You will admit that the *importance* of such scenes needs no further proof; to this may now be added that, in every instance, you will be able to discover in the details of the scenes the *determining* factors which you may have found lacking in the other scenes—the scenes which occurred later and were reproduced earlier.

(pp. 202–203)

This led Freud to affirm the thesis that he often calls the "sexual aetiology of the neuroses" but I will call the "sexual theory of the neuroses" (STN) both for the category of hysteria and the psychoneuroses in general:

I therefore put forward the thesis that at the bottom of every case of hysteria there are *one or more occurrences of premature sexual experience,* occurrences which belong to the earliest years of childhood but which can be reproduced through the work of psycho-analysis in spite of the intervening decades. I believe that this is an important finding, the discovery of a *caput Nili* in neuropathology.

(p. 203)

Combined with his theory of the actual neuroses, Freud thus proposed a general sexual theory of the neuroses in which the difference between actual neuroses and the psychoneuroses concerned whether the sexual cause was somatic and in the present or psychologically mediated and in repressed unconscious memories of the past:

it was possible at that time to draw a contrast between the common neuroses as disorders with a *contemporary* aetiology and psychoneuroses whose aetiology was chiefly to be looked for in the sexual experiences of the remote past. The theory culminated in this thesis: if the *vita sexualis* is normal, there can be no neurosis.

(1906, pp. 273–274)

Freud held that such early sexual experience was not only sometimes what explained hysteria but that it was a necessary condition for development of hysteria: "a person who has not had sexual experiences earlier can no longer become disposed to hysteria" (1896, p. 212).

Freud was to embrace the STN as his core clinical theory thesis for the rest of his life. For example, ten years later, after Freud had given up the seduction theory and shifted to the Oedipal theory, he offered basically the same core thesis and his rationale for holding it:

> [E]xperiences were eventually reached which belonged to the patient's childhood and related to his sexual life. And this was so, even in cases in which the onset of the illness had been brought about by some commonplace emotion of a non-sexual kind. Unless these sexual traumas of childhood were taken into account it was impossible either to elucidate the symptoms (to understand the way in which they were determined) or to prevent their recurrence. In this way the unique significance of sexual experiences in the aetiology of the psychoneuroses (hysteria and obsessions) seemed to be established beyond a doubt; and this fact remains to this day one of the cornerstones of my theory.
>
> (1906, p. 273)

Despite emphasizing that the recalled scenes were "sexual experiences in childhood consisting in stimulation of the genitals, coitus-like acts" (1896, p. 206), Freud recognized that locating the original sexual traumas in early childhood invited the fatal objection that the experiences, however brutal and traumatic, were not truly sexual for the child, given the Victorian doctrine that childhood is "a period before the development of sexual life; and this would seem to involve the abandonment of a sexual aetiology" (1896, p. 201). To address this potential falsification, Freud developed an auxiliary assumption, the "deferred action" hypothesis, that the childhood trauma is perhaps minimally sexual at the time due to the lack of maturity of the sexual organs, but is later unconsciously retroactively understood as sexual and thus has sexual-traumatic effects:

> Our view then is that infantile sexual experiences are the fundamental precondition for hysteria ... but that they do not do so immediately, but remain without effect to begin with and only exercise a pathogenic action later, when they have been aroused after puberty in the form of unconscious memories.
>
> (1896, p. 212)

> But they produce their effect only to a very slight degree at the time at which they occur; what is far more important is their deferred effect, which can only take place at later periods of growth.
>
> (1898, p. 281)

He also argued that even slight excitations in an immature organ could cause lasting sexual trauma:

> But have we not a right to assume that even the age of childhood is not wanting in slight sexual excitations, that later sexual development may perhaps be decisively influenced by childhood experiences? Injuries sustained by an organ which is as yet immature, or by a function which is in process of developing, often cause more severe and lasting effects than they could do in maturer years.
>
> (1896, p. 202)

Freud's early theory that childhood sexual abuse is the uniform cause of the psychoneuroses has come to be known as the "seduction theory." Despite all of Freud's theoretical legerdemain, this theory was subsequently falsified by Freud himself, when he became convinced that some cases of hysteria lacked any such childhood seduction etiology, for reasons that remain unclear: "This aetiology broke down under the weight of its own improbability and contradiction in definitely ascertainable circumstances" (1914, p. 17); "almost all my women patients told me that they had been seduced by their father. I was driven to recognize in the end that these reports were untrue" (1933, p. 120). This falsification was a major blow to Freud's theoretical ambitions, and in later accounts he sometimes expressed the painfulness of the experience:

> When, however, I was at last obliged to recognize that these scenes of seduction had never taken place, and that they were only phantasies which my patients had made up or which I myself had perhaps forced on them, I was for some time completely at a loss.
>
> (1925, p. 34)

Freud offered a host of reasons for his error—for example, that he was misled by the unrepresentative nature of his sample, or fooled by a couple of confirmed genuine cases. However, he resisted the obvious explanation—that he suggested the seduction scenes to his patients in the course of psychoanalysis. Given Freud's assertive use of his method to ferret out sexual memories and his belief in the seduction theory, critical-minded observers could hardly fail to notice that the outcome Freud obtained—in which all of the patients acknowledged histories of childhood sexual seduction even when it was not true—is exactly what one would predict based on the theory that the outcome is due to suggestion. In other words, the nature of the failure of the seduction theory appears to provide a dramatic confirmation of the suggestion objection to Freud's psychoanalytic method. Freud fully understood this challenge not only to his theory but to the method by which he gathered evidence: "my confidence alike in my technique and in its results suffered a severe blow" (1925, p. 34). This, then, is the beginning of Freud's Lakatosian moment in which both his theory and his method faced a seemingly fatal falsification.

Freud's Continuous Commitment to His Core Thesis, the Sexual Theory of the Neuroses

In this section, I argue that Freud's shift from the seduction theory to the Oedipal theory is a prototypical instance of the process Lakatos described, and that Freud himself saw it in roughly Lakatosian-type terms. I document that Freud had a primary core thesis to which he was committed across theory changes—the sexual theory of the neuroses—plus several connected core theses, and that he saw the seduction and Oedipal hypotheses as two versions of this one core continuous doctrine. In response to the falsification of the seduction theory, he altered some background auxiliary hypotheses, especially those concerning childhood sexuality, to obtain his revised theory and avoid falsification of his core thesis. In this section, I will consider the continuity of Freud's views from before to after the formulation of the Oedipal hypothesis. I will delay a consideration of how Freud actually arrived at the Oedipal theory itself and the implications of that process until a subsequent section.

In his historic paper of 1896 announcing the seduction theory of hysteria, Freud refers to his sexual theory of the neurosis (STN)—which ambiguously varies by context, sometimes referring to hysterical neuroses, sometimes to all psychoneuroses, but ultimately to a universal claim about all the neuroses, both actual and psychoneuroses. The STN constitutes Freud's core doctrine:

> But the most important finding that is arrived at if an analysis is thus consistently pursued is this. Whatever case and whatever symptom we take as our point of departure, in the end we infallibly come to the field of sexual experience. So here for the first time we seem to have discovered an aetiological precondition for hysterical symptoms.
>
> (p. 199)

He insists, based on his experience with eighteen cases, on the "universal validity of the sexual aetiology," and asserts that "I have come to regard the participation of sexual motive forces as an indispensable premiss" (1896, p. 200). These statements are not explicitly tied to the seduction hypothesis but are more general and abstract in nature, asserting sexual etiology and leaving seduction to fill in an open parameter specifying the nature of the sexual experience.

In a paper published in 1898, after Freud had privately rejected the seduction hypothesis and was moving on to an Oedipal interpretation of childhood sexual experience, he repeated the STN as if nothing had changed—because in this regard it hadn't:

Exhaustive researches during the last few years have led me to recognize that the most immediate and, for practical purposes, the most significant causes of every case of neurotic illness are to be found in factors arising from sexual life ... I have tried to give an indication of the ... scientific support for the theory of the "sexual aetiology of the neuroses".

(1898, p. 263)

Thus, in every case of neurosis there is a sexual aetiology.

(1898, p. 268)

When Freud finally publicly detailed the changes to his theory in 1906, he was explicit that he considered the changes to be adjustments to a continuous core sexual theory of the neuroses that he termed "my theory" in the singular:

My theory of the aetiological importance of the sexual factor in the neuroses can best be appreciated, in my opinion, by following the history of its development. For I have no desire whatever to deny that it has gone through a process of evolution and been modified in the course of it.

(1906, p. 271)

[I]t is not to be wondered at that, in the course of ten years of continuous effort at reaching an understanding of these phenomena, I have made a considerable step forward from the views I then held, and now believe that I am in a position, on the basis of deeper experience, to correct the insufficiencies, the displacements and the misunderstandings under which my theory then laboured.

(1906, p. 274)

Freud made it crystal clear in the 1906 paper that the STN constituted the essence of his theory: "This theory might be expressed by saying that the cause of life-long hysterical neuroses lies in what are in themselves for the most part the trivial sexual experiences of early childhood" (1906, p. 273); "the essence of these illnesses lies solely in a disturbance of the organism's sexual processes" (p. 279); "[T]he aetiology of the neuroses comprises everything which can act in a detrimental manner upon the processes serving the sexual function" (p. 279).

In later accounts, Freud describes the shift as due not to the failure of his earlier theory but to an isolated "mistaken idea" (1914, p. 17) or "error" (1925, p. 33) in taking the reports of seductions as literally true. He indicates his strategy of reinterpreting the reports as reports of spontaneous Oedipal sexual fantasies, thus retaining the STN:

When I had pulled myself together, I was able to draw the right conclusions from my discovery: namely, that the neurotic symptoms were not related directly to actual events but to wishful phantasies, and that as far as the neurosis was concerned psychical reality was of more importance than material reality. I do not believe even now that I forced the seduction-phantasies on my patients, that I "suggested" them. I had in fact stumbled for the first time upon the Oedipus complex, which was later to assume such an overwhelming importance, but which I did not recognize as yet in its disguise of phantasy. Moreover, seduction during childhood retained a certain share, though a humbler one, in the aetiology of neuroses.

(1925, p. 34–35)

In addition to the STN, repression, and the psychoanalytic method, Freud also continued to embrace as a core doctrine what he referred to as "infantilism," the thesis of childhood etiological origin—that "the events and influences which lie at the root of every psychoneurosis belong ... to the time of early childhood" (1898, p. 267), which was the basis for his rejection of earlier hereditarian degeneracy views:

In tracing back the vicissitudes of an individual's illness to the experiences of his ancestors, we have gone too far; we have forgotten that between his conception and his maturity there lies a long and important period of life—his childhood—in which the seeds of later illness may be acquired. And that is what in fact happens with a psycho-neurosis. Its true aetiology is to be found in childhood experiences, and, once again—and exclusively—in impressions concerned with sexual life.

(1898, p. 280)

This may be a case where there are degrees of "core-ness." In his letter to Fliess in September 1897 explaining his doubts about the seduction theory, Freud said that in view of the problems confronting him, he had considered giving up the doctrine of childhood origin. He never gave up infantilism, but, even in that pessimistic letter to Fliess, Freud did not even hint at the possibility of giving up the STN.

What, then, are the peripheral or auxiliary elements that Freud manipulates to protect the core? The most important one by far, and the one most heralded by Freud, is the nature of childhood sexuality.

The idea that the false reports of seduction were the patient's fantasies led immediately to a rethinking of the auxiliary hypothesis of childhood asexuality, for why would the child have such fantasies when there was no seduction to trigger them unless the child had spontaneous sexual feelings? To save the STN, Freud challenged a standard Victorian background hypothesis about child sexuality:

But since these experiences of childhood were always concerned with sexual excitations and the reaction against them, I found myself faced by the fact of infantile sexuality—once again a novelty and a contradiction of one of the strongest of human prejudices. Childhood was looked upon as "innocent" and free from the lusts of sex, and the fight with the demon of "sensuality" was not thought to begin until the troubled age of puberty. Such occasional sexual activities as it had been impossible to overlook in children were put down as signs of degeneracy or premature depravity or as a curious freak of nature. Few of the findings of psycho-analysis have met with such universal contradiction.

(1925, p. 33)

In 1896, Freud had accepted the Victorian view and reasoned that child sexual experience must always originate in the actions of adults either immediately or through arousing sexuality in children who then abuse other children:

I am inclined to suppose that children cannot find their way to acts of sexual aggression unless they have been seduced previously. The foundation for a neurosis would accordingly always be laid in childhood by adults, and the children themselves would transfer to one another the disposition to fall ill of hysteria later.

(1896, pp. 208–209)

But there is already a hint of Freud's changing views in the 1898 paper, in what for the time was a rather startling comment:

We do wrong to ignore the sexual life of children entirely; in my experience, children are capable of every psychical sexual activity, and many somatic sexual ones as well ... [H]uman sexual life does not begin only with puberty, as on a rough inspection it may appear to do.

(1898, p. 280)

Freud here departs from his earlier view of at most only "slight" sexual feelings in childhood, and prepares the way for the Oedipal theory by hypothesizing spontaneous natural child sexuality.

In *Three Essays* (1905b), Freud develops the natural child sexuality auxiliary hypothesis to its full extent. He is explicit about natural internal causes being sufficient to arouse child sexuality: "Obviously seduction is not required in order to arouse a child's sexual life; that can also come about spontaneously from internal causes" (1905b, p. 190). Nevertheless, he continues to observe that seduction can be a traumatic etiology: "I cannot admit that in my paper on 'The Aetiology of Hysteria' I exaggerated the frequency or importance of that influence ... though I consequently overrated the importance of seduction in comparison with the factors of sexual constitution and development" (1905b, pp. 190–191).

Freud alerts us to the fact that the shift to the Oedipal hypothesis requires him to adjust another peripheral assumption as well:

> After I had made this correction, "infantile sexual traumas" were in a sense replaced by the "infantilism of sexuality". A second modification of the original theory lay not far off. Along with the supposed frequency of seduction in childhood, I ceased also to lay exaggerated stress on the accidental influencing of sexuality on to which I had sought to thrust the main responsibility for the causation of the illness ... the factors of constitution and heredity necessarily gained the upper hand once more; but there was this difference between my views and those prevailing in other quarters, that on my theory the "sexual constitution" took the place of a "general neuropathic disposition".
>
> (1906, pp. 275–276)

The issue of constitution becomes salient again because the Oedipal theory postulates a universal Oedipus complex as a normal developmental stage, thus requiring some further distinction between those who do and do not become neurotic. Seduction cannot explain all cases, so Freud assumes that sexual constitution may be a salient additional factor. In *Introductory Lectures* he argues that sexual constitution as reflected in the natures and relative strengths of various sexual component instincts is a prior and currently inaccessible causal factor beyond the resulting repressed Oedipal conflicts to which psychoanalysis can gain access.

I have argued that the way Freud thought about his shift from the seduction theory to the Oedipal theory is consistent with Lakatos's description of how scientists react to falsification of a theory. The falsified theory is conceptualized as part of a larger continuous research program with core doctrines that are defended when falsification strikes. From this perspective, Freud embraced and was devoted to protecting certain core hypotheses, above all his STN. Freud does not see the Oedipal hypothesis as a new theory replacing his earlier seduction theory that he has abandoned, but as the result of an improvement in his core theory by adjusting some peripheral hypotheses that he sees as malleable elements. Freud followed Lakatos's positive and negative heuristics to the letter, keeping the core constant at all costs even when it meant proposing highly controversial corrections to widely accepted auxiliary hypotheses.

The scientifically very challenging problem facing Freud at this point was two-fold. First, the falsification of the seduction theory cast into doubt Freud's psychoanalytic method, as I explain in the next section, so that his ability to generate new evidence that was scientifically acceptable was blocked. Second, although there was a minor prediction about natural child phallic sexuality that Freud was able to confirm (see Chapter 4), this was largely independent of the Oedipal hypothesis and not as bold and risky as one might like. And, as I argue in a later section, the fact was that the Oedipal theory, due to the way it was generated and applied, seemed to generate no bold novel prediction that would save it from being a manifestly ad hoc theory. Freud thus confronted the second challenge of his Lakatosian moment, in which he had to show that his solution for saving his core hypothesis is not purely ad hoc.

Freud's Psychoanalytic Method in Doubt

The stakes in Freud's response to the falsification of the seduction theory were raised even higher by the fact that it was not only his substantive STN that was cast into doubt but also his psychoanalytic method for revealing unconscious contents, a point, we saw, that he appreciated: "My confidence alike in my technique and in its results suffered a severe blow" (1925, p. 34). Freud's exploration of the patient's unconscious memories depended entirely on his use of his psychoanalytic method to get the patient to recall formerly unconscious memories. The method evolved over time and is described in Chapter 2. The reliability and validity of this method was open to doubt from the beginning, due to the obvious possibility that the resulting insights by the patient might reflect suggestion by the analyst rather than veridical memories. However, the psychoanalytic method was the only technique Freud had for supporting his claims about unconscious mental states and their role in the etiology of the psychoneuroses. For him, it was an irreplaceable methodology that he vigorously promoted and defended, both before and after his theoretical shift from the seduction theory to Oedipal theory.

For example, in his major seduction theory paper, Freud wrote:

> What is even more important to me than the value you put on my results is the attention you give to the procedure I have employed. This procedure is new and difficult to handle, but it is nevertheless irreplaceable for scientific and therapeutic purposes ... The new method of research gives wide access to a new element in the psychical field of events, namely, to processes of thought which have remained unconscious ... I cannot believe that psychiatry will long hold back from making use of this new pathway to knowledge.
>
> (1896, pp. 220–221)

Yet, when he later contemplates the falsification of the seduction theory and grapples with what it means, he recognizes that a correct use of his method and the application of his signature suitability-as-a-determinant methodology for establishing causal relevance (see Chapter 9) have apparently failed him: "it could not be disputed that I had arrived at these scenes by a technical method which I considered correct, and their subject-matter was unquestionably related to the symptoms from which my investigation had started" (1925, p. 34).

After Freud's theoretical shift, Freud continued to assert that the psychoanalyses of his patients provided "convincing evidence" for his etiological theory:

> The question may, however, be raised of where convincing evidence is to be found in favour of the alleged aetiological importance of sexual factors in the psychoneuroses, in view of the fact that the onset of these illnesses may be observed in response to the most commonplace emotions or even to somatic precipitating causes ... To such a question I would reply that the psycho-analytic examination of neurotics is the source from which this disputed conviction of mine is derived. If we make use of that irreplaceable method of research, we discover that *the patient's symptoms constitute his sexual activity.*
>
> (1906, p. 278)

Note that here and elsewhere Freud characterizes the psychoanalytic method as "irreplaceable." Once Freud gave up the use of hypnosis for clinical purposes, there existed no technology other than psychoanalysis for revealing a patient's unconscious mental states. Without such a method, Freud's project would have collapsed.

Despite his affirmations of his method, Freud was of course entirely aware of the inevitable doubts about his method that arose from the failure of the seduction theory. If the psychoanalytic method had led to insights that he publicly touted as major empirically supported discoveries revealed by his method, and those insights turned out to be invalid, then how could the method be trusted?

For example, if Freud had announced that with further psychoanalytic exploration he had discovered that it was not seductions after all but Oedipal fantasies that were at the origin of hysterical neuroses, who other than his acolytes would have believed that this was anything other than the workings of suggestion? Keeping up appearances, Freud only rarely acknowledged the widespread doubts about the psychoanalytic method. A clear indication appears in 1908, with the Hans report in hand but not yet published, in a paper on the sexual theories of children based largely on the parents' prephobic diary of Hans's sexual development. Freud began by observing that there were three sources of information about childhood sexuality: direct observation of children, adults' conscious memories of their childhoods, and information gained from psychoanalysis, where the information comes "from the inferences and constructions, and from the unconscious memories translated into conscious material, which result from the psycho-analysis of neurotics" (1908, p. 209). Rather than embracing the latter evidence consistent with his earlier statements, Freud instead acknowledged that insights gained during psychoanalysis had become open to so many doubts that they were best ignored:

> The material that comes from the third source is open to all the criticisms which it is the custom to marshal against the trustworthiness of psycho-analysis and the reliability of the conclusions that are drawn from it. Thus I cannot attempt to justify it here.
>
> (1908, p. 209)

In the following year, by using the Hans case's more direct evidence from the observation of a child to verify the results of his adult psychoanalyses, Freud made his one significant attempt to answer the criticisms of his method that had been amplified by falsification of the seduction theory.

The Oedipal Hypothesis as a Purely Ad Hoc Theory Initially Lacking Novel Evidence and Requiring a Bold Novel Prediction

The first step at a Lakatosian moment is to develop a new theory that saves one's core hypothesis from falsification. For Freud, that new theory was the Oedipal theory. In this section I am going to examine the birth of the Oedipal theory, as documented in Freud's letters to Wilhelm Fliess. My point is to understand the evidential status of the Oedipal hypothesis at the time it was proposed so that it can then be placed within Lakatos's framework. Freud's letters record quite vividly the dramatic process by which Freud crystallized the Oedipal theory over the course of a few weeks in 1897. I briefly review that history and then consider its philosophy of science implications.

First, Freud's achievement from a Lakatosian perspective must be appre-ciated. Freud's seemingly impossible challenge was to develop a new theory that accomplished three goals: preserve his core STN hypothesis that had been falsified in its seduction theory version; explain all the data that his earlier seduction theory had explained, *but also explain the false reports of seductions* that resulted from his analyses so that he would not fatally undermine his core psychoanalytic method; and avoid immediate falsification of the new theory itself. In the same letter of September 21, 1897, in which Freud famously explained to his friend Wilhelm Fliess the reasons why he had come to doubt his seduction theory (he had expressed doubts previously, but only vaguely and without any explanation), he showed that he was already on the path that would lead to a solution to this puzzle in the form of the Oedipal theory. He admitted to Fliess that there was a problem with his psychoanalytic method when exploring early unconscious mental contents, namely,

> there are no indications of reality in the unconscious, so that one cannot distinguish between truth and fiction that has been cathected with affect. (Accordingly, there would remain the solution that the sexual fantasy invariably seizes upon the theme of the parents.)
>
> (1985a, pp. 264–265)

That is, patients might shift the subject of their emerging unconscious memory from a variety of other people to seduction by the father, yielding a spurious result of frequent fantasies of seduction by the father, without Freud being able to tell whether the resulting fantasy was a memory or a shift of object.

It would not escape Freud that once the fantasy representing an emerging unconscious memory was allowed to be shifted in object, it could also be shifted in other ways as well. This points to the radical possibility that the memory's object—the parent—was real but the reality of the event was not, and that the patient was remembering not an actual incident but a sexual fantasy from childhood, perhaps a masturbatory fantasy. Given this interpretive ambiguity, it is possible for the same evidence to mean quite different things, and a change of meaning can change whether the evidence falsifies a given theory.

Indeed, in his 1906 paper explaining his theoretical shift, Freud deploys precisely this strategy to evade the falsification of his revised theory. He indicates that the problem at the time of the seduction theory was that he did not then know how to distinguish distorted fantasy from reality so that he got the meanings of the seduction fantasies wrong, but in his new theory the very same evidence via auxiliary assumptions about transformations of meanings turns out to be confirming of his theory:

> I was at that period unable to distinguish with certainty between falsifications made by hysterics in their memories of childhood and traces of real events. Since then I have learned to explain a number of phantasies of seduction as attempts at fending off memories of the subject's own sexual activity (infantile masturbation).
>
> (1906, p. 274)

With this brilliant but admittedly rather arbitrary-seeming twist, the data of the old theory—including the false reports of seductions—are fully explained by the new theory (as transformations of Oedipal fantasies when not veridical), and none of the existing data falsifies the new theory. And the core STN thesis is preserved.

However, this solution demands that children can be spontaneously sexual without first being stimulated by seducers. Conjoined with Freud's continuing insistence on his core thesis of infantilism, this leads to child sexuality and something like the Oedipus complex as a necessary part of a full solution. Indeed, looking back many years later, Freud described precisely this two-phase shift as follows:

> [Y]ou will recall an interesting episode in the history of analytic research which caused me many distressing hours. In the period in which the main interest was directed to discovering infantile sexual traumas, almost all my women patients told me that they had been seduced by their father. I

was driven to recognize in the end that these reports were untrue and so came to understand that hysterical symptoms are derived from phantasies and not from real occurrences. It was only later that I was able to recognize in this phantasy of being seduced by the father the expression of the typical Oedipus complex in women.

(1933, p. 120)

To continue with Freud's reports of his development of the Oedipal thesis, in a letter to Fliess on October 3, 1897 (Freud, 1897/1985b), just two weeks after Freud's letter discussing his doubts about the seduction theory, Freud reported on his ongoing self-analysis to Fliess. He announced that he had discovered what he claimed to be the occasion of the triggering of his own Oedipus complex:

[T]he old man plays no active part in my case … [L]ater (between two and two and a half years) my libido toward *matrem* was awakened, namely, on the occasion of a journey with her from Leipzig to Vienna, during which we must have spent the night together and there must have been an opportunity of seeing her *nudam*.

(1897/1985b, p. 268)

(Note that Ernest Jones [1956] later claimed that the train trip to which Freud refers in fact occurred when Freud was four years old.)

The wording suggests that Freud did not, in fact, recall seeing his mother naked or recall having sexual feelings awakened towards her but rather inferred what "must" have happened (they "must" have spent the night together on the train and therefore he "must" have seen his mother naked). Note that Freud performed his self-analysis primarily by free-associating to his dreams ("my self-analysis, which I consider indispensable for the clarification of the whole problem, has continued in dreams and has presented me with the most valuable elucidations and clues" [p. 268]). It is not surprising that Freud arrived at meanings of the kind that he was seeking. Even Freud seems to have been aware of the possibility of self-suggestion, observing after a rather free-handed interpretation that "A harsh critic might say of all this that it was retrogressively fantasied instead of progressively determined" (p. 270).

In a letter on October 15, 1897, Freud (1897/1985c) informed Fliess once again that he had developed a new theory, in essence the Oedipal theory (although he did not yet use that specific phrase). Noting of his self-analysis both that "I have got much further" and "I have found nothing completely new," Freud went on to say:

A single idea of general value dawned on me. I have found, in my own case too, [the phenomenon of] being in love with my mother and jealous of my father, and I now consider it a universal event in early childhood …

If this is so, we can understand the gripping power of *Oedipus Rex* ... [T]he Greek legend seizes upon a compulsion which everyone recognizes because he senses its existence within himself. Everyone in the audience was once a budding Oedipus in fantasy and each recoils in horror from the dream fulfillment here transplanted into reality.

(1897/1985c, p. 272)

The new idea is the universality of the Oedipus complex, not just that such feelings might occur, for it appears Freud already knew of such instances ("I have found, in my own case too"). In other words, based on self-suggestible interpretations of his dreams that are questionable even in their veridicality about Freud, Freud leaped to a universal generalization. His primary "evidence" seems to have been his idiosyncratic interpretation of the Oedipus play and myth.

What conclusions can one draw from Freud's reports of the birth of the Oedipal theory? I emphasize that the immediate point is not an evaluation of the truth or falsity of the Oedipal hypothesis, for Freud's self-analysis was in the context of discovery, not of justification, so no such evaluation is yet appropriate. However, the evidential status of the hypothesis at its inception is of interest because it reveals the hypothesis's initial degree of "ad hoc"-ness. Sometimes the context of discovery contains some serious evidence or novel facts that provide some initial evidential credence for a newly proposed hypothesis. However, as far as one can tell, the discovery of the Oedipal hypothesis by Freud involves no cogent scientifically acceptable evidence for the truth of the hypothesis. At its inception, the Oedipal hypothesis is pure speculation, scientifically speaking. Moreover, there is no immediately obvious and testable scientifically bold prediction from the new theory of neurosogenesis, especially given that the validity of psychoanalytic insight cannot be assumed.

The problem of the Oedipal theory's ad hoc nature is challenging to overcome. The Oedipal hypothesis is designed to explain precisely the same data that emerged during the seduction theory episode by reinterpreting the patients' memories and fantasies. Assuming that the Oedipal theory successfully accomplishes this goal without incurring falsification, the theory is thus far purely ad hoc, without any novel predictions. If one tries to get around this problem by predicting the clinical emergence of more overtly Oedipal fantasies and memories than one has gotten before, the scientific reply will be that the seduction theory episode has cast doubt on the methodology of psychoanalytic investigation of unconscious contents. For why did such novel results not emerge earlier? And, if fantasies can be distorted, then who is to say how exactly they can be distorted, and can't one dream up other explanations of the seduction fantasies that do not involve Oedipal explanations, if one is not wedded to the goal of saving the STN at all cost? The most immediately plausible explanation for why the seduction memories produced in psychoanalysis did not correspond with reality is that the fantasies were suggested to the patient by Freud, and this means that the psychoanalytic method cannot be trusted. Thus, novel predictions that depend on the same psychoanalytic method for their confirmation do not constitute independent, bold, potentially scientifically persuasive predictions.

In sum, Freud thus far fails to take the second step in responding to a Lakatosian moment. When Freud deploys the Oedipal thesis to save his sexual theory of the neuroses, it is a pure ad hoc move. The only "evidence" for the hypothesis is that it saves Freud's cherished sexual theory of the neuroses. Unless Freud can produce novel predictions from the Oedipal theory that also evade the suggestion objection to the psychoanalytic method, his Oedipal theory will be a degenerative and implausible revision that arguably renders his theory pseudoscientific.

After documenting in the next chapter that Freud was focused throughout his career on responding to the suggestion objection, I will argue in Chapter 3 that in the unique circumstance of the failure of the seduction theory, he attempted to provide an answer to the ad hoc and suggestion objections in the Hans case. It is there and only there that Freud admitted that what was needed was evidence that to the degree possible circumvents the complexities and suggestion opportunities of adult psychoanalyses, and a child analysis was his answer:

> But even a psycho-analyst may confess to the wish for a more direct and less roundabout proof of these fundamental theorems. Surely there must be a possibility of observing in children at first hand and in all the freshness of life the sexual impulses and wishes which we dig out so laboriously in adults.
>
> (1909a, p. 6)

In Chapter 4, I review Freud's Oedipal-theoretic interpretation of the Hans case, and in Chapter 5 I present the history of the primary rival theory to Freud's that I am calling the "fright theory"—which, we shall see, Freud vigorously attempted to rebut in his Hans analysis. Chapters 6 through 10 will be concerned with reconstructing and analyzing four key arguments in the Hans case, the first two of which—the "undirected anxiety" and "day the horse fell down" arguments in Chapters 6 and 7, respectively—are primarily "negative" arguments aimed at rebutting the fright theory. Two other arguments are explicit attempts to confirm the Oedipal theory with novel, bold predictions that are not derivable from the fright theory or from a suggestion account. The first, the "sexual repression" argument analyzed in Chapter 8, is a potentially powerful but previously unrecognized N=1 argument that attempts to confirm the Oedipal theory's predictions of the pattern of Hans's sexual desires over time. The second, concerning the "detailed characteristics" of Hans's phobic symptoms, is analyzed in Chapter 10. This last argument holds that Hans's symptoms have otherwise inexplicable detailed characteristics that require the Oedipal hypothesis for an adequate explanation. The intervening Chapter 9 is exclusively concerned with understanding Freud's "suitability of a determinant" methodology of psychoanalytic interpretation that Freud proposed as an epistemological foundation to rebut the suggestion objection and that is the basis for Chapter 10's argument. Chapter 11 offers a critique of Adolf Grunbaum's influential "Tally Argument" analysis of Freud's attempt to rebut the suggestion objection, which is the most prominent rival to my "suitability" analysis.

Caveats

A few caveats may be useful before proceeding. First, for ease of exposition, I consider the Oedipus complex here only in its original form relevant to the Hans case, of the sexual desire of a son for his mother, before it was expanded to daughters and to same-sex parents. Second, I limit myself in this book to case material that is not based on interpreting Hans's fantasies and dreams. Such evidence raises unique interpretive challenges and is certainly not "more direct" evidence, and I address Hans's fantasy and dream evidence elsewhere (Wakefield, 2007; 2008; forthcoming).

In addition, several minor textual caveats are also worth noting. First, many of the writers I quote, including Freud, use italics liberally for emphasis. Rather than stating each time whether italics are in the original text or added by me for emphasis, I adopt the convention that any italics appearing in quoted passages are in the original unless otherwise stated. Second, when quoted writers cite others within the quoted passage, I often eliminate the reference citations from within quoted passages without the addition of ellipses. Third, with apologies, I omit the umlaut modifier in the spelling of German words, and to retain consistency of spelling across original and secondary texts, I do not add the traditional "e" as a replacement. Finally, although I generally use APA style, for Freud's much-cited works I use a briefer style common in psychoanalytic journals, listing only the original year of publication and using the abbreviation "SE" for the Standard Edition of Freud's works—the full reference is J. Strachey (Ed. & Trans.), *The Standard Edition of the Complete Psychological Works of Sigmund Freud*. London: Hogarth Press—followed by volume and page numbers.

References

Breuer, J. (1895). Fraulein Anna O. *SE* 2, 21–47.
Eagle, M. (2018). *Core concepts in classical psychoanalysis: Clinical, research evidence and conceptual critiques*. Abingdon, UK: Routledge.
Freud, S. (1896). The aetiology of hysteria. *SE* 3, 187–221.
Freud, S. (1898). Sexuality in the aetiology of the neuroses. *SE* 3, 259–285.
Freud, S. (1900). The interpretation of dreams (first part). *SE* 4.

Freud, S. (1905a). Fragment of an analysis of a case of hysteria. *SE* 7, 1–122.

Freud, S. (1905b). Three essays on the theory of sexuality. *SE* 7, 123–246.

Freud, S. (1906). My views on the part played by sexuality in the aetiology of the neuroses. *SE* 7, 269–279.

Freud, S. (1908). On the sexual theories of children. *SE* 9, 205–226.

Freud, S. (1909a). Analysis of a phobia in a five-year-old boy. *SE* 10, 1–150.

Freud, S. (1909b). Notes upon a case of obsessional neurosis. *SE* 10, 151–318.

Freud, S. (1911). Psycho-analytic notes on an autobiographical account of a case of paranoia (Dementia Paranoides). *SE* 12, 1–82.

Freud, S. (1918). From the history of an infantile neurosis. *SE* 17, 1–124.

Freud, S. (1923). Two encyclopaedia articles. *SE* 18, 233–260.

Freud, S. (1933). New introductory lectures on psycho-analysis. *SE* 22, 1–182.

Freud, S. (1940). An outline of psycho-analysis. *SE* 23, 141–208.

Freud, S. (1985a). Letter from Freud to Fliess, September 21, 1897. In J. M. Masson (Ed. & Trans.), *The complete letters of Sigmund Freud to Wilhelm Fliess, 1887–1904* (pp. 264–266). Cambridge, MA: Harvard University Press. (Original work 1897.)

Freud, S. (1985b). Letter from Freud to Fliess, October 3, 1897. In J. M. Masson (Ed. & Trans.), *The complete letters of Sigmund Freud to Wilhelm Fliess, 1887–1904* (pp. 267–270). Cambridge, MA: Harvard University Press. (Original work 1897.)

Freud, S. (1985c). Letter from Freud to Fliess, October 15, 1897. In J. M. Masson (Ed. & Trans.), *The complete letters of Sigmund Freud to Wilhelm Fliess, 1887–1904* (pp. 270–273). Cambridge, MA: Harvard University Press. (Original work 1897.)

Gay, P. (1988). *Freud: A life for our time.* New York: W. W. Norton & Co.

Jones, E. (1956). *Sigmund Freud: Life and work*, Vol. I, revised edition. London: Hogarth Press.

Kitcher, P. (1992). *Freud's dream: A complete interdisciplinary science of mind.* Cambridge, MA: MIT Press.

Lakatos, I. (1968). Criticism and the methodology of scientific research programmes. *Proceedings of the Aristotelian Society*, 69, 149–186.

Lakatos, I. (1970). Falsification and the methodology of scientific research programmes. In I. Lakatos & A. Musgrave (Eds.), *Criticism and the growth of knowledge* (pp. 91–196). Cambridge: Cambridge University Press.

Mahony, P. (1986). *Freud and the Rat Man.* New Haven, CN: Yale University Press.

Midgley, N. (2006). Re-reading "Little-Hans": Freud's case study and the question of competing paradigms in psychoanalysis. *Journal of the American Psychoanalytic Association*, 54(2), 537–559.

Schreber, D. P. (2000). *Memoirs of my nervous illness* (I. Macalpine & R. A. Hunter, Ed. and Trans.). New York: New York Review of Books. (Original work 1903).

Spitzer, R. L., Gibbon, M., Skodol, A. E., Williams, J. B. W., & First, M. B. (2002). *DSM-IV-TR casebook: A learning companion to the diagnostic and statistical manual of mental disorders (4th ed.) Text Revision.* Arlington, VA: American Psychiatric Publishing.

Wakefield, J. C. (2007). Max Graf's "Reminiscences of Professor Sigmund Freud" revisited: New evidence from the Freud Archives. *Psychoanalytic Quarterly*, 76, 149–192.

Wakefield, J. C. (2007). Attachment and sibling rivalry in Little Hans: The "phantasy of the two giraffes" reconsidered. *Journal of the American Psychoanalytic Association*, 55, 821–849.

Wakefield, J. (2008). Little Hans and the thought police: The "Policeman Fantasies" as the first supervisory transference fantasies. *International Journal of Psychoanalysis*, 89, 71–88.

Wakefield, J. C. (2022). *Attachment, sexuality, power: Oedipal theory as regulator of family affection in Freud's case of Little Hans*. New York: Routledge.

Wakefield, J. C. (forthcoming). *Freud's interpretation of dream and fantasy evidence: A hypothesis testing approach to the case of Little Hans*. New York: Routledge.

Chapter 2

"All My Efforts Valueless"

Freud's Lifelong Concern with the
Suggestion Objection as the Major Threat
to Psychoanalytic Theory

The Suggestion Objection as a Central Preoccupation in Freud's Work

In this chapter, I document Freud's concern about and sustained entanglement with the suggestion objection. As philosopher of psychoanalysis Michael Lacewing observes, "From its inception, psychoanalysis has been troubled by the problem of suggestion" (2013, p. 718). Indeed, from Freud's and Breuer's (1893) initial "Preliminary Communication" reporting the first cases of cathartic therapy ("It is plausible to suppose that it is a question here of unconscious suggestion" [p. 7]) to Freud's summing up of his theory in "The Outline of Psycho-Analysis" (1938) in the year before his death ("The therapeutic successes that occurred under the sway of the positive transference are open to the suspicion of being of a *suggestive* nature" [p. 176]), the suggestion objection was continually on Freud's mind.

Adolf Grunbaum (1984) performed a service by drawing attention to the centrality of the problem of suggestion for Freud's theory and the lack of an adequate reconstruction and evaluation of Freud's response, leaving us without an understanding of the epistemological foundations of Freud's theory. For reasons I present in a later chapter, Grunbaum's own much-discussed reconstruction of Freud's response to the suggestion objection—Freud's supposed "Tally Argument"—is not a defensible reading of Freud. Grunbaum's challenge thus remains unmet, and I undertake to meet it in this book. I agree with Grunbaum on one crucial point: even at this late date, a correct understanding of Freud's response to the suggestion objection yields surprising insights into the nature and status of his overall argument. In this chapter, I start by documenting Freud's acute awareness of and chronic concern about the suggestion objection.

Interpreting Suggestion Broadly

The concept of suggestion was a prominent one in Freud's day. Like others, Freud's interest in hypnotic suggestion as a psychologically potent process was initially stoked by the craze for stage mesmerism in Europe:

DOI: 10.4324/9781003272472-2

While I was still a student I had attended a public exhibition given by Hansen the "magnetist", and had noticed that one of the subjects experimented upon had become deathly pale at the onset of cataleptic rigidity and had remained so as long as that condition lasted. This firmly convinced me of the genuineness of the phenomena of hypnosis.

(1925, p. 16)

Freud's acquaintance with suggestion occurred at the end of about a century of development of the idea. At first the term had been used descriptively by British Associationists simply to label the process by which one idea called up an associated idea in the mind. However, by Freud's day it was firmly associated with the craze for mesmerism and hypnosis. Mesmerism originated in the eighteenth century with the Viennese physician Franz Mesmer, who postulated a mysterious biological fluid or force that conferred "animal magnetism." He claimed that a therapist's manipulation of the patient's animal magnetism could cure various ailments. The doctrine of animal magnetism was discredited late in the eighteenth century by a scientific panel formed by Louis XVI. The panel, which included Benjamin Franklin and Antoine Lavoisier, performed scientific experiments and concluded that mesmerism's claimed medical effects were due not to animal magnetism but to the patient's imagination and suggestion by the therapist. Thus, the scientific panel ironically discredited mesmerism's animal magnetism but provided a rationale for taking suggestion seriously. Mesmerism continued to be influential in stage demonstrations of the power of suggestion. Later renamed "hypnotism" and shorn of animal-magnetism pseudoscience by Scottish physician James Braid, both stage demonstrations and medical usage gained in popularity. In the late nineteenth century, both Charcot in Paris and Liébeaut and Bernheim in Nancy systematically exploited hypnosis and hypnotic suggestion for medical purposes and greatly influenced Freud, as we shall see.

Since then, the notion of suggestion has gradually broadened to become a vague and malleable concept covering many modes of nonrational personal and social influence on individuals' beliefs. The vagueness was already present in Freud's time. In the Hans case history, in the course of rebutting the objection that Hans's insights must be attributed to suggestion, Freud takes a moment to deride the concept's vagueness and its overuse as an all-purpose explanation for psychological phenomena that we don't understand:

A singular thing. I can remember, when I first began to meddle in the conflict of scientific opinions twenty-two years ago, with what derision the older generation of neurologists and psychiatrists of those days received assertions about suggestion and its effects. Since then the situation has fundamentally changed. The former aversion has been converted into an only too ready acceptance ... [I]t has since been discovered how great an economy of thought can be effected by the use of the catchword "suggestion". Nobody knows and nobody cares what suggestion is, where it comes from, or when it arises,—it is enough that everything awkward in the region of psychology can be labelled "suggestion".

(1909, p. 102)

If construed as an attempt at rebuttal of the suggestion objection, these complaints have no substance. One need not understand suggestion at a theoretical level or in a precise way to reasonably believe on the basis of existing evidence that there is some such process or set of processes that, whatever they are, explain Hans's inclination to be influenced in his avowals by his father. Social psychology has confirmed that social influence phenomena induce individuals to endorse what they perceive as socially desirable, even when it may be blatantly false. Suggestion thus must be taken seriously as an alternative hypothesis in the Hans case. Collins (1980) rightly criticizes the "disingenuousness" of Freud's claim that suggestion is a confused or meaningless concept given that throughout his career Freud regularly used the term with seeming confidence as to its meaning. Even if we lack a theoretical understanding of suggestion, it can be a perfectly good concept if it refers to at least some empirically specifiable domain of phenomena, and that it clearly does.

What, then, is suggestion? Despite his dismissive comment above about the meaning of "suggestion," Freud himself offered the following definition in the preface to his translation of Bernheim's book on hypnosis as suggestion:

What distinguishes suggestion from other kinds of psychic influence, such as a command or the giving of a piece of information or instruction, is that in the case of a suggestion an idea is aroused in another person's brain which is not examined in regard to its origin but is accepted just as though it had arisen spontaneously in that brain.

(Freud, 1888, p. 82)

In a similar spirit, Lacewing (2013) says:

suggestion comprises communications and features of the structure and setting of communication that, while bypassing the subject's critical and/ or conscious reflection, lead to a change in their mental states (beliefs, memories, desires, etc.), mental state reports, and/or behavior

(p. 721)

This covers a lot of potential territory. For example, Grunbaum (1984) encompasses placebo effects of treatment that influence symptoms or behavior within suggestion.

If we conceptualize psychoanalysis as issuing in an explicit or implicit agreement by the patient with certain of the analyst's interpretations, then any cause of agreement that involves the analyst's influence or other influences on the patient and is not based on veridical memories or logically persuasive reasoning might be considered suggestion. Accordingly, Grunbaum (1984) characterizes the suggestion objection as follows: "analysts induce their docile patients by suggestion to furnish the very clinical responses needed to validate the psychoanalytic theory of personality" (p. 130). Lacewing (2013) puts the suggestion challenge this way: "The challenge is a methodological one: how can psychoanalysis legitimately infer its theoretical claims from clinical data, if these data could be biased, through suggestion, by the theory they are meant to independently support?" (p. 721).

If one requires an influence on the patient's beliefs for suggestion, then the fact that Freud implausibly attributes Oedipal mental contents to Hans based on what Hans says but without Hans's avowals or knowledge would not be a matter of suggestion. Lacewing (2013) draws a useful distinction between *suggestion* as influence that contaminates the clinical data produced by the patient and *confirmation bias* as biased use of the clinical data by the analyst in reaching theoretical conclusions. However, these are difficult to separate in the Hans case, given that Hans is a child who cannot be expected to confront explicit statements of Oedipal and other contents such as sexual desire for his mother or the wish to kill his father, although at times the interpretations do approach these contents. In any event, the real question in the end is whether Freud's interpretations are veridical and his defenses against the suggestion objection argue broadly for veridicality. Consequently, I will construe "suggestion" in an extremely broad way that encompasses both standard suggestion and confirmation bias in assessing Freud's defense of the validity of his etiological claims.

Freud fully appreciated the potentially devastating nature of the threat posed by the suggestion objection. If one has any doubt about his acute awareness and passionate engagement with this issue, one need only look at how he characterized the suggestion objection's potential impact on his theory in the following passages in his *Introductory Lectures*. The passages occur after Freud admits that to some extent suggestion is used in psychoanalysis by exploiting the patient's positive transference to the analyst to persuade the patient to accept the analyst's interpretations:

It must dawn on us that in our technique we have abandoned hypnosis only to rediscover suggestion in the shape of transference.

But here I will pause, and let you have a word; for I see an objection boiling up in you so fiercely that it would make you incapable of listening if it were not put into words: "Ah! so you've admitted it at last! You work with the help of suggestion, just like the hypnotists! That is what we've thought for a long time. But, if so, why the roundabout road by way of memories of the past, discovering the unconscious, interpreting and translating back distortions—this immense expenditure of labour, time and money—when the one effective thing is after all only suggestion?

Why do you not make direct suggestions against the symptoms, as the others do—the honest hypnotists? Moreover, if you try to excuse yourself for your long detour on the ground that you have made a number of important psychological discoveries which are hidden by direct suggestion—what about the certainty of these discoveries now? Are not they a result of suggestion too, of unintentional suggestion? Is it not possible that you are forcing on the patient what you want and what seems to you correct in this field as well?"

What you are throwing up at me in this is uncommonly interesting and must be answered.

(1917, pp. 446–447)

If [the suggestion objection] were justified, psycho-analysis would be nothing more than a particularly well-disguised and particularly effective form of suggestive treatment and we should have to attach little weight to all that it tells us about what influences our lives, the dynamics of the mind or the unconscious. That is what our opponents believe; and in especial they think that we have "talked" the patients into everything relating to the importance of sexual experiences—or even into those experiences themselves—after such notions have grown up in our own depraved imagination.

(1917, p. 452)

There is an irony in the suggestion objection becoming the major threat to psychoanalysis, given that Freud's early work relied on hypnotic suggestion and other direct suggestion processes to eliminate hysterical symptoms. However, when Freud left direct suggestion behind as a therapeutic technique and claimed to use psychoanalysis to reveal unconscious etiologically relevant memories, suggestion became a potent objection to the validity of his findings. As Collins (1980) observes: "Though Freud discarded hypnosis and suggestion early in his career, he continued to be preoccupied with suggestion throughout his life, not as a therapeutic method, but as an idea with the capacity to discount his work" (p. 436). The problem was especially acute after the seduction theory fiasco in which some of the memories of childhood sexual abuse that Freud claimed to have uncovered via psychoanalysis in his patients turned out to be bogus, which seemed to confirm the suggestion theory.

Note that the suggestion objection applies across the board to all psychoanalytically generated clinical evidence. A standard defense of the Oedipal theory is that since Freud's time, many other psychoanalysts have verified the reality of the Oedipus complex as a cause of neurosis. However, if suggestion is a problem inherent to the psychoanalytic method, then trying to verify the validity of the Oedipal-theoretic results of one analysis by referring to the Oedipal-theoretic results of other analyses is as futile as trying to verify the accuracy of a New York Times article by checking whether other copies of the same edition of the same newspaper agree. Instead, one needs independent evidence not subject to the same potentially distorting influences. After documenting Freud's engagement with the suggestion objection in this chapter, I will argue in the next chapter that such independent verification is precisely what Freud sought and thought he found in the Hans case. Freud thus embraced the Hans case as an epistemological foundation for his entire clinical project.

Freud's Early Awareness of the Power of Suggestion

In understanding the Hans case in the context of Freud's concern about the suggestion objection, it is useful to understand Freud's longstanding engagement with, and understanding of the challenge of, the problem of suggestion. Long before his mature psychoanalytic theorizing, Freud was already acutely aware of the power of suggestion and the potential problems posed by suggestion to etiological theorizing and claims of therapeutic efficacy. When he first began treating hysterical patients, in addition to direct hypnotic suggestion, Freud used the then-popular treatment of electrical stimulation. However, Freud soon concluded that this treatment was not helpful and worked only by suggestion:

> I put my electrical apparatus aside, even before Moebius had saved the situation by explaining that the successes of electric treatment in nervous disorders (in so far as there were any) were the effect of suggestion on the part of the physician.
>
> (1925, p. 16)

An initial link between hypnotic suggestion and hysteria was forged for Freud during his visit in 1885–1886 to Jean-Martin Charcot's neurology clinic at the Salpêtrière hospital in Paris. Charcot postulated that hysterics suffered from a hereditary brain pathology such that a physical trauma could cause a splitting of mental processing, and that hysterical symptoms occurred when the split-off part intruded into consciousness. He used hypnosis to recreate the splitting and thus induce hysterical seizures, and demonstrated what he called "major hypnosis," a form of trance distinctive to hysterics that occurred in several stages with certain physical symptoms associated with each stage: "these hysterical patients are said to exhibit three stages of hypnosis, each of which is distinguished by special physical signs of a most remarkable kind (such as enormous neuro-muscular hyper-excitability, somnambulistic contractures, etc.)" (Freud, 1888, p. 77). Although Charcot used hypnosis to demonstrate his theory and not as a treatment, the potential power of hypnotic suggestion was not lost on Freud: "In Paris I had seen hypnotism used freely as a method for producing symptoms in patients and then removing them again" (Freud, 1925, p. 17).

Early in his career, Freud embraced the purposeful use of suggestion as a curative treatment and was enthralled with the power to hypnotically suggest away a patient's hysterical symptoms: "[T]here was something positively seductive in working with hypnotism. For the first time there was a sense of having overcome one's helplessness" (1925, p. 17). This eventually morphed into direct suggestion without hypnosis but with Freud applying pressure to the head of the patient and insisting on the patient's remembering. Freud's initial revelation that hysterical symptoms might be directly eliminated by hypnotic or other suggestion was again borrowed from the French:

> [T]he news reached us that a school had arisen at Nancy which made an extensive and remarkably successful use of suggestion, with or without hypnosis, for therapeutic purposes. It thus came about ... that in the first years of my activity as a physician my principal instrument of work ... was hypnotic suggestion.
>
> (p. 17)

Freud visited Hippolyte Bernheim's clinic in Nancy in 1889 for the purpose of improving his hypnotic technique. Notably, Freud's view that the mind includes unconscious mental states was also influenced by Bernheim's demonstrations: "I was a spectator of Bernheim's astonishing experiments upon his hospital patients, and I received the profoundest impression of the possibility that there could be powerful mental processes which nevertheless remained hidden from the consciousness of men" (p. 17).

The year before his visit to Bernheim's clinic, Freud published a German translation of Bernheim's book, *Suggestion and its Therapeutic Effects*. In the introduction, Freud summarizes the dispute between the Bernheim and Charcot schools on the relation of hypnosis to hysteria. The analysis reveals Freud's clear grasp of the potential powers of suggestion. He notes that Bernheim demystifies hypnosis and elevates suggestion to "the key to its understanding," and that "convincing evidence is offered that the use of hypnotic suggestion provides the physician with a powerful therapeutic method" (Freud, 1888, p. 75). Freud explains that, contrary to Charcot's notion of a distinct hysterical form of major hypnosis resulting from a hereditary neurological abnormality, Bernheim

> maintains that all the phenomena of hypnotism have the same origin: they arise, that is, from a suggestion, a conscious idea, which has been introduced into the brain of the hypnotized person by an external influence and has been accepted by him as though it had arisen spontaneously.
>
> (p. 77)

This would imply that what Charcot takes to be a discovery of an objective mental reality is in fact an artifact of his own suggestion to the patient. Freud thus concludes: "If the supporters of the suggestion theory are right, all the observations made at the Salpêtrière are worthless; indeed, they become errors in observation" (pp. 77–78) because they are due to the physician's suggestion and nothing inherent in the disorder. This is the very objection that Freud would later see lodged against his own theoretical claims.

Freud was thus acutely aware of the danger of inadvertent suggestion yielding false evidence supporting an etiological theory. Although Freud defends Charcot against Bernheim's suggestion objection, he acknowledges the power of the suggestion objection, prophetically concluding that Bernheim's "criticisms will show their importance in the fact that in every future investigation of hysteria and hypnotism the need for excluding the element of suggestion will be more consciously kept in view" (Freud, 1888, p. 78). This presages Freud's own later attempt to rebut the suggestion objection. As Grunbaum (1984) points out, "Thus, even as early as 1888, Freud patently had a sophisticated grasp of the *epistemic* problem of spurious data as posed by the patient's susceptibility to the doctor's influence" (p. 283).

Even during his visit to Bernheim's clinic, there were portents of the limits of the power of direct suggestion to eliminate hysterical symptoms despite some successes. Freud had convinced a patient with whom he had limited success to accompany him to Nancy:

> Bernheim now attempted several times to bring this about, but he too failed. He frankly admitted to me that his great therapeutic successes by means of suggestion were only achieved in his hospital practice and not with his private patients.
>
> (Freud, 1925, pp. 17–18)

Eventually, Freud became disillusioned with direct hypnotic suggestion and adopted the technique of insisting that the patient recall the desired unconscious memories while placing pressure on the patient's forehead. This nonhypnotic pressure technique was also inspired by something Freud witnessed at Nancy:

> When I found that, in spite of all my efforts, I could not succeed in bringing more than a fraction of my patients into a hypnotic state ... I set about working with them in their normal state. At first, I must confess, this seemed a senseless and hopeless undertaking. I was set the task of learning from the patient something that I did not know and that he did not know himself. How could one hope to elicit it? But there came to my help a recollection of a most remarkable and instructive experiment which I had witnessed when I was with Bernheim at Nancy [in 1889]. Bernheim showed us that people whom he had put into a state of hypnotic somnambulism, and who had had all kinds of experiences while they were in that state, only appeared to have lost the memory of what

they had experienced during somnambulism; it was possible to revive these memories in their normal state. It is true that, when he questioned them about their somnambulistic experiences, they began by maintaining that they knew nothing about them; but if he refused to give way, and insisted, and assured them that they did know about them, the forgotten experiences always reappeared. So I did the same thing with my patients. When I reached a point with them at which they maintained that they knew nothing more ... I ventured to declare that the right memory would occur to them at the moment at which I laid my hand on their forehead. In that way I succeeded, without using hypnosis, in obtaining from the patients whatever was required for establishing the connection between the pathogenic scenes they had forgotten and the symptoms left over from those scenes. But it was a laborious procedure.

(Freud, 1910a, pp. 22–23)

Yet, despite intense efforts, at times "Insistence was of no further help" (1910a, p. 29). Eventually, Freud moved on to interpreting the patient's free associations, the rationale for which he explains as follows (note that by "complex" Freud refers simply to any group of linked ideas cathected with a common affect):

I found it impossible to believe that an idea produced by a patient ... could be an arbitrary one and unrelated to the idea we were in search of ... In the patient under treatment two forces were in operation against each other: on the one hand, his conscious endeavour to bring into consciousness the forgotten idea in his unconscious, and on the other hand, the resistance we already know about, which was striving to prevent what was repressed or its derivatives from thus becoming conscious. If this resistance amounted to little or nothing, what had been forgotten became conscious without distortion ... [T]he greater the resistance against what we were in search of becoming conscious, the greater would be its distortion. The idea which occurred to the patient in place of what we were in search of had thus itself originated like a symptom: it was a new, artificial and ephemeral substitute for what had been repressed, and was dissimilar to it in proportion to the degree of distortion it had undergone under the influence of the resistance. But, owing to its nature as a symptom, it must nevertheless have a certain similarity to what we were in search of; and if the resistance were not too great, we ought to be able to guess the latter from the former ... We see, then, that if in our search for a repressed complex in one of our patients we start out from the last thing he remembers, we shall have every prospect of discovering the complex, provided that the patient puts a sufficient number of his free associations at our disposal. Accordingly, we allow the patient to say whatever he likes.

(1910a, pp. 29–31)

The analyst thus brings the patient's unconscious memories into consciousness by interpretation, that is, by verbally formulating, or guessing, what the patient is repressing. The analyst's interpretation associates to the repressed memory and provides an attractive force or eased associative pathway, so to speak, for the repressed content to emerge into consciousness.

A problem with this account is that the eased associative pathway applies to anything that associates to the interpretation, so associations by the patient may appear confirmatory of the interpretation but in fact be associations triggered by the interpretation. Given that the analyst determines the interpretations, this procedure is highly vulnerable to suggestion. Moreover, because the patient is hypothesized to be actively defending against remembering the unconscious material, some further prodding by the analyst might seem justified. As we shall see, Freud was not reluctant to add such pressure to his interpretations, yielding a heightened danger of suggestive influence on the patient's reports.

The Suggestion Objection as the Main Objection Posed by Critics to Freud's Clinical-Etiological Claims

The suggestion theory of Freud's clinical "data" was immediately the most obvious and persuasive objection to Freud's etiological claims, as well as the most devastating. This criticism came even from Freud's closest confidante and friend, Wilhelm Fliess, and Freud complained to Fliess that "you take sides against me and tell me that 'the reader of thoughts merely reads his own thoughts into other people', which renders all my efforts valueless" (Freud, 1901/1985c, p. 447).

The suggestion account of Freud's results continued to be the standard critical view at the time of the Hans case and beyond. Carl Jung implies as much when, in a lecture delivered in 1912 in which Jung attempts to defend Freud's shift from the seduction theory to the Oedipal theory, he says, "You will perhaps be inclined to share the suspicion of the critics that the results derived from analytic researches were based on suggestion" (Jung, 1915, p. 11). At around the same time, articles posing the suggestion objection to Freud's theory were appearing in medical journals. Here are two examples:

> Freud asserts that his method ... is, in contrast to all other methods of psychotherapy, characterized by the fact that its therapeutic efficacy is not due to suggestion, a statement which the facts attested by Freud himself lead us frankly to question ... [I]t is extremely probable that Freud by his method suggests the memories of sexual occurrences to his patients; in other words, that he elicits from them a fictitious memory of sexual events in their childhood, of events that have never occurred. Indeed, Loewenfeld gives an instance of a patient of Freud who subsequently came into his (Loewenfeld's) hands. The woman stated to him

that the sexual events which she had related to Freud when under his treatment had really never occurred. She declared that the whole thing had been a piece of pure imagination ... The physician already believes, and the patient is involuntarily led to believe, that a cure ... will supervene when a sexual trauma or aggression has been revealed ... Surely here is suggestion, involuntary and unintentional perhaps, but none the less suggestion.

(Dercum, 1911, pp. 1373, 1375, 1376)

The father ... asks a five-year-old boy—three months after its occurrence—"Did you, as the horse fell, think of your daddy?" for he, namely, is of the absolute conviction that the boy had the wish to see his father ... drop over dead. The boy answers: "Maybe, yes. It is possible." And this ... should not be suggestion? If this sort of thing is already done in the case of a child, then just imagine ... the way the sexual trauma suffered in childhood is gradually foisted upon the credulity of the adult.

(Haberman, 1913, p. 425)

We also have Freud's testimony in the prime of his theorizing that the challenge of the suggestion objection is the primary objection to his psychoanalytic claims. After acknowledging a component of suggestion in the use of transference to overcome patient resistances, Freud comments:

But you will now tell me that, no matter whether we call the motive force of our analysis transference or suggestion, there is a risk that the influencing of our patient may make the objective certainty of our findings doubtful. What is advantageous to our therapy is damaging to our researches. This is the objection that is most often raised against psychoanalysis, and it must be admitted that, though it is groundless, it cannot be rejected as unreasonable.

(1917, p. 452)

The suggestion objection is also influential among philosophers of science. Karl Popper asks:

[H]ow much headway has been made in investigating the question of the extent to which the (conscious or unconscious) expectations and theories held by the analyst influence the 'clinical responses' of the patient? (To say nothing about the conscious attempts to influence the patient by proposing interpretations to him, etc.)

(Popper, 1962, p. 3, n. 3)

Adolf Grunbaum (1984) argues that the suggestion objection is fatal to Freud's reliance on clinical psychoanalytic data, even when the analyst brings together several convergent lines of evidence:

[C]ontamination by suggestion does undermine the probative value of clinical data ... [T]he purported consilience of clinical inductions has the presumption of being *spurious,* and this strong presumption derives from the fact that the *independence* of the inferentially concurring pieces of evidence is grievously jeopardized by a *shared* contaminant: the analyst's influence. For *each* of the *seemingly* independent clinical data may well be more or less alike confounded by the analyst's suggestion so as to conform to his construction, at the cost of their epistemic reliability or probative value.

(Grunbaum, 1984, p. 285)

Psychoanalysis's Prima Facie Vulnerability to the Suggestion Objection

Freud's claims regarding the unconscious meanings he uncovered in his patients' minds were extraordinarily vulnerable to the suggestion objection due to three features of his psychoanalytic method: Freud's method was complex in ways that gave him many degrees of freedom in shaping the direction of the patient's thoughts; by his own description, Freud was assertive in influencing the patient in the direction that his theory predicted the patient should go; and, most provocatively, Freud suggested to the patient beforehand the specific content that the patient must remember and thus blatantly led the patient. A selection of passages from Freud will illustrate these points and make clear why the suggestion objection is so prima facie appealing.

First, then, it is clear from Freud's descriptions of his method that the complexity and malleability of the psychoanalytic process offer many opportunities for the analyst to exert influence. For example, in an essay in *Studies on Hysteria* (Breuer & Freud, 1895), Freud describes his method as follows:

[B]y detecting lacunas in the patient's first description ... we get hold of a piece of the logical thread at the periphery, and from this point on we clear a further path by the pressure technique.

In doing this, we very seldom succeed in making our way right into the interior along one and the same thread. As a rule it breaks off half-way: the pressure fails and either produces no result or one that cannot be clarified or carried further in spite of every effort ... [I]f we cannot promptly overcome the resistance ... [w]e drop it and take up another thread, which we may perhaps follow equally far ...

It is easy to imagine how complicated a work of this kind can become. We force our way into the internal strata, overcoming resistances all the time; we get to know the themes accumulated in one of these strata and the threads running through it, and we experiment how far we can advance with our present means and the knowledge we have acquired; we obtain preliminary information about the contents of the next strata by means of the pressure technique; we drop threads and pick them up again ... every time that we pursue a file of memories we are led to some side-path, which nevertheless eventually joins up again. By this method we at last reach a point at which we can stop working in strata and can penetrate by a main path straight to the nucleus of the pathogenic organization. With this the struggle is won, though not yet ended. We must go back and take up the other threads and exhaust the material.

(Freud, 1895, pp. 294–295)

Freud's description of "how complicated a work of this kind can become" makes clear the therapist's potential influence, for example, in deciding which thread is promising and when a thread has or has not culminated in adequate insight. He says, "we get hold of a piece of the logical thread," "we clear a further path by the pressure technique," and if that fails, "we drop it and take up another thread," all of which involves pivotal judgments and decisions by the analyst. Freud's language of "force," "struggle," and "overcoming resistance" reveals the assertiveness of the procedure, discussed below.

In "The Aetiology of Hysteria," Freud provides another vivid description of his method, including the following:

If the memory which we have uncovered does not answer our expectations, it may be that we ought to pursue the same path a little further; perhaps behind the first traumatic scene there may be concealed the memory of a second, which satisfies our requirements better ...

If we take a case which presents several symptoms ... [t]o begin with, the chains of memories lead backwards separately from one another; but, as I have said, they ramify. From a single scene two or more memories are reached at the same time, and from these again side-chains proceed whose individual links may once more be associatively connected with links belonging to the main chain ... In short, the concatenation is far from being a simple one ...

If the analysis is carried further, new complications arise. The associative chains belonging to the different symptoms begin to enter into relation with one another ... [A] particular symptom ... calls up not only the earlier links in its own chain but also a memory from another chain ... This experience accordingly belongs to both series, and in this way it constitutes a *nodal point* ... from which two or more symptoms have proceeded; one chain has attached itself to one detail of the scene, the second chain to another detail.

(1896c, pp. 195–198)

As Freud says, this criss-crossing maze of linkages is "far from being a simple one." As "new complications arise," the therapist must judge whether a claimed memory "does not answer our expectations" versus "satisfies our requirements," and when the final termination points of an associative thread are reached. These judgments offer enormous degrees of freedom for the therapist's influence. It is within the analyst's power to drop the threads that disconfirm and pursue the ones that confirm the analyst's theory.

Second, the plausibility of the suggestion objection is greatly increased by the aggressive way in which Freud pressured the patient to arrive at the kinds of memories that Freud postulated must exist. An episode from early in Freud's career is suggestive. It is well known that Freud sent his friend, Wilhelm Fliess, a letter in September 1897 in which he announced doubts about his seduction theory based largely on his failure to bring his patients' analyses to successful conclusions (Freud, 1897/1985a). Less well known is that just a month later he sent a further letter to Fliess temporarily backtracking on those doubts, explaining that "several, though not yet all, doubts about my conception of neurosis are being resolved" (Freud, 1897/1985b, p. 274). What had occurred to resolve those doubts? Freud explains that the key was simply his taking a more aggressive stance in overcoming the patient's resistance to accepting his interpretations:

> An idea about resistance has enabled me to put back on course all those cases of mine that had gone somewhat astray, so that they are now proceeding satisfactorily. Resistance, which finally brings the [analytic] work to a halt, is nothing other than the child's former character, the degenerative character ... I dig it out by my work; it struggles; and the person who initially was such a good, noble human being becomes mean, untruthful, or obstinate, a malingerer—until I tell him so and thus make it possible for him to overcome this character.
>
> (Freud, 1897/1985b, p. 274)

To obtain the evidence he required, Freud accused the patient of harboring a resistant degenerate inner self from childhood that is "mean, untruthful, or obstinate, a malingerer" in order to "dig it out" of the patient despite the patient's initial vigorous denials. His patients succumbed and Freud temporarily regained some confidence in his seduction theory, although not for long.

The aggressiveness of Freud's technique is revealed in many of his descriptions. Rather than repeat them, I will quote part of Grunbaum's (1984) colorful summary statement about Freud's assertive technique:

> [W]e must not overlook that he avowedly coaxed, coached, and even browbeat the patient in the quest for the theoretically expected data ... Numerous other statements ... show that he felt entitled on theoretical grounds to hector the patient relentlessly for not having retrieved the desired sort of memory ... Clearly, the analysand is admonished beforehand as to what is expected of him. And this avowed brain washing is conducive to yielding only spurious confirmations of etiologic hypotheses.
>
> (p. 151)

The third and by far most problematic feature of psychoanalysis from the perspective of the suggestion objection is that, prior to the patient's recall, Freud offers anticipatory ideas—interpretations—that explicitly present the patient with the precise contents of what he expects the patient to remember, making the suggestion process painfully evident. Consequently, Freud's method is a virtual prototype of what one would expect of a process in which one exercises influence and suggestion to get the results one wants. Of course, Freud has a rationale for this provocative practice, as we saw in a passage above: stating ahead of time the memory that is expected to emerge is a technique for overcoming resistance. Nonetheless, this raises bright red flags with regard to the possibility of suggestion, as Freud understood.

That Freud literally suggested the memory he was looking for in the patient before the patient recalled it is made explicit in many passages throughout his work, including Freud's commentary on the Hans case:

> In a psycho-analysis the physician always gives his patient (sometimes to a greater and sometimes to a less extent) the conscious anticipatory ideas by the help of which he is put in a position to recognize and to grasp the unconscious material. For there are some patients who need more of such assistance and some who need less; but there are none who get through without some of it.
>
> (1909, p. 104)

Giving the patient "the conscious anticipatory ideas" that the patient is then expected to recall as memories is endorsed throughout Freud's writings, starting with *Studies in Hysteria*, where Freud wrote: "it is of use if we can guess the way in which things are connected up and tell the patient before we have uncovered it. If we have guessed right, the course of the analysis will be accelerated" (Freud, 1895, p. 295). Shortly after the Hans publication, in an address to a psychoanalytic conference, Freud commented on the routine use of anticipatory interpretation and acknowledged that this weakened the knowledge claims of psychoanalysis due to the possibility of suggestion, but alluded to the recent Hans case as independent evidence for his views:

> The treatment is made up of two parts—what the physician infers and tells the patient, and the patient's working-over of what he has heard. The mechanism of our assistance is easy to understand: we give the patient the conscious anticipatory idea [the idea of what he may expect to find] and he then finds the repressed unconscious idea in himself on the basis of its similarity to the anticipatory one. This is the intellectual help which makes it easier for him to overcome the resistances between conscious and unconscious.
>
> (1910b, p. 141)

Later, in *Introductory Lectures* (1917), writing of the challenges of treating narcissistic neuroses, Freud says: "we … give the same help by the offer of anticipatory ideas" (p. 438). He explains the rationale for anticipatory interpretations as follows:

> There is no doubt that it is easier for the patient's intelligence to recognize the resistance and to find the translation corresponding to what is repressed if we have previously given him the appropriate anticipatory ideas. If I say to you: "Look up at the sky! There's a balloon there!" you will discover it much more easily than if I simply tell you to look up and see if you can see anything. In the same way, a student who is looking through a microscope for the first time is instructed by his teacher as to what he will see; otherwise he does not see it at all, though it is there and visible.
>
> (1917, p. 437)

A few years later, in "Remarks on the Theory and Practice of Dream Interpretation" (1923), Freud emphasizes the need for the therapist to take an active role in leading the resistant patient to the repressed contents. Such patients, Freud says,

> reproduce the forgotten experiences of their childhood only after one has constructed them from their symptoms, associations and other signs and has propounded these constructions to them … [W]ith these patients unless one interprets, constructs and propounds, one never obtains access to what is repressed in them.
>
> (p. 115)

And, in his late work, *Constructions in Analysis* (1937), Freud says,

> The analyst finishes a piece of construction and communicates it to the subject of the analysis so that it may work upon him; he then constructs a further piece out of the fresh material pouring in upon him, deals with it in the same way and proceeds in this alternating fashion.
>
> (p. 260)

Freud's repeated assertions along these lines make psychoanalysis an ideal target of the suggestion objection.

Freud's Polemical Responses to the Suggestion Objection

Freud repeatedly attempted to refute the suggestion objection polemically. His comments in the Hans case imply that he did not think the brief polemical rebuttals entirely succeeded. To see why, I briefly review a few of them.

In "Further Remarks on the Neuro-Psychoses of Defence" (1896b), Freud anticipates the suggestion objection to his seduction theory: "The most immediate objections to this conclusion will probably be ... that one must beware of forcing on patients supposed reminiscences of this kind by questioning them, or of believing in the romances which they themselves invent" (p. 164). Freud says:

> In reply ... we may ask that no one should form too certain judgements in this obscure field until he has made use of the only method which can throw light on it—of psycho-analysis for the purpose of making conscious what has so far been unconscious.
>
> (p. 164)

This response baldly begs the question by assuming that Freud's psychoanalytic method is valid. In fact, both the method and its results were cast into doubt by the failure of the seduction theory.

In "Heredity and the Aetiology of the Neuroses" (1896a), Freud defends first against the related objection that patients make up the sexual stories. Oddly enough, Freud cites his patients' vigorous resistance to his interpretations as evidence for their correctness:

> How is it possible to remain convinced of the reality of these analytic confessions ... [T]he fact is that these patients never repeat these stories spontaneously ... One only succeeds in awakening the psychical trace of a precocious sexual event under the most energetic pressure of the analytic procedure, and against an enormous resistance. Moreover, the memory must be extracted from them piece by piece.
>
> (p. 153)

Freud's argument that only enormous pressure from the analyst can extract the memories from the patient may argue against purposeful confabulation, which was a stereotypical property of hysterics. However, it only encourages the suggestion objection that the analyst forces his view on the reluctant patient.

Freud addresses the suggestion objection at length in his main presentation of the seduction theory, "The Aetiology of Hysteria" (1896c). He first comments again on the objection that patients may be inventing their stories of sexual abuse and presents a series of reasons the scenes acknowledged by his patients are likely genuine, largely variations on arguments considered above: "Before ... analysis the patients know nothing about these scenes"; they "are reproduced with the greatest reluctance"; the patients "are indignant ... if we warn them that such scenes are going to emerge"; "only the strongest compulsion of the treatment" gets them to agree; and, despite reviewing the excavated memories repeatedly, "they still attempt to withhold belief from them, by emphasizing the fact that, unlike what happens in the case of other forgotten material, they have no feeling of remembering the scenes." Freud takes this latter point, the patient's lack of recall, as "conclusive proof" that the patient is not making up the scene: "Why should patients assure me so emphatically of their unbelief, if what they want to discredit is something which—from whatever motive—they themselves have invented" (pp. 204–205). However, all of these arguments—the patient's reluctance, indignation, lack of recall, and such—could be taken to support the suggestion objection. This seems like a diversion from the more threatening objection. Freud also mentions here and elsewhere the intense emotions and feelings experienced by the patient: "While they are recalling these infantile experiences to consciousness, they suffer under the most violent sensations, of which they are ashamed and which they try to conceal" (p. 204). However, the patient's intense emotions and sensations do not imply the veridicality of the patient's memories and could be entirely expectable feelings when patients reluctantly acquiesce to and reiterate Freud's narratives of incestuous sexual abuse.

When Freud finally turns to the suggestion objection, his response is disappointing. He acknowledges that this objection is not as easy to refute as the confabulation concern, and then simply denies that it occurs:

> Is it not very possible either that the physician forces such scenes upon his docile patients, alleging that they are memories …
>
> It is less easy to refute the idea that the doctor forces reminiscences of this sort on the patient, that he influences him by suggestion to imagine and reproduce them. Nevertheless it appears to me equally untenable. I have never yet succeeded in forcing on a patient a scene I was expecting to find, in such a way that he seemed to be living through it with all the appropriate feelings. Perhaps others may be more successful in this.
>
> (1896c, p. 204)

Freud's disclaimer is worthless because the suggestion objection does not accuse Freud of explicitly or knowingly forcing a memory on a patient.

Freud then goes on to argue that "there are, however, a whole number of other things that vouch for the reality" of the excavated sexual contents. These include "the uniformity which they exhibit in certain details … which would otherwise lead us to believe that there were secret understandings between the various patients" (p. 205), as well as details the intimate implications of which patients might not even understand. The problem with such arguments is that patients did not come up with the seduction scenarios by themselves. The consistencies and details to which Freud refers can be explained as features that the therapist subtly or explicitly suggested to multiple patients (see Grunbaum's comment above about consilience of evidence as pseudo-convergence driven by the common source of suggestion).

In "Constructions in Analysis" (1937), Freud dismisses the suggestion objection on the basis that only an incompetent analyst who does not listen to the patient could succumb to this problem:

> The danger of our leading a patient astray by suggestion, by persuading him to accept things which we ourselves believe but which he ought not to, has certainly been enormously exaggerated. An analyst would have had to behave very incorrectly before such a misfortune could overtake him; above all, he would have to blame himself with not allowing his patients to have their say. I can assert without boasting that such an abuse of "suggestion" has never occurred in my practice.
>
> (1937, p. 262)

To modern psychologists as well as to most of Freud's contemporaries, this passage would seem naïve and defensive—and, yes, boastful. Social psychologists have documented the power of social desirability and person-to-person influence, even to the extent that under suggestion from others, individuals assert what is plainly contradicted by their own perception (e.g., Asch, 1951; 1956). Suggestion is simply more powerful and less obvious than Freud is willing to admit. As Collins (1980) observes, this remark is "astonishing" from someone who pioneered the description of our "unawareness of behaviour" (p. 433). Macmillan (2001) points out that such rationalizations ignore the vast body of scientific literature on the subtlety, power, and omnipresence of social influence factors that can hardly be claimed to be controlled by the analyst's intentions or within awareness.

Freud presents an additional polemical response to the suggestion objection based on the centrality of transference to psychoanalysis. He argues in *Introductory Lectures* that analysis uses suggestion, but only in exploiting the transference neurosis to motivate the patient to accept the analyst's reconstructions. He claims that the fact that analysis isolates the use of suggestion within the analysis of the transference and then analyzes and dispels the transference reaction insulates the broader etiological investigation from suggestion.

This "transference" argument simply begs the question of whether suggestion influences the broader psychoanalytic etiological exploration, let alone whether the analysis of transference itself is subject to such processes. Even Freud seems ultimately to have realized that the exploitation of transference to persuade the patient cuts both ways on the suggestion issue: "The therapeutic successes that occurred under the sway of the positive transference are open to the suspicion of being of a *suggestive* nature" (1938, p. 176).

Freud also argued that the process of free association "guarantees to a great extent that ... nothing will be introduced into it by the expectations of the analyst" (1925, p. 41). This defense underestimates the reach of suggestion. Judd Marmor reminds us how subtly suggestion can be exercised:

In face-to-face transactions the expression on the therapist's face, a questioning glance, a lift of the eyebrows, a barely perceptible shake of the head or shrug of the shoulder all act as significant cues to the patient. But even behind the couch, our 'uh-huhs' as well as our silences, the interest or the disinterest reflected in our tone of voice or our shifting postures all act like subtle radio signals influencing the patients' responses, reinforcing some responses and discouraging others.

(1962, 291–292)

Conclusion

In sum, Freud fully understood the threat from the suggestion objection from the beginning and was concerned throughout his career to rebut it. He recognized it as a cardinal objection to his psychoanalytic claims that required a response. However, his frequent attempts at brief polemical rebuttals were evasive and unpersuasive. Their inconclusiveness underscores how crucially important it was for Freud to mount a larger nonpolemical, evidence-driven, programmatic argument. I consider that argument in the next chapter.

References

Asch, S. E. (1951). Effects of group pressure upon the modification and distortion of judgment. In H. Guetzkow (ed.), *Groups, leadership and men*. Pittsburgh, PA: Carnegie Press.

Asch, S. E. (1956). Studies of independence and conformity: I. A minority of one against a unanimous majority. *Psychological monographs: General and applied*, 70 (9), 1–70.

Breuer, J., & Freud, S. (1893). On the psychical mechanism of hysterical phenomena: Preliminary communication. *SE* 2, 1–17.

Breuer, J., & Freud, S. (1895). Studies on hysteria. *SE* 2.

Collins, S. (1980). Freud and "the riddle of suggestion." *International Review of Psychoanalysis*, 7, 429–437.

Dercum, F. X. (1911). The role of dreams in etiology. *JAMA*, 56(19), 1373–1376.

Freud, S. (1888). Preface to the translation of Bernheim's Suggestion. *SE* 1, 73–87.

Freud, S. (1893). On the psychical mechanism of hysterical phenomena: A lecture. *SE* 3, 25–39.

Freud, S. (1895). The psychotherapy of hysteria. *SE* 2, 253–305.

Freud, S. (1896a). Heredity and the aetiology of the neuroses. *SE* 3, 141–156.

Freud, S. (1896b). Further remarks on the neuro-psychoses of defence. *SE* 3, 157–185.

Freud, S. (1896c). The aetiology of hysteria. *SE* 3, 187–221.

Freud, S. (1909). Analysis of a phobia in a five-year-old boy. *SE* 10, 1–150.

Freud, S. (1910a). Five lectures on psycho-analysis. *SE* 11, 1–56.

Freud, S. (1910b). The future prospects of psycho-analytic therapy. *SE* 11, 139–152.

Freud, S. (1917). Introductory lectures on psycho-analysis, part 3. *SE* 16.

Freud, S. (1923). Remarks on the theory and practice of dream interpretation. *SE* 19, 107–122.

Freud, S. (1925). An autobiographical study. *SE* 20, 1–74.

Freud, S. (1937). Constructions in analysis. *SE* 23, 255–270.

Freud, S. (1938). An outline of psycho-analysis. *SE* 23, 139–208.

Freud, S. (1985a). Letter from Freud to Fliess, September 21, 1897. In J. M. Masson (Ed. & Trans.), *The complete letters of Sigmund Freud to Wilhelm Fliess, 1887–1904* (pp. 264–266). Cambridge, MA: Harvard University Press. (Original work 1897.)

Freud, S. (1985b). Letter from Freud to Fliess, October 27, 1897. In J. M. Masson (Ed. & Trans.), *The complete letters of Sigmund Freud to Wilhelm Fliess, 1887–1904* (pp. 273–275). Cambridge, MA: Harvard University Press. (Original work 1897.)

Freud, S. (1985c). Letter from Freud to Fliess, August 7, 1901. In J. M. Masson (Ed. & Trans.), *The complete letters of Sigmund Freud to Wilhelm Fliess, 1887–1904* (pp. 446–448). Cambridge, MA: Harvard University Press. (Original work 1901.)

Grunbaum, A. (1984). *The foundations of psychoanalysis: A philosophical critique.* Berkeley, CA: University of California Press.

Haberman, J. V. (1913). The psychoanalytic delusion. *Medical Record*, 84(10), pp. 421–427.

Jung, C. G. (1915) *The theory of psychoanalysis.* New York: The Journal of Nervous and Mental Disease Publishing Company.

Lacewing, M. (2013). The problem of suggestion in psychoanalysis: An analysis and solution. *Philosophical Psychology*, 26(5), 718–743.

Macmillan, M. (2001). Limitations to free association and interpretation. *Psychological Inquiry*, 12(3), 113–128.

Marmor, J. (1962). Psychoanalytic therapy as an educational process. In J. Masserman (ed.), *Psychoanalytic education: Science and psychoanalysis* (Vol. 5) (pp. 286–299). New York: Grune and Stratton.

Popper, K. R. (1962). *Conjectures and refutations.* New York: Basic Books.

Chapter 3

"A More Direct and Less Roundabout Proof"

The Hans Case as Freud's Response to the Suggestion Objection

Why the Little Hans Case History is the Most Important Clinical Theory Paper Freud Wrote

In this chapter, I explain the primary reason why Freud's "Little Hans" case history (1909) is uniquely important for an evaluation of Freud's signature Oedipal theory of neurosogenesis. Indeed, I hold that from the perspective of a philosophy of science reconstruction of Freud's argument and evaluation of his theory, it is the most important clinical theory paper Freud ever wrote. Some reasons for this judgment were already provided in Chapter 1. One reason is obvious: the theory of the Oedipus complex was at the heart of Freud's clinical theory, and the Hans case is the most sustained and direct clinical discussion specifically aimed at demonstrating the Oedipus complex.

A second reason mentioned in Chapter 1 is that the Hans case constitutes what I called "Freud's Lakatosian moment." That is, the Oedipal hypothesis was proposed as a way of saving Freud's sexual theory of the neuroses after the failure of the seduction theory by adjusting peripheral elements of the theory to save its core thesis. Under such circumstances, the new hypothesis would typically be dismissed as ad hoc unless it gave rise to a novel, bold prediction. The Hans case provides that novel prediction, namely, that Hans's phobia is best explained by the Oedipal theory. Consequently, the scientific credibility of Freud's strategy of saving his sexual theory of the neuroses by switching from the seduction theory to the Oedipal theory is at stake.

However, by far the primary reason why the Hans case history is so important for evaluating Freud's overall argument, which I focus on in this chapter, is simply that the Hans case is Freud's only serious, evidence-driven attempt to reply to what he correctly recognized as the most threatening objection to his Oedipal theory as well as to his theorizing in general, the "suggestion objection" (as I am calling it). This is the objection that the supposed memories that Freud retrieved from his patients, the agreement he obtained from his patients with his interpretations, and the etiological insights he had into his patients' conditions during psychoanalysis that he cited as the evidence for his Oedipal theory of sexual development and neurosogenesis

DOI: 10.4324/9781003272472-3

were in fact bogus evidence. In fact, the objection claims, rather than discovering genuine etiological factors in his patients' minds, Freud either influenced his patients to accept his interpretations or embraced biased readings of the evidence his patients produced to yield the conclusions he desired.

Freud was quite explicit that the insights yielded by psychoanalytic treatment provided the evidential support on which he based his Oedipal theory:

> The question may, however, be raised of where convincing evidence is to be found in favour of the alleged aetiological importance of sexual factors in the psychoneuroses ... I would reply that the psychoanalytic examination of neurotics is the source from which this disputed conviction of mine is derived.
>
> (1906, p. 278)

Yet, as we saw in the last chapter, the nature of psychoanalysis itself as Freud practiced it—including the use of anticipatory ideas and interpretations to let the patient know beforehand what the analyst expects the patient to remember, the many subjective judgments by the analyst regarding likely associative pathways and meanings, and the general assertiveness and tenacity with which the analyst pursues the patient's appropriate responses—raises the possibility that the supposed insights are not veridical and that Freud's insights and his patients' reports are hopelessly epistemologically contaminated by Freud's influence and biases. Thus, doubt is cast on the very heart of Freud's evidential argument, including the validity of the psychoanalytic method of exploring the unconscious and the substantive evidence derived from that method that is claimed to support the Oedipal theory.

To respond to this objection, Freud attempted in the Hans case to provide evidence for the Oedipal theory that was not as vulnerable as his adult cases to the suggestion objection. The Hans case history is Freud's only serious attempt to provide such an evidence-based response to the suggestion objection. It is an attempt that, I will argue, he took to be a success and thus one on which he rested the epistemic warrant for his clinical-theoretic claims for the remainder of his life. Rather than this being merely a way of construing Freud's argument, the textual evidence I present later in this chapter clearly shows that this is the way that Freud himself firmly saw the importance of the Hans case. It is thus fair to say that from the perspective of a philosophical evaluation of Freud's argument, the Hans case is the single most important clinical theory paper that Freud wrote.

The argument I will put forward in this chapter on the Hans case's role in Freud's overall argument for the Oedipus complex is only part—but a crucial part—of a larger analysis of Freud's response to the suggestion objection. The other aspects of the argument that are most important are Freud's methodological claims that a comprehensive understanding of the psychoanalytic evidence in a case often yields a unique evidentially compelling solution to the etiological puzzle, and that the lynchpin of such a solution is a singular causal explanation of otherwise inexplicable detailed features of the patient's neurotic symptoms in terms of their specific sexual etiology. These epistemologically crucial aspects of Freud's interpretive methodology are reviewed in Chapter 9, and their success or failure when applied in the Hans case is evaluated in Chapter 10. However, as I argue in Chapter 9's analysis of Freud's interpretive methodology, whatever methodological arguments Freud provides, he still needs the Hans case to provide the anchor that secures his overall account from obvious potential ripostes.

All of that lies ahead. In this chapter, I focus exclusively on examining Freud's framing of the Hans case's argument and demonstrating Freud's epistemological reliance on the Hans case as a unique guarantor of his adult clinical findings.

The Hans Case as a Response to the Suggestion Objection

I now turn to the Hans case and its role in addressing the suggestion objection. At the case study's outset, Freud makes clear that his point in publishing the case is no less than saving psychoanalysis from the suggestion objection. His aim is to present evidence that is more direct and observational than his usual evidence from his adult cases, and thus to avoid the complex, multi-layered series of inferences, interpretations, associative linkages, and reconstructions of the past that occur in a typical adult analysis that leave such analyses open to the suggestion objection:

> But the peculiar value of this observation lies in the considerations which follow. When a physician treats an adult neurotic by psycho-analysis, the process he goes through of uncovering the psychical formations, layer by layer, eventually enables him to frame certain hypotheses as to the patient's infantile sexuality; and it is in the components of the latter that he believes he has discovered the motive forces of all the neurotic symptoms of later life. I have set out these hypotheses in my *Three Essays on the Theory of Sexuality*, and I am aware that they seem as strange to an outside reader as they seem incontrovertible to a psycho-analyst. But even a psycho-analyst may confess to the wish for a more direct and less roundabout proof of these fundamental theorems. Surely there must be a possibility of observing in children at first hand and in all the freshness of life the sexual impulses and wishes which we dig out so laboriously in adults from among their own debris—especially as it is also our belief that they are the common property of all men, a part of the human constitution, and merely exaggerated or distorted in the case of neurotics.
>
> (1909, pp. 5–6)

In characterizing the Hans case's "peculiar value," Freud tells us why this case is important. Freud acknowledges that adult psychoanalysis is a process of "laboriously" "uncovering the psychical formations, layer by layer" in an attempt to "dig out" the relevant insights from the patient's "own debris" of a lifetime of accumulated meanings and complex associative pathways so as to eventually "frame certain hypotheses as to the patient's infantile sexuality." Given the complexity of the process, the result could easily be seen as coming more from the analyst than from the patient. Although Freud saves face by insisting that the results are "incontrovertible to a psycho-analyst" and strange only to non-analysts, he implicitly acknowledges that there are genuine epistemic challenges to the results that analysts may be reluctant to confront but that make the results potentially controvertible, admitting that "even a psycho-analyst may confess to the wish for a more direct and less roundabout proof of these fundamental theorems."

So, Freud's goal in the Hans case report is to provide "a more direct and less roundabout proof" of Freud's theoretical claims that places them on more solid epistemological ground. What does Freud mean here by "more direct"? He clearly means the opposite of the problems with adult analysis that he complains about in the passage—the uncovering of psychical formations layer by layer and the laborious digging out of insights from among the patient's extensive psychological debris that are part of what make the results dubious and open to the suggestion objection. By "observing in children at first hand and in all the freshness of life the sexual impulses and wishes," the lesser number of inferential steps from observation to theory confirmation in a child analysis offers the possibility of greater epistemological confidence. Thus, the analysis of a child offers a way to check the validity of adult analyses and, indirectly, the validity of the psychoanalytic method used in the adult analyses.

One must not be misled into thinking that Freud is saying that the evidence in the Hans case is "direct" in some absolute logical-positivist sense. Interpretation of unconscious material behind a child's behavior is still interpretation and thus inferential and not direct observation. Freud carefully states that the child case data is "more direct and less roundabout," not that it is self-evidently observational in some absolute sense. Neu (1995) gets this point exactly right when he agrees that a child case can offer more confident inferences, but cautions that "the observation of children is itself of course theory-laden, that is, involves interpretation ... the demand for neutral, uninterpreted, data involves ... a fundamental misunderstanding of the nature of evidence ... especially in relation to psychoanalytic claims" (1995, p. 138).

It should be kept in mind that Freud's theory of neurosogenesis in adults generally postulated multiple traumatic incidents and production of fantasies that cumulatively lead to symptom formation and take part in determining the nature of the symptoms. Although Freud later emphasized the unresolved early childhood Oedipal sexual fantasies as the crucial "specific causes" of later hysteria and downplayed the sequence of postpubertal experiences that activated those earlier memories and led more directly to symptoms, in fact he held from the beginning that symptoms are shaped by the entire sequence and most immediately by the later experiences. Thus, the nature of the symptoms as reflections of the earliest determining traumas may be obstructed and distorted by the overlaying influences of later determinants. It might even happen that the primary determination of symptom details is due virtually entirely to the later experiences:

> Indeed, in the great majority of instances we find that a first trauma has left no symptom behind, while a later trauma of the same kind produces a symptom, and yet that the latter could not have come into existence without the cooperation of the earlier provoking cause; nor can it be cleared up without taking all the provoking causes into account.
>
> (1895, p. 173)

Freud writes of the complexity of the relationship between the earliest Oedipal and later postpubertal sexual and other precipitating causes and the complex inferences that are needed to disentangle such multicausal structures, for example:

> It may happen that the determining power of the infantile scenes is so much concealed that, in a superficial analysis, it is bound to be overlooked. In such instances we imagine that we have found the explanation of some particular symptom in the content of one of the later scenes—until, in the course of our work, we come upon the same content in one of the *infantile* scenes, so that in the end we are obliged to recognize that, after all, the later scene only owes its power of determining symptoms to its agreement with the earlier one. I do not wish because of this to represent the later scene as being unimportant; if it was my task to put before you the rules that govern the formation of hysterical symptoms, I should have to include as one of them that the idea which is selected for the production of a symptom is one which has been called up by a combination of several factors and which has been aroused from various directions simultaneously. I have elsewhere tried to express this in the formula: *hysterical symptoms are overdetermined.*
>
> (1896b, p. 216)

Later, after Freud's transition to the Oedipal theory, he again emphasizes how distant the determination of symptom features may be from the original specific Oedipal cause:

> [H]ysterical symptoms ... were now no longer to be regarded as direct derivatives of the repressed memories of childhood experiences; but

between the symptoms and the childish impressions there were inserted the patient's phantasies (or imaginary memories), mostly produced during the years of puberty, which on the one side were built up out of and over the childhood memories and on the other side were transformed directly into the symptoms. It was only after the introduction of this element of hysterical phantasies that the texture of the neurosis and its relation to the patient's life became intelligible.

(1906, p. 274)

Freud laments that the sequence of meaning transformations over time are a major challenge that sometimes the analyst may be unable to meet, going so far as to opine that older patients may become untreatable because of this:

[I]n practice ... the therapeutic operation was almost always compli- cated by the circumstance that it was not a single ("traumatic") impression, but in some cases a series of impressions—not easily scanned—which had participated in the creation of the symptom ... If the patient's age is in the neighbourhood of the fifties the conditions for psycho-analysis become unfavourable. The mass of psychical material is then no longer manageable.

(1904, pp. 249, 254)

The Hans case offered the uniquely favorable opportunity to examine a less overdetermined relationship between the earliest Oedipal desires and symptom formation as it took place directly from one to the other without mediation by postpubertal layers of meaning and symptom determination. It thus constituted a uniquely potent test of the specific Oedipal doctrines by examining symptoms that are unmediated by postpubertal cooperating traumas and thus must have the direct imprinting of the original, and in this case co-occurring, Oedipal trauma on them.

Freud's intentions for the Hans case become clearer in his summations of what he thinks he has accomplished. At the beginning of his Discussion sec- tion, he states,

My impression is that the picture of a child's sexual life presented in this observation of little Hans agrees very well with the account I gave of it (basing my views upon psychoanalytic examinations of adults) in my *Three Essays*.

(p. 101)

Freud's parenthetical remark reminds us that the point here is not merely that the Hans case confirms the account in *Three Essays*. The point is also that the earlier account was based wholly on the results of adult analyses and was thus open to the suggestion objection. The congruence of the

Hans case's findings with the results of Freud's interpretations in his adult cases is Freud's crucial point. If the "picture of a child's sexual life" that results from more direct and less questionable "observation" of a child agrees with the picture that emerges from the more elaborate and questionable reconstructions and analyses of the many layers of an adult's meaning system, this is potentially powerful support for the claim that the adult analyses and the method by which they were carried out may be scientifically valid.

In the final passage with which he ends his discussion of the case, Freud again attempts to explain the special value of the Hans case and is even more explicit regarding the epistemological point of the case:

> I cannot take leave of our small patient's phobia without giving expression to a notion which has made its analysis, leading as it did to a recovery, seem of especial value to me. Strictly speaking, I learnt nothing new from this analysis, nothing that I had not already been able to discover (though often less distinctly and more indirectly) from other patients analysed at a more advanced age. But the neuroses of these other patients could in every instance be traced back to the same infantile complexes that were revealed behind Hans's phobia. I am therefore tempted to claim for this neurosis of childhood the significance of being a type and a model, and to suppose that the multiplicity of the phenomena of repression exhibited by neuroses and the abundance of their pathogenic material do not prevent their being derived from a very limited number of processes concerned with identical ideational complexes.
>
> (1909, p. 147)

It is not true that Freud learned nothing substantively new from the Hans case. In a note added just a year later to *Three Essays*, he explicitly states that "'Analysis of a Phobia in a Five-Year-Old Boy' has taught us much that is new for which we have not been prepared by psycho-analysis" (1905, p. 193). Rather, Freud is underscoring that the case's "especial value" to him lies not in some novel substantive discovery but in the epistemological implications of the congruence of its findings with the findings of his adult cases. Freud reminds us of the superior epistemic basis for the conclusions in the Hans child case relative to his adult cases in which the conclusions are "less distinctly and more indirectly" and thus more questionably obtained. The case's primary value lies in the fact that with its superior epistemic foundation, the case duplicates Freud's findings with "other patients analyzed at a more advanced age"—that is, with all of Freud's other patients. It thus supports Freud's previous conclusions with adults against the suggestion objection.

Freud's Polemical Responses to the Suggestion Objection in the Hans Case

Although the Hans case in fact addresses the suggestion objection via its more direct evidence, Freud still goes through the motions of polemically defending the case from standard suggestion objection type criticisms. In his Discussion section, Freud takes up the suggestion issue as his first topic, and he immediately turns to a point that complicates his use of the case as a response to the suggestion objection, namely, the fact that Hans was analyzed by his own father. Freud formulates the potential objection as follows:

> [A]n analysis of a child conducted by his father, who went to work instilled with my theoretical views and infected with my prejudices, must be entirely devoid of any objective worth. A child, it will be said, is necessarily highly suggestible, and in regard to no one, perhaps, more than to his own father; he will allow anything to be forced upon him, out of gratitude to his father for taking so much notice of him; none of his assertions can have any evidential value, and everything he produces in the way of associations, phantasies, and dreams will naturally take the direction into which they are being urged by every possible means. Once more, in short, the whole thing is simply "suggestion"—the only difference being that in the case of a child it can be unmasked much more easily than in that of an adult.
>
> (1909, pp. 101–102)

Whereas Freud usually writes with disarming clarity about potential objections, he seems to exaggerate the nature of this potential objection. The fact that a child is highly open to suggestion from his father does not imply that "he will allow *anything* to be forced upon him," that "*none* of his assertions can have any evidential value," that "*everything* he produces ... will naturally take the direction into which they are being urged," and so "in short, the *whole thing* is simply 'suggestion'" (emphases added). Framing the objection in an inflated way allows Freud to more easily rebut it. The question is rather whether enough of Hans's avowals might be due to suggestion so as to cast doubt on the soundness of Freud's inferences. And certainly there is some merit in the concern that the child's father would be in a particularly good position to influence his son, although it is also true that Hans demonstrates rather impressive independence.

In any event, as we shall see, some of Freud's arguments are structured so as to be immune to the suggestion objection so that this never becomes a crucial issue. Moreover, as I discuss below, when the possibility of suggestion does arise, Freud provides guidelines to help decide the issue—namely, that it is not the patent's avowal per se but the flow of corroborating associations after the patient's agreement with an interpretation that supports the correctness of the interpretation.

Nonetheless, in his Discussion section, Freud responds polemically to some versions of the suggestion objection. He first defends the general truthfulness of children's assertions against the accusation that one cannot trust what a child says, although acknowledging that resistance might bring about some misleading statements:

> I do not share the view which is at present fashionable that assertions made by children are invariably arbitrary and untrustworthy. The arbitrary has no existence in mental life. The untrustworthiness of the assertions of children is due to the predominance of their imagination, just as the untrustworthiness of the assertions of grown-up people is due to the predominance of their prejudices. For the rest, even children do not lie without a reason, and on the whole they are more inclined to a love of truth than are their elders ... [T]he observations made during the period before the phobia admit of no doubt or demur. It was with the outbreak of the illness and during the analysis that discrepancies began to make their appearance between what he said and what he thought; and this was partly because unconscious material, which he was unable to master all at once, was forcing itself upon him, and partly because the content of his thoughts provoked reservations on account of his relation to his parents.
>
> (1909, pp. 102–104)

It is true that some of the reports of Hans's development and spontaneous statements prior to the phobia appear to be safe from suggestion. However, even here one might worry about the parents throwing out hints of how Hans ought to respond to satisfy Freud's theory at least verbally, for testing that theory was the point of keeping the diary.

As to Freud's comments on the truthfulness of children, Freud's formulation borders on a strawman argument. No one except Freud in his hyperbolic statements is saying that Hans's statements are "invariably arbitrary or untrustworthy." Moreover, there is an equivocation in Freud's counter-argument between two senses of arbitrariness. One can agree with Freud that mental states are psychologically determined and thus not arbitrary relative to psychological laws, so "the arbitrary has no existence in mental life"—and still hold that Hans gives (psychologically determined) false responses to his father's pressuring questions that are arbitrary relative to the truth of the matter. Indeed, Freud's point that children's assertions are not arbitrary because they are determined by imagination leaves open the possibility that imagination does not correspond to reality and thus there is arbitrariness in the veridicality sense. As to the implication that resistance may have led Hans to mislead his father at times, this does not address the question of how to identify the truth in such cases.

How to Distinguish Veridical Avowals from Avowals Due to Suggestion

Following these rather unpersuasive polemical passages, Freud addresses the issue of suggestion with unusual directness. In one of his clearest statements on the issue, Freud acknowledges that Hans was told things by his father and by Freud that might be considered prima facie instances of suggestion of Oedipal themes to Hans. Freud not only admits that this is true but argues, consistent with the last chapter's survey, that such anticipatory interpretation is a general and necessary feature of psychoanalysis given that the mental contents the analyst is seeking are repressed. In effect, Freud is admitting that there is a prima facie basis for the suggestion objection in the Hans case and elsewhere:

> It is true that during the analysis Hans had to be told many things that he could not say himself, that he had to be presented with thoughts which he had so far shown no signs of possessing, and that his attention had to be turned in the direction from which his father was expecting something to come. This detracts from the evidential value of the analysis; but the procedure is the same in every case. For a psychoanalysis is not an impartial scientific investigation, but a therapeutic measure. Its essence is not to prove anything, but merely to alter something. In a psycho-analysis the physician always gives his patient (sometimes to a greater and sometimes to a less extent) the conscious anticipatory ideas by the help of which he is put in a position to recognize and to grasp the unconscious material. For there are some patients who need more of such assistance and some who need less; but there are none who get through without some of it. Slight disorders may perhaps be brought to an end by the subject's unaided efforts, but never a neurosis—a thing which has set itself up against the ego as an element alien to it. To get the better of such an element another person must be brought in, and in so far as that other person can be of assistance the neurosis will be curable … It is true that a child, on account of the small development of his intellectual systems, requires especially energetic assistance.
>
> (1909, pp. 104–105)

As noted, such apparent suggestions in the form of anticipatory questions or interpretations regarding central Oedipal meanings were offered to Hans multiple times during the analysis. For example, Hans's father was the first to suggest to Hans that when Hans saw the horse fall down, Hans thought of his father falling down and being dead. Hans's father is the first to raise the question of whether Hans wants to replace his father with Mummy as well as the question of whether Hans is afraid of his father. Moreover, during Freud's one meeting with Hans and his father, Freud put forward the Oedipal interpretation: "I then disclosed to him that he was afraid of his father, precisely because he was so fond of his mother. It must be, I told him, that he thought his father was angry with him on that account" (p. 42). Freud later commented,

> I thought the right moment had now arrived for informing him that he was afraid of his father because he himself nourished jealous and hostile wishes against him—for it was essential to postulate this much with regard to his unconscious impulses. In telling him this, I had partly interpreted his fear of horses for him: the horse must be his father—whom he had good internal reasons for fearing.
>
> (p. 123)

The hypothesized symbolic link between the horse and Hans's father was repeatedly raised by the father without Hans having proposed it himself. So, the central Oedipal hypotheses did not originate in the case material with Hans but with Freud and the father.

Freud offers two responses to the suggestion objection in relation to such anticipatory interpretations in the Hans case. First, Freud emphasizes that Hans demonstrated his independence of thought because in some instances Hans spontaneously came forward with material that was not suggested ahead of time by Hans's father:

> And yet, even during the analysis, the small patient gave evidence of enough independence to acquit him upon the charge of "suggestion". Like all other children, he applied his childish sexual theories to the material before him without having received any encouragement to do so.
>
> (1909, p. 105)

Freud cites Hans's "excremental" theory of childbirth, his concern about his own bowel movements that Freud interprets as a manifestation of libido, and two "plumber" fantasies that Freud claims to have castration-anxiety meanings.

This is a weak argument. The plumber fantasies require extensive and debatable interpretation and so cannot be considered the "more direct" evidence Freud seeks (see Wakefield, forthcoming). The truth of the theory that children initially develop an excremental theory of childbirth, as well as the theory that anal pleasure is specifically sexual, are independent of the truth of the Oedipal theory. Also, one should not overestimate Freud's self-professed cleverness in anticipating that Hans would come up with the excremental theory of childbirth because Freud likely derived the idea from Hans himself, in earlier interactions with Hans that were reported in a prior paper (Freud, 1908). In any event, the fact that a child being treated for constipation should bring up feelings about excrement is not surprising. Even if Freud is correct that these statements or behaviors indicate that Hans was forthright and spontaneous at times, his polemical gloss on them does not address the legitimacy of the evidence for Freud's specific argument that Hans has an Oedipus complex.

Second and more promisingly, Freud comments on how to distinguish Hans's genuine agreement with an interpretation from his feigned agreement or his acquiescent agreement due to suggestion. One imagines that Freud is implying that such a discrimination might be easier to make in a child patient than in an adult, but the guidelines he puts forward are general ones and elsewhere he states them as applying generally. In putting forward these guidelines, Freud offers an invaluable method for evaluating Freud's own interpretations of the case material. One can think of the suggestion objection as a claim that there is a generic epistemological contaminant of the psycho-analytic situation that threatens the validity of the claimed insights that result from psychoanalytic interpretation. Alternatively, one can conceptualize it as a rival theory of each of the conclusions agreed to by the patient or reached by the analyst during psychoanalysis. Taking the latter course, the question becomes, for each instance of claimed insight, whether the overall evidence better supports the veridical-insight or suggestion explanation of the patient's avowal. In the Hans case, Freud provides some rough and fallible but data-anchored guidelines from his own perspective for drawing the distinction between insight and acquiescence:

> If we were to reject little Hans's statements root and branch we should certainly be doing him a grave injustice. On the contrary, we can quite clearly distinguish from one another the occasions on which he was fal-sifying the facts or keeping them back under the compelling force of a resistance, the occasions on which, being undecided himself, he agreed with his father (so that what he said must not be taken as evidence), and the occasions on which, freed from every pressure, he burst into a flood of information about what was really going on inside him and about things which until then no one but himself had known.
>
> (1909, p. 103)

Thus, it is not the patient's mere "yes" to an interpretation but above all whether the patient follows up the "yes" with fresh spontaneous confirming associations that fill out the picture that allows the analyst to have some confidence in the patient's avowal. As noted, this criterion is not a passing rationalization on Freud's part but rather an approach he affirmed to the end of his life, as in this statement from *Constructions in Analysis*:

> A plain "Yes" from a patient is by no means unambiguous. It can indeed signify that he recognizes the correctness of the construction that has been presented to him; but it can also be meaningless, or can even deserve to be described as "hypocritical", since it may be convenient for

his resistance to make use of an assent in such circumstances in order to prolong the concealment of a truth that has not been discovered. The "Yes" has no value unless it is followed by indirect confirmations, unless the patient, immediately after his "Yes", produces new memories which complete and extend the construction. Only in such an event do we consider that the "Yes" has dealt completely with the subject under discussion

(1937, p. 262)

Freud also says that "if nothing further develops we may conclude that we have made a mistake and we shall admit as much to the patient at some suitable opportunity" (1937, p. 261). Thus, again, the sign of a mistaken interpretation is that "nothing further develops"—that is, no corroborating evidence emerges. This criterion should be kept in mind as we approach and evaluate the Hans case material.

Does Freud Contradict Himself About the Purpose of Psychoanalysis?

Some commentators have pointed to an apparent tension in Freud's discussion of suggestion in the Hans case, with one commentator concluding that "in his anxiety to respond to the charge of suggestion, Freud gives multiple and perhaps contradictory responses" (Neu, 1995, p. 145). This charge is prompted by two seemingly opposed claims about the nature of psychoanalysis that occur in the passage about suggestion quoted above:

1 "For a psychoanalysis is not an impartial scientific investigation, but a therapeutic measure. Its essence is not to prove anything, but merely to alter something."
2 "Therapeutic success, however, is not our primary aim; we endeavour rather to enable the patient to obtain a conscious grasp of his unconscious wishes."

Freud was fond of reminding his readers that psychoanalysis uniquely links a method of psychological research with medical treatment, for example: "[T]he attempt at discovering the determining cause of a symptom was at the same time a therapeutic manoeuvre" (1893, 35); "the laborious but completely reliable method of psycho-analysis used by me in making ... investigations which also constitute a therapeutic procedure" (1896a, p. 162); "the uncovering of this unknown meaning is accompanied by the removal of the symptoms—so that in this case scientific research and therapeutic effort coincide" (1923, 236); and "In psycho-analysis there has existed from the very first an inseparable bond between cure and research. Knowledge brought therapeutic success" (1926, p. 256). This link raises the question of the precise relationship of these two goals, and whether one goal takes precedence over the other. The purported contradiction in the Hans case record thus begs for clarification.

So, the puzzle goes, on the one hand, Freud says that therapeutic success is *not* the "primary aim" of psychoanalysis, but on the other hand he says that aiming for therapeutic success is the "*essence*" of psychoanalysis! Freud is too talented a rhetorician to blatantly contradict himself in the way commentators have suggested. There are various convoluted glosses that one can use to try to explain Freud's apparently conflicting statements, but it turns out that these are not needed because there is a simple translational point that can resolve the problem.

The translation, "*primary aim*," appears to be potentially misleading and to create the illusion of a tension. The second passage above reads in German: "*Es ist aber nicht der therapeutische Erfolg, den wir an erster Stelle anstreben, sondern wir wollen den Patienten in den Stand setzen, seine unbewußten Wunschregungen bewußt zu erfassen.*" The use here of "ersten Stella" (literally, "first point" or "first job") need not be translated as the "primary aim" of psychoanalysis but as the less loaded "initial task," "first step," "immediate goal," or "preliminary goal," or something similar. This would be consistent with Freud's tendency to portray insight and cure as going together, with cure a sort of epiphenomenon of insight: "understanding and cure almost coincide ... a traversable road leads from the one to the other" (1933, p. 145). It would thus allow the two cited sentences to be consistent. Yes, Freud is saying, therapy is the ultimate purpose of psychoanalysis in the medical context, but the way the analyst actually pursues that "essence" is to focus entirely on overcoming the patient's resistances, gaining insight into the patient's unconscious wishes, and resolving the patient's conflicts. Cure is an epiphenomenon of insight for Freud, and this is why throughout his writings Freud cites research and therapy as going together in psychoanalysis.

The same idea appears elsewhere in Freud's work with less ambiguity. For example, in *Introductory Lectures*, Freud says:

> I will digress for a moment to ask if you know what is meant by a causal therapy. That is how we describe a procedure which does not take the symptoms of an illness as its point of attack but sets about removing its *causes*. Well, then, is our psycho-analytic method a causal therapy or not? ... In so far as analytic therapy does not make it its first task to remove the symptoms, it is behaving like a causal therapy.
>
> (1917, p. 435)

And, in a 1923 encyclopedia article on psychoanalysis, Freud says:

> It may be laid down that the aim of the treatment is to remove the patient's resistances and to pass his repressions in review and thus to bring about the most far-reaching unification and strengthening of his ego, to enable him to save the mental energy which he is expending upon

internal conflicts ... The removal of the symptoms of the illness is not specifically aimed at, but is achieved, as it were, as a by-product if the analysis is properly carried through.

(1923, p. 251)

In an early paper, Freud said that "the task the psycho-analytic method seeks to perform may be formulated in different ways, which are, however, in their essence equivalent," and he offers the following three definitions of the aim: "the task of the treatment is to remove the amnesia"; "all repressions must be undone"; and "the task consists in making the unconscious accessible to consciousness, which is done by overcoming the resistances" (1904, pp. 252–253). All of these are focused on insight and intrapsychic change, not therapeutic symptom cure, although that is certainly expected to follow.

I conclude that no contradiction is lurking in Freud's two sentences when properly interpreted and seen in the context of his view of the relationship of insight and cure. The aim of psychoanalysis is insight, and the Hans case is presented as a vindication of Freud's method of obtaining insight. It is a wonderful benefit that the resulting insight can yield therapeutic cure as a side effect, but that is not of the essence of the epistemological justification for and importance of psychoanalysis as a method of scientific research. Indeed, as Freud over time became less optimistic about the therapeutic benefits of psychoanalysis, he was quite clear that psychoanalysis remained of just as much interest due to its being a unique methodology for exploring the mind and wanted assurance "that the therapy will not destroy the science" (1926, p. 254).

Freud's Reliance on the Hans Case to Answer the Suggestion Objection and Secure the Epistemological Foundations of His Clinical Theory

In light of the manifest weaknesses of Freud's typical polemical responses to the suggestion objection discussed in the last chapter, most observers would agree with Collins (1980) that "Freud offers no theoretical rebuttal of the possibility that what is at work is suggestion" (p. 434). I will argue that this is not at all the case. Rather, the nature and locus of Freud's most rigorous response to the suggestion objection has gone unrecognized by his defenders and critics alike. Moreover, Freud's response is tactically brilliant and in principle scientifically relevant. Freud took on the suggestion objection by attempting to show that the same results gotten through his supposedly contaminated method in his adult psychoanalyses are arrived at in a child case in which the presumed influence of suggestion, although present, is vanishingly small or can be evaded or corrected for when it does occur.

Freud believed that the Hans case provided evidence less vulnerable than his adult analyses to the suggestion objection, and that it succeeded in confirming both his Oedipal theory and the validity of his psychoanalytic method. He thus rested his subsequent claims about adult analyses on the Hans case as an epistemological warrant.

How reliant was Freud on the Hans case to support his rejection of the suggestion objection to his Oedipal theory? The answer is that he was virtually totally reliant on it throughout his remaining career. Whenever Freud reviewed his success in discovering infantile sexuality and the Oedipus complex using his method of psychoanalysis, he added the point that these discoveries—and thus his method—were confirmed by the direct observation of children. Why repeat the reference to Hans over and over in every retelling of his discoveries? Freud knew that when he mentioned the discoveries he had made through analyses of adults, the standard skeptical reaction would be: "sure, that's because you suggested these ideas to your patients, just like you did with the seduction scenes you had 'discovered' earlier using your same method." Freud possessed no other answer to this skeptical dismissal than the Hans case. Freud needed to reference Hans whenever he made claims about what he had established in adult analyses in order to vouch for the epistemological validity of his method and thus the scientific validity of his claimed discoveries. Hans is Freud's one answer to the otherwise devastating suggestion objection.

Did Freud really place such weight on the Hans case in making his argument for the Oedipus complex? In this section, I survey selected passages from various years throughout his career that show that he did so. Although not a systematic review of all such passages, the cited passages are sufficient to document Freud's routine and repetitive reliance throughout his career on the Hans case to vouch for his analytic results with adults and to support the epistemological validity of his overall argument despite the suggestion objection.

1908. Freud began making his case for the epistemological importance of the Hans case even before the case was published. In 1908, Freud published a preliminary paper on the sexual theories of children that was based on the case:

> Recently, the analysis of a five-year-old boy, which his father undertook and which he has handed over to me for publication, has given me irrefutable proof of the correctness of a view towards which the psycho-analysis of adults had long been leading me.
>
> (1908, p. 214)

In this paper, Freud summarized his theories about how children—specifically, boys ("the following observations apply chiefly to the sexual development of one sex only, that is, of males" [p. 211])—develop their understanding of sexuality and of where babies come from. Many of the ideas that make their appearance in the full Hans case history appear in this preliminary paper, such as: the child's view that both sexes have a penis; the child's view that the mother's growing belly during pregnancy means that the baby comes from inside the mother and not, for example, from the stork; the child's view that babies, growing in the belly, are thus likely delivered through the anus in the same way as excrement; the child's view that intercourse, which Freud hypothesizes to be generally witnessed by the child, is conceptualized as a sadistic and violent act; the child's view, due to the boy's eventual discovery that girls do not in fact have penises, that castration should be feared as a potential punishment; and, triggered by the boy's puzzlement that the baby is said to be the father's but the child knows nothing of the vagina, the child's sexual investigations aimed at explaining the father's role in having children.

Freud begins by observing that there are three sources of information about childhood sexual theories and childhood sexuality:

> Firstly, from the direct observation of what children say and do; secondly, from what adult neurotics consciously remember from their childhood and relate during psycho-analytic treatment; and thirdly, from the inferences and constructions, and from the unconscious memories translated into conscious material, which result from the psycho-analysis of neurotics.
>
> (p. 209)

Freud acknowledges the intrinsic objections to information from the latter two sources. He notes that what adult neurotics consciously remember from their childhood and relate during psychoanalytic treatment is problematic because "it is subject to the objection that it may have been falsified in retrospect." Similarly, he observes that material derived from psychoanalytic interpretation such as "the inferences and constructions" and "unconscious memories translated into conscious material" that emerge in psychoanalysis of neurotics "is open to all the criticisms which it is the custom to marshal against the trustworthiness of psycho-analysis and the reliability of the conclusions that are drawn from it" due to the problem of suggestion. In contrast, Freud asserts that the "direct observation of what children say and do" provides "the most unequivocal and fertile source of all" (p. 209) of evidence regarding childhood sexual ideas and experiences. The evidential fruitfulness of direct observation is only limited, Freud says, by the fact that people have ignored and suppressed children's sexual thoughts. Without these restraints, direct observation of children could have "by itself supplied all that is worth knowing on the subject" (p. 209). In this regard, Freud observes in the 1909 report that Hans was raised with as few restraints as possible in sexual matters, so we can expect to learn much from him.

1910. In a footnote added in the 1910 edition of his *Three Essays*, Freud writes:

> When the account which I have given above of infantile sexuality was first published in 1905, it was founded for the most part on the results of psycho-analytic research upon adults. At that time it was impossible to make full use of direct observation on children: only isolated hints and some valuable pieces of confirmation came from that source. Since then it has become possible to gain direct insight into infantile psycho-sexuality

by the analysis of some cases of neurotic illness during the early years of childhood. It is gratifying to be able to report that direct observation has fully confirmed the conclusions arrived at by psycho-analysis—which is incidentally good evidence of the trustworthiness of that method of research. In addition to this, the "Analysis of a Phobia in a Five-Year-Old Boy" (1909b) has taught us much that is new for which we have not been prepared by psycho-analysis.

(Freud, 1905, p. 193, n. 2)

Note that Freud here expresses his belief that the Hans case plays a dual role. First, it confirms his substantive theory of the Oedipus complex in a child through direct observation. Second, because the evidence is more direct than in adult cases, in doing so it simultaneously vindicates and proves trustworthy his psychoanalytic methodology for exploring the mind by which he reached parallel conclusions in the psychoanalysis of adults.

1910. Again, the year after the Hans case was published, in an address to a psychoanalytic conference, Freud says: "[I]n speaking to you I need not rebut the objection that the evidential value in support of the correctness of our hypotheses is obscured in our treatment as we practise it to-day; you will not forget that this evidence is to be found elsewhere, and that a therapeutic procedure cannot be carried out in the same way as a theoretical investigation" (1910, p. 142). Freud thus acknowledged that suggestion poses a prima facie problem for psychoanalytic evidence given that therapy is not a pure experiment regarding psychoanalysis versus the suggestion theory because it requires anticipatory statements by the analyst of what the analyst expects the patient to remember. He alludes, however, to the independent evidence recently provided by the Hans case: "This evidence is to be found elsewhere."

1914. In recounting the history of his discoveries, Freud says:

In the beginning, my statements about infantile sexuality were founded almost exclusively on the findings of analysis in adults which led back into the past. I had no opportunity of direct observations on children. It was therefore a very great triumph when it became possible years later to confirm almost all my inferences by direct observation and the analysis of very young children.

(Freud, 1914, p. 18)

1917. In his *Introductory Lectures*, Freud explains:

For psycho-analytic research has had to concern itself, too, with the sexual life of children, and this is because the memories and associations arising during the analysis of symptoms [in adults] regularly led back to the early years of childhood. What we inferred from these analyses was later confirmed point by point by direct observations of children.

[Strachey notes: "The earliest of these direct observations were made in the case of 'Little Hans.'"]

(Freud, 1917, p. 310)

Freud later relies on the Hans case in spelling out the features of the Oedipus complex:

What, then, can be gathered about the Oedipus complex from the direct observation of children at the time of their making their choice of an object before the latency period? Well, it is easy to see that the little man wants to have his mother all to himself, that he feels the presence of his father as a nuisance, that he is resentful if his father indulges in any signs of affection towards his mother and that he shows satisfaction when his father has gone on a journey or is absent.

(p. 332)

1918. A decade after the Hans case, Freud published the "Wolf Man" case (1918) in which he retrospectively analyzed an infantile neurosis reported by an adult patient. Freud attempted to justify his retrospective approach in contrast to the Hans case's direct observation by identifying distinctive virtues of each approach. In the course of doing so, he reiterated the epistemological advantages of "direct" observation during childhood due to one's not having to wade through all the intervening time's distortions and alterations of material:

My description will therefore deal with an infantile neurosis which was analysed not while it actually existed, but only fifteen years after its termination. This state of things has its advantages as well as its disadvantages in comparison with the alternative. An analysis which is conducted upon a neurotic child itself must, as a matter of course, appear to be more trustworthy, but it cannot be very rich in material; too many words and thoughts have to be lent to the child ... An analysis of a childhood disorder through the medium of recollection in an intellectually mature adult is free from these limitations; but it necessitates our taking into account the distortion and refurbishing to which a person's own past is subjected when it is looked back upon from a later period. The first alternative perhaps gives the more convincing results; the second is by far the more instructive. In any case it may be maintained that analysis of children's neuroses can claim to possess a specially high theoretical interest ... [S]o many of the later deposits are wanting in them that the essence of the neurosis springs to the eyes with unmistakable distinctness.

(Freud, 1918, pp. 8–9)

Thus, Freud holds that although problematic in various ways, a direct analysis of a child as in the Hans case provides the most "trustworthy" and "convincing" results. In fact, "the essence of the neurosis springs to the eyes with unmistakable distinctness," exposing the sexual sources that lie behind all psychoneuroses.

1923. In an encyclopedia article aimed at explaining psychoanalysis to the general public, Freud writes:

> Science had become accustomed to consider sexual life as beginning with puberty and regarded manifestations of sexuality in children as rare signs of abnormal precocity and degeneracy. But now psycho-analysis revealed a wealth of phenomena, remarkable, yet of regular occurrence, which made it necessary to date back the beginning of the sexual function in children almost to the commencement of extra-uterine existence; and it was asked with astonishment how all this could have come to be overlooked. The first glimpses of sexuality in children had indeed been obtained through the analytic examination of adults and were consequently saddled with all the doubts and sources of error that could be attributed to such a belated retrospect; but subsequently (from 1908 onwards) a beginning was made with the analysis of children themselves and with the unembarrassed observation of their behaviour, and in this way direct confirmation was reached for the whole factual basis of the new view.
>
> (Freud, 1923a, pp. 243–244)

1925. In his *Autobiographical Study*, Freud writes:

> My surprising discoveries as to the sexuality of children were made in the first instance through the analysis of adults. But later (from about 1908 onwards) it became possible to confirm them fully and in every detail by direct observations upon children. [Strachey inserts a footnote here: "Cf. the analysis of 'Little Hans.'"]
>
> (Freud, 1925, p. 39)

1926. In *The Question of Lay Analysis*, Freud imagines an interlocutor asking: "Now tell me, though, what certainty can you offer for your analytic findings on the sexual life of children? Is your conviction based solely on points of agreement with mythology and history?" Freud answers:

> Oh, by no means. It is based on direct observation. What happened was this. We had begun by inferring the content of sexual childhood from the analysis of adults—that is to say, some twenty to forty years later. Afterwards, we undertook analyses on children themselves, and it was no small triumph when we were thus able to confirm in them everything that we had been able to divine, in spite of the amount to which it had been overlaid and distorted in the interval.
>
> (1926, p. 214)

When Freud's imagined interlocutor raises the further question: "What? You have had small children in analysis? children of less than six years? Can that be done? And is it not most risky for the children?" Freud answers:

> It can be done very well ... [A]s regards the damage done by early analysis, I may inform you that the first child on whom the experiment was ventured, nearly twenty years ago, has since then grown into a healthy and capable young man, who has passed through his puberty irreproachably, in spite of some severe psychical traumas ... Much that is of interest attaches to these child analyses; it is possible that in the future they will become still more important. From the point of view of theory, their value is beyond question. They give unambiguous information on problems which remain unsolved in the analyses of adults; and they thus protect the analyst from errors that might have momentous consequences for him. One surprises the factors that lead to the formation of a neurosis while they are actually at work and one cannot then mistake them ... We have become quite generally convinced from the direct analytic examination of children that we were right in our interpretation of what adults told us about their childhood.
>
> (Freud, 1926, pp. 215–216)

Three things become clear from this review. The first is that Freud continued throughout his life to be well aware of the threat to his views from the suggestion objection and related objections regarding the epistemological contamination of clinical psychoanalytic investigations into etiology of psychoneurotic symptoms. Second, he relied on the Hans case as his "ace in the hole" to support and justify the conclusions he reached in his adult cases. Third, as we have seen, at the moments when he acknowledges this problem and addresses it, Freud does not—as Grunbaum (1984) would maintain— rebut the potential suggestion objections on the basis of therapeutic success, which Grunbaum calls Freud's "Tally Argument." Rather, he rebuts the objection by citing the Hans case's conclusions in themselves as proof that such epistemological contamination cannot be generating his results. Freud clearly relied on the Hans case not as just one piece of supporting data among others but rather as an integral part of his basic argument for his Oedipal theory that must be consistently cited when referring to the mass of data from adult analyses to make that mass of data evidentially credible.

Conclusion

The suggestion objection was, and remains, the most commonly cited reason for rejecting Freud's clinical theorizing about the etiology of the psychoneuroses based on suspicions that the data from his psychoanalytic cases is epistemologically contaminated. This is in part because Freud's method of psychoanalytic investigation is particularly vulnerable to the suggestion objection, as we saw in the last chapter. As we also saw in the last chapter, Freud was well aware of his theory's vulnerability to the suggestion objection from early in his career and appreciated its seriousness, and his many attempts to respond polemically were not persuasive.

I have not yet reconstructed Freud's arguments in the Hans case. Rather, I have argued for seeing the Hans case as Freud's only major *evidentially grounded* attempt to refute the suggestion objection, vindicate his psychoanalytic method, and support his Oedipal theory. He attempted to do this by showing that the very same conclusions yielded by his method with adults could be arrived at in a more direct and defensible manner with a child case that lacks the many layers of interpretation and thus the inordinate opportunity for suggestion in adult cases. The case's special features make it possible to construct arguments that are largely immune to or plausibly able to evade the suggestion objection. Thus, from an epistemic-evidential perspective, it is fair to say that the Hans case is the most important clinical theory paper Freud wrote.

Thinking that he succeeded in demonstrating in the Hans case that his Oedipal theory had been shown to be verified independently of suggestion, Freud relied on the Hans case for the rest of his career as an epistemological undergirding for his theoretical claims about adult cases that, he recognized, were by themselves vulnerable to the suggestion objection. The evaluation of the Hans case as evidence for the Oedipal theory is thus in effect an evalua-tion of the evidence and argument for the Oedipal theory itself.

References

Collins, S. (1980). Freud and "the riddle of suggestion." *International Review of Psychoanalysis*, 7, 429–437.

Freud, S. (1893). On the psychical mechanism of hysterical phenomena: A lecture. *SE* 3, 25–39.

Freud, S. (1895). Fraulein Elisabeth von R. *SE* 2, 135–181.

Freud, S. (1896a). Further remarks on the neuro-psychoses of defence. *SE* 3, 157–185.

Freud, S. (1896b). The aetiology of hysteria. *SE* 3, 187–221.

Freud, S. (1904). Freud's psychoanalytic procedure. *SE* 7, 249–254.

Freud, S. (1905). Three essays on the theory of sexuality. *SE* 7, 123–246.

Freud, S. (1906). My views on the part played by sexuality in the aetiology of the neuroses. *SE* 7, 269–279.

Freud, S. (1908). On the sexual theories of children. *SE* 9, 205–226.

Freud, S. (1909). Analysis of a phobia in a five-year-old boy. *SE* 10, 1–150.

Freud, S. (1910). The future prospects of psycho-analytic therapy. *SE* 11, 139–152.

Freud, S. (1914). On the history of the psycho-analytic movement. *SE* 14, 6–66.

Freud, S. (1917). Introductory lectures on psycho-analysis, part 3. *SE* 16.

Freud, S. (1918). From the history of an infantile neurosis. *SE* 17, 1–124.

Freud, S. (1923a). Two encyclopaedia articles. *SE* 18, 233–260.

Freud, S. (1923b). Remarks on the theory and practice of dream interpretation. *SE* 19, 107–122.

Freud, S. (1925). An autobiographical study. *SE* 20, 1–74.

Freud, S. (1926). The question of lay analysis. *SE* 20, 177–258.

Freud, S. (1933). New introductory lectures on psycho-analysis. *SE* 22, 1–182.

Freud, S. (1937). Constructions in analysis. *SE* 23, 255–270.

Grunbaum, A. (1984). *The foundations of psychoanalysis: A philosophical critique.* Berkeley, CA: University of California Press.

Neu, J. (1995). "Does the Professor talk to God?" Learning from Little Hans. *Philosophy, Psychiatry & Psychology,* 2, 137–158.

Wakefield, J. C. (forthcoming). *Freud's interpretation of dream and fantasy evidence: A hypothesis testing approach to the case of Little Hans.* New York: Routledge.

Chapter 4

"A Little Oedipus"
Freud's Analysis of the Hans Case

In Freud's discussion of the Hans case history, he presents his theory of the etiology of Hans's phobia, which I review here. All citations are to the Hans case history (Freud, 1909), unless otherwise specified. The evidence he presents for his etiological theory is reviewed in the following chapters. Obviously I cannot cover every aspect of Freud's explanation but just central strands.

Freud hopes to demonstrate both the plausibility of the Oedipal theory of neurosogenesis and the reliability of his method of psychoanalytic inquiry, while minimizing the potential interference from suggestion. He sets himself three goals: (1) to "consider how far it supports the assertions which I put forward in my *Three Essays on the Theory of Sexuality*" about childhood sexuality; (2) to demonstrate how the Oedipal theory of phobia "can contribute towards our understanding of this very frequent form of disorder"; and, (3) to illuminate normal childhood development and thus see "whether it can be made to shed any light upon the mental life of children" in general (p. 101). My primary concern is the Oedipal explanation of Hans's phobia, but first I consider how Freud thinks that the Hans case supports his general child sexual developmental hypotheses in *Three Essays*.

Hans and Normal Child Sexual Development

Prior to the development of Hans's phobia, Hans's parents were keeping a diary of Hans's sexual development at Freud's behest for the purpose of verifying Freud's claims about child sexuality. In his *Three Essays* (1905), Freud had argued that young children naturally develop sexual feelings, contrary to the common Victorian medical doctrine that children are naturally lacking in sexual feeling and that all childhood sexuality is pathological, induced either by physiological disorder or premature stimulation (which was the position Freud himself had embraced during his earlier "seduction theory" period). Freud argues that Hans is basically normal and not hereditarily tainted, for otherwise his use of the Hans case to understand normal development would face the "objection ... according to which Hans was a neurotic, a 'degenerate' with a bad heredity, and not a normal child, knowledge about whom could be

DOI: 10.4324/9781003272472-4

applied to other children" (p. 141). To the objection that Hans is tainted because he develops a phobia, Freud points to how common such phobias are among presumptively normal children and cites Hans's cheerful healthiness in every other respect; he "was well formed physically, and was a cheerful, amiable, active minded young fellow who might give pleasure to more people than his own father" (p. 142); he "is described by his parents as a cheerful, straightforward child" (p. 103); and he "had an unusually kind-hearted and affectionate disposition ... he was never unmoved if any one wept in his presence" (p. 112).

One can readily grant Freud that Hans is a hereditarily normal boy who developed a phobia. Consequently, the potential evidential value of the Hans case cannot be dismissed merely because it is just one case. As Anna Freud later insisted in an introduction to an English translation of the Hans case, "The issue ... is not the illness of a child who may be hereditarily tainted, or sexually overstimulated, or abnormally precocious, or otherwise individually predisposed; rather, it is a more or less typical occurrence" (1980, p. 280).

Regarding Freud's claims about sexual development, Freud's theory of childhood sexuality vastly extends the category of sexuality to encompass oral, anal, phallic, Oedipal, and latency developmental stages as well as many component sexual zones such as skin contact, scopophilia (sexual arousal at seeing a sexual object), exhibitionism, muscular exertion or infliction of pain as a form of sexual aggression and sadism, and many others. Freud needs this extraordinarily broad conception of what is specifically sexual to justify his signature claim that hysterical symptoms, which can take endless forms, are all of sexual origin. However, the non-Oedipal aspects of the component theory of sexuality play a relatively minor role in the main argument of the Hans case regarding the etiology of his phobia. The "excretory complex" enters significantly into the case's explanation of Hans's phobia, but this is primarily in relation to Hans's excretory theory of childbirth and is thus more an Oedipal derivative than a direct issue of anal sexuality. Given that the component theory of sexuality raises complex conceptual issues of its own and plays a relatively minimal role in the case, I largely ignore it here.

Other than the Oedipus complex, the one aspect of child sexuality that plays a major role in the Hans case history is Hans's clearly documented phallic sexuality. Starting during the prephobia period at about age three, Hans's parents document Hans's early fascination with penises ("widdlers"), including curiosity about the genitals of his parents and his friends, excitement at observing the penises of various animals, and, of course, interest in his own penis, including repeated pleasurable self-touching. When his mother scolds and threatens him for masturbating, he answers rather dismissively, "But it's great fun."

Freud observes:

> The first trait in little Hans which can be regarded as part of his sexual life was a quite peculiarly lively interest in his "widdler" ... This interest aroused in him the spirit of enquiry ... little Hans began to try to get a sight of other people's widdlers; his sexual curiosity developed, and at the same time he liked to exhibit his own widdler.
>
> (pp. 106–107)

Freud concludes that these evidences of sexuality in the straightforward sense of genital pleasure confirm his claim about childhood sexuality, observing that "in little Hans's sexual constitution the genital zone was from the outset the one among his erotogenic zones which afforded him the most intense pleasure" (pp. 106–107), and that for Hans "this period is marked ... by a primacy of the phallus" (p. 110, n. 2). To this extent, the Hans case vindicates Freud's view that children naturally experience sexual pleasure. Freud later used such pleasures as a knock-down argument, albeit of limited scope, for the existence of child sexuality:

> On the whole you will have gained very little for what you want to assert—the sexual purity of children—even if you succeed in convincing me that it would be better to regard the activities of infants-in-arms as non-sexual. For the sexual life of children is already free from all these doubts from the third year of life onwards: at about that time the genitals already begin to stir, a period of infantile masturbation—of genital satisfaction, therefore—sets in, regularly perhaps.
>
> (1917, p. 325)

To this extent, Freud is quite justified in concluding at the outset of his Discussion that "the picture of a child's sexual life presented in this observation of little Hans agrees very well with the account I gave ... in my *Three Essays*" (p. 101).

The Hans case is, however, ultimately about the Oedipal theory of neurosogenesis, not childhood phallic sexuality. Freud makes clear that Hans's fascination with widdlers is not ultimately what his phobia is about:

> [W]e must remark that it was Hans's parents who had extracted from the pathogenic material operating in him the particular theme of his interest in widdlers. Hans followed their lead in this matter, but he had not yet taken any line of his own in the analysis. And no therapeutic success was to be observed.
>
> (p. 120)

Freud allows that the suppression of Hans's masturbation had a role in causing the accumulation of excess libidinal tension that led to the phobia, but insists that it is deeply suppressed Oedipal themes alone that emerge symbolically in horse phobia symptom formation:

We have seen how our little patient was overtaken by a great wave of repression ... He gave up masturbation ... But these were not the components which were stirred up by the precipitating cause of the illness (his seeing the horse fall down) or which provided the material for the symptoms, that is, the content of the phobia ... We shall probably come to understand the case more deeply if we turn to those other components which do fulfil the two conditions that have just been mentioned. These other components were tendencies in Hans which had already been suppressed and which, so far as we can tell, had never been able to find uninhibited expression: hostile and jealous feelings towards his father, and sadistic impulses (premonitions, as it were, of copulation) towards his mother.

(pp. 138–139)

Freud's Explanation of Hans's Phobia

According to Freud, Hans's neurosis is a result of increasing Oedipal sexual desire that is repressed, causing the transformation of libido into anxiety, and then the fixation of the anxiety onto horses. Similar to what modern-day cognitive scientists might propose, he postulates an interacting network of unconscious thoughts, emotions, and desires that are linked via associational pathways of activation and yield Hans's conscious meanings and symptoms. However, unlike modern cognitivist views, Freud claims that the specific meanings activating the associative web underlying Hans's phobic symptoms are repressed sexual and aggressive meanings elaborated in Freud's Oedipal theory of child development.

Freud distinguishes the precipitating cause of Hans's phobia—his witnessing a horse accident in which a horse pulling a bus-wagon fell down in the street—from the specific cause that explains why the precipitating cause had the inordinate effect that it did. In earlier writing, Freud analogized this relationship to how a superficial trauma to a foot might trigger an episode of gout due to deeper underlying causes. Today's brain-disorder oriented psychiatrist might similarly argue that there must exist brain features that explain why the same psychologically traumatic precipitating event causes post-traumatic stress disorder in one individual and not in another. Freud wields similar logic, but at a psychological level. He accepts that witnessing the horse accident triggered Hans's phobia ("he recalled the event, insignificant in itself, which immediately preceded the outbreak of the illness and may no doubt be regarded as the precipitating cause of its outbreak" [p. 125]; "the neurosis took its start directly from this chance event" [p. 136]), but observes that such an event would not necessarily cause a similar outcome in others ("In itself the impression of the accident which he happened to witness carried no 'traumatic force'" [p. 136]).

Freud also argues that the horse accident cannot be the primary cause of Hans's anxiety because Hans experienced episodes of anxiety about separation from his mother prior to witnessing the horse accident ("Chronological considerations make it impossible for us to attach any great importance to the actual precipitating cause of the outbreak of Hans's illness, for he had shown signs of apprehensiveness long before he saw the bus-horse fall down in the street" [p. 136]; this argument is examined in Chapters 6 and 7). The accident merely focused Hans's prior more diffuse anxieties onto horses with "the horse being exalted into the object of his anxiety" (p. 136). However, the Oedipal theory is required for a full explanation because the detailed features of the horses and horse situations that trigger Hans's fear bear unmistakable evidence of their origins in Oedipal associations, the details of which were transferred onto horses: "I will reveal at once that all these characteristics were derived from the circumstance that the anxiety originally had no reference at all to horses but was transposed on to them secondarily and had now become fixed upon those elements of the horse-complex which showed themselves well adapted for certain transferences" (p. 51; this fundamental argument is examined in Chapter 10).

The associative web postulated by Freud that yields Hans's phobia when he witnesses the horse accident can be divided into two components. The first is the Oedipus complex that explains Hans's basic sexual and emotional desires, such as Hans's sexual longing for his mother and the wish to kill his father. The Oedipus complex is entirely independent of the horse phobia but provides the foundation for Hans's phobic reaction to the horse accident. The second component consists of other memories that mediate between and connect the unconscious Oedipal components and the falling horse accident. These associative linkages imbue the horse accident with Oedipal meanings, causing Hans's phobic-level anxiety about horses that is in fact derived from his Oedipus complex.

To start with the first component, according to Freud, the Oedipus complex is a universal developmental stage that differs from child to child only in the relative strengths of its various components. Such variations may be brought about by circumstances but are often constitutionally based. The Hans case provides one of the most vivid characterizations Freud offers of this developmental stage. Freud claims that

> In his attitude towards his father and mother Hans confirms in the most concrete and uncompromising manner what I have said ... with regard to the sexual relations of a child to his parents. Hans really was a little Oedipus who wanted to have his father "out of the way"... so that he might be alone with his beautiful mother and sleep with her.
>
> (p. 111)

For Freud, it is an expectable outcome that Hans would initially fixate his erotic attachments on his mother due to their physical intimacy and the pleasure Hans received during Hans's infancy when he was taken care of by her: "The boy had found his way to object-love in the usual manner from the care he had received when he was an infant" (p. 111). Indeed, Hans experienced an ongoing erotic need for cutaneous pleasure (i.e., skin contact) with his mother as one component of sexuality, expressed as the desire to be in bed and cuddle or sleep with her: "a new pleasure had now become the most important for him—that of sleeping beside his mother. I should like to emphasize the importance of pleasure derived from cutaneous contact as a component in this new aim of Hans's" (p. 111).

Freud claims that Hans's wish to be alone with his mother was amplified during the summer before the phobia's outbreak, when the family stayed at a summer house in Gmunden. Hans's father frequently traveled into Vienna for work, leaving Hans alone with his mother. This allowed Hans to crawl into her bed and cuddle or sleep with her more frequently than the father usually allowed, a correlation that, Freud suggests, Hans noticed ("This wish had originated during his summer holidays, when the alternating presence and absence of his father had drawn Hans's attention to the condition upon which depended the intimacy with his mother which he longed for" [p. 111]). As well, Hans would sometimes express separation anxiety that caused his mother to take him into her bed to soothe him. As Hans's father puts it, "Unfortunately, when he got into an elegiac mood of that kind, his mother used always to take him into bed with her" (p. 23)—"unfortunately" because Hans's father, steeped in Freud's theory, was concerned about excessive sexual stimulation from too much contact between mother and son and tried to prevent it when he was present (this aspect of the case is considered in detail in Wakefield, 2022). Freud hypothesizes that Hans's greater access to his mother when his father was away increased Hans's Oedipal sexual arousal:

> During the preceding summer Hans had had similar moods of mingled longing and apprehension … and at that time they had secured him the advantage of being taken by his mother into her bed. We may assume that since then Hans had been in a state of intensified sexual excitement, the object of which was his mother.
>
> (p. 118)

Hans, Freud argues, naturally then wished his father to be away more often.

Freud cites three pieces of evidence for Hans's heightened sexual arousal after Hans's summer opportunities for intimacy with his mother (these are discussed in detail in Chapter 8): Hans's increased masturbation ("On the same day his mother asked: 'Do you put your hand to your widdler?' and he answered: 'Yes. Every evening, when I'm in bed'" [p. 24]) and two talks with his mother that Freud construes as attempts at seduction ("The intensity of this excitement was shown by his two attempts at seducing his mother" [p. 118]). In one, Hans asks his mother why she so carefully avoids touching his penis when powdering him after his bath, and in another he reports an overheard comment by a visiting aunt that Hans "has got a dear little thingummy" (p. 23). Hans's repeated attempts to cuddle with his mother despite his father's objections also evidences his sexual longing for his mother, according to Freud.

Hans's increased sexual drive due to increased access to his mother during the summer was abruptly frustrated when the family returned to Vienna, where Hans's father was continuously present and discouraged such physical closeness. Hans then had to contend with a great amount of undischarged sexual tension. Thinking back to what allowed his access to his mother during the summer, Hans's wishing that his father should be away changed to wishing "that his father should be *permanently* away— that he should be 'dead'" (p. 112). This altered wish gave rise in Hans to conflict and anxiety because Hans also loved and depended on his father. Moreover, Hans became frightened that his father would find out about his hostile wish and severely punish him, perhaps by cutting off the very organ that became aroused when thinking about possessing his mother (i.e., castration anxiety).

Another strand in Hans's growing Oedipal desire starts with the birth of Hans's sister Hanna when Hans was three-and-a-half years old, which Freud says had several important consequences: "The arrival of his sister brought into Hans's life many new elements, which from that time on gave him no rest" (p. 132). Both during his mother's confinement and afterward when she cared for Hanna, Hans did not have the same access to her:

> In the first place he was obliged to submit to a certain degree of priva-
> tion: to begin with, a temporary separation from his mother, and later a
> permanent diminution in the amount of care and attention which he had
> received from her and which thenceforward he had to grow accustomed
> to sharing with his sister.
>
> (p. 132)

This deprivation left Hans with increased longing and decreased satisfaction. Moreover, in watching his infant sister cared for by his mother, Hans was reminded of the pleasures he had enjoyed when he was looked after as an infant: "In the second place, he experienced a revival of the pleasures he had enjoyed when he was looked after as an infant; for they were called up by all that he saw his mother doing for the baby" (p. 132). Freud concludes that "As a result of these two influences his erotic needs became intensified, while at the same time they began to obtain insufficient satisfaction" (p. 132).

Freud suggests that an alternative source of intimate satisfaction for Hans was his relationships with other children and that Hans redirected his erotic longing for his mother onto his friends:

> He made up for the loss which his sister's arrival had entailed on him by
> imagining that he had children of his own; and so long as he was at

Gmunden—on his second visit there—and could really play with these children, he found a sufficient outlet for his affections.

(p. 132)

This outlet, too, was lost upon the family's return to Vienna. Not only did Hans not have his summer Gmunden friends to play with, but the family had moved to a new flat in Vienna as well, and so Hans was now without close friends at the new location. Hans thus redirected his search for sexual gratification back onto his mother:

> His affection had moved from his mother on to other objects of love, but at a time when there was a scarcity of these it returned to her, only to break down in a neurosis. It was not until this happened that it became evident to what a pitch of intensity his love for his mother had developed.
> (p. 110)

Even more immediately impacting Hans was the fact that at the new flat Hans had been moved into his own bedroom where he slept alone, and no longer slept near his parents with ready access to his mother. All of this served to amplify his unsatisfied longing for his mother who had become the only available outlet for his sexual needs: "But after his return to Vienna he was once more alone, and set all his hopes upon his mother. He had meanwhile suffered another privation, having been exiled from his parents' bedroom" (pp. 132–133).

Hans attempted to compensate for his frustrated sexual desires by masturbatory gratification: "His intensified erotic excitability now found expression … in regular auto-erotic satisfaction obtained by a masturbatory stimulation of his genitals" (p. 133). Hans also attempted to satisfy these sexual longings in his friendships:

> The sexual aim which he pursued with his girl playmates, of sleeping with them, had originated in relation to his mother. It was expressed in words which might be retained in maturity, though they would then bear a richer connotation.
> (pp. 110–111)

Another consequence of Hanna's birth was that it left Hans with an intense curiosity about where children come from: "his sister's birth stimulated him to an effort of thought … impossible to bring to a conclusion … He was faced with the great riddle of where babies come from" (p. 133). Hans's persistent inquiry into how children are created yielded an excretory model of birth in which a child is inside the mother and pushed out like feces (or "lumf"). However, the excretory theory of childbirth left Hans with the puzzle of the nature of the father's role in having children, a question of great interest to Hans given his rivalry with his father for his mother's affections:

But there was something else, which could not fail to make him uneasy. His father must have had something to do with little Hanna's birth, for he had declared that Hanna and Hans himself were his children. Yet it was certainly not his father who had brought them into the world, but his mother. This father of his came between him and his mother. When he was there Hans could not sleep with his mother, and when his mother wanted to take Hans into bed with her, his father used to call out. Hans had learnt from experience how well-off he could be in his father's absence, and it was only justifiable that he should wish to get rid of him. And then Hans's hostility had received a fresh reinforcement. His father had told him the lie about the stork and so made it impossible for him to ask for enlightenment upon these things. He not only prevented his being in bed with his mother, but also kept from him the knowledge he was thirsting for. He was putting Hans at a disadvantage in both directions, and was obviously doing so for his own benefit.

But this father, whom he could not help hating as a rival, was the same father whom he had always loved and was bound to go on loving, who had been his model, had been his first playmate, and had looked after him from his earliest infancy: and this it was that gave rise to the first conflict. Nor could this conflict find an immediate solution. For Hans's nature had so developed that for the moment his love could not but keep the upper hand and suppress his hate—though it could not kill it, for his hate was perpetually kept alive by his love for his mother.

(pp. 133–134)

Freud portrays Hans's sexually tinged curiosity ("epistemophilia") about reproduction as being experienced not just intellectually but also viscerally, in a sexual manner involving penile arousal and an inchoate anticipation of intercourse:

But his father not only knew where children came from, he actually per-formed it—the thing that Hans could only obscurely divine. The widdler must have something to do with it, for his own grew excited whenever he thought of these things—and it must be a big widdler too, bigger than Hans's own. If he listened to these premonitory sensations he could only suppose that it was a question of some act of violence performed upon his mother, of smashing something, of making an opening into some-thing, of forcing a way into an enclosed space—such were the impulses that he felt stirring within him. But although the sensations of his penis had put him on the road to postulating a vagina, yet he could not solve the problem, for within his experience no such thing existed as his widdler required. On the contrary, his conviction that his mother possessed a penis just as he did stood in the way of any solution. His attempt at dis-covering what it was that had to be done with his mother in order that she might have children sank down into his unconscious; and his two active impulses—the hostile one towards his father and the sadistic-tender one towards his mother—could be put to no use, the first because of the love that existed side by side with the hatred, and the second because of the perplexity in which his infantile sexual theories left him.

This is how, basing my conclusions upon the findings of the analysis, I am obliged to reconstruct the unconscious complexes and wishes, the repression and reawakening of which produced little Hans's phobia.

(pp. 134–135)

The striking view that a five-year-old boy has an inchoate sense or premonition of intercourse based on bodily sensations was a doctrine Freud held throughout his career. For example, in 1924 in his paper on the dissolution of the Oedipus complex, Freud reiterates: "The child may have had only very vague notions as to what constitutes a satisfying erotic intercourse; but certainly the penis must play a part in it, for the sensations in his own organ were evidence of that" (1924, p. 176). Regarding the hypothesized sadistic nature of Hans's sexual longings, Freud holds that this emerges when Hans expresses to his father a wish to tease and whip a horse, and then to do the same to his mother: "'Which would you really like to beat? Mummy, Hanna, or me?' Hans: 'Mummy'" (p. 81). Freud comments that "the boy's wish ... was compounded of an obscure sadistic desire for his mother" (p. 83).

One of the few places where Freud is critical of Max is in his failure fully to explain to Hans the nature of the reproductive act and thus allow his curiosity to abate. In response to Freud's urging, Max does explain to Hans that females have no widdlers like Hans's, but he never explains the existence of the vagina and the act of intercourse, leaving Hans to continue his puzzled inquiries even after the phobia and the analysis end. Freud differs with Max on this decision and disputes the general attitude of his time against sexual enlightenment of children:

If matters had lain entirely in my hands, I should have ventured to give the child the one remaining piece of enlightenment which his parents withheld from him. I should have confirmed his instinctive premonitions, by telling him of the existence of the vagina and of copulation; thus I should have still further diminished his unsolved residue, and put an end to his stream of questions. I am convinced that this new piece of enlightenment would have made him lose neither his love for his mother nor his own childish nature, and that he would have understood that his preoccupation with these important, these momentous things must rest for the present—until his wish to be big had been fulfilled. But the educational experiment was not carried so far.

(p. 145)

Freud thus claims that Hans repressed both of the core conflictual Oedipal contents, the "sadistic-tender" sexual impulse directed at his mother in an inchoate form of desire for copulation and Hans's hostility towards his father and desire to be rid of him so he could possess his mother. Freud considers Hans's fear of his father to be somewhat more accessible to Hans's consciousness than his proto-copulatory desire for his mother. Freud thus first addresses Hans's fear hoping to allow the deeper incestuous desires to emerge: "Having partly mastered his castration complex, he was now able to communicate his wishes in regard to his mother" (p. 121); "it is evident that at every point Hans's hostile complex against his father screened his lustful one about his mother, just as it was the first to be disclosed and dealt with in the analysis" (p. 137).

As evidence for the notion of castration anxiety, Freud cites Hans's unwillingness to acknowledge that his baby sister Hanna did not have a penis (see Wakefield, 2017, for a critique of this interpretation). Freud also interprets Hans's self-reassurance that his penis, despite the fact that it will get bigger over time, is "fixed in, of course" (p. 34), as evidence for castration anxiety provoked by his mother's castration threat over a year before when she noticed Hans masturbating:

> a remark made by him in conversation, to the effect that his widdler was "fixed in, of course", allow us our first glimpse into the patient's unconscious mental processes. The fact was that the threat of castration made to him by his mother some fifteen months earlier was now having a deferred effect upon him.
>
> (p. 120)

Fritzl, Lizzi, and the Black Around the Mouth: The Associational Web that Links Hans's Death Wish Against His Father to the Horse Accident

This brings us to Freud's answer to the critical explanatory question in the Hans case: What precisely explains the transformation of Hans's anxiety into a phobia directed at horses? The event that triggered Hans's phobia was witnessing a horse accident in which a large horse pulling a bus-wagon fell down in the streets of Vienna, kicking wildly (see Chapter 10).

Hans says that he is afraid of horses falling down as well as of their biting. To provide an Oedipal explanation of the phobic level of these fears, Freud relies on two incidents that are reported in the course of the analysis to provide associational links between Hans's unconscious Oedipal thoughts and the horse accident, the Fritzl and Lizzi incidents (discussed below). Freud attempts to show that the phobic object has features that ease the way for the underlying sexual and aggressive Oedipal material to attach to it, with the mediating associations providing the pathway. He argues that the feared objects bear unmistakable evidence of their origins in Oedipal sexual material, with the horse content incidental and secondary: "[I]t does no harm to make acquaintance at close quarters with a phobia of this sort ... the anxiety originally had no reference at all to horses but was transposed on to them secondarily" (p. 51). Thus, in addition to unknown constitutional features, it is the preexisting associative web of mental states with attached amounts of sexual energy that determine the causation of Hans's neurosis. Freud summarizes the big picture of how he sees the associational pathway from the Oedipus complex to the horse phobia in the following passage:

> Nevertheless, the neurosis took its start directly from this chance event and preserved a trace of it in the circumstance of the horse being exalted into the object of his anxiety ... [T]he impression of the accident ... acquired its great effectiveness only from the fact that horses had formerly been of importance to him as objects of his predilection and interest, from the fact that he associated the event in his mind with an earlier event at Gmunden which had more claim to be regarded as traumatic, namely, with Fritzl's falling down while he was playing at horses, and lastly from the fact that there was an easy path of association from Fritzl to his father. Indeed, even these connections would probably not have been sufficient if it had not been that, thanks to the pliability and ambiguity of associative chains, the same event showed itself capable of stirring the second of the complexes that lurked in Hans's unconscious, the complex of his pregnant mother's confinement. From that moment the way was clear for the return of the repressed; and it returned in such a manner that the pathogenic material was remodelled and transposed on to the horse-complex, while the accompanying affects were uniformly turned into anxiety.
>
> (pp. 136–137)

For Freud, a potent associative link between Hans's father and the horse accident is the horse's falling down, linking the horse accident and Hans's Oedipal feelings of wanting his father to fall down dead so he can be with his mother. Freud construes Hans as acknowledging this association under his father's questioning ("I: 'When the horse fell down, did you think of your daddy?' Hans: 'Perhaps. Yes. It's possible'" [p. 51]). Freud embraces this route of association: "[T]he boy saw a big heavy horse fall down ... Hans at that moment perceived a wish that his father might fall down in the same way—and be dead" (pp. 51–52).

As to how a horse falling down could link so firmly in Hans's mind to Hans's death wish toward his father, Freud finds the answer in an incident that occurred at Gmunden when Hans was playing horses with Fritzl, his favorite friend. Fritzl "ran ever so fast and all at once he hit his foot on a stone and bled" (p. 58) and, Freud suggests, fell down (there is in fact an issue of whether Fritzl fell down, but I leave this issue to be addressed in Chapter 10's assessment of Freud's evidence):

> His father ... elicited from Hans the recollection of an event at Gmunden, the impression of which lay concealed behind that of the falling bus-horse. While they were playing at horses, Fritzl, the playmate of whom he was so fond, but at the same time, perhaps, his rival with his many girl friends, had hit his foot against a stone and had fallen down, and his foot had bled. Seeing the bus-horse fall had reminded him of this accident.
>
> (p. 126)

Freud suggests that Fritzl's falling down bleeding while playing horses with Hans—especially given that Hans's father used to play horses with Hans—was a crucial mediating associative link between Hans's fantasies about his father's dying and the horse accident in which the horse fell down ("this was the event which formed the connection between the two scenes" [p. 126]). Freud thus takes the Fritzl incident to be one of the key associative pathways that gave meaning to the horse accident.

A second incident at Gmunden served as a link between Hans's fear of horses biting and Hans's repressed Oedipal fears. A neighbor girl, Lizzi, was leaving and her luggage was being taken to the station in a horse-drawn cart. When Hans tried to pet the horse, Lizzi's father told him to be careful because horses bite. Freud suggests, first, a link between Lizzi's departing from Gmunden and Hans's wish that his father would go away so he could be alone with his mother. Building on that equivalence, there is a further link between Hans wanting his father to be gone and his fear of potential retribution in the form of being bitten (or castrated), given that Lizzi's departure was associated with that danger:

> At that time the form taken by the wish had been merely that his father should "go away" and at a later stage it became possible for his fear of being bitten by a white horse to attach itself directly on to this form of the wish, owing to a chance impression which he received at the moment of some one else's departure.
>
> (p. 111)

This link is then responsible for the fear of being bitten to emerge from the horse accident: "Soon afterwards he traced back his fear of being bitten by a horse to an impression he had received at Gmunden. A father had addressed his child on her departure with these words of warning: 'Don't put your finger to the horse; if you do, it'll bite you'" (p. 119). This event had served to further solidify a link between horses, Hans's father, and the horse accident. The warning about a horse biting alerted Hans to the fact that horses can be dangerous. The little neighbor girl, Lizzi, was departing, the very thing that Hans wished for his father to do while at Gmunden. Yet the horse that provided the means for her going away could bite, a form of revenge for the wished-for departure by an animal already linked to Hans's father. In sum, Freud sees Hans's fear of a horse biting as an expression of Hans's castration anxiety, that is, his fear of his father's revenge for Hans wanting him out of the way. Freud also thinks that the fear of a horse falling down expresses Hans's ambivalence about his death wish towards his father.

In addition to the Fritzl and Lizzi incidents, there is a third crucial piece of evidence that Freud deploys to establish associative links between Hans's Oedipus complex and the horse accident. This evidence emerged in Freud's one session with Hans and his father:

> We were also forced to confess that the connections between the horses he was afraid of and the affectionate feelings towards his mother which had been revealed were by no means abundant. Certain details which I now learnt—to the effect that he was particularly bothered by what horses wear in front of their eyes and by the black round their mouths—were certainly not to be explained from what we knew. But as I saw the two of them sitting in front of me and at the same time heard Hans's description of his anxiety-horses, a further piece of the solution shot through my mind, and a piece which I could well understand might escape his father. I asked Hans jokingly whether his horses wore eyeglasses, to which he replied that they did not. I then asked him whether his father wore eyeglasses, to which, against all the evidence, he once more said no. Finally I asked him whether by "the black round the mouth" he meant a moustache; and I then disclosed to him that he was afraid of his father, precisely because he was so fond of his mother. It must be, I told him, that he thought his father was angry with him on that account; but this was not so, his father was fond of him in spite of it, and he might admit everything to him without any fear. Long before he was in the world, I went on, I had known that a little Hans would come who would be so fond of his mother that he would be bound to feel afraid of his father because of it; and I had told his father this.
>
> (pp. 41–42)

The father repeatedly attempts to identify the kinds of harnesses or other gear on horses to which Hans is referring. In response to his father's questions, Hans says that he is "most afraid of horses with a thing on their mouths" that is black, that it is not a moustache, and that only a few horses have it. Hans's father comments, "I think in reality it must be the thick piece of harness that dray-horses wear over their noses" (p. 49). However, the next day,

> At every horse that passed I asked him if he saw the "black on its mouth"; he said "no" every time ... I asked him if the "black" reminded him of a moustache, and he said: "Only by its colour." So I do not yet know what it really is.
>
> (p. 52)

The day after that,

> I asked again to-day what the "black on the horses' mouths" looked
> like. Hans said: "Like a muzzle." The curious thing is that for the
> last three days not a single horse has passed on which he could point
> out this "muzzle" ... I suspect that some sort of horses' bridle—the
> thick piece of harness round their mouths, perhaps—really reminded
> him of a moustache, and that after I alluded to this this fear dis-
> appeared as well.
>
> (p. 53)

Finally, on April 14, Hans "called out, almost with joy: 'Here comes a
horse with something black on its mouth!' And I was at last able to
establish the fact that it was a horse with a leather muzzle" (p. 69), and
the mystery of the origin of the material for the association to the father
was solved. Freud relies on the moustache-and-glasses association to lock
down his interpretation of Hans's fear of horses as a fear of his father:

> Certain details of which Hans had shown he was afraid, the black on
> horses' mouths and the things in front of their eyes (the moustaches
> and eyeglasses which are the privilege of a grown-up man), seemed to
> me to have been directly transposed from his father on to the horses.
>
> (p. 123)

Freud sums up:

> Let me summarize the results that had so far been reached. Behind the
> fear to which Hans first gave expression, the fear of a horse biting him,
> we had discovered a more deeply seated fear, the fear of horses falling
> down; and both kinds of horses, the biting horse and the falling horse,
> had been shown to represent his father, who was going to punish him for
> the evil wishes he was nourishing against him. Meanwhile the analysis
> had moved away from the subject of his mother.
>
> (p. 126)

The Excretory Theory of Childbirth: The Associative Web Linking Hans's Desire for His Mother and the Horse Accident

Freud's comment that the analysis had moved away from the mother presages
a further construction of Hans's associative web that links his Oedipal feelings
about his mother to the horse accident. Freud claims that all of the horse
accident associations to the father, including associations to both the death
wish aimed at him and the fear of castration by him, would likely not have
been sufficient to transform Hans's anxiety into a horse phobia if it had not

been for the added power of another line of associations to the mother: "Hans at that moment perceived a wish that his father might fall down in the same way—and be dead. May there not have been yet another meaning concealed behind all this?" (p. 52). Multiple streams of converging associative chains can compound a feature's emotional power and yield a combined meaning ("In the process of the formation of a phobia from the unconscious thoughts underlying it, condensation takes place" [p. 83]).

The second major line of association that links Hans's Oedipal desires to the horse accident runs through what Freud calls the "lumf" (Hans's word for feces) complex, by way of association to the excretory theory of childbirth. We saw above that Hanna's birth caused Hans to puzzle over where children come from. Freud concludes that Hans, rejecting the "stork" story told to him by his father, inferred an excretory model of birth according to which babies are pushed out like a turd ("lumf"). In fact, Freud claims to have predicted this path of the analysis:

> I had predicted to his father that it would be possible to trace back Hans's phobia to thoughts and wishes occasioned by the birth of his baby sister. But I had omitted to point out that according to the sexual theory of children a baby is a "lumf", so that Hans's path would lie through the excremental complex.
>
> (pp. 74–75)

However, the lumf theory of childbirth left Hans with the unresolved mystery of what role the father might play in having children.

Hans's "lumf" theory of childbirth is linked to the horse accident in two ways. First, like his mother when she was pregnant, the horse that fell down is quite fat, suggesting it is carrying a baby-lumf that perhaps it wants to expel lying down, the position Hans's mother had been in during her confinement ("I: 'Was it big or little?' Hans: 'Big.' I: 'Fat or thin?' Hans: 'Fat. Very big and fat'" [p. 51]; "We have learned the immediate precipitating cause after which the phobia broke out. This was when the boy saw a big heavy horse fall down" [p. 51]). The horse's undoubted whinnying as it kicked may well have evoked Hans's mother's pained groaning during childbirth ("Hans's bed was moved into the next room. He woke up there at seven, and, hearing his mother groaning, asked: 'Why's Mummy coughing?' Then, after a pause, 'The stork's coming to-day for certain'" [p. 10]). As well, the horse itself was black, evocative of the color of lumf.

I: "I say, wasn't the bus-horse the same colour as a lumf?" …
HE: (very much struck) "Yes."

(p. 64)

Second, when asked what frightened him so about the horse falling down, Hans identified the fact that the horse was kicking and making a row with its feet that scared him:

I: "Why did it give you such a fright?"

HANS: "Because the horse went like this with its feet." (He lay down on the ground and showed me how it kicked about.) "It gave me a fright because it made a row with its feet."

(p. 50)

Freud comes up with the hypothesis that the kicking of feet reminds Hans of his reaction to having to go the W.C., and it subsequently emerges that Hans would kick his feet both when he needed to go to the W.C. and when he was angry at being forced to go to the W.C., and that the loud sound itself appears to remind him of the sound of going lumf.

I: "What does a loud row remind you of?"

HE: "That I've got to do lumf in the W.C." ...

I: "Why?"

HE: "I don't know. A loud row sounds as though you were doing lumf. A big row reminds me of lumf."

(p. 64)

Indeed, lumf also makes a sound or "row" as it drops. At one point the father interprets the black falling horse as itself associated with a lumf:

The bus-horse that falls down and makes a row with its feet is no doubt—a lumf falling and making a noise. His fear of defaecation and his fear of heavily loaded carts is equivalent to the fear of a heavily loaded stomach.

(p. 66)

Freud approvingly comments, "In this roundabout way Hans's father was beginning to get a glimmering of the true state of affairs" (p. 66). It also may be the case that kicking occurred when Hans was in discomfort when being given an enema ("There has been trouble with his stools from the very first; and aperients and enemas have frequently been necessary ... Recently the constipation has again made its appearance more frequently" [pp. 55–56])

A further important link of Hans's sexuality to lumf emerges when Hans's father investigates and finds that his wife often takes Hans into the W.C. with her ("I asked my wife whether Hans was often with her when she went to the W.C. 'Yes,' she said, 'often. He goes on pestering me till I let him. Children are all like that'" [p. 57]; "We learn that formerly Hans had been in the habit of insisting upon accompanying his mother to the W.C." [p. 127]). This moment of intimacy, anatomical curiosity, and likely arousal ("Pleasure taken in looking on while someone one loves performs the natural functions is once more a 'confluence of instincts'" [p. 127]), links the "lumf" context to Hans's sexual closeness to his mother and thus to his fear of his father's wrath ("it is worth bearing carefully in mind the desire, which Hans had already repressed, for seeing his mother doing lumf" [p. 57]).

In sum, Hans's fear of horses pulling heavy carts and buses falling was in fact a fear of his own incestuous desire to sleep with and have a child with his mother—"heavily loaded carts represented his mother's pregnancy to him, and the horse's falling down was like having a baby" (p. 131).

It is also true that Hans clearly had aggressive feelings towards his little sister Hanna, given that she too took his mother away from him, so that anything reminding him of lumf would also provoke associations to her birth and to guilty aggressive feelings, a point that emerges frequently in the case record:

I: "When you were watching Mummy giving Hanna her bath, perhaps you wished she would let go of her so that Hanna should fall in?"
HANS: "Yes."

(p. 67)

In the evening my wife told me that Hans had been out on the balcony and had said: "I thought to myself Hanna was on the balcony and fell down off it." … Hans's repressed wish was very transparent. His mother asked him if he would rather Hanna were not there, to which he said "Yes."

(p. 68)

I: "Are you fond of Hanna?"
HANS: "Oh yes, very fond."
I: "Would you rather that Hanna weren't alive or that she were?"
HANS: "I'd rather she weren't alive."
I: "Why?"
HANS: "At any rate she wouldn't scream so, and I can't bear her screaming."

(pp. 71–72)

This completes the major pieces of the puzzle of the origin of Hans's phobia.

Freud's Conception of Psychopathology

In the last two sections of this review, Freud's conceptualization of Hans's pathological condition will be explored, both generally and in terms of his specific diagnosis.

Freud's concept of psychopathology can be confusing because sometimes he describes a categorical distinction in which a conflict that does not produce symptoms is not a disorder, and other times he describes a vague quantitative continuum. Rebutting the theory that some people are inherently hereditarily neurotic, Freud comments that "no sharp line can be drawn between 'neurotic' and 'normal' people" and "our conception of 'disease' is a purely practical one and a question of summation, that disposition and the eventualities of life must combine before the threshold of this summation is overstepped" (1909, p. 146). This is often misunderstood as asserting that there is no categorical distinction between disorder and health and that the notion of disorder is arbitrary. However, Freud is rejecting the common medical doctrine of his times that neurotic individuals are hereditarily tainted and form a separate class of individuals from the healthy. Freud is not denying that there can be a reasonably clear distinction between *conditions* that are healthy versus those that are neurotic. However, even here, he is arguing that the distinction is based not on one simple essential process, like an infection, but rather on the complex balance among a great many libidinal forces, so that the Oedipal theory lacks the clear-cut causal account of his earlier seduction theory.

Moreover, the constellation of forces determining the moment that the overall summation of unsatisfied libido transforms into intractable anxiety is so complex and involves so many strands of causation that it cannot be predicted. Freud explained this situation in a paper a few years before the Hans case:

> [T]he aetiology of the neuroses comprises everything which can act in a detrimental manner upon the processes serving the sexual function ... A single pathogenic influence is scarcely ever sufficient; in the large majority of cases a number of aetiological factors are required, which support one another and must therefore not be regarded as being in mutual opposition. For this reason a state of neurotic illness cannot be sharply differentiated from health. The onset of the illness is the product of a summation and the necessary total of aetiological determinants can be completed from any direction. To look for the aetiology of the neuroses exclusively in heredity or in the constitution would be just as one-sided as to attribute that aetiology solely to the accidental influences brought to bear upon sexuality in the course of the subject's life—whereas better insight shows that the essence of these illnesses lies solely in a disturbance of the organism's sexual processes.
>
> (1906, p. 279)

Freud offers several theories of what put Hans over that threshold (e.g., increasing affection for his mother, his mother's rejection of his advances, stopping his masturbation, Hans's intellectual inability to solve the puzzle of reproduction), but in the end declares that "we cannot decide; and, indeed, it is a matter of indifference, for ... [t]he fact remains that his sexual excitement suddenly changed into anxiety" (p. 119). Freud is conceptually sophisticated enough to understand that the existence of a fuzzy boundary of ambiguous cases between categories does not imply that there is no categorical distinction that applies to a range of clear cases on either side of the boundary (e.g., night versus day, child versus adult). For example, when Freud considers the ambiguity of whether a seemingly healthy individual's Oedipus complex is completely dissolved or just deeply and enduringly repressed, he says, "We may plausibly assume that we have here come upon the borderline—never a very sharply drawn one—between the normal and the pathological" (1924, p. 177). In addition to rejecting the doctrine that neurosis is due to a lifelong hereditary taint, Freud is also acknowledging in this passage that the Oedipal theory lacks the clear-cut causal account of his earlier seduction theory.

One indicator to Freud of pathology in Hans is Hans's anxiety when out walking with his mother, implying that even when Hans gets what he originally longed for, he can no longer experience satisfaction, demonstrating a pathological transformation:

> Longing can be completely transformed into satisfaction if it is presented with the object longed for. Therapy of that kind is no longer effective in dealing with anxiety. The anxiety remains even when the longing can be satisfied ... He was with his mother, and yet he still suffered from anxiety—that is to say, from an unsatisfied longing for her ... [H]is anxiety had stood the test.
>
> (p. 26)

Freud appends the following note:

> To speak quite frankly, this is actually the criterion according to which we decide whether such feelings of mingled apprehension and longing are normal or not: we begin to call them "pathological anxiety" from the moment at which they can no longer be relieved by the attainment of the object longed for.
>
> (p. 26, n. 1)

More generally, for Freud, repression itself is a normal process for internal regulation and is not inherently pathological. Only when repression goes wrong and leads to anxiety or other symptoms is it pathological:

> no experience could have a pathogenic effect unless it appeared intolerable to the subject's ego and gave rise to efforts at defence ... If the defence was successful, the intolerable experience with its affective consequences was expelled from consciousness and from the ego's memory. In certain circumstances, however, what had been expelled pursued its activities in what was now an unconscious state, and found its way back into consciousness by means of symptoms and the affects attaching to them, so that *the illness corresponded to a failure in defence.*
>
> (Freud, 1906, p. 276; emphasis added)

He reiterated this view in his later reanalysis of Hans in his revised theory of anxiety:

The anxiety felt in animal phobias is, therefore, an affective reaction on the part of the ego to danger; and the danger which is being signaled in this way is the danger of castration. *This anxiety differs in no respect from the realistic anxiety which the ego normally feels in situations of danger, except that its content remains unconscious and only becomes conscious in the form of a distortion.*

(1926, p. 126; emphasis added)

In that later work, Freud argues in a famous "servant/master" analogy that, given Hans's love for his mother and consequent desire to have his father out of the way, "It would then be eminently natural for him to dread his master's vengeance and to develop a fear of him" (1926, p. 103). Freud concludes that even Hans's fear of castration is not itself a neurotic symptom because nothing has gone wrong with emotional processing:

We cannot, therefore, describe the fear belonging to this phobia as a symptom. If "Little Hans", being in love with his mother, had shown fear of his father, we should have no right to say that he had a neurosis or a phobia. His emotional reaction would have been entirely comprehensible. What made it a neurosis was one thing alone: the replacement of his father by a horse. It is this displacement, then, which has a claim to be called a symptom.

(1926, p. 103)

Anxiety Hysteria: Freud's Diagnosis of Little Hans

A final point in Freud's understanding of the Hans case is his diagnosis of Hans's phobic condition as an "anxiety hysteria," the first time he gave extended attention to this diagnosis. Freud had initially considered most phobias to be "actual neuroses" due to direct transformation of excessive sexual desire into anxiety, basically an anxiety neurosis attached to an object: "The anxiety ... which underlies all phobias, is not derived from any memory ... *Phobias, then, are a part of the anxiety neurosis*" (1895a, p. 81).

However, Freud clearly considers Hans's anxiety to result from repression of his Oedipal desires, thus to be based on a psychological component of repressed memory, even though instead of typical hysterical symptoms it eventuates in anxiety. This appears to be a psychoneurotic, hysterical element with an essential memory component, even though it does not eventuate in typical somatic hysterical conversion symptoms but only in anxiety.

From what condition, then, is Hans suffering, given that there are elements of both actual neurosis and psychoneurosis? Freud had always observed a close affinity between hysteria and anxiety neurosis in their shared symptoms such as paresthesias, hyperesthesias, exaggerated pain, and shortness of breath, and argued that the mechanism of the two neuroses ... suggest that anxiety neurosis is actually the somatic counterpart to hysteria: ... the difference is merely that in anxiety neurosis the excitation ... is purely somatic (somatic sexual excitation), whereas in hysteria it is psychical (provoked by conflict). Thus it is not to be wondered at that hysteria and anxiety neurosis regularly combine with each other.

(1895b, pp. 114–115)

In the Hans case, Freud gives up this duality by diagnosing Hans with a novel hybrid disorder category of "anxiety hysteria." Aside from some earlier letters to Jung and discussions with Stekel, the Hans case is the first published account of this category, which Freud claims is the most common neurotic condition:

Disorders of this kind are called "phobias", and we *might* classify Hans's case as an agoraphobia if it were not for the fact that it is a characteristic of that complaint that the locomotion of which the patient is otherwise incapable can always be easily performed when he is accompanied by some specially selected person—in the last resort, by the physician. Hans's phobia did not fulfil this condition; it soon ceased having any relation to the question of locomotion and became ... concentrated upon horses.

In the classificatory system of the neuroses no definite position has hitherto been assigned to "phobias". It seems certain that they should only be regarded as syndromes which may form part of various neuroses and that we need not rank them as an independent pathological process. For phobias of the kind to which little Hans's belongs, and which are in fact the most common, the name of "anxiety-hysteria" seems to me not inappropriate ... It finds its justification in the similarity between the psychological structure of these phobias and that of hysteria—a similarity which is complete except upon a single point ... For in anxiety-hysteria the libido which has been liberated from the pathogenic material by repression is not *converted* (that is, diverted from the mental sphere into a somatic innervation), but is set free in the shape of *anxiety* ... [T]here are cases of simple anxiety-hysteria, which exhibit feelings of anxiety and phobias, but have no admixture of conversion. The case of little Hans is one of the latter sort.

Anxiety-hysterias are the most common of all psychoneurotic disorders ... [I]t is the least dependent upon a special constitutional disposition and ... the most easily acquired at any time of life. One essential characteristic of anxiety-hysterias is very easily pointed out. An anxiety-hysteria tends to develop more and more into a "phobia".

(pp. 115–116)

This, then, is a pathway to phobic neurosis that Freud had not elaborated in his previous work. It starts as the generation of undirected anxiety that is not an "actual neurosis" but rather hysterical in nature (i.e., involving repression). This is followed by the subsequent fixation of the anxiety upon a feared object.

References

Freud, A. (1980). Foreword to *Writings of Anna Freud* (Vol. 8, pp. 277–282). New York: International Universities Press.

Freud, S. (1904). Freud's psychoanalytic procedure. *SE* 7, 249–254.

Freud, S. (1905). Three essays on the theory of sexuality. *SE* 7, 123–246.

Freud, S. (1906). My views on the part played by sexuality in the aetiology of the neuroses. *SE* 7, 269–279.

Freud, S. (1909). Analysis of a phobia in a five-year-old boy. *SE* 10, 1–150.

Freud, S. (1917). Introductory lectures on psycho-analysis, part 3. *SE* 16.

Freud, S. (1924). The dissolution of the Oedipus complex. *SE* 19, 171–180.

Freud, S. (1926). Inhibitions, symptoms and anxiety. *SE* 20, 75–176.

Wakefield, J. C. (2017). Concept representation in the child: What did Little Hans mean by "widdler"? *Psychoanalytic Psychology*, 34(3), 352–360.

Wakefield, J. (2022). *Attachment, sexuality, power: Oedipal theory as regulator of family affection in the case of little Hans.* New York: Routledge.

Chapter 5

Freud Versus the Fright Theory

Wolpe and Rachman's Behaviorist Challenge to Freud's Oedipal Analysis of the Little Hans Case

It was not from a methodological objection based on suggestion or from an alternative psychoanalytic perspective but from learning theory that the most powerful attack on Freud's interpretation of the Hans case was to come. In 1960, Joseph Wolpe and Stanley Rachman, two prominent behaviorist theorists, published what remains today by far the most influential critique of Freud's account of the etiology of Hans's phobia. More importantly, they presented a plausible alternative account of their own anchored in learning theory.

Wolpe and Rachman noted that late in Hans's analysis it emerged that, just prior to the onset of his horse phobia, Hans had witnessed a horse accident in the streets of Vienna in which a horse pulling a large bus-wagon fell down, kicking his feet. Hans reports that he was terribly frightened by this event and that his horse anxiety began immediately afterward. Based on this revelation and relying on Pavlovian/Watsonian classical conditioning theory, Wolpe and Rachman postulated that one-trial learning of fear of horses occurred when Hans witnessed the horse accident. This conditioning, they argue, fully explains the phobia without the need to appeal to Oedipal dynamics or other psychoanalytic factors. Partisans on both sides of the "Freud wars" have generally lined up either in their agreement with Wolpe and Rachman's rival analysis or their acceptance of Freud's pointed counterarguments, to be considered in later chapters.

But how could Freud possibly present counterarguments to an objection that was not stated until half a century after his case history was published and long after he was dead? Wolpe and Rachman's rival account of Hans's anxiety symptoms in terms of the traumatic emotional experience of fright, although framed in technical learning-theoretic terms, is anchored in folk psychology that anyone might understand. In Freud's time, the "fright theory" of anxiety symptoms (as I shall call the view that nonsexual emotions such as extreme fear can cause an anxiety neurosis) was commonly accepted in medical circles based on psychiatric observations of anxiety symptoms following life-threatening circumstances, as in war neuroses or train-wreck neuroses. Indeed, the fright theory had been an early objection to Freud's sexual theory of the neuroses, leading to Freud's rift with his mentor Breuer

DOI: 10.4324/9781003272472-5

and a published interchange with Leopold Lowenfeld (Freud, 1895b; Lowenfeld, 1895; see below).

Regarding Breuer, in his own theoretical contribution to *Studies on Hysteria*, Breuer (1895) went to great lengths to accommodate Freud's emphasis on sexual etiologies, for example: "I do not think I am exaggerating when I assert that *the great majority of severe neuroses in women have their origin in the marriage bed*" (Breuer, 1895, p. 246); "it is perhaps worth while insisting again and again that the sexual factor is by far the most important and the most productive of pathological results" (pp. 246–247). Nonetheless, he could not help but state what he really believed, that the "fright theory" is correct that not all neurotic etiologies need be sexual: "It is self-evident and is also sufficiently proved by our observations that the non-sexual affects of fright, anxiety and anger lead to the development of hysterical phenomena" (p. 246); "Alongside sexual hysteria we must at this point recall hysteria due to fright—traumatic hysteria proper—which constitutes one of the best known and recognized forms of hysteria" (p. 247). For Breuer, Wolpe and Rachman's horse accident explanation of Hans's horse phobia would likely have been very plausible.

The fright theory continued to be a common view after publication of the Hans case history. For example, the eminent American neurologist Morton Prince, who embraced a version of the idea of unconscious mental states, nevertheless dismissed Freud's sexual etiology theory when describing a case of phobia in which he failed to identify any sexual etiological factors: "The impulses of instincts other than sexual are sufficient to induce psychical trauma, insistent ideas, and emotion. To hold otherwise is to substitute dogma for the evidence of experience" (1914, p. 408). Consequently, long before Hans was a gleam in the eye of Max Graf, Freud already had developed a strategy for addressing this sort of objection and he deployed it preemptively in the Hans case.

Victor Haberman's (1913) "Common Sense" Objection as Precursor to Wolpe and Rachman

In fact, the horse accident objection did not wait half a century to appear. It entered the literature within a few years of the publication of the Hans case. This is not surprising given that Wolpe and Rachman's "fright" account is just a technical version of common sense. Victor Haberman, a Columbia University physician, in a 1913 critique of psychoanalysis in a New York medical journal, ridiculed Freud's account as follows:

> There is, however, a limit at which, despite ever so well meant scientific explanations, *common sense* has a right to interpose its veto ... This limit is also reached in the case of a five-year-old boy ... which case is certainly maintained to be documental evidence of the highest kind by disciples of

Freud ... This boy gets a phobia of horses, and the father—a physician—writes to Freud: "Sexual over-excitement through coddling by the mother undoubtedly prepared the soil..." Now the fact is later established that the fear dates from the moment that the boy once saw a horse fall over. Before one however discovered this simple incident, one had analyzed almost three months – an example of the objectivity of these analyses. It is but by pure chance that this occurrence is at all learned in the analysis; yet this fact which would sufficiently explain for the majority the source of the fear cannot forsooth be the basis of it but only the "actual incitant" (Anlass) – and the analysis is again begun anew. The father who himself makes the analysis doesn't seem at all to be moved by the discovery of the actual fright occasioned by the falling horse, but he asks a five-year-old boy – three months after its occurrence – "Did you, as the horse fell, think of your daddy?"

(1913, p. 425)

Freud anticipated when writing up the Hans case that this would be a common response to the horse accident revelation. As we shall see in later chapters, he devoted considerable energy to arguing that his Oedipal account was superior to its commonsense rival.

Wolpe and Rachman's Learning Theory Account of Hans's Phobia

Wolpe and Rachman offered a cogent and in some respects devastating critique of Freud's analysis of Hans's phobia. However, they also understood that a theory is generally not given up despite its inadequacies and disconfirmations (or what Thomas Kuhn called a theory's "anomalies") unless a superior rival theory is available to take its place. They knew that their critique of Freud's account of Hans's phobia, no matter how brilliant, might fall flat unless they offered an alternative account that provided a rival theory with superior empirical support. And this is what they attempted to do, using empirically anchored behaviorist learning theory: "In case it should be argued that, unsatisfactory as it is, Freud's explanation is the only available one, we shall show how Hans's phobia can be understood in terms of learning theory ... based on experimental findings" (1960, p. 145).

Their account is succinctly formulated in terms of learning theory, but in essence it is a sophisticated version of Haberman's commonsense objection that fright from the horse accident caused the neurosis:

In brief, phobias are regarded as conditioned anxiety (fear) reactions. Any "neutral" stimulus, simple or complex, that happens to make an impact on an individual at about the time that a fear reaction is evoked acquires the ability to evoke fear subsequently. If the fear at the original conditioning situation is of high intensity or if the conditioning is many times repeated the conditioned fear will show the persistence that is characteristic of *neurotic* fear; and there will be generalization of fear reactions to stimuli resembling the conditioned stimulus.

(1960, pp. 146–147)

Wolpe and Rachman note that Hans apparently had a constitutional tendency to experience anxiety, given that Freud reports that he was a sensitive child who was empathic when others wept and was disturbed as a child when he saw merry-go-round horses being beaten. Thus, they imply, Hans was likely high in what we now call "neuroticism," the easy arousal of intense negative emotion such as anxiety. It is known that such individuals are more prone to the development of phobias and other anxiety disorders under stress. Wolpe and Rachman also allow that Hans's memories of earlier anxiety-provoking experiences related to horses, such as those in the Fritzl and Lizzi incidents over the previous summer (see Chapter 4), likely prepared Hans to react as he did with one-trial anxiety learning to the horse accident he witnessed.

After rejecting Freud's claims regarding Hans's sexual desire for his mother (see below), Wolpe and Rachman claim that the conditioning associated with the experience of seeing the horse fall down was not merely a precipitating trigger of Hans's phobia but was in fact the fundamental cause—in interaction with Hans's disposition—of the entire neurotic condition. Noting that Hans says, "No. I only got it [the phobia] then. When the horse in the bus fell down, it gave me such a fright, really! That was when I got the nonsense" (Freud, 1909, p. 50), and that this was confirmed by Hans's mother, they state: "It is our contention that the incident to which Freud refers as merely the exciting cause of Hans's phobia was in fact the cause of the entire disorder" (1960, p. 146).

Wolpe and Rachman emphasize that the process of one-trial conditioning they are proposing as the explanation of Hans's neurosis is experimentally supported by the classic study of "Little Albert" by Watson and Raynor (1920) in which a child was conditioned to fear a white rat, as well as other studies. Moreover, their account links into a vast background literature on learning, offering empirical anchoring of a sort lacking in Freud's theory.

Freud on the Distinction Between a "Precipitating Cause" and "Specific Cause"

Freud, we shall see later in detail, dismisses the type of horse accident account of Hans's phobia put forward by Haberman and by Wolpe and Rachman by arguing that the accident is a mere "precipitating cause" or "releasing cause" of the symptoms and not a specific etiology of the neurotic pathology. Freud was not creating the concept of a precipitating cause as opposed to a specific etiology in an ad hoc manner for his Hans commentary but rather using an analysis of neurotic causation that he had developed years before, starting from his work with Breuer. However, this distinction became central after Freud's (1895a) article proposing that the diagnosis of anxiety neurosis should be separated from the broader category of neurasthenia because of different sexual etiologies. Freud's sexual theory of anxiety neurosis was attacked by Viennese physician Leopold Lowenfeld (1895), who insisted that emotional experiences such as traumatic frights are enough to cause an anxiety neurosis without the involvement of sexual factors. In his response to Lowenfeld, Freud (1895b) elaborated the concept of a precipitating cause as a major part of his defense. (Freud borrowed here Charcot's notion that physical traumas were only the precipitating causes of hysterical symptoms; Charcot took the specific causes to be hereditary neurological deficits.)

Freud's goal in responding to Lowenfeld, as in the Hans case, was to defend against the accusation that frights that immediately precede neurotic symptoms must be the cause of the neurosis. He elaborated a framework for considering the various components in the causation of a neurosis in a cogent and persuasive way, with analogies from physical medicine:

> I think we can arrive at a picture of the probably very complicated aetiological situation which prevails in the pathology of the neuroses if we postulate the following concepts:
>
> (a) Precondition, (b) Specific Cause, (c) Concurrent Causes, and, as a term which is not equivalent to the foregoing ones, (d) Precipitating or Releasing Cause ...
>
> [W]e may characterize as the *precipitating* or releasing cause the one which makes its appearance last in the equation, so that it immediately precedes the emergence of the effect. It is this chronological factor alone which constitutes the essential nature of a precipitating cause. Any of the other causes, too, can in a particular case play the role of precipitating cause ...
>
> The factors which may be described as *preconditions* are those in whose absence the effect would never come about, but which are incapable of producing the effect by themselves alone, no matter in what amount they may be present. For the specific cause is still lacking.
>
> The *specific cause* is the one which is never missing in any case in which the effect takes place, and which moreover suffices, if present in the required quantity or intensity, to achieve the effect, provided only that the preconditions are also fulfilled.
>
> As *concurrent causes* we may regard such factors as are not necessarily present every time, nor able, whatever their amount, to produce the effect by themselves alone, but which operate alongside of the preconditions and the specific cause in satisfying the aetiological equation.
>
> (1895b, pp. 135–136)

Freud goes on to present an example of his "complete aetiological schematic picture" in physical medicine:

Effect: Phthisis pulmonum; Precondition: Disposition, for the most part laid down through heredity, by the organic constitution;

Specific Cause: Bacillus Kochii; Auxiliary Causes: Anything that diminishes the powers—emotions as well as suppurations or colds.

(1895b, p. 137)

He then elaborates this disease model for neuroses:

The schematic picture for the aetiology of anxiety neurosis seems to me to be on the same lines. Precondition: Heredity. Specific Cause: A sexual factor, in the sense of a deflection of sexual tension away from the psychical field. Auxiliary Causes: Any stock noxae—emotion, fright, and also physical exhaustion through illness or over-exertion.

(1895b, p. 137)

In this passage, Freud does not mention the precipitating cause as such because any auxiliary or specific cause could be the precipitating cause, which is distinguished by its temporal role in relation to symptom onset rather than by any essential nature. This omission emphasizes Freud's basic point that the precipitating cause is relatively unimportant from a scientific perspective. What is important is the specific cause, which captures the essence of the particular condition. In Freud's analysis, heredity became an auxiliary cause that made it easier or more difficult to develop a neurosis once the specific sexual cause occurred. Note that Freud specifically dismisses fright as one of the "stock noxae," like exhaustion or physical illness, that often play a generic role in the triggering of a neurosis when the specific cause is present, but do not by themselves have any relationship to the structure of the resulting symptoms. In the psychoneuroses, in which, according to Freud, symptoms come about as a result of the defensive processing of meanings, the evidence for the claim that the precipitating cause is not the full or specific cause emerges in the details of the neuroses' symptoms, which must bear the stamp of the specific cause in the nature of the symptoms themselves.

Freud's Response to Lowenfeld's Fright Theory

In defending his sexual theory of the neuroses from Lowenfeld's (1895) fright theory, Freud (1895b) deployed his distinction between precipitating causes and specific etiology. The response to Lowenfeld provides a foundation for Freud's response to the fright theory in the Hans case. Freud observes that Lowenfeld argues that known nonsexual factors such as emotional traumas, especially severe frights, are also capable of causing anxiety neuroses:

With an unerring eye Lowenfeld (1895) detects the essential feature of my paper—namely, my assertion that anxiety-symptoms have a specific and uniform aetiology of a sexual nature ... What arguments, then, does Lowenfeld use to support his objection to my theory? ... I emphasized as a point essential to an understanding of anxiety neurosis that... the preparedness for anxiety, which constitutes the nucleus of the neurosis, cannot be acquired by a single or repeated affect of psychically justified fright ... Against this, Lowenfeld insists on the fact that in a number of cases "states of anxiety appear immediately or shortly after a psychical shock (fright alone, or accidents which were accompanied by fright), and in such situations there are sometimes circumstances which make the simultaneous operation of sexual noxae of the kind mentioned extremely improbable." [O]ne clinical observation ... concerns a woman of thirty ... [H]er husband had an attack of illness which frightened her, and in her agitation she ran about the cold room in her chemise. From that time on she was ill. First she had states of anxiety and palpitations in the evening, then came attacks of convulsive trembling, and after that phobias, and so on. It was the picture of a fully-developed anxiety neurosis. "Here," concludes Lowenfeld, "the anxiety states are obviously of psychical origin, brought about by the single fright."

(1895b, pp. 125–126)

Freud agrees with Lowenfeld that anxiety neuroses are often triggered by such traumatic frights or other emotions:

I do not doubt that my respected critic can produce many similar cases. I myself can supply a long list of analogous examples. Anyone who has not seen such cases—and they are extremely common—of an outbreak of anxiety neurosis after a psychical shock, ought not to regard himself as qualified to take part in discussions about anxiety neurosis ... About the facts themselves, which Lowenfeld uses against me, there is not the slightest doubt.

(1895b, p. 127)

Freud then recounts multiple cases in which a neurosis was triggered by intense emotions or stressors.

Having acknowledged that neuroses are triggered by frights and other nonsexual traumatic experiences, Freud then argues that precipitating triggers are often of a general nature—"stock noxae," he dismissively calls them—operating across many disorders. Such stock noxae precipitate an attack of symptoms without providing the specific etiology that explains the patient's pathological condition that disposes the patient to such attacks:

But there is doubt about their interpretation. Are we to accept the *post hoc ergo propter hoc* conclusion straight away and spare ourselves any critical consideration of the raw material? There are examples enough in which the final, releasing cause has not, in the face of critical analysis, maintained its position as the *causa efficiens*. One has only to think, for instance, of the relationship between trauma and gout. The role of a trauma in provoking an attack of gout in the injured limb is probably no different from the role it plays in the aetiology of tabes and general paralysis of the insane; only in the case of gout it is clear to the meanest capacity that it is absurd to suppose that the trauma has "caused" the gout instead of having merely provoked it. ... Emotion, fright, is also a stock factor of this kind. Fright can provoke chorea, apoplexy, paralysis agitans and many other things just as well as it can provoke anxiety neurosis ... [I]f the same specific cause can be shown to exist in the aetiology of all, or the great majority, of cases of anxiety neurosis, our view of the matter need not be shaken by the fact that the illness does not break out until one or other stock factor, such as emotion, has come into operation ...

If anyone wants to prove to me that in these remarks I have unduly neglected the significance of the stock aetiological factors, he must confront me with observations in which my specific factor is missing—that is, with cases in which anxiety neurosis has arisen after a psychical shock although the subject has (on the whole) led *a normal vita sexualis*.

(Freud, 1895b, pp. 125–128)

Freud acknowledges in this early paper that anxiety neuroses are often preceded by traumatic emotions such as intense fright, so the fact that Hans's phobia emerges after he witnesses the horse accident is not so surprising. He explains that such standard emotional precipitating causes can trigger a large variety of pathological conditions without being the cause to which the specific pathology can be attributed. So, analogous to the triggering of an episode of gout by a minor physical trauma, Freud can insist that the precipitating cause need not be the specific cause that is necessary for the condition to develop. He then challenges his critics to show him a case of anxiety disorder in which there is fright but no deeper sexual factor.

This is precisely what Wolpe and Rachman attempt to do. They offer a rival account in terms of fright in which they also attempt to systematically demolish Freud's argument for a sexual factor lurking in the etiology of Hans's neurosis.

Wolpe and Rachman's Critique of Freud's Account of Hans's Phobia

Wolpe and Rachman attack Freud's claim that there is a deeper sexual-specific etiology lying behind the precipitating cause of fright:

We shall show that although there are manifestations of sexual behavior on the part of Hans, there is no scientifically acceptable evidence showing any connection between this behavior and the child's phobia for horses; that the assertion of such connection is pure assumption; that the elaborate discussions that follow from it are pure speculation.

(1960, p. 135)

Note that Wolpe and Rachman acknowledge that Hans was found to have some sexual feelings in early childhood. They focus instead on Freud's failure to demonstrate the Oedipal nature of the sexual feelings and that there was a causal connection between those feelings and Hans's phobia. Asserting that "It is our contention that Freud's view of this case is not supported by the data, either in its particulars or as a whole" (1960, p. 143), Wolpe and Rachman formulate six central Freudian theses at which they direct their critique:

The major points that he regards as demonstrated are these: 1) Hans had a sexual desire for his mother, 2) he hated and feared his father and wished to kill him, 3) his sexual excitement and desire for his mother were transformed into anxiety, 4) his fear of horses was symbolic of his fear of his father, 5) the purpose of the illness was to keep near his mother and finally 6) his phobia disappeared because he resolved his Oedipus complex.

(1960, p. 143)

Wolpe and Rachman consider these six Freudian theses and offer replies to each. First, they reject Freud's claim that Hans had a sexual desire for his mother:

That Hans derived satisfaction from his mother and enjoyed her presence we will not even attempt to dispute. But nowhere is there any evidence of his wish to copulate with her. Yet Freud says that, "if matters had lain entirely in my hands ... I should have confirmed his instinctive premonitions, by telling him of the existence of the vagina and of copulation". The "instinctive premonitions" are referred to as though a matter of fact, though no evidence of their existence is given.

(Wolpe & Rachman, 1960, p. 143)

Second, Wolpe and Rachman are also severely critical of Freud's claim that Hans hated and feared his father and wished to kill him. They argue that any seeming evidence to the contrary was obtained by suggestion:

Never having expressed fear or hatred of his father, Hans was told by Freud that he possessed these emotions. On subsequent occasions Hans denied the existence of these feelings when questioned by his father. Eventually, he said "Yes" to a statement of this kind by his father. This simple affirmative obtained after considerable pressure on the part of the

father and Freud is accepted as the true state of affairs and all Hans's
denials are ignored.

(1960, pp. 143–144)

Third, regarding Freud's claim that Hans's anxiety was a transformation of
his repressed sexual desire for his mother, Wolpe and Rachman assert that
there is no case evidence of a change in Hans's attitude to his mother from
before to after the onset of the phobia. Freud in fact argues that there is a
marked change in Hans's sexual behavior from before to after the phobia's
onset, and I examine that argument in a later chapter.

Fourth, Wolpe and Rachman argue that the symbolic relationship proposed
by Freud between the horse and Hans's father is not supported. In rejecting
Freud's equation of horse and father, Wolpe and Rachman cite the experimental and research evidence from learning theory to support their rejection
of Freud's claim that such fears must *always* involve symbolic gratification.
However, knocking down Freud's overgeneralization is not equivalent to
showing that *in this case* the fear does not involve symbolic gratification, and
I will shortly discuss how behavioral theory itself has evolved to allow such
symbolism. More specifically, Wolpe and Rachman critique Freud's main
arguments for such a symbolic relationship, the "moustache and glasses"
argument, which, along with other evidence presented by Freud, I evaluate in
a later chapter.

Fifth, Freud claims that the purpose of Hans's phobia was to keep him
close to his mother. Wolpe and Rachman (1960) reply that this interpretation
fails to explain why Hans continued to feel anxiety even when he was out
walking with his mother. They do not, however, address Freud's own explanation of this fact, which he recognized as a potential objection and addressed in an argument I discuss in a later chapter.

Finally, to the sixth contention, that the analysis of Hans's Oedipal problems cured his phobia, Wolpe and Rachman answer that there is no coherent
temporal relationship in the case record linking Oedipal interpretations to
symptom improvement. Responding to Freud's statement that he hopes to
provide a more direct proof of psychoanalytic theorems, they conclude:

> The chief conclusion to be derived from our survey of the case of Little
> Hans is that it does not provide anything resembling direct proof of psy-
> choanalytic theorems. We have combed Freud's account for evidence that
> would be acceptable in the court of science, and have found none ...
>
> Freud fully believed that he had obtained in Little Hans a direct con-
> firmation of his theories, for he speaks towards the end of "the infantile
> complexes that were revealed behind Hans's phobia" ... Infantile com-
> plexes were not *revealed* (demonstrated) behind Hans's phobia: They
> were merely hypothesized ... Freud's claim of "a more direct and less
> roundabout proof" of certain of his theories is not justified by the

evidence presented. No confirmation by direct observation is obtained for any psychoanalytic theorem, though psychoanalysts have believed the contrary for 50 years. The demonstrations claimed are really interpretations that are created as facts.

(1960, pp. 146–147)

Despite its brilliance and its celebrated status in psychology as the death blow to Freud's Oedipal theory of Hans's phobia, Wolpe and Rachman's critique has some serious limitations. The main one, I will show in later chapters, is that Wolpe and Rachman did not accurately and completely formulate Freud's central arguments in the Hans case. This is not to say whether they were right or wrong, only that they offer insufficient evidence to decide whether they are right or wrong. In my reassessment of Freud's major claims in this book, the limitations of Wolpe and Rachman's paper will be rectified by carefully and charitably formulating and assessing Freud's arguments.

Note that Wolpe and Rachman do not criticize Freud for basing his conclusions on one case study. Behaviorists also frequently use single case designs and thus exercise caution about such a criticism. For example, Eysenck and Wilson, although behaviorist critics of Freudian theory, acknowledge that such caution is warranted:

It seems to us that it would be quite unfair to Freud and psychoanalysis to exclude the type of evidence on which he placed the greatest stress, on the arbitrary grounds that this evidence relied on single case reports. What is required, however, is to look at these case reports with a critical eye, to discover whether they do in fact provide the kind of experimental evidence which Freud believes they furnish.

(1973, p. 338)

As Eysenck and Wilson argue, the question is not whether the data came from a single case. Skinner and Pavlov, for example, rely heavily on single case designs in which variables are manipulated over time. Rather, the question is whether proper evidence "can be found in the type of case history offered by Freud," and "Are there alternative hypotheses which would explain the facts equally well, or better, than those considered by Freud?" (1973, pp. 338–339). This is the approach I will take in later chapters in assessing Freud's argument in the Hans case and whether he succeeded in showing his account to be superior to the fright theory.

Further Development of the Conditioning Theory of Phobias Since Wolpe and Rachman: Is the Fright Theory Still a Challenge to Freud's Oedipal Account?

The question of whether Wolpe and Rachman's criticisms of Freud are correct will be evaluated in various chapters to come. A separate issue is whether

Wolpe and Rachman's rival account of Hans's phobia in terms of one-trial fear conditioning is still a viable alternative account. I briefly consider some subsequent developments in the behavioral theory of phobias in order to address this question.

Wolpe and Rachman's classical conditioning account of Hans's horse phobia turned out to be a watershed not only in Freud criticism but also in behaviorist theory. For a while, it became the standard model of phobias.

Menzies and Clarke recounted this history as follows:

> Though proposed as early as 1917, the Pavlovian model of phobic reactions was not to become the dominant etiological account until well after the Second World War. It was not until publication of Wolpe and Rachman's classic critique of Freud's famous case study, "Little Hans," that the conditioning account was to take centre stage ... Its influence on the growth of interest and acceptance of the conditioning model, and the demise of the analytic account, cannot be overestimated ... [P]rior to onset of Hans' concerns, he had suffered a traumatic experience involving horses. Hans had been startled by an accident in which a horse pulling a bus had fallen. By his own account, the event had caused him great distress. Furthermore, as confirmed by his mother, his fear of horses had broken out immediately afterwards. Unlike Freud, Wolpe and Rachman saw the complete cause of Hans' disorder in this event, arguing that his phobic concerns, and all phobias, were due to traumatic Pavlovian conditioning. In the basic Pavlovian case, a neutral stimulus (the conditioned stimulus or CS) may acquire the capacity to elicit fear (the conditioned response or CR) if it occurs in contiguity with a second stimulus (the unconditioned stimulus or UCS) that inherently elicits fear or pain (unconditioned response or UCR). Hence, in Hans' case, horses (CS) had supposedly acquired the capacity to elicit fear (CR) after being involved in the accident (UCS) that had caused the initial startle and distress (UCR).
>
> (Menzies & Clarke, 1995, pp. 24–25)

However, the conditioning model as a general theory of phobias has subsequently faced serious challenges. Menzies and Clarke (1995) observe that "there are several problems for the traditional conditioning account of phobic onset and maintenance. The persistence, resistance to corrective information, and selective nature of phobias are genuine problems for the Pavlovian explanation" (p. 31). Seligman (1971) similarly identified inadequacies of the classical conditioning analysis of phobias:

> phobias are highly resistant to extinction, whereas laboratory fear conditioning, unlike avoidance conditioning, extinguishes rapidly; phobias comprise a nonarbitrary and limited set of objects, whereas fear

conditioning is thought to occur to an unlimited range of conditioned stimuli. Furthermore, phobias, unlike laboratory fear conditioning, are often acquired in one trial and seem quite resistant to change by 'cognitive' means.

(p. 307)

He proposed adding both biological preparedness and symbolic meaning to behaviorist accounts of phobias.

These and other problems have driven theoreticians within the broadly behaviorist camp to propose new accounts of how phobias are formed that are less anchored in conditioning. Indeed, it is fair to say that Wolpe and Rachman's theory is effectively dead as a *general complete* theory of phobias. Rachman (1977) himself has gone beyond the earlier theory, positing three pathways to phobia formation: classical conditioning of the kind proposed in Wolpe and Rachman, vicarious learning by modeling others, and learning through information or instruction.

Subsequent work, while acknowledging that experience and conditioning enter into fear formation in a variety of ways, has emphasized biological preparedness for quick conditioning of specific fears and "nonassociative" innate fear formation without any specific traumatic trigger at all. Rethinking laboratory results where one-trial conditioning of fear to a neutral stimulus was difficult, Seligman (1971) wondered why Hans's phobia was so easily conditioned in one trial. He questioned whether the theory proposed by Wolpe and Rachman is adequate as a general theory of phobia formation, and noted that subsequent attempts to replicate Watson and Raynor's study with Little Albert have met with mixed results:

Furry things, like rats and rabbits, became aversive to Little Albert, but Watson and Rayner themselves probably did not ... Conditioning occurred in two trials, making it operationally prepared and it was also selective ... English (1929) did not get fear conditioning to a wooden duck, even after many pairings with a startling noise.

(p. 315)

Seligman's question of why Hans became afraid of horses rather than the other things that were present when he experienced his fright remains a serious challenge to a classical behaviorist account which holds that all stimuli are initially equal. Seligman concluded that there must be biologically shaped "prepared" linkages, having evolutionary roots, that make some stimuli—such as, perhaps, large animals in a state of acute distress—more easily conditionable than others. To this extent, conditioning would be influenced by the evolved "meanings" that we are programmed to experience more easily. Thus, Seligman suggests that not all stimuli are created equal. Seligman suggests that horses were salient because human beings are biologically shaped to be more sensitive to some stimuli relevant to our survival—like large animals—than to others.

There is an irony here because in effect the ease of conditionability of a stimulus indicates its "symbolic meaning" based on biologically prepared linkages:

In some ways, we have come full circle. We began by concurring in the rejection of the psychoanalytic interpretation of phobias, e.g., that horses were fearful to Little Hans because they symbolized his father's retribution. We modified the learning reconstruction of phobias by suggesting a modification of general process learning theory. Phobias, in our view, are not instances of unprepared fear conditioning, but of prepared fear conditioning. Nonarbitrary stimuli seem particularly ready to become phobic objects for human beings and this may also be true of "soteria," the opposite number from phobias (e.g., Linus' blanket). Particular CSs are readily conditioned to particular UCSs. Perhaps this is a way of reconstructing symbolism. Is it possible that there really is something to horses and wolves, etc., that makes them highly associable with certain kinds of traumas, perhaps even sexual ones? Does anyone have a lamb phobia? This is testable. When Little Hans acquired his phobia, there were not only horses around, but other things, such as his nurse or a bus and yet these did not become phobic objects. Why only horses? If children were given horses and blackboards, both paired with anxiety-arousal, would they learn readily to be afraid of horses but not of blackboards?

So, for a biologically oriented learning theorist, to what can the notion of symbolism amount? A is symbolic of B, if and only if human beings are prepared, in the sense defined, to learn that A is associated with B. If humans can acquire with A the properties of B after only minimal input, then it is meaningful to say that A is symbolic of B.

(1971, pp. 317–318)

Rachman (1977) also later critiqued the conditioning model and developed a new multipathway model of phobia formation that attempted to deal with the problems confronting the Wolpe-Rachman classical conditioning model, especially the fact that many phobics report no history of direct Pavlovian conditioning of their fear. Rachman moved toward the position that, to account for the details of phobia formation, one must look at idiosyncratic meanings in a way reminiscent of Freud's idiographic approach:

[W]e are moving towards a position in which it is postulated that there is an ease of connection between certain people and certain stimuli—and contrariwise, that some people are particularly invulnerable to certain fear stimuli. In addition to postulating an appropriate fit between the person and the stimulus, we also have to take into account the occurrence of "critical moments". In attempting to explain those fears which have an acute onset, one needs to know why the fear emerges at the particular time that it does ... [Q]uite frequently these same people have been exposed to the same stimulus repeatedly in the past without acquiring the fear. It seems that for acute onset fears, there are certain psychological states in which the person is vulnerable to the acquisition of fear … [O]ne needs to know why the fear arose on the day that it did, at the time that it did. And why do they acquire a fear of public transport, crowded or open spaces, or whatever the content of their phobia is, when on hundreds or thousands of previous exposures to the same set of stimuli, they remained unaffected? … [I]t seems likely that the critical incident occurs when the person is in an emotionally upset or apprehensive state before the critical incident occurs … The Seligman hypothesis is of some utility in that biologically non-significant stimuli are said to be "poorly prepared" for fear. Also, people are considerably more resilient than the conditioning theory allows.

(pp. 384–386)

That is, the conditioning theory has moved from a universal generalization straightforwardly applied to Hans's circumstances to an idiographic single-event causal explanation of a very different kind that takes into account Hans's prior emotional state, but still a conditioning explanation. Rachman's analysis suggests the same sort of process of matching explanatory proposals to the details of the phobia that, we shall see, Freud attempts. Both Rachman and Seligman, in suggesting biologically based linkages between meanings, come closer to the psychoanalytic view that stimuli have symbolic meanings that explain rapid fear conditioning as a precipitating cause of a deeper process, even if they do not agree with the Oedipal contents Freud proposes.

Menzies and Clarke (1995) go a step further than Seligman's preparedness theory by arguing for biologically based "non-associative"—that is, non-conditioning—processes in some phobia formation. They argue that the conditioning theory cannot possibly account for all of phobia formation due to a variety of empirical challenges:

There are six arguments against acceptance of the conditioning theory of fear acquisition. They are: (1) The failure of people to acquire fears in what are theoretically, undoubtedly fear-evoking situations (e.g. air raids). (2) It is difficult to produce conditioned fear reactions in human subjects, even under controlled laboratory conditions. (3) The conditioning theory rests on the equipotentiality premise (Seligman and Hager, 1972), which is now recognized to be untenable. (4) The distribution of fears in normal and neurotic populations is difficult to reconcile with the conditioning theory. (5) A significant number of phobic patients, psychiatric and military, recount histories that cannot be accommodated by the conditioning theory. (6) Fears can be reduced by vicarious processes and it seems highly likely that they can be acquired by similar processes.

(1995, p. 379)

The nonassociative account postulates innate fears that depend only on maturation and perhaps on certain triggering experiences such as a mother's fear, but not on fear conditioning even of the minimal sort required by Seligman's preparedness model:

> [I]n many clinical cases, traumatic conditioning episodes do not appear to have preceded onset ... In human subjects, it appears that aversive asso-ciative learning need not be a precipitant of fear of water, heights, spiders, strangers, and separation, to name but a few.
>
> (Menzies & Clarke, 1995, pp. 34, 38, 43)

The Continued Relevance of the Wolpe-Rachman Critique and the Challenge of the "Precipitating Cause" or "Fright" Account

With all these changes to the behavioral theory of phobias since the original Wolpe and Rachman model, where do we stand with regard to their critique of Freud? Based on the above developments, one might be tempted to declare that the Wolpe-Rachman analysis has been disconfirmed and the conditioning theory has failed. This would be misleading. Despite suggesting complexities undreamed of in Wolpe and Rachman's simple characterization of fear con-ditioning, these developments leave intact the proposed conditioning pathway to Hans's phobia formation, albeit with the possibility of supplementary explanatory constructs such as biological preparedness, idiosyncratic condi-tions that promote conditioning, and emotional background that explains why conditioning yielding phobia formation took place on that particular occasion. The modifications in no way return us to a specifically Oedipal or Freudian explanation of Hans's phobia.

In the conditioning model's development over time, there are three critical points regarding its challenge to the Oedipal account of Hans's phobia: (1) the original simple conditioning model has been abandoned as a general theory of phobia formation in the light of much evidence at odds with it; (2) modifications to the conditioning model—including the importance of biological prepared-ness, but especially individual emotional preparedness, symbolic meanings, and nonconditioned fears in the development of a phobia—bring it closer to the richness of the Freudian-type model in which idiosyncratic meanings and inter-nal emotional variables play a large role in the explanation of phobia formation; and, most importantly for present purposes, (3) despite all the changes, the essential mortal challenge of the "fright theory" to Freud's Oedipal account, based on the horse accident as a conditioning opportunity, remains more or less what it was.

The last point is crucial. These new views do not deny that the conditioning account is still part of the overall explanation of phobias. For example, Menzies and Clarke (1995), despite defending the existence of some uncon-ditioned innate fears, insist on the continued importance of conditioned fears:

To continue to support the associative position as a comprehensive account of phobic etiology in the face of this growing list seems pointless. Of course, this does not mean that the nonassociative model can account for all fears and phobias ... Addition of the nonassociative pathway should not be taken to eliminate the possibility of conditioned fears.

(p. 43)

Where do all these developments leave us with regard to the rivalry between Freud's and Wolpe and Rachman's claims about the primary cause of Hans's phobia? We know that Hans's fear was not entirely innate and nonassociative because Hans did not have the phobia prior to the horse accident. Even Wolpe and Rachman agree with Freud that Hans's experiences prior to the horse accident prepared him to respond so extremely to his experience, but they place such earlier sensitizing experiences as secondary etiologically to the accident itself and consider those experiences to be specific to horses and not Oedipal. Perhaps a strong reaction to a large animal was biologically prepared, but even Freud admits that the horse accident was at least a precipitating cause of Hans's phobia while insisting it was not the primary cause. None of the newer developments in behaviorist thinking dissolve the question of whether the horse accident might have been the primary etiology rather than a mere incidental precipitant of Hans's phobia. In essence, then, the tradition of challenge to Freud that I am calling the "fright theory" that runs from Breuer through Lowenfeld and Haberman on to Wolpe and Rachman and myriad others, is intact. The "fright theory" is still the major challenge to Freud's account of Hans's phobia that he recognized it to be.

References

Breuer, J. (1895). Theoretical. In J. Breuer & S. Freud, Studies on hysteria. *SE* 2, 183–251.
Eysenck, H. J., & Wilson, G. D. (1973). Comment. In H. J. Eysenck & G. D. Wilson (Eds.), *The experimental study of Freudian theories* (pp. 338–339). London: Methuen.
Freud, S. (1895a). On the grounds for detaching a particular syndrome from neurasthenia under the description "anxiety neurosis". *SE* 3, 85–115.
Freud, S. (1895b). A reply to criticisms of my paper on anxiety neurosis. *SE* 3, 119–139.
Freud, S. (1909). Analysis of a phobia in a five-year-old boy. *SE* 10, 1–150.
Freud, S. (1926). Inhibitions, symptoms and anxiety. *SE* 20, 75–176.
Haberman, J. V. (1913, September 6). The psychoanalytic delusion. *Medical Record*, 84(10), 421–427.
Lowenfeld, L. (1895). Über die Verknüpfung neurasthenischer und hysterischer Symptome in Anfallsform nebst Bemerkungen über die Freudsche Angstneurose. *Münchener Medicinische Wochenschrift*, 42, 282–285.
Menzies, R. G., & Clarke, J. C. (1995). The etiology of phobias: A non-associative account. *Clinical Psychology Review*, 15, 23–48.
Prince, M. (1914). *The unconscious: The fundamentals of human personality, normal and abnormal*. New York: Macmillan.

Rachman, S. (1977). The conditioning theory of fear acquisition: A critical examination. *Behavior Research & Therapy*, 15, 375–387.

Seligman, M. E. P. (1971). Phobias and preparedness. *Behavior Therapy*, 2, 307–320.

Watson, J. B., & Rayner, R. (1920). Conditioned emotional reactions. *Journal of Experimental Psychology*, 3, 1–14.

Wolpe, J., & Rachman, S. (1960). Psychoanalytic "evidence": A critique based on Freud's case of little Hans. *Journal of Nervous and Mental Disease*, 131(2), 135–148.

Chapter 6

"Without an Object to Begin With"

Does the Case Evidence Support Freud's Claim that Hans's Disorder Started with a Period of Free-Floating Anxiety Preceding the Phobia?

In the last chapter, we saw that the "fright" theory of the etiology of Hans's horse phobia is a compelling rival and real threat to Freud's Oedipal theory in terms of evidential support and explanatory power. Freud responds directly to this threat with two "negative" arguments that attempt to use the case data to preemptively falsify the fright account. These negative arguments are purely aimed at eliminating the fright theory from contention and are independent of Freud's positive arguments in support of his own Oedipal account, to be considered in later chapters.

In this chapter, I consider the first of Freud's negative arguments, the "undirected anxiety" argument. Essentially, the argument is that the case description of the phobia's onset reveals that Hans's anxiety disorder started with a period of free-floating anxiety not directed at any particular object. Freud claims that the fixation of this undirected anxiety onto the object of horses, and thus the transformation of the disorder into a phobia, occurred only later. He says, for example:

> The first thing we learn is that the outbreak of the anxiety-state was by no means so sudden as appeared at first sight. A few days earlier the child had woken from an anxiety-dream to the effect that his mother had gone away, and that now he had no mother to coax with.
>
> (1909, p. 23)

> In the evening he seems to have had another attack similar to that of the previous evening, and to have wanted to be "coaxed" with ... Here, then, we have the beginning of Hans's anxiety as well as of his phobia. As we see, there is good reason for keeping the two separate.
>
> (p. 24)

and

> Chronological considerations make it impossible for us to attach any great importance to the actual precipitating cause of the outbreak of

DOI: 10.4324/9781003272472-6

Hans's illness, for he had shown signs of apprehensiveness long before he saw the bus-horse fall down in the street.

(p. 136)

The undirected anxiety argument is based on the case report's description of Hans's symptoms prior to treatment by his father. It is thus immune to the suggestion objection. There is no plausible way that such undirected anxiety prior to the horse accident could have been suggested to Hans by his father during the analysis, which occurred later.

The undirected anxiety argument has become a mainstay in the literature on the Hans case, with other prominent interpreters building on Freud's observations. For example, Jonathan Lear, accepting Freud's argument, states that, regarding the emergence of Hans's fear of horses,

> the outbreak of the phobia was preceded by a period of anxiety ... And, Freud argues, anxiety naturally strives toward conceptualization: by its nature it tends to look for an object and thus transform itself into fear ... His anxiety was free-floating; his fear was of horses.
>
> (Lear, 1990, p. 107)

Jerome Neu states: "Hans' problem began as an unfocused anxiety, and only emerged as a specific phobia gradually" (p. 139). And John Bowlby (1973), reinterpreting the case in terms of attachment theory, and thus seeing separation anxiety rather than undirected anxiety in Hans's pre-phobic behavior, follows Freud's strategy for dismissing the fright theory by asserting: "Thus, both the sequence of events leading up to the phobia and Hans's own statements make it clear that, *distinct from and preceding any fear of horses,* Hans was afraid" (p. 286; for a full examination of Bowlby's reinterpretation of the Hans case, see Wakefield, 2022).

This argument is presented early in Freud's running commentary on the case report at the point reporting the onset of Hans's phobia, which is long before the horse accident comes to light in the analysis. Although Freud consequently does not mention the fright theory or the horse accident when constructing this argument, nevertheless the argument's primary logical target is clearly the fright theory's horse accident account of Hans's phobia. Paralleling Freud's presentation, I will consider the undirected anxiety argument as an independent argument about the phenomenology of Hans's symptoms independent of closely related arguments about the timing of the horse accident and the phobia's onset to be considered in the next chapter.

Freud's Prediction of Possible Undirected Anxiety

The undirected anxiety argument asserts that prior to the fixation of Hans's anxiety onto the object of horses, Hans experienced a period of free-floating anxiety not directed at any particular object. As Freud summarizes it later in his commentary when dismissing the horse accident's importance: "[T]he anxiety originally had no reference at all to horses but was transposed on to them secondarily and had now become fixed upon those elements of the horse-complex" (p. 51). The sort of free-floating anxiety that Freud attributes to those with Hans's diagnosis of anxiety hysteria consists of sheer anxious somatic and affective activation without any particular object of fear. It thus resembles the modern category of "generalized anxiety disorder" before it was transformed under pressure from cognitive behaviorists into what amounts to a "worry disorder" that involves multiple diffuse objects of concern.

The logical structure of the undirected anxiety argument appears to be valid. If indeed Hans's anxiety disorder started with a period of free-floating anxiety prior to the horse phobia, then the horse accident, after which the phobia started, cannot fully explain the overall disorder's onset. Moreover, the fright theory offers no reason to expect the occurrence of a period of undirected, free-floating anxiety prior to phobia formation. It claims that the terror experienced during the horse accident leads directly to the fear of horses, with the object of the fear presumably continuous from the content of the triggering incident to the resulting phobic content. Thus, if Hans experienced an initial period of undirected anxiety followed by the phobia as continuous parts of one larger anxiety disorder, then this is a prima facie disconfirmation of the fright account of Hans's overall disorder.

In contrast, a period of undirected anxiety preceding the phobia is not only consistent with Freud's theory but predicted as a possibility by his "repression" theory of symptom formation. At the time of the Hans case, Freud held that phobia formation in cases of anxiety hysteria involves four steps: repression of Oedipal sexual desire; availability of the sexual energy formerly attached to the repressed desire; transformation of the available sexual energy into free-floating anxiety; and attachment of the free-floating anxiety to a chosen phobic object at which it becomes directed. As his theory of anxiety matured, the sequence changed to reflect the fact that anxiety is an ego-generated signal of danger, and became: repression of Oedipal sexual desire; repression of an anxiety-provoking idea associated with the repressed Oedipal sexual desire (in the boy's Oedipal case, fear of castration by the father due to the boy's desire for the mother and desire to be rid of the father); availability of the anxiety affect that was attached to the repressed fear; transformation of the available anxiety into a free-floating experience of anxiety; attachment of the free-floating anxiety to a chosen phobic object at which the anxiety becomes directed through displacement.

Freud's theory, early or late, thus predicts a possible stage of undirected anxiety prior to choice of a phobic object. Freud holds that such undirected anxiety tends to seek an object partly because there are defensive advantages if the anxiety is focused on a specific object (e.g., the anxious individual can then avoid the anxiety-provoking object). Consequently, although Freud's theory of phobogenesis allows for a period of undirected anxiety, it does not predict that the period of undirected anxiety will be prolonged enough to be observable. In any specific case, repression could be almost immediately followed by fixation of anxiety upon an object, so the phase of undirected anxiety would be unexperienced and unobservable. Consequently, Freud's theory would not be falsified by the lack of a period of undirected anxiety. But the rival fright theory would be falsified and Freud's theory confirmed if such a period of undirected anxiety were to be observed as part of the overall anxiety condition that included the horse phobia.

The Undirected Anxiety Argument as Freud's Antidote to the Causal Illusion

One of the most compelling points in favor of explaining Hans's phobia by his witnessing a horse accident is that Hans indicates that the horse phobia broke out immediately following the horse accident. The idea that temporal sequencing (one event following another) suggests a cause-effect relationship seems to be part of our built-in psychological causation-detection mechanisms, and was famously identified by David Hume as one of the essential features of our notion of causation. Nevertheless, most things that follow other things are not caused by them. Freud (1895) dismisses such arguments for a causal relationship between fright and anxiety disorder as fallacious *post hoc ergo propter hoc* ("after this, therefore because of this") reasoning that ignores potential deeper causes: "Are we to accept the *post hoc ergo propter hoc* conclusion straight away and spare ourselves any critical consideration of the raw material?" (p. 127). Freud, we saw in an earlier chapter, argues that this makes no more sense than saying that an attack of gout is caused by hitting one's toe, and ignoring the underlying medical condition. Or, think here of the World War II Londoner who pulled the W.C. flush cord just as a buzz bomb destroyed his house; the illusion of causality from the temporal sequence kept him from pulling such cords for the rest of his life, or so the story goes. Temporal sequence arguments for causation are potentially intellectual versions of such causal illusions.

However, there is more than sheer Humean temporal sequence at work here shaping our intuitions. The experience of witnessing the horse accident and the experience of the phobia share the intentional content of fear of horses, suggesting on plausible background behavioral and folk-psychological grounds that the two are linked by mental causation. It simply makes sense that witnessing a horse accident might cause a child such a fright as to bring about horse phobia symptoms for a few months. The horse accident account thus offers a straightforward, prima facie plausible answer to the pivotal question: Why did Hans's phobia occur when it did?

The undirected anxiety argument is part of an ingenious attempt by Freud to undo the potency of the causal-sequence impression. If Hans's disorder did not start with phobic content, then the power of the horse accident to explain the phobia is undermined. Freud's attempt to challenge the simple "content" argument and to turn the phobia's content, or lack thereof, to his own advantage by uncovering a contentless phase of Hans's disorder is part of the power and the point of the undirected anxiety argument.

The Case Record's Description of the Onset of the Phobia

Freud's argument that Hans experienced a period of free-floating anxiety before the phobia's onset rests on his reading of the case history's description of the initial occurrences of Hans's anxiety. The case record up to the time of the phobia's onset mentions four occasions of anxiety (counting a day and that evening as one occasion). Here are the relevant passages, labeled for easy reference:

(P1) Hans (aged four and three-quarters) woke up one morning in tears. Asked why he was crying, he said to his mother: "When I was asleep I thought you were gone and I had no Mummy to coax [cuddle-JW] with." An anxiety dream, therefore.
(p. 23; we are told that this report dates "from the first days in January")

(P2) I had already noticed something similar at Gmunden in the summer ... Once he made a remark to this effect: "Suppose I was to have no Mummy", or "Suppose you were to go away", or something of the sort. I cannot remember the exact words. Unfortunately, when he got into an elegiac mood of that kind, his mother used always to take him into bed with her.
(p. 23; this is a comment by the father on P1)

(P3) On January 7th he went to the Stadtpark with his nursemaid as usual. In the street he began to cry and asked to be taken home, saying that he wanted to "coax" [cuddle-JW] with his Mummy. At home he was asked why he had refused to go any farther and had cried, but he would not say. Till the evening he was cheerful, as usual. But in the evening he grew visibly frightened; he cried and could not be separated from his mother, and wanted to "coax" with her again. Then he grew cheerful again, and slept well.
(pp. 23–24)

(P4) On January 8th my wife decided to go out with him herself, so as to see what was wrong with him. They went to Schonbrunn, where he always likes going. Again he began to cry, did not want to start, and was frightened. In the end he did go; but was visibly frightened in the street. On the way back from Schonbrunn he said to his mother, after much internal struggling: "I *was afraid a horse would bite me*." (He had, in fact, become uneasy at Schonbrunn when he saw a horse.) In the evening he seems to have had another attack similar to that of the previous evening, and to have wanted to be "coaxed" with. He was calmed down. He said, crying: "I know I shall have to go for a walk again to-morrow." And later: "The horse'll come into the room."

(p. 24)

I am going to limit the examination here to P3 and P4, the anxiety experienced on Hans's walks with his nursemaid and his mother on January 7 and 8, respectively. The reasons for this focus are several.

First, one would imagine that the point is to explain Hans's anxiety disorder, and that encompassing other anxieties within the target domain of explanation could confuse things. P1 and P2 are expressions of anxiety but both are transient expressions of Hans's apprehensiveness about his mother's presence, a common child concern. These anxieties occur before the onset of the intense anxiety in P3 that plausibly constitutes an anxiety disorder and are not nearly severe, enduring, or unusual enough to be considered an anxiety disorder. In contrast, P3 and P4 appear to be likely instances of anxiety disorder. There is a danger that if one simply reaches back to noncontiguous incidents and tosses various moments of anxiety into the disorder Freud is trying to explain, then of course one can trivially show that the entire disorder was not caused by any recent incident. Second, the timing of the earlier incidents raises questions. One of them (P2) occurred several months before the walk with the nursemaid and its precise nature and circumstances are vague. The other occurred a few days before the walk with the nursemaid, but whether it was part of the same condition or an instance of anxiety unrelated to the later outbreak is unclear. In contrast, the continuity from one day to the next of P3 and P4 offers a strong prima facie case that they are part of one overall disorder. Third, it is within that continuous period of the two instances, P3 and P4, that, as we shall shortly see, Freud locates what he believes is the transition from undirected anxiety to phobic anxiety. Indeed, Freud claims that it is during the walk with his mother on January 8 that Hans developed his phobic fear. Thus, if there is evidence for a change in the nature of Hans's anxiety, it should be recognizable within the two-day period of January 7 and 8 during which, according to Freud, on one day Hans experienced undirected anxiety and on part of the next he experienced phobic content.

There is an additional compelling reason for focusing on P3 and P4 and keeping P1 and P2 separate. In my book, *Attachment, Sexuality, Power* (Wakefield, 2022), I establish the likely trigger for both of these incidents of Hans's anxiety about his mother. One of them (P2) occurred when the family was at their summer home at Gmunden, and the other (P1) occurred in Vienna in the days prior to the phobia's outbreak. In both instances, Hans's father was assertively interfering with Hans's attachment relationship with his mother and preventing him from cuddling with her for soothing purposes. An attachment-theoretic explanation of Hans's anxiety appears to be compelling here. Such an explanation would combine two elements. First, Bowlby (1973) argues that Hans's mother tended to threaten to leave him when he misbehaved, and this may have caused some degree of anxious attachment and proneness to separation anxiety. One can supplement this with multiple other potential separation anxiety provoking events, such as that Hans attended his first funeral that summer in Gmunden, and that his father was in fact leaving and going into Vienna during the week (note that Hans expresses anxiety about his father going away). During the time in Vienna after the summer, the father continued his blocking Hans from cuddling with his mother. The combination of background factors disposing to separation anxiety along with the immediate disruption of Hans's access to his mother—or, to put it another way, the combination of Hans's mother's threats to leave with her actual unavailability due to the father's interference—could easily have led to the described morning or bedtime anxieties.

I conclude that the serious and persuasive evidence, if there is any, for Freud's undirected anxiety argument occurs in the descriptions of Hans's two walks, one with his nursemaid and one with his mother, on January 7 and 8, to which I now turn.

When Did Hans's Phobia Begin? Freud's Commentary on the Phobia's Onset

Immediately after the reports of the first days of the anxiety condition (reproduced above), Freud comments: "Here, then, we have the beginning of Hans's anxiety as well as of his phobia. As we see, there is good reason for keeping the two separate" (p. 24). Freud's grounds for saying that the onset of Hans's anxiety and of his phobia must be kept separate become clear in Freud's subsequent description of Hans's first reports of anxiety on the walk with the nursemaid (P3), as follows:

> Hans's anxiety, which thus corresponded to a repressed erotic longing, was, like every infantile anxiety, without an object to begin with: it was still anxiety and not yet fear. The child cannot tell [at first] what he is afraid of; and when Hans, on the first walk with the nursemaid, would not say what he was afraid of, it was simply that he himself did not yet know.
>
> (p. 25)

Using Hans's reaction to the nursemaid's questions as evidence, Freud asserts that Hans's anxiety was "without an object" and "not yet [phobic] fear" during the walk with the nursemaid on January 7, the day before he first reported his horse fear. However, Freud presents no evidence for his claim beyond the interchange between Hans and his nursemaid. Freud thus moves without argument from the fact that on the walk with the nursemaid Hans *would not say* what he was afraid of to the conclusion that Hans *could not say* because he *did not know* what he was afraid of. Freud claims that Hans was not merely ignorant of the object of his fear, but that there was no object of his fear because Hans was not yet afraid of anything specific. Freud continues:

> *He said all that he knew*, which was that in the street he missed his mother, whom he could coax with, and that he did not want to be away from her. In saying this he quite straightforwardly confessed the primary meaning of his dislike of streets.
>
> (p. 25; emphasis added)

In asserting that Hans said "all that he knew," Freud again claims that Hans did not yet possess a fear of horses, of which he presumably would have been aware. As to Hans's request that he wants to go home to his mother, Freud interprets this longing as revealing the true underlying meaning of the anxiety, namely, Hans's sexual desire for his mother. But Hans's request could also be interpreted as an anxious child's desire to be soothed by his attachment figure.

The next day, Hans's mother took him for a walk to see what was wrong. On the way home, Hans admitted for the first time that he was afraid of horses. Freud makes clear in his commentary on the description of this walk that he is assuming that it was on this day that Hans first attached his anxiety, formerly undirected, onto the object of horses:

> His anxiety, then, corresponded to repressed longing ... This was shown to be so in the case of Hans on the occasion of his next walk, when his mother went with him. He was with his mother, and yet he still suffered from anxiety ... *But his anxiety had stood the test; and the next thing for it to do was to find an object.* It was on this walk that he first expressed a fear that a horse would bite him.
>
> (p. 26; emphasis added)

Freud uses this discussion of Hans's anxiety when with his mother to pursue his agenda of arguing that Hans's anxiety started prior to the phobia. He suggests that, having been present for some time, at the time of this walk the anxiety was ready to be attached to an object ("But his anxiety had stood the test; and the next thing for it to do was to find an object"). It is on this walk that Freud places the phobia's onset, simply because Hans first reported his fear on this walk: "It was on this walk that he first expressed a fear that a horse would bite him." That is, Freud implicitly equates Hans's expressing that he was afraid of horses with Hans acquiring a fear of horses.

In sum, Freud assumes without argument that before Hans reported the phobia, any anxiety was undirected anxiety and not phobic anxiety. He infers that Hans began suffering from his phobia on January 8 based solely on the fact that Hans first reported his fear of horses to his mother on that day. Freud's inference is not valid on its face. Anxiety prior to Hans's report of his phobia could be phobic anxiety, if Hans was resistant to admitting the nature of his fear—as, I will argue, his behavior suggests he was. I thus reconsider Freud's evaluation of Hans's anxiety prior to the report of the phobia by considering the alternative hypothesis that Hans was reticent about admitting his phobia. If the anxiety before January 8 was really so different in nature, one would expect to find some hint of this in the case report. I thus focus on whether the symptomatic descriptions or any other information in the case report warrant Freud's claim that the anxieties preceding the walk with the mother were a different free-floating pre-phobic kind of anxiety, versus the alternative hypothesis that it was simply phobic anxiety prior to Hans being willing to tell his mother about his phobia.

Is There Evidence in Hans's Symptoms on His Walks with the Nursemaid and His Mother for Freud's Hypothesis of Pre-Phobia Undirected Anxiety?

We know that by the end of the walk on January 8 with his mother, Hans had the horse phobia. Freud claims Hans did not have the phobia during his walk with the nursemaid on January 7, despite intense anxiety symptoms. Considering the evidence from the case description, does Freud's claim that Hans's anxiety on the two walks was so radically different stand up to close examination?

Both walks were characterized by destinations that were among Hans's favorites (Stadtpark and Schonbrunn) and companions with whom he was familiar (nursemaid and mother), so no explanation for Hans's anxieties can readily be found in such circumstances. Freud assumes that Hans does not say what he is afraid of on the 8th because there is no such thing, but we know that Hans is often a reluctant reporter. Indeed, he remains similarly reticent for most of the next day as well (see below), even though he eventually does tell his mother of his fears. So the obvious rival hypothesis is that he already has the phobia and is simply unwilling to say.

How can we explore which of these hypotheses is most plausible? If the anxiety conditions on the two days were very different in their nature, one might expect this to emerge in some way in Hans's behavior or verbal reports. So, one way to test the hypothesis that the phobia already existed on the 7th is to put aside Hans's explanations or lack thereof and compare the symptoms that occurred during the two walks and their aftermath. To the degree that the symptoms and the language used by Hans to describe them are similar, this suggests the likelihood that they have the same type of source. In contrast, lack of similarity or other revealing distinctive features could be suggestive of different types of sources. I shall examine the two days' symptoms with this in mind, looking for similarities and divergences and what might explain them.

If one compares the reports of the walk with the nursemaid and the walk with the mother, then except for the fact that the mother was able to insist on completing the walk despite Hans's resistance, whereas the nurse yielded to Hans's desire to return home, the pattern of behavior and the symptoms displayed by Hans are markedly similar. On both days, the symptoms consisted of crying, fear, reluctance to either begin or continue walking in the streets, and desire to return home. Indeed, when describing the symptoms on the walk with the mother, the father indicates by the term "again" that the symptoms were a repetition of those experienced the day before ("Again he began to cry, did not want to start, and was frightened"). Moreover, upon reflection, it is unclear why undirected anxiety would be manifested so intensely and specifically while walking in the streets. Undirected anxiety can occur at home as well as in the streets. So, the symptoms seem to make more sense if there is already a horse phobia.

But what of Hans's confession of the nature of his fear on the 8th but not on the 7th? The fact that on January 7 Hans would not say why he was afraid is summarily interpreted by Freud as implying that Hans did not yet know the source of his anxiety. However, Hans strongly resisted explaining his fear on both days. On the day he confessed the nature of his fear, he was clearly afraid at the outset of the walk ("he did not want to start, and was frightened" and "was visibly frightened in the street"). He did not admit to his phobia until the walk was nearly over and he and his mother were on their way home, and even then, he explained the problem to his mother only "after much internal struggling." We know that he had the phobia earlier on that day because "he had, in fact, become uneasy at Schonbrunn when he saw a horse." Except for the fact that Hans admitted the truth to his mother, these events seem similar to what happened after the walk with the nursemaid the day before: "At home he was asked why he had refused to go any farther and had cried, but he would not say." Given that on January 8 Hans manifested strong resistance to explaining his fear, Freud's conclusion that he lacked the phobia on the 7th just because he did not explain his fear that day is unwarranted. Hans resisted explaining his phobia on the 7th just as he did on the 8th, except that on the 8th he eventually came around.

Is There Evidence for the Undirected Anxiety Thesis in Hans's Evening Symptoms on January 7 and 8?

So far, I have considered only the symptoms during the two walks on January 7 and 8, and concluded that the symptom evidence offers no support for Freud's claim of undirected anxiety on the 7th. The same conclusion emerges from an examination of Hans's symptoms and behavior in the evenings following the walks.

Hans's father indicates that Hans's behavior on the two evenings was quite similar ("In the evening he seems to have had another attack similar to that of the previous evening"). Specifically, on the evening after the walk with the nursemaid, before Hans had admitted to a horse phobia, Hans went through a cycle of fear, crying, wanting to cuddle with his mother, and being soothed and calmed down once he did ("But in the evening he grew visibly frightened; he cried and could not be separated from his mother, and wanted to 'coax' with her again. Then he grew cheerful again, and slept well"). Similarly, the next evening, after the walk with his mother, by which point Hans had admitted to being afraid of horses, Hans experienced the same cycle of fear-need for cuddling-calming down ("In the evening he seems to have had another attack similar to that of the previous evening, and to have wanted to be 'coaxed' with. He was calmed down"). The symptoms and behaviors are the same on both nights, and due to Hans's reluctant admission, we know that the symptoms were generated by fear of horses in the second case. Nothing in the case evidence suggests that the cause was different on the first night. It is worth noting that attachment theory predicts that a boy experiencing anxiety over a phobic fear would long for contact with his mother to produce a sense of safety.

In regard to these evening attacks, Freud argues that they were not due to the phobia, as follows:

> Then again, there were the states into which he fell on two consecutive evenings before going to sleep, and which were characterized by anxiety mingled with clear traces of tenderness. These states show that at the beginning of his illness there was as yet no phobia whatever present, whether of streets or of walking or even of horses. If there had been, his evening states would be inexplicable; for who bothers at bedtime about streets and walking?
>
> (p. 25)

There are two problems with this argument. First, in claiming that the two evenings were before the phobia's outbreak, Freud mischaracterizes the case report. The evenings of the 7th and 8th are the only "two consecutive evenings" on which Hans is described as having the sort of anxiety symptoms described by Freud, and Hans had already reported his phobia prior to the second evening. Thus, Freud's main point—that the nature of the evening states shows that there was as yet no phobia—is incorrect. Second, Freud's suggestion that Hans's evening anxieties cannot be understood as part of a horse phobia because there are no horses in the home ("for who bothers at bedtime about streets and walking?") conflicts with Hans's explicit testimony. On the evening of the 8th, Hans explains why he is anxious in bed at night: "He said, crying: 'I know I shall have to go for a walk again to-morrow.' And later: 'The horse'll come into the room.'" Hans explains that he is afraid that a horse may come after him, and he is thinking fearfully about the next day's challenges in confronting horses in the street. So, nothing in Freud's comments challenges the conclusion, supported by the marked similarity of the symptoms on the two walks and during the two following evenings, that Hans's phobia already existed on the 7th.

Why Did Hans Continue to Experience Anxiety When He Was Out Walking with His Mother?

The hypothesis that Hans had his phobia on the 7th has a distinct explanatory advantage in resolving a paradox faced by Freud. On the walk with the nursemaid, Hans says he wants to coax with his Mummy. Both Freud and Bowlby jump on that statement as revealing that Hans's desire to be with his mother is the primary cause of Hans's anxiety. However, they are then faced with the seeming inconsistency that the next day Hans experiences the same anxiety symptoms during a walk with his mother. If the meaning of Hans's fear is that he wants to be with his mother, then why should Hans still show intense fear when he is with her?

Freud recognizes the explanatory challenge and makes a valiant attempt to explain how it is possible that Hans's desire to be with his mother could be the source of Hans's continued anxiety even when the desire is seemingly satisfied on the walk with his mother:

> His anxiety, then, corresponded to repressed longing ... This was shown to be so in the case of Hans on the occasion of his next walk, when his mother went with him. He was with his mother, and yet he still suffered from anxiety—that is to say, from an unsatisfied longing for her. It is true that the anxiety was less; for he did allow himself to be induced to go for the walk, whereas he had obliged the nursemaid to turn back. Nor is a street quite the right place for "coaxing", or whatever else this young lover may have wanted. But his anxiety had stood the test; and the next thing for it to do was to find an object. It was on this walk that he first expressed a fear that a horse would bite him.
>
> (p. 26)

Freud's explanation is that the anxiety condition is pathological precisely because the anxiety has become autonomous and no longer subsides in the presence of the originally longed-for object. This explanation is not implausible on its face; unsatisfied emotions surely can become detached from the original object. But it seems ad hoc, for why then is Hans soothed by his mother's presence at home in the evening? That is, why should his anxiety be undischargeable during the walks with the mother in the street but dischargeable when at home with the mother? A plausible explanation is that when Hans was on the walk with his mother, he was suffering from a horse phobia, so her presence did not address the source of his anxiety, whereas at home the lack of horses allowed his mother's soothing presence to have the desired effect. The facts point not to free-floating anxiety soothed by mother's presence but anxiety fixed on some object on the streets other than mother.

Another proposal floated by Freud is that at first the anxiety was not undirected and free-floating but rather directed at walking in the street generally ("locomotion"), and only later became directed at horses. This meshes with Freud's notion that Hans was averse to locomotion because such muscular movement was suggestive of the sexual act that, in some vaguely conceptualized form, he desired with his mother ("The content of his phobia was such as to impose a very great measure of restriction upon his freedom of movement, and that was its purpose ... since this pleasure in movement included the impulse to copulate" [p. 139]).

However, the evidence does not easily comport with the hypothesis of an inhibition of locomotion. Hans has no general problem of locomotion or movement, only a problem when there are horses actually or possibly present. For example, the father notes that Hans had little problem going out in the streets on Sunday morning (and this was without the mother, because she did not accompany Hans and his father on their Sunday visits to Hans's grandmother in Lainz), because there were few horses around at that time, an observation inconsistent with the existence of a general locomotion issue independent of the horse phobia.

I conclude that the symptoms experienced by Hans on the day preceding the identification of the phobia on January 8 are consistent with the hypothesis that he already had the horse phobia. The only consideration against this alternative is that the phobia was not reported before the 8th, and Freud, along with other commentators such as Bowlby and Neu, all assume that it did not exist before this date. Given that the horse accident immediately preceded the phobia's outbreak, they thus implicitly assume that the horse accident must have happened on the walk with the mother that day—perhaps, they might suggest, this is what she refers to when she says that Hans showed some anxiety that day when seeing a horse?—and the phobia then began. Oddly enough, the whole dispute comes down to this assumption about the precise day that Hans saw the horse fall down, which nurtures the idea that the disorder existed before the phobia. The fact that the precise day that the horse fell down is not explicitly specified in the case record has allowed for this century-long ambiguity and disagreement about whether the disorder preceded, followed, or was simultaneous with phobia formation. In the next chapter, I will attempt to resolve this issue to the degree possible based on the available evidence.

Conclusion

Freud takes it as manifest from the case record that Hans's phobia was preceded by a period of undirected anxiety. The main basis for Freud's conclusion seems to be that Hans's phobia was not reported until January 8, whereas intense anxiety was reported on January 7. This does not by itself imply or even support that the anxiety on January 7 was pre-phobic and not the same phobic anxiety experienced on the 8th. The alternative hypothesis is that Hans had his phobia on the 7th but did not report it, consistent with his resistance to reporting it until late into the next day.

To assess Freud's claim, I examined the details of the symptoms manifested by Hans on the two days in question to consider whether there is any evidence that Hans was suffering from different forms of anxiety disorder on the two days. I found that the striking similarity of the symptoms on the walks on the two days and during the following evenings on the 7th and 8th, as well as other lines of evidence discussed above, suggest similar, not divergent, causes and concerns, and there is no evidence whatever that favors Freud's hypothesis. We know that on the 8th the cause was a horse phobia, so it is most plausible and parsimonious to assume that Hans already had his phobia on the 7th. I conclude that the undirected anxiety argument fails to provide the refutation of the fright theory that Freud was seeking.

In this chapter, I have focused exclusively on Freud's argument that there occurred a period of undirected anxiety preceding Hans's phobia. I set aside reference to the horse accident witnessed by Hans, because that emerges later in the case history. However, analyzing the undirected anxiety argument as a stand-alone argument is somewhat artificial because it is also part of a larger "chronology" argument in which Freud claims that the timing of the horse accident witnessed by Hans shows that Hans's anxiety began before the phobia. This is the second of Freud's "negative" arguments against the rival fright account that I mentioned earlier, which I examine in the next chapter.

References

Bowlby, J. (1973). *Attachment and loss (Vol. 2): Separation: Anxiety and anger.* New York: Basic Books.
Freud, S. (1895). A reply to criticisms of my paper on anxiety neurosis. *SE* 3, 119–139.
Freud, S. (1909). Analysis of a phobia in a five-year-old boy. *SE* 10, 1–150.
Grunbaum, A. (1984). *The foundations of psychoanalysis: A philosophical critique.* Berkeley, CA: University of California Press.
Lear, J. (1990). *Love and its place in nature: A philosophical interpretation of Freudian psychoanalysis.* New York: Farrar, Straus & Giroux.
Wakefield, J. C. (2022). *Attachment, sexuality, power: Oedipal theory as regulator of family affection in Freud's case of Little Hans.* New York: Routledge.

Chapter 7

"Chronological Considerations Make It Impossible"

The Day the Horse Fell Down: Resolving a Century-Old Puzzle

In this chapter, I confront and resolve a century-old dispute about what day Little Hans saw a horse fall down, which was the incident that triggered his horse phobia. Strangely enough, the answer to this question determines whether Freud can preemptively protect his Oedipal theory of Hans's horse phobia from its primary rival, the "fright theory" or conditioning theory. The answer will turn out to have been staring us in the face all this time.

Return of the Fright Theory

What did Freud feel on that day in Vienna in early April 1908 as he read the latest notes sent to him by his follower Max Graf? Max was reporting on his psychoanalytic treatment of his five-year-old son, Herbert Graf (aka "Little Hans") for a horse phobia. The notes came to Freud week by week in the form of the father's transcriptions of his sessions with Hans in which, with Freud's occasional guidance, he explored the Oedipal roots of Hans's fear. Freud did not know what would be revealed each week as the case unfolded, although fitting each week's events into his Oedipal framework had not proven difficult. On this particular day, as Freud read the installment recounting Max's discussions with Hans on April 5, he came to a part of the report that contained an unexpected and disorienting revelation. Hans reported that his phobia had started immediately after he witnessed a terrifying accident in which a horse pulling a bus-wagon fell down in the streets, kicking loudly. Hans's father interrogated Hans's mother, who had been with Hans at the time, and she confirmed Hans's description in full. (Surely Freud wondered: why hadn't Max known about this from the beginning? Hans's mother, a former patient of Freud's, had been with Hans when the accident occurred and saw that he became afraid of horses immediately afterward, yet never mentioned it. The answer to this puzzle lies in the Grafs' family dynamics, and is addressed in my companion volume, *Attachment, Sexuality, Power* [Wakefield, 2022].)

Despite Freud's self-confidence and penchant for rationalization, it is difficult to believe that he was not sorely disappointed by what he read that day. Hans's phobia had started three months before, in early January, seemingly

DOI: 10.4324/9781003272472-7

out of the blue, to his father's bewilderment accompanied by Oedipal speculations:

> No doubt the ground was prepared by sexual over-excitation due to his mother's tenderness; but I am not able to specify the actual exciting cause ... I cannot see what to make of it ... [I]s the whole thing simply connected with his mother?
>
> (1909, p. 22)

No hint of a specific triggering experience had been evident at the time. This had provided Freud with a reassuringly simple case that perfectly suited his goal of confirming his Oedipal theory of the sexual roots of the neuroses. It seemed to be a case lacking any distracting nonsexual emotional noxae to complicate the etiological picture. However, the standard skeptical objection to Freud's sexual theory of the neuroses even among those who accepted psychogenic etiology was that surely not just sexuality but also intense emotions such as fear could cause neurosis, as in the railroad-accident and shell-shock neuroses—an objection I am calling the "fright theory" that Freud had confronted in his split with Breuer and in a published exchange with Lowenfeld in 1895 (see Chapter 5). In the Hans case, he thought he had escaped from this objection, but here it was again to complicate his account of the case that, using direct child evidence, Freud hoped would vindicate his sexual-Oedipal theory of neurosogenesis.

Freud was aware that medical opinion as well as common sense would hold that if Hans saw a terribly frightening incident concerning a horse just before the outbreak of a horse phobia, likely that explained the phobia without any need for the added theoretical paraphernalia of a psychoanalytic explanation. Consequently, he would now be forced to clutter up his Oedipal-theoretic commentary with defensive theoretical finessing to reject the fright theory's rival explanation. Freud was of course ready with his standard rebuttal that such emotional shocks merely precipitated or reshaped the neurosis but were not its deeper specific cause, just as hitting one's foot might trigger an attack of gout but not reflect the underlying cause of the disease. Such explanatory contortions distinguishing triggering nonsexual causes from deeper and more lawful specific sexual etiologies offered potentially legitimate distinctions to be sure, but could easily be applied in a questionable ad hoc manner. The horse accident was an evidential wild card that would inevitably raise these causation issues and, disappointingly, had to be addressed once again.

Or was Freud so convinced of the correctness of his theory and his ability to defend it from this old and familiar theoretical foe that he felt nothing and saw in the latest developments only a minor bump along the interpretive road? We will never know how Freud felt. But we can reconstruct and evaluate what Freud actually did about this revelation from the text of his commentary on the Hans case record.

The Strategic Situation Freud Confronted

The revelation of the horse accident altered the strategy of Freud's commentary, forcing him to mount a preemptive attack on the fright theory. As we saw in Chapter 5, half a century after Freud's Oedipal account of the Hans case was published, Wolpe and Rachman (1960) argued that Hans's phobia was caused not by an Oedipus complex but by Hans witnessing the horse accident, and, oddly enough, Freud had already replied to their argument in his case commentary. For, once Freud became aware of the horse accident and anticipated the appeal of attributing Hans's phobia to it, he set about laying the groundwork in his commentary for dismissing the accident as an unimportant side issue.

For convenience of exposition and analysis, I am dividing Freud's overall riposte to the fright theory into two separate arguments. Freud's first argument, regarding qualitative distinctions in the nature of Hans's anxiety, is that Hans's symptoms started with a period of intense undirected anxiety prior to his phobic symptoms directed at horses, so the explanation of his overall anxiety disorder must be distinct from the explanation of the specific phobic form that it eventually took. I addressed this argument in the last chapter and concluded that there is no evidence in the case record for Freud's contention that Hans experienced a period of intense undirected anxiety immediately prior to and continuous with his phobia. However, I did not attempt to determine the specific timing of the phobia's onset but only argued that the uniformity of the symptoms over two continuous days suggested one continuous phobic disorder for that time period.

Freud's second and core argument is based on his interpretation of the chronology of events in the case record. The argument is that the horse accident itself occurred after the onset of Hans's intense anxiety, making it impossible for the horse accident to explain the overall disorder. I address this chronology argument in this chapter. I focus here on the events of January 7 and 8, when Hans took anxious walks with his nursemaid and mother, respectively, and during which Freud thinks the horse accident and the phobia onset occurred.

As an aside, later in his theoretical development, Freud would find ways to theoretically finesse the fright-theory objection by expanding the domain of sexual energy to encompass narcissism and other realms. He thus, for example, recast affects such as fear in defense of the self as themselves ultimately sexual processes of libido discharge. However, the move of libidinizing all emotions has no independent plausibility. It not only yields an underdeveloped and impoverished psychoanalytic theory of emotions but also, because it is a manifestly ad hoc maneuver to save the sexual theory of the neuroses, further transforms libido theory into a pseudoscience. Freud eventually admitted as much when he added a death instinct to the sexual or life instinct, finally capitulating to a long-time criticism by Jung that Freud's notion of sexual libido had in effect become equivalent to all human motivation, making his sexual theory of the neuroses a vacuous tautology.

Despite his efforts, there was no way that Freud could prevent the horse accident from becoming the focal point of the primary objection to Freud's Oedipal analysis. The importance of the horse accident in the etiology of Hans's phobia has been at the center of debate ever since. However, Freud's critics have uniformly rejected or ignored Freud's argument that the horse accident occurred on January 8, after the onset of Hans's anxiety, but without much in the way of counterargument. I will attempt to resolve the century-long dispute about when the horse fell down and thus resolve whether Freud can, on this basis, reject the fright theory out of hand.

"Insignificant in Itself": The Emergence of the Horse Accident and Freud's Dismissive Response to the "Precipitating Cause"

Hans revealed on April 5 that he had witnessed a horse accident that triggered his horse phobia. This was three months after the beginning of his phobia and less than one month before the analysis ended on May 2. In the following dialogue, Hans serendipitously revealed that his phobia, which he called his "nonsense," had started immediately after he saw the frightening scene of the horse falling down in the street:

I: "So you're not afraid with a small cart?"

HANS: "No. I'm not afraid with a small cart or with a post-office van. I'm most afraid too when a bus comes along."

I: "Why? Because it's so big?"

HANS: "No. Because once a horse in a bus fell down."

I: "When?"

HANS: "Once when I went out with Mummy in spite of my 'nonsense', when I bought the waistcoat."

(This was subsequently confirmed by his mother.)

I: "What did you think when the horse fell down?"

HANS: "Now it'll always be like this. All horses in buses'll fall down."

I: "In all buses?"

HANS: "Yes. And in furniture-vans too. Not often in furniture-vans."

I: "You had your nonsense already at that time?"

HANS: "No. I only got it then. When the horse in the bus fell down, it gave me such a fright, really! That was when I got the nonsense."

I: "But the nonsense was that you thought a horse would bite you. And now you say you were afraid a horse would fall down."

HANS: "Fall down and bite." [Freud notes here: "Hans was right, however improbable this collocation may sound. The train of thought, we shall see, was that the horse (his father) would bite him because of his wish that it (his father) should fall down."]

I: "Why did it give you such a fright?"

HANS: "Because the horse went like this with its feet." (He lay down on the ground and showed me how it kicked about.) "It gave me a fright because it made a row with its feet."

I: "Where did you go with Mummy that day?"

HANS: "First to the Skating Rink, then to a cafe, then to buy a waistcoat, then to the pastry-cook's with Mummy, and then home in the evening; we went back through the Stadtpark [i.e., city park]." (All of this was confirmed by my wife, as well as the fact that the anxiety broke out immediately afterwards.)

(1909, pp. 49–50)

Hans asserts that it was when he witnessed the horse accident that he got his horse phobia. This sequence, and specifically "the fact that the anxiety broke out immediately afterwards," is confirmed by Hans's mother. Given the convergence of Hans's and his mother's testimony, Hans's report is not disputed by Freud or any other commentator. Given the spontaneous and surprising emergence of the story, and the fact that such a potentially traumatic factor would be anything but welcome in this case report, there is no reason to suspect that suggestion is a factor.

Hans's explanation of how the accident affected him is striking and has the ring of truth. He says that when the horse fell down, he thought: "Now it'll always be like this. All horses in buses'll fall down," expressing a generalized belief of the kind emphasized in cognitive-behavioral theory. Phenomenologists would describe Hans's new sense that horses pulling buses and other large, heavy wagons are inherently unstable and dangerous as a transformation of Hans's way of experiencing the world. In any event, the accident clearly had a great impact on Hans.

The emergence of such information about a potentially traumatic incident at the time of the onset of Hans's phobia would seem to be a bombshell with potentially devastating implications for Freud's Oedipal account of Hans's phobia. However, Freud reacts dismissively. Freud's first comment is that "it does no harm to make acquaintance at close quarters with a phobia of this sort—which we may feel inclined to name after its new objects" (1909, p. 51). In referring to the phobia's "new objects," Freud implies that horses are chosen as the objects after the anxiety already exists and are merely grafted on to the preexisting anxiety.

Freud frames the horse accident as a "precipitating cause" in contrast to deeper etiological causal processes, thus limiting its etiological importance:

We must specially acknowledge one most important result of the boy's examination by his father. We have learned the immediate precipitating cause after which the phobia broke out. This was when the boy saw a big heavy horse fall down.

(1909, p. 51)

Similarly, Freud comments:

> It was at this stage of the analysis that he recalled the event, insignificant in itself, which immediately preceded the outbreak of the illness and may no doubt be regarded as the precipitating cause of its outbreak. He went for a walk with his mother, and saw a bus-horse fall down and kick about with its feet [p. 49]. This made a great impression on him. He was terrified, and thought the horse was dead; and from that time on he thought that all horses would fall down.
>
> (p. 125)

The claim that the horse accident was merely a precipitating cause is supported by the claim that what was precipitated was only the phobic form of the disorder, not the overall anxiety disorder itself, which, Freud asserts, existed prior to the horse accident:

> Chronological considerations make it impossible for us to attach any great importance to the actual precipitating cause of the outbreak of Hans's illness, for he had shown signs of apprehensiveness long before he saw the bus-horse fall down in the street. Nevertheless, the neurosis took its start directly from this chance event and preserved a trace of it in the circumstance of the horse being exalted into the object of his anxiety.
>
> (pp. 136–137)

Freud argues that he is entitled to be dismissive of the horse accident because Hans had his anxiety disorder before it. He seems to think this for reasons overlapping with those presented in the analysis of his undirected anxiety argument in the last chapter. Recall that Freud claims that Hans's anxiety had not yet found an object on the walk with the nanny on the 7th ("Hans's anxiety ... was, like every infantile anxiety, without an object to begin with: it was still anxiety and not yet fear" [1909, p. 25]), nor at the beginning of the walk with his mother on the 8th, but became phobic only during that walk ("But his anxiety had stood the test; and the next thing for it to do was to find an object. It was on this walk that he first expressed a fear that a horse would bite him" [p. 26]). Freud's grounds for these claims were that Hans does not report a phobia until late in the day on the 8th, and his mother reports that Hans displayed some anxiety in relation to a horse at Schonbrunn: "On the way back from Schonbrunn he said to his mother, after much internal struggling: 'I *was afraid a horse would bite me.*' (He had, in fact, become uneasy at Schonbrunn when he saw a horse.)" (p. 24). Freud appears to equate Hans's reported uneasiness at seeing a horse at Schonbrunn and his later report of his fear with his seeing the horse accident and the start of the phobia. This is the grounds for Freud's claim that Hans was intensely anxious before the accident or the phobia, for he was indeed apprehensive the day before the report, when walking with his nursemaid. In dismissing the horse accident as "insignificant in itself," Freud relies heavily on these "chronological considerations."

Freudians Versus Behaviorists on the Onset of Hans's Phobia

Wolpe and Rachman's Lack of Response to Freud's Chronology Argument

As we saw in an earlier chapter, Wolpe and Rachman (1960) argue that the fright caused by the horse accident is sufficient to explain Hans's phobia based on the behavioral theory of one-trial fear conditioning, without any need to invoke the Oedipus complex for which, they argue, there is no evidence. What, then, do Wolpe and Rachman make of Freud's "chronology" counterargument that the accident cannot be the cause of Hans's anxiety disorder, which preexisted the accident, although it did trigger the anxiety's focus on the phobic content? Surprisingly, in their otherwise systematic and carefully argued paper, Wolpe and Rachman do not even mention let alone respond to Freud's riposte.

Without any argument, Wolpe and Rachman (1960) simply assume that Freud's crucial premise regarding the timing of phobia onset is false and that the horse phobia had started by the time of the walk with the nursemaid. They thus start their description of the clinical course of the phobia with the events of January 7:

> The first signs appeared on January 7, when Hans was being taken to the park by his nursemaid as usual. He started crying and said he wanted to "coax" (caress) with his mother. At home "he was asked why he had refused to go any further and had cried, but he would not say".
>
> (1960, p. 137)

After describing the symptoms on Hans's walk with his mother the next day, they allude to the similarity of the symptoms ("*As on the previous day*, Hans showed fear in the evening and asked to be 'coaxed'" [p. 137; emphasis added]), indicating their conclusion that the condition causing the symptoms is the same. In sum, Wolpe and Rachman implicitly assume that the phobia already existed on January 7 based on the marked similarity of the symptoms to those on January 8, and they ignore Freud's argument to the contrary. Nor do they comment on when the falling horse may have been observed. They do not seem to have identified this as an issue in evaluating the relative merits of their account versus Freud's. Those who attempt to take seriously and evaluate Freud's argument against Wolpe and Rachman's position are on their own.

Neu on the "Chronological Impossibility" of Wolpe and Rachman's Hypothesis

Freud's argument against the etiological relevance of the horse accident has generally been assumed to be sound by those who are sympathetic to his account of the Hans case. Consequently, the discussion of the validity of Wolpe and Rachman's hypothesis has not advanced much within the psychoanalytic community since Freud's preemptive attack a century ago. One exception is a recent reanalysis of the Freud versus Wolpe and Rachman dispute by philosopher Jerome Neu, who, in a vigorous defense of Freud's Oedipal-theoretic explanation of Hans's anxiety, attempts to present some novel evidence in defense of Freud.

Neu comes down strongly on Freud's side against Wolpe and Rachman: "I believe that Freud's account ... is powerful and persuasive, and that it is the behaviorist approach that fundamentally misunderstands and distorts the character of evidence and argument in cases such as Little Hans'" (Neu, 1995, p. 146). Neu follows Freud in making the claimed onset of the anxiety disorder prior to the phobia's onset the pivotal element in his rebuttal of Wolpe and Rachman's etiological claim, going so far as to ridicule Wolpe and Rachman for violating the principle that causes temporally precede their effects:

> But one should not attribute too much to the chance precipitating event of seeing a horse fall down. Those who think the "entire disorder" (Wolpe and Rachman, 216) can be explained by this incident are mistaken. For one thing, Hans' apprehensiveness started *before* that "precipitating" incident. If one takes a comprehensive enough view of Hans' disorder, attributing exclusive causal force to seeing the horse falling would involve the nonsensical notion of the onset of the symptoms preceding their supposed cause.
> (Neu, 1995, p. 139)

Elaborating on this theme, Neu follows Freud in asserting that the Wolpe-Rachman account is "chronologically impossible":

> But the most severe problem with the conditioning alternative was pointed out by Freud fifty years before Wolpe and Rachman put it forward: "Chronological considerations make it impossible for us to attach any great importance to the actual precipitating cause of the outbreak of Hans' illness, for he had shown signs of apprehensiveness long before he saw the bus-horse fall down in the street" (136; cf. 26, 49, 118) ... [T]he general anxiety that is really the larger problem ... began earlier and has to be explained, as Freud insists, by something other than the incident of the horse falling. As Freud puts it, "... at the beginning of his illness there was as yet no phobia whatever present, whether of streets or of walking or even of horses" (25) ...

The oversimple and chronologically impossible interpretation persists ... Awareness of the role of general anxiety in the case should save one from confusion ... Despite differing emphases, Bowlby and Freud agree that Hans' "enormously intensified affection" for his mother is "the fundamental phenomenon in his condition" (24–25; 96, 114) and that his problems significantly precede the apparent "precipitating incident."

(Neu, 1995, pp. 148–149)

So, a century after Freud's preemptive attack, the argument that the disorder started before the phobia and thus before the horse accident, and thus that the accident cannot be the disorder's cause, remains Neu's primary response to Wolpe and Rachman's etiological claim. The persuasiveness of Neu's as well as Freud's rejection of Wolpe and Rachman's hypothesis hangs on the soundness of this rebuttal.

As an aside, Neu misreads Bowlby when he claims that Bowlby agrees with Freud that Hans's intensified affection was essential to his condition. Bowlby's view is that Hans's mother's threats to leave when he misbehaved caused Hans to suffer from separation anxiety and anxious attachment to his mother, and this predisposed Hans to develop a phobia in response to the stressor of seeing the horse accident. (For a full analysis of Bowlby's views on Hans, see my *Attachment, Sexuality, Power* [Wakefield, 2022].) In fact, Bowlby explicitly disagrees with Freud on whether Hans has an intensified affection for his mother. According to Bowlby, Hans is feeling intensified anxiety about separation, not increased affection:

On all these issues, it is evident that Freud was thinking along lines very different from those proposed here. Hans's insistent desire to remain with his mother is seen, not in terms of anxious attachment, but as the expression of the love for his mother, held to have been genitally sexual in character, having reached an 'extreme pitch of intensity' (SE 10: 110–11).

(Bowby, 1973, p. 287)

In addition to quoting Freud, Neu claims to find additional evidence for Freud's chronological claim in the passage in which Hans first describes the horse accident. The evidence consists of a contradiction between two of Hans's assertions about when he got his nonsense. Hans initially says he went out on the walk with his mother the day of the horse accident "in spite of my nonsense," seemingly implying that he already had his phobia prior to that walk. But later, in response to a direct clarifying question from his father ("You had your nonsense already at that time?"), Hans says, "No. I only got it then. When the horse in the bus fell down ... That was when I got the nonsense." This apparent contradiction—Hans seemingly both did and did not already have his nonsense on the day he saw the horse accident—is resolved by Neu by arguing that Hans is equivocating on the meaning of "nonsense":

Hans' apprehensiveness ... crucially precedes the proposed precipitating incident. There may be some confusion about the matter because, when the incident of the bus horse falling is first mentioned, Hans claims both (1) that he saw the horse fall "Once when I went out with Mummy in spite of my 'nonsense'..." (49)—which suggests, as his father says, that Hans already had his "nonsense," and (2) that "No. I only got it then. When the horse in the bus fell down, it gave me such a fright, really! That was when I got the nonsense" (50). The apparent contradiction is most simply resolved if we understand that "nonsense" in the second statement refers to the fear specifically of horses (which Hans describes as a compound fear that horses would "Fall down and bite" [50]), rather than the general anxiety that is really the larger problem, which began earlier and has to be explained, as Freud insists, by something other than the incident of the horse falling.

(p. 149)

So, according to Neu, the simplest way to resolve the seeming contradiction is by giving "nonsense" two different meanings in the two statements—meanings that fit with the Freud-Neu thesis that Hans had intense anxiety symptoms before the onset of the phobia. In the first report about going out on the walk with his mother in spite of his nonsense, Hans means he already had his undirected anxiety prior to seeing the horse accident. In the second report about getting the nonsense when he saw the horse fall down during the walk with his mother, he means that when he saw the horse fall down, he got his phobia.

Neu's argument is not supported by any independent evidence. More importantly, it is at odds with other evidence of the text. First, from the time that Freud initially suggested that the horse phobia—and *specifically* the horse phobia—should be represented to Hans as a piece of nonsense ("I arranged with Hans's father that he should tell the boy that *all this business about horses* was a piece of nonsense and nothing more" [p. 28; emphasis added]), the term "nonsense" was used throughout the case by Hans and all concerned to refer to Hans's horse phobia, e.g., "'This nonsense of yours' (*that is how he speaks of his phobia*) 'will get better if you go for more walks'" (p. 30; emphasis added). "Nonsense" is never used in an alternative sense to refer to other anxiety problems, nor would it seem an apt description because it is precisely the fact that the fear is of more or less harmless horses that makes it nonsense; there is nothing that is nonsense about generalized anxiety. Second, Hans brings up the horse accident in the discussion with his father specifically in the context of explaining the details of the horse phobia. Given this immediate context of his reference to his nonsense, it is most plausibly a reference to this issue. Third, when the father attempts to clarify by asking Hans, "You had your nonsense already at that time?" it is clear that he is referring to what he and Hans have just been discussing in elaborate detail, namely, the horse phobia, so it seems that Hans would respond using the same meaning of "nonsense", which is the meaning that Hans had used three sentences before. Finally, note that the father is quite explicit that the "nonsense" they are discussing refers to the phobia: "But the nonsense was that you thought a horse would bite you." Given this context, Neu's explanation of Hans's inconsistency is not simple to rectify with the evidence. Neu's claimed evidence is in fact merely an unsupported ad hoc hypothesis aimed at shoring up the Freudian reading of the case.

There is a much simpler alternative hypothesis that is more consistent with the overall text than Neu's. Hans intended in both instances to refer to his horse phobia, but in starting to talk about the walk, the horse accident, and the phobia onset, all of which occurred three months earlier, Hans made an innocent mistake about the temporal sequencing of events in the first statement. When the father, perplexed by Hans's statement or perhaps detecting some sense of confusion or doubt on Hans's part, requested clarification of when the phobia started, Hans focused his attention on the sequencing and immediately realized he had made an error when he said he went out with Mummy in spite of his nonsense. When Hans says, "no, I only got it then," he is answering his father's clarifying question by correcting his earlier error. It is easy to see how Hans might have gotten momentarily confused in his recollection. Supposing that Hans already had his phobia and therefore had already witnessed the horse fall down on a walk with his mother prior to the walks on January 7 and 8, there were two walks with his mother around the same time to distinguish, and Hans initially may have confused the walk with his mother on the day he saw the horse fall down with the walk with his mother on January 8 when he went out in spite of having his phobia. In his second statement, Hans corrected his earlier error and placed the onset of the nonsense during the earlier walk. According to this reading, the seeming contradiction is an error and its subsequent correction, and the assertions cited by Neu offer no evidence that Hans had substantial anxiety symptoms prior to and contiguous with his phobia.

There is another minor bit of evidence that is contrary to Neu's and Freud's argument. Hans's father reports in the same passage that Hans's entire story about the day of the accident was confirmed by his wife, and specifically that she confirmed "that the anxiety broke out immediately afterwards." The fact that the father says that the mother reported that Hans's *anxiety*—not specifically the phobia—broke out immediately after the accident seems to suggest that the phobia and the anxiety are the same and that there likely was not a separate anxiety disorder occurring before the horse accident. But, of course, the father might have been substituting his own word for his wife's, or in context his wife might have meant "the anxiety of the phobia."

A Question Unresolved

Is Freud's dismissive reaction to the horse accident, based on the chronology argument, justified? His supporters clearly think it is. Freud's riposte has been widely accepted as definitive within the psychoanalytic camp to this day. A recent review of psychoanalytic perspectives on the Hans case does not even mention Wolpe and Rachman's alternative proposal that the horse accident might have been etiologically primary (Midgley, 2006). Freud's view is obviously still very much alive in defenders such as Neu despite the fact that, putting it generously, the text on which Neu bases his argument does not resolve the question of whether Hans's overall disorder or just the phobia broke out immediately after the horse accident.

On the other side, Freud's Oedipal interpretation has been summarily dismissed by his critics on the grounds that the horse accident was obviously the cause of the phobia, yet they have not directly addressed Freud's chronology counterargument. They have relied on the statements by Hans ("I only got it then. When the horse in the bus fell down, it gave me such a fright, really! That was when I got the nonsense") and his mother ("All of this was confirmed by my wife, as well as the fact that the anxiety broke out immediately afterwards") to allow them to dismiss Freud's counterargument (e.g., Eysenck, 2004; Erwin, 2003). This may seem to be a knock-down argument until one realizes that Freud is not denying that the *phobia* started immediately after the horse accident, but rather asserting that an anxiety disorder existed prior to the horse accident and the phobia.

Freud's argument relies on the assumption that one can equate the onset of Hans's phobia with Hans's first verbal report that he was afraid of horses. Hans was clearly suffering from an anxiety disorder the day before that first verbal report, so if Freud's equation is right, then he is right about the disorder starting before the horse accident. However, this argument is inconclusive to say the least because, as we have seen, Hans was quite reluctant to explain his fear even on the second day, and may merely have refrained from explaining his problem on the first day. The various pieces of evidence presented by both sides are ambiguous enough that either position remains conceivable. Despite the ardor on both sides, the arguments on both sides are weak and the 100-year-old dispute remains unsettled. I will try to put this dispute to rest by presenting fresh evidence that is independent of any of the evidence thus far provided by the disputants.

The Day the Horse Fell Down

So, is Freud correct that the horse accident occurred, and Hans's phobia thus came into existence, on January 8, the day Hans first reported the phobia to his mother, and that it had not existed the day before, when Hans manifested anxiety symptoms of a similar nature and intensity? Surprisingly, this question can be resolved with a high degree of confidence. More remarkably, the crucial evidence has been hiding in plain sight in the case record itself. To answer the question, we merely need to put side by side two different descriptions of outings Hans went on with his mother. The first is the description provided near the beginning of the case record of the day the mother took Hans for a walk to see what was wrong with him after the nursemaid's report of problems the previous day. This is the day that Hans admitted he was afraid of horses, and this is the day claimed by Freud to be the day that Hans got the phobia and thus, by implication (given the mother's comment that the anxiety broke out immediately after the horse accident), the day the horse fell down:

> On January 8th my wife decided to go out with him herself, so as to see what was wrong with him. They went to Schonbrunn, where he always likes going. Again he began to cry, did not want to start, and was frightened. In the end he did go; but was visibly frightened in the street. On the way back from Schonbrunn he said to his mother, after much internal struggling: "I *was afraid a horse would bite me.*" (He had, in fact, become uneasy at Schonbrunn when he saw a horse.)
>
> (p. 24)

As an enticement to the anxious Hans, this outing was to one of his favorite destinations, the Imperial Palace, zoo, and gardens at Schonbrunn. From the text, it appears they went directly to Schonbrunn and back. On that day, the mother reports that there was an incident in which Hans became uneasy when he saw a horse at Schonbrunn. If one adopts Freud's account, this incident can be interpreted as the very incident in which Hans became anxious when he saw the horse fall down. However, the mother says nothing about such an accident. So, this incident could just be one in which Hans is responding phobically to a horse, his phobia having been acquired earlier.

The fact that Hans did not want to start out on this excursion with his mother suggests that the phobic object had been determined prior to this walk. Otherwise, if he suffered only from undirected anxiety, it is unclear why he would not be as happy to be walking with his mother as to be at home with her. If Hans was suffering from undirected anxiety at the day's beginning, one would expect on attachment-theoretic grounds that Hans would just want to be near his attachment object, his mother. In any event, he clearly did have the phobia by the time he arrived home. So, given that the mother said that the anxiety broke out immediately after the horse accident, we know the horse accident occurred either on this day or earlier. Freud's claim is that it occurred on this day, not before.

The second description of Hans's outing with his mother is the detailed account provided by Hans later in the case record of the day on which the horse accident was witnessed by Hans, described when the horse accident is first revealed, the details of which were confirmed by Hans's mother. Hans initially refers to its happening on the day "when I bought the waistcoat." Later in the passage, his father asks him, "Where did you go with Mummy that day?" of the accident, and Hans elaborates in precise detail as follows:

"Hay market" area right outside of the Stadtpark, just 100 meters from the Stadtpark's train station. The rink's location on the edge of the Stadtpark is consistent with Hans's comment that he and his mother returned home from the rink by walking though the Stadtpark. The other errands that Hans and his mother went on that day, including buying Hans a waistcoat and picking up pastries, are also the sorts of activities that would be likely to occur close to home and that are time consuming, casting further doubt on the combined-excursion idea. Moreover, the ice rink is located about four miles from the Schonbrunn zoo but was convenient to Hans's home for a visit any time. Certainly any support for the combined-excursion hypothesis based on the location of ice rinks evaporates, and the time element makes such an idea additionally unlikely.

In sum: We know from both Hans and his mother that Hans got the phobia immediately after the horse accident. And we know from the case record that Hans had the phobia toward the end of January 8. So, we know the accident happened on or before January 8. Freud assumes the accident happened on that very day and attributes Hans's disorder-level anxieties of January 7 to pre-accident anxieties not due to the horse accident. However, contrary to Freud's assumption, we know from the comparison of the descriptions of the two outings in the case record that the accident did not happen on January 8 because that is the day the mother took Hans to Schonbrunn, whereas the accident happened on the day they went to the ice rink near the Stadtpark and on a series of other local errands. We know that these excursions were unlikely to have occurred on the same day based on textual, geographical, and logistic considerations.

We also know that the accident did not occur on January 7 because the case record is clear that the accident was witnessed on a walk with the mother, whereas the only walk reported on January 7 is Hans's walk with his nursemaid. There were surely no walks between the one with the nursemaid on January 7 and the one with Hans's mother on January 8 because the very point of the walk with the mother was to find out what was going on with Hans based on the nursemaid's report. Thus, the horse accident must have occurred on a walk with the mother that took place before the walk with the nursemaid on January 7. The latest possible date is Monday, January 6, on which the case report does not comment.

This conclusion resonates with a detail not previously noted. Hans's first reported marked anxiety symptoms took place on January 7 when he was walking with the nursemaid. According to the case report, when these symptoms occurred, the nursemaid was taking Hans to the Stadtpark, and Hans refused to proceed. These events would make particular sense if Hans had previously, as he and his mother report, experienced the horse accident at the Stadtpark.

Consequently, the anxiety symptoms Hans manifested on January 7—the ones that are claimed by Freud to have been undirected anxiety that preceded the formation of the phobia—in fact occurred after the horse accident and thus after the formation of the phobia and can be attributed to Hans's growing fear of horses, even though he did not state as much on that day. Our finding in the last chapter of the phenomenological congruence of the symptoms on the days and evenings of January 7 and 8 as well as the fact that Hans was afraid initially to go into the streets even with his mother on January 8 support the conclusion that Hans already had his phobia, not just undirected anxiety or separation anxiety, prior to January 8.

These findings render unsound Freud's and Neu's primary counterargument against Wolpe and Rachman's etiological claim. They are consistent with Wolpe and Rachman's theory of the case. I conclude that Freud's chronological considerations fail to eliminate from contention the rival fright-theory hypothesis.

Further Speculations on Precisely Which Day the Horse Fell Down

When did the horse accident actually occur? In principle it might have happened on any day prior to Tuesday, January 7. So, Monday, January 6 is the most conservative guess. But, conceivably, it might have occurred even before Hans's anxiety dream on about the 2nd. If so, then that anxiety dream, too, like the difficulties experienced with Hans by the nursemaid on the 7th, might have been an expression of attachment longing intensified by Hans's new and growing fear of horses.

There is one consideration in favor of such an earlier-onset chronology. The day of the accident, Hans and his mother were engaged in a series of errands that included purchasing a new waistcoat for Hans as well as a visit to the pastry shop. This suggests the possibility of a special occasion, and in particular that Hans's mother was preparing for the New Year's Eve ("Silvester") holiday celebration. At that time, prior to the current tradition of public concerts in Vienna on New Year's Day, the New Year's celebration generally involved multiple social gatherings and visiting and traditional foods. A new waistcoat for Hans and the purchase of pastries would fit with what one might expect in the preparation.

However, if the phobia already existed starting on New Year's Day—even, let us suppose, in an initially less severe form that intensified over a number of days until the events of the 7th—how could Hans's difficulties not have been noticed and mentioned by someone prior to the 7th? There is one fatal flaw in this line of reasoning: the two people who were most likely to know about the problem at its early stages, Hans and his mother, were clearly not interested in communicating this information. From the case record, we know that Hans resisted explaining what he was experiencing. Moreover, his mother would likely have been reticent about Hans's difficulties as well. After all, she did not even mention the horse accident until directly asked after it came up in therapy three months later. The case record reveals that she hid other things as well from her husband (the family dynamic behind these facts is thoroughly explored in Wakefield, 2022). It is perhaps understandable that, given the parents' marital disputes over a wide range of issues including child rearing and what constituted a threat to Hans's mental health, the last thing Hans's mother would want her husband to know is that Hans was possibly harmed mentally on her watch. If the mother noticed the symptoms, she may well not have communicated them to others as long as they had not yet been noticed, hoping they would subside. Given the nature of Hans's problem, as the problem grew in intensity there is a limit to how long the mother could have gotten away with this, but it is not implausible that several days might have passed this way if the phobia was initially at a weaker strength.

Even if Hans's mother had failed to report the problem and the nursemaid had not yet noticed it, wouldn't Hans's father have noticed it? After all, the father took Hans to visit the father's mother in Lainz every Sunday, and Hans's mother generally did not accompany them. He would presumably have visited his mother with Hans in his charge on Sunday, January 5. However, it is easily possible that even if Hans had an incipient horse phobia on that outing, his father might not have noticed it. The trip was by train from a station quite close to their home, and we know from the case record that even at the height of his phobia Hans was able to make this trip with minimal discomfort because on Sunday Vienna's streets were relatively empty of horses:

> [H]is phobia increased again so much that he could not be induced to go out, or at any rate no more than on to the balcony. Every Sunday he went with me to Lainz, because on that day there is not much traffic in the streets, and it is only a short way to the station.
>
> (p. 29)

> Hans had promised to go with me to Lainz the next Sunday, March 15th. He resisted at first, but finally went with me all the same. He obviously felt all right in the street, as there was not much traffic, and said: "How sensible God's done away with horses now."
>
> (p. 31)

It is thus possible that Hans's phobia began prior to the 2nd, likely on December 31 while shopping for the New Year celebration. In this case, all the reported anxiety, with the exception of the single instance of separation anxiety the summer before, was a result of the growing phobia. However, what the evidence establishes is that the phobia started prior to the walk with the nursemaid on the 7th, and thus the horse accident could have occurred as late as Monday, January 6.

Conclusion

The fact that Hans witnessed the horse accident before the occurrence of his intense anxiety on January 7 and 8 means that it is highly likely that all of

Hans's intense anxiety was triggered by Hans's witnessing the horse accident. Consequently, Freud's preemptive attack on the fright theory fails.

The failure of Freud's preemptive attack on the fright theory does not mean that Freud's Oedipal account is incorrect. It just means that the Oedipal theory and the fright theory remain prima facie viable rivals that must be judged against each other for their evidential support and explanatory power. And it means that the emphasis in evaluating Freud's theory must be on the persuasiveness of whatever positive arguments he presents for his theory, because his attempt to eliminate the main rival theory has failed. In the following chapters, I present and evaluate what I take to be Freud's two main arguments for his Oedipal theory of Hans's phobia.

References

Bowlby, J. (1973). *Attachment and loss (Vol. 2): Separation: Anxiety and anger.* New York: Basic Books.

Erwin, E. (Ed.) (2003). *The Freud encyclopedia.* New York: Routledge.

Eysenck, H. J. (2004). *Decline and fall of the Freudian empire.* New Brunswick, NJ: Transaction.

Freud, S. (1905). Three essays on the theory of sexuality. *SE* 7, 123–246.

Freud, S. (1909). Analysis of a phobia in a five-year-old boy. *SE* 10, 1–150.

Midgley, N. (2006). Re-reading "Little Hans": Freud's case study and the question of competing paradigms in psychoanalysis. *Journal of the American Psychoanalytic Association,* 54, 538–559.

Neu, J. (1995). "Does the Professor talk to God?" Learning from Little Hans. *Philosophy, Psychiatry & Psychology,* 2, 137–158.

Wakefield, J. C. (2022). *Attachment, sexuality, power: Oedipal theory as regulator of family affection in Freud's case of Little Hans.* New York: Routledge.

Wolpe, J., & Rachman, S. (1960). Psychoanalytic "evidence": A critique based on Freud's case of Little Hans. *Journal of Nervous and Mental Disease,* 131, 135–148.

Chapter 8

"A Repressive Process of Ominous Intensity"

Freud's N=1 Sexual Repression Argument

In this chapter, I reconstruct and evaluate what I will call the "repression argument." Unlike the two "negative" arguments considered in the last two chapters that were aimed at eliminating the rival "fright theory" of Hans's phobia, the repression argument is the first of two "positive" arguments directly in support of the Oedipal account of Hans's horse phobia that I will reconstruct from Freud's commentary on the Hans case. The repression argument is Freud's most direct attempt to empirically confirm his core and most provocative Oedipal-theoretic claim that Hans's anxiety symptoms are caused by repressed sexual desire for his mother. He does this by testing the theory's predictions about changes in Hans's sexual behavior over time. The repression argument is best understood as an N=1 empirical study that tests the hypothesis that *the pattern of Hans's sexual feelings over the time covered in the case history confirms the distinctive predictions of Freud's Oedipal account of Hans's phobia.* Remarkably, despite its power, salience, and pivotal nature, this argument has been entirely overlooked in the literature and has not been subject to serious reconstruction and evaluation. Note that although in previous chapters I argued that Freud's negative arguments failed to demonstrate that the fright theory is false, Freud's failure to falsify the fright theory does not resolve the issue of whether the Oedipal or fright theory is superior. It just leaves the question open and increases the importance of Freud's positive arguments for the superior evidential support and explanatory power of his Oedipal theory.

Freud's Three Testable Predictions About Hans's Pattern of Sexual Behavior

At the heart of Freud's account is the claim that Hans's symptoms are due to the repression of his sexual desire for his mother. As Jonathan Lear (1990) succinctly puts it, "Freud attributed the outbreak of anxiety to the increase and subsequent repression of Hans's affection for his mother" (p. 104), with the proviso that Freud insists on the specifically sexual nature of this affection.

DOI: 10.4324/9781003272472-8

Freud's narrative explanation of the sequence of events leading to Hans's phobia consists essentially of the following. First, due to time spent alone with his mother at their vacation house the summer before, Hans had an upsurge of sexual desire for his mother manifested in and amplified by his spending time cuddling or sleeping in bed with her. This was accompanied by Hans's increased masturbation as a form of release. Then, something occurred that caused Hans to enter into a state of conflict over his sexual desires and consequently to repress his desires and to suppress his masturbation. Freud remains noncommittal about the exact nature of the trigger for repression, but perhaps earlier threats of castration were reawakened in his mind by his parents' renewed pressure to stop his self-touching, or possibly Hans just felt overwhelmed by his increasing desires. Finally, the resulting diminution in masturbation and other sexual gratification such as cuddling with his mother led to undischarged sexual desire which was transformed into or caused Hans's heightened anxiety. The heightened anxiety, interacting with Hans's witnessing the horse accident, gave rise to Hans's phobic symptoms.

Thus, Freud's Oedipal hypothesis predicts that the case report will reveal a pattern in which Hans's sexual desire for his mother first becomes increasingly intense, followed by conflict and repression, followed by decreased overt desire accompanied by symptoms. That is, the sequence of events expectable on the basis of the repression hypothesis is: (1) Hans's heightened sexual desire in the period prior to the phobia's onset; (2) Hans's internal conflict over sexual strivings at the time of the phobia onset; (3) Hans's diminished sexual striving simultaneous with and proportional to symptom formation after the phobia's onset.

Freud holds that Hans's witnessing of the horse accident shapes Hans's subsequent horse-phobia symptoms, thus incorporating the horse accident into his overall explanation of the phobia's causation as a "precipitating cause" of the specific horse-phobia form of Hans's anxiety disorder. In effect, Freud integrates his repression-argument observational schema with the fright theory's observational sequence of the horse phobia emerging after the horse accident. Simplifying somewhat (I am leaving out the "undirected anxiety" phase Freud claimed to occur prior to the phobia that is discussed in a previous chapter, as well as various associative links between Oedipal meanings and horse accident meanings that I will consider in a later chapter), this yields the following temporal sequence proposed as a predicted observable Oedipal temporal sequence:

Heightened sexual desire for the mother => *struggle to repress heightened desires* + *horse accident* => *horse phobia* + *marked decrease in sexual desire for mother*

Freud never explicitly put together all these elements into one concisely stated argument in the way I am doing it here. However, he does explicitly argue for each component at various points in his commentary. The overall argument is clearly part of his intentions.

Note that I refer to claims about the case data that follow from Freud's theory as *predictions*, even though, because Freud was making claims about past events during Hans's phobia, they are technically *retrodictions* or *postdictions*. Nor are these "predictions" strict derivations from Freud's general theory plus the initial conditions prior to the phobia's outbreak. Rather, they are *post hoc* explanations of a singular causal relationship. As I shall explain in the next chapter, I agree with Frank Cioffi that such singular causal claims can be made and evaluated in a reasonably sensible and scientific way. The explanation must be *post hoc* because none of the etiological theories in play in the Hans case—whether Freud's, Bowlby's, or Wolpe and Rachman's—can adequately predict the phobia's occurrence based on the factors that existed before the onset of Hans's pathology. However, each of their *post hoc* explanations does have its own degree of explanatory power and evidential persuasiveness, and each predicts certain observable consequences.

The repression argument addresses a particular explanatory challenge faced by Freud. One of the great strengths of the "fright" theory is that it explains why Hans's phobia occurred precisely when it did, making it difficult for other theories to display equal or greater explanatory power. The repression argument potentially meets this challenge by offering an equally precise explanation of the timing of the onset of Hans's phobia that overlaps with the horse accident, namely, the point at which Hans's sexual conflict causes the repression of his sexual desire, yielding symptom formation.

Unlike the horse-accident account, Freud cannot rely on commonsense background assumptions to justify his Oedipal approach. He must offer an explanation that has observable consequences that might not be expectable on independent grounds. The strength of Freud's approach lies precisely in the boldness and riskiness of his predictions. Because of their riskiness, the confirmational payoff of a successful prediction would be high and go a long way toward placing Freud's thesis into the explanatory running. All of this, of course, depends on linking the Freudian hypotheses to empirically observable indicators.

Freud's Operational Definition of "Oedipal Sexual Desire"

The repression argument is an elegant attempt by Freud to show that his theory can generate empirically testable predictions about the case data that are as precise and impressive as those generated by the fright theory but would not be expected on the horse-accident account. However, the Oedipal theory is highly theoretical whereas the fright theory is based on observable events such as Hans witnessing the horse accident and its features. To test Freud's hypotheses using the Hans case report in a persuasive way, observable behaviors must be linked to each of the central terms of Freud's predictions, including conflict, repression, and sexual desire.

Conflict in Hans may be inferred from observable external parental pressures that go against Hans's spontaneously expressed preferences, or Hans's verbalization of internal worries regarding sexual activity. Repression may be operationalized as a sudden diminution of expression of sexual desire during or immediately following conflict. Note that the distinction between repression and suppression seems not to be of concern to Freud in this context, and apparently was generally less important to him than usually supposed (Erdelyi, 2006), and will be set aside here.

Sexual desire, the concept on which the test of Freud's theory most depends, is the most challenging variable to operationalize. It is arguably a theoretical entity that is not directly observable. Moreover, it is not immediately obvious how to measure hypothesized sexual desire in a four-year-old boy who cannot self-report it. Obviously, some behavioral operationalization is necessary. In searching for a way to test Freud's distinctive predictions, I take the approach of granting Freud as much leeway as possible in defining what is "sexual" as long as the definition does not prejudice the evidential relevance of Freud's prediction of the trajectory of sexual feelings.

In combing through Freud's statements about the case, it becomes apparent that Freud handles the challenge of operationalizing Hans's sexual desire quite ingeniously, albeit implicitly. One can initially identify four indicators of the levels of Hans's sexual desire for his mother that Freud cites: (1) Hans's self-touching of his penis, or "masturbation"; (2) Hans's verbal or behavioral expressions of wanting to be with and to cuddle with his mother; (3) Hans's specific verbal references to his penis when in the presence of his mother; (4) dream expressions that are interpreted as symbolic disguised manifestations of his sexual desire for his mother.

Each of these indicators is of interest but can be challenged as begging the question in one way or another. Regarding masturbation, it is an assumption based on Freud's own theory, not an independently verified fact, that Hans's masturbation is generally stimulated by his sexual fantasies about his mother and is directed at relieving the tension brought about by his sexual desire for her. Nevertheless, Hans's masturbation is at least a form of sexual expression. Given Freud's insistence on the specifically sexual nature of the desires leading to the phobia, this seems his strongest indicator.

Regarding Hans's yearnings to cuddle with his mother in bed, here at least Hans's desires are clearly directed towards his mother. The problem is that these desires are not obviously sexual and they need not be sexual because Bowlby's attachment theory can explain such yearnings as nonsexually motivated. However, as with the masturbation indicator, one can provisionally grant Freud his auxiliary assumption about the sexual nature of Hans's desire to be with his mother and evaluate whether Freud's prediction is confirmed. Separately, one can assess whether the evidence would be better explained by Bowlby's theory. If Freud is right, then the case report should reveal an inverse relationship between measures of desire to be with the mother and measures of symptom intensity, and this would be of interest because Bowlby's attachment theory predicts precisely the opposite, that symptom intensity should trigger greater yearning in the child for the safety of the mother.

Hans's overt references to his penis when talking to his mother are prima facie evidence of sexual interest, and Freud, leaping to Oedipal conclusions, refers to them as attempts by Hans to seduce his mother. However, there are only two such instances, so they contribute little to broader generalizations. In principle, they also must be examined for whether they represent sexual longing directed at the mother, but erring on the side of inclusion, these seem to be acceptable indicators for Freud's purposes.

The dream reports considered by Freud are interpreted to be concerned with the expression of specifically sexual longings for the mother. However, the dreams are heavily interpreted and do not reflect sexual material at the manifest content level. Thus, Freud's interpretations must be assessed for their evidential cogency. This is a daunting task in its own right and is best considered elsewhere (see Wakefield, forthcoming).

In sum, allowing Freud various auxiliary hypotheses to facilitate an operationalized prediction, Hans's level of sexual desire for his mother can be defined primarily in terms of frequency of masturbation and frequency of seeking cuddling with his mother. According to Freud's account, there should be evidence of rising desire before the phobia, explaining why repression might prove to be necessary at that particular time. There should then be evidence of a struggle to repress the sexual desire just prior to or at the time of phobia symptom formation. This should be followed by evidence of decreased sexual desire as symptoms occur. Using Freud's operational criteria, each of these components is a testable prediction of Freud's theory.

Distinctiveness and Scientific Viability of Freud's Predictions

Before turning to the further reconstruction and evaluation of Freud's repression argument, I briefly consider two virtues of the argument that make it a strong test. These are, first, that it distinguishes Freud's theory from prominent rival theories, and second, that it evades some common methodological criticisms of Freudian theory.

Regarding distinctiveness, the sequence of Hans's behaviors that Freud's Oedipal theory predicts—namely, heightened sexual desire measured by masturbation and desire for cuddling, followed by conflict over sexual desire, followed by phobia onset accompanied by decreased sexual desire—is a novel prediction that is not derivable from other available theories. It is not predicted by either the horse-accident (fright) account (Wolpe & Rachman, 1960) or the nonsexual attachment-theory account (Bowlby, 1973), the two most serious rivals to the Oedipal theory.

The fright theory asserts that Hans's horse phobia originated in a frightening experience with a horse. According to this account, the sequence of relevant events would have content specific to horses. The theory predicts nothing about Hans's relationship with his mother, his sexual behavior, or the period prior to phobia onset. Nor does it predict a period of conflict over sex at the time of phobia onset. Regarding the period after the phobia appears, it does not predict that symptom onset is accompanied by reduced sexual desire in the form of reduced frequency of masturbation or reduced longing for cuddling with the mother. Consequently, if Freud's predictions should be confirmed, this would be a reason to prefer the Oedipal theory to the fright theory.

The predictions of attachment theory are not as univocal as the fright and Oedipal theories' predictions, but one can identify some broad expectations (for a full discussion, see *Attachment, Sexuality, Power* [Wakefield, 2022]). According to Bowlby, children have a biologically designed nonsexual attachment motivational system that causes them to seek proximity to an attachment figure who provides comforting when the child faces threats or is anxious. Attachment soothing lowers the intensity of fear and allows the child to tolerate anxiety and learn to cope with threats. If access to the attachment figure is blocked or the soothing response by the attachment figure is unsatisfactory, fears can rise unchecked and dispose a child to the development of an anxiety disorder.

There is nothing in Bowlby's theory that would imply heightened sexual desire before or reduced sexual desire after a phobia's onset, nor would a phobia be linked to sexual conflict, for Bowlby's theory says nothing about sexual desire. Thus, there would be no congruence in predictions with the Oedipal theory about explicitly sexual indicators such as masturbation. With regard to Hans's desire to cuddle with his mother, for Bowlby this would be an indicator of attachment need, not sexual desire. Both Bowlby and Freud would predict heightened longing for the mother prior to phobia onset, but in Bowlby's case it would be because the development of an anxiety disorder is generally preceded by problems in the attachment relationship that would tend to increase the child's desire for soothing and contact with the attachment figure. Bowlby would not predict a conflict in the child over such longing, except in some pathological forms of attachment relating. Most importantly, Bowlby would not predict a diminution of longing for cuddling after symptom formation. In fact, attachment theory would predict the opposite, an increase of longing for the attachment figure's comforting and safe haven as anxiety increases after phobia formation.

In sum, Freud's predicted pattern of sexual behavior over the course of phobia onset is quite distinctive as compared with the predictions of rival theories. It represents a novel and risky prediction that puts his theory to a legitimate scientific test.

In regard to the scientific legitimacy of the repression argument's test of Freud's theory, many philosophers of science and Freud critics have expressed general doubts about the scientific viability of Freud's arguments on a variety of grounds. However, I believe that his overlooked repression argument in the Hans case escapes these criticisms. I will briefly comment on several of the most prominent such objections.

The *suggestion objection*, discussed in an earlier chapter, is not a plausible explanation of the phenomena predicted by the repression argument. None of the standard sources of suggestion emphasized in the literature, such as the therapist's influence on, anticipation of, or biased interpretation of, the patient's free associations apply to the repression argument as reconstructed here. For one thing, the evidence consists of Hans's behavior, not his purported memories or agreement to interpretations. As well, much of the evidence occurred before, during, and immediately after the onset of his phobia, before the analysis could start or have time to influence him.

The *case study objection* holds that case studies, as opposed to controlled studies, cannot provide scientifically relevant evidence for an etiological theory. However, Freud's logic in formulating and testing his repression hypothesis using the Hans case data is impeccably scientific and consistent with the resurgence in psychology of methodologically legitimate N=1 case studies. As to generalization, this depends on background assumptions. Hans is a quasi-randomly selected instance of the theory's target domain (Freud goes out of his way to argue that Hans is normal and representative within that domain), and the prediction is highly unexpectable for anyone in that domain. The area of the prediction involves developmental theory which is arguably potentially lawful for that domain. It is not uncommon in developmental theory to study one or a few instances in a domain and provisionally generalize. If Freud's predictions are verified, that would be prima facie probatively relevant to consideration of how seriously his theory should be taken.

Adolf Grunbaum (1984) argues that Freud relied on therapeutic effectiveness to demonstrate the validity of his sexual etiological theories. But, Grunbaum objects, cure can occur for all sorts of other reasons, especially suggestion of various kinds, so Freud's etiological theories have no real support from the evidence of the couch. However, Grunbaum's objections are not relevant to the testing of the repression hypothesis in the Hans case because therapeutic success has no role in the repression argument, which depends entirely on a certain predicted pattern of Hans's sexual activity before, during, and immediately after the onset of his phobia, independent of any later cure. Grunbaum's critique focuses on "on the couch" tests of Freud's hypotheses in ongoing treatment, which is usually contrasted with more scientific controlled experimental data. However, the repression argument fits neither category, being an N=1 naturalistic analysis that involves data external to therapy. Additionally, suggestion, which is the main reason why on the couch data can be misleading, is not an issue in regard to the repression argument (see above, and see Chapter 11 for a critique of Grunbaum's analysis of Freud's argument).

Karl Popper (1963) famously claimed that Freudian hypotheses are pseudoscientific because they are *unfalsifiable*, Popper's criterion for pseudoscience. Popper held that Freud's hypotheses about repression are impossible to falsify because if the patient responds the opposite of what is expected based on a hypothesized impulse, then that is because of a defense against the impulse:

> Whatever anybody may do is, in principle, explicable in Freudian or Adlerian terms ... Whether a man sacrificed his life to rescue a drowning child (a case of sublimation) or whether he murdered the child by drowning him (a case of repression) could not possibly be predicted or excluded by Freud's theory; *the theory was compatible with everything that could happen ...*
>
> (1974, p. 985)

In fact, it would not be a problem if all possible actions, including "opposite" altruistic and murderous actions, were potentially explainable by Freud's theory, as long as the theory provided testable predictions or explanations of which of the opposite reactions would occur. Presumably, it is not a strike against Einsteinian mechanics that it can explain opposite motions of objects.

In any event, the repression argument does not suffer from the problem of unfalsifiability. A specific sequence is being predicted by Freud's theory, and alternative sequences would disconfirm the theory. Obviously, no falsification is absolute; as even Popper acknowledged, every theory has recourse to various auxiliary hypotheses and other maneuvers to avoid immediately yielding to apparent falsification, and the Oedipal theory is no different. However, the prediction in this case is relatively clear-cut—as clear-cut as in many other sciences. I conclude that the repression argument shows that Popper's claim that Freudian psychoanalysis is unfalsifiable is incorrect.

Observing that "no moment of time is so favourable for the understanding of a case as its initial stage" (p. 24), Freud tests his repression argument primarily using the case report's description of the initial days of Hans's phobic condition and the days immediately preceding it. Fortunately, these events are described in detail in the father's case notes (Freud observes that "the material seems to be amply sufficient for giving us our bearings" [p. 24]). I now consider in turn each of Freud's three predictions concerning Hans's sexual life and whether they are confirmed by the case report.

Prediction 1: Does the Case Record Provide Evidence of Increased Sexual Desire in the Period Before the Phobia Began?

Freud postulates that Hans's sexual desire for his mother greatly increased in the months before the phobia's outbreak in January. The change, Freud says, began during the summer holiday in Gmunden, when Hans's father generally was in Vienna on business during the week. Consequently, Hans and his mother were left alone together ("In the summer I used to be constantly leaving Gmunden for Vienna on business, and he was then the father" [p. 45]). During this time, Hans often cuddled with his mother in bed ("I: 'Did you often get into bed with Mummy at Gmunden?' Hans: 'Yes'" [p. 90]). Freud sees this summer period of intimacy as the occasion for intensified Oedipal feelings:

> Hans's desires for his mother had consequently been awakened to an unusual degree: Hans really was a little Oedipus who wanted to ... be alone with his beautiful mother and sleep with her. This wish had originated during his summer holidays, when the alternating presence and absence of his father had drawn Hans's attention to the condition upon which depended the intimacy with his mother which he longed for.
>
> (p. 111)

Freud reiterates his claim that Hans's desires for his mother were awakened "to an unusual degree" many times. According to Freud, Hans's "increased affection for his mother" (p. 25) caused him to experience "enormously intensified" (p. 25) affection at "such a high pitch of intensity" (p. 110) that his "state of intensified sexual excitement" (p. 118) and the "intensity of the child's emotions" (p. 25) grew "greater than he could control" (p. 25) and thus Hans "was overwhelmed by an intensification of his libido" (p. 25) and by an "intensified erotic excitability" (p. 133). Consequently, "[A] new pleasure had now become the most important for him—that of sleeping beside his mother" (p. 110). Indeed, Freud holds that this intensification of incestuous desire "was the fundamental phenomenon in his condition" (p. 24) during this pre-phobic period.

According to Freud, Hans's intensified desire became ripe for repression when Hans's sources of erotic gratification became grossly inadequate to the level of his desires: "his erotic needs became intensified, while at the same time they began to obtain insufficient satisfaction" (p. 132). Freud offers two reasons for the development of this marked disparity between desire and gratification. First, the Graf family had moved to a new apartment shortly before the summer holiday, so when they returned to Vienna, Hans was in a new environment and had few playmates or other acquaintances nearby. Thus, sexual feelings that had become distributed among friends and away from his mother before and during the time at Gmunden, where he had many friends, now became directed entirely at her once again:

> His affection had moved from his mother on to other objects of love, but at a time when there was a scarcity of these it returned to her, only to break down in a neurosis ... [A]fter his return to Vienna he was once more alone, and set all his hopes upon his mother.
>
> (pp. 110, 132)

Second, the move to the new apartment also entailed a change in sleeping arrangements. Hans, whose bed had previously been in his parents' bedroom, was now for the first time moved into a bedroom of his own: "Hans was about four years old when he was moved out of our bedroom into a room of his own" (p. 99); "He had meanwhile suffered another privation, having been exiled from his parents' bedroom" (pp. 132–133). This new experience of being alone without easy access to his parents seems to have made Hans lonely or anxious, for the case report suggests that he sought his parents' affection after waking up by himself in the morning and when going to bed at night.

The result of these various changes, Freud claims, is that Hans's heightened sexual feelings were deprived of their former outlets. I now examine the evidence, based on three indicators of sexuality identified earlier, that Freud cites to support his claim that Hans experienced markedly increased sexual desire for his mother.

Does Hans's Masturbation Reveal an Increase in Sexual Desire Prior to the Phobia?

According to his parents' diary of his sexual development, Hans had displayed an interest in his penis and the penises of animals and curiosity about his parents' genitals, and he had been touching his genitals, for a long time. His mother's reported castration threat to try to stop him from touching his penis occurred a year-and-a-quarter before the onset of the phobia ("When he was three and a half his mother found him with his hand on his penis. She threatened him … " [p. 7]). Relative to this long-term interest, it is challenging to discern an overall upsurge of self-touching in the period immediately before the phobia. Freud himself speculates that Hans's level of masturbatory activity had remained constant at a high level for a long time, leaving little room for an upsurge: "we may presume that Hans, who was now four and three-quarters, had been indulging in this pleasure every evening for at least a year" (p. 27). (This latter speculation that masturbation had been continuous for over a year was aimed at disputing the standard medical view at the time that masturbation was responsible for the onset of the neurosis.)

However, a closer look allows a case to be made for an increase in Hans's masturbation shortly before the phobia onset. Max asked Hans about masturbation during the summer at Gmunden: "I: 'Did you put your hand to your widdler at Gmunden, when you were in bed?' He: 'No. Not then; I slept so well at Gmunden that I never thought of it at all'" (pp. 61–62). Daily play with friends and unfettered access to his mother seem to have *lowered* Hans's inclination to touch his penis during the summer prior to his phobia's onset. Moreover, during the summer at Gmunden, Hans spent more time in bed with his mother during his father's absences, so masturbation seems less likely; in Vienna, Hans's only reported masturbation was when he was in his own bed alone. If we take Hans at his word and take his lack of self-touching during the summer as the baseline, then there certainly is an upsurge closer to the phobia. On the day that he first admitted on a walk with his mother that he was afraid of being bitten by a horse, his mother asked him, "Do you put your hand to your widdler?" and he answered: "Yes. Every evening, when I'm in bed" (p. 24). This appears to imply that the self-touching has been ongoing daily prior to the phobia's outbreak, in sharp contrast to the summer. This could be interpreted as supporting Freud's case that the deprivations upon returning to Vienna were sufficient to cause an increase in ungratified sexual need that translated into an upsurge—or return to a previous higher level—of masturbation.

Do Hans's Two Instances of Separation Anxiety Reveal "Enormously Intensified" Sexual Need for His Mother Prior to the Phobia's Outbreak?

A few days before the phobia began, Hans had an anxiety dream about his mother not being available for cuddling: "When I was asleep I thought you were gone and I had no Mummy to coax with" (p. 23). Freud argues that this anxiety dream revealed heightened sexual longing:

> The disorder set in with thoughts that were at the same time fearful and tender, and then followed an anxiety dream on the subject of losing his mother and so not being able to coax with her any more. His affection for his mother must therefore have become enormously intensified.
>
> (p. 24)

Putting this dream together with a similar incident reported by the father to have occurred about six months before at Gmunden ("Suppose I were to have no Mummy" [p. 23]), Freud argues that they are evidence that Hans experienced a sustained period of "increased affection for his mother" (p. 25) in the months before the phobia:

> But the beginnings of this psychological situation go back further still. During the preceding summer Hans had had similar moods of mingled longing and apprehension, in which he had said similar things; and at that time they had secured him the advantage of being taken by his mother into her bed. We may assume that since then Hans had been in a state of intensified sexual excitement, the object of which was his mother.
>
> (p. 119)

Freud thus assumes that the two incidents are part of the same causal sequence and joined by a continuous period of intensified sexual excitement aimed at the mother, with the earlier incident being the "beginnings of this [current] psychological situation" at which time the recent "disorder set in." This would be an extraordinary leap if there really was just one earlier incident ("Once he made a remark ... ") and thus two incidents total separated by months, neither of which alone rises to the level of a disorder. It could easily be the case that each of the two incidents was caused by some immediate situation (e.g., the mother's occasional threats to leave when Hans misbehaved, or Hans witnessing his first funeral). However, when Freud writes in the plural of earlier "similar moods of mingled longing and apprehension, in which he had said similar things," he relies on the fact that the father, although recalling only one explicit remark, indicates that Hans was frequently similarly moody at bedtime: "When he was in bed in the evening he was usually in a very sentimental state ... Unfortunately, when he got into an elegiac mood of that kind, his mother used always to take him into bed with her" (p. 23). Hans was clearly unhappy about being alone in bed at Gmunden and longing for his mother's attention. Freud thus can make his case for a generally increased desire on Hans's part for contact with his mother.

This particular indicator is explainable in other ways. In my parallel volume, *Attachment, Sexuality, Power,* I provide an alternative explanation for why Hans's longing for his mother increased during the prephobia period. Hans's father, motivated by Oedipal theory, began blocking Hans from coming into bed with his mother for their usual cuddling and thus was disrupting Hans's usual attachment soothing. This bond disruption likely started just before the summer, when Hans was moved into his own bedroom. Hans assumed that his father must be angry at him ("You're cross. I know you are" [p. 83]) despite his father offering him the "explanation that only *little* boys come into bed with their Mummies and that *big* ones sleep in their own beds" (p. 83). The father reveals his attitude towards mother-son intimacy when he says that "unfortunately" (p. 23) his wife responded to Hans's longing by taking him into bed with her. This deprivation and disruption by Hans's father of Hans's attachment relationship with his mother coincides with precisely the period during which Freud says that Hans's desire for his mother increased. Thus, Hans's behavior was likely simply an attempt to maintain the status quo of the mother as a secure base. Nonetheless, I conclude that, taking Freud's indicator at face value, the prediction of Hans's increased intensity of longing for his mother and thus, in Freud's terms, sexual desire in the months preceding the phobia's outbreak is arguably weakly confirmed by the evidence of Hans's reported longings for his mother.

Do Hans's Two Attempts at "Seducing" His Mother Reveal Intensified Sexual Desire?

Freud presents an additional line of evidence in support of the hypothesis of Hans's greatly increased sexual needs aimed at the mother prior to the phobia, namely, two purported attempts by Hans six months apart to "seduce" his mother:

> His affection for his mother must therefore have become enormously intensified ... In support of this, we may recall his two attempts at seducing his mother, the first of which dated back to the summer, while the second (a simple commendation of his penis) occurred immediately before the

outbreak of his street-anxiety. It was this increased affection for his mother which turned suddenly into anxiety—which, as we should say, succumbed to repression.

(pp. 24–25)

The first incident occurred during the summer at Gmunden. After Hans's bath, his mother was "powdering round his penis and taking care not to touch it," and Hans asked her, "Why don't you put your finger there?" When she responded "because that'd be piggish ... Because it's not proper," Hans laughed and said, "But it's great fun" (p. 19). In the other incident, in Vienna, Hans repeated to his parents his visiting aunt's overheard compliment about his penis that "He *has* got a dear little thingummy" (p. 23).

These interactions with the mother surely do contain elements of sexuality, consistent with Hans's general long-term interest in widdlers. They thus can be taken to support Freud's claim of Hans's increased sexual interest. The question remains whether these behaviors represent Hans's sexual feelings directed at his mother versus an opportunistic and essentially autoerotic desire for stimulation and for admiration.

Conclusion Regarding Freud's Prediction of Intensification of Hans's Sexual Desire

The evaluation of Freud's first prediction is provisionally supportive of Freud, given the charitable way the test has been set up. So far as one can tell from the case record, it does seem as though Hans's sexual behavior as operationally defined did increase before the phobia, at Gmunden, or when back in Vienna. Whether Hans's sexuality was intensified at the dramatic levels suggested by Freud's rhetoric is uncertain. Whether Freud's explanation for what caused these alterations in behavior is the best explanation also remains questionable. However, comparison to rival theories aside, Freud's first prediction can be considered weakly confirmed or at least not disconfirmed.

Prediction 2: Does the Case Record Evidence Indicate that Hans Repressed His Sexual Needs Immediately Prior to Phobia Onset?

I now examine the evidence Freud offers for his second prediction, that Hans repressed his sexual desires just prior to the phobia's outbreak. This is a pivotal prediction for Freud because it is the specific act of repression that, according to Freud, triggers Hans's anxiety disorder ("It was this increased affection for his mother which turned suddenly into anxiety—which, as we should say, succumbed to repression" [p. 24]). Consequently, if evidence for repression of sexuality just prior to or simultaneous with symptom formation is lacking, then the heart of Freud's repression argument is threatened.

Does Hans's Response to Parental Prohibitions of Masturbation Reveal Conflict About or Suppression of Masturbation Proximal to Phobia Onset?

Freud thinks that masturbation accompanied by fantasy is Hans's main outlet for his Oedipal sexual desires. If Freud's second prediction is correct, then one would expect to see a conflict about and diminution in Hans's masturbation at the time of the phobia's emergence. Freud maintains that Hans's parents' fresh prohibitions and threats about masturbation were the immediate event that triggered Hans's repression of his sexual desires, which in turn caused the phobia.

Freud thus asserts that Hans gave up masturbation at the time of phobia onset. Freud is quite explicit in claiming that the case data reveals a cessation of masturbatory activity due to repression at the time of phobia onset: "We have seen how our little patient was overtaken by a great wave of repression and that it caught precisely those of his sexual components that were dominant. He gave up masturbation" (p. 138). At another point, in the course of defending his repression account against the standard anti-masturbation medical orthodoxy of the time, Freud challenges the view that masturbation itself is intrinsically harmful to a child and leads to anxiety disorders such as Hans's. He suggests that it is not masturbation but sexual repression and the consequent cessation of masturbation that caused the phobia:

> Hans admitted that every night before going to sleep he amused himself with playing with his penis. "Ah!" the family doctor will be inclined to say, "now we have it. The child masturbated: hence his pathological anxiety." But gently. That the child was getting pleasure for himself by masturbating does not by any means explain his anxiety; on the contrary, it makes it more problematical than ever. States of anxiety are not produced by masturbation or by getting satisfaction in any shape ... And we shall find that at this moment he was actually engaged in a struggle to break himself of the habit—a state of things which fits in much better with repression and the generation of anxiety.
>
> (p. 27)

Freud asserts that at the time of phobia outbreak, Hans was engaged in the process of stopping the self-touching habit. This would imply that Hans either had just recently given up masturbation or was in a state of deep conflict over it prior to giving it up. However, the facts revealed in the case record do not support either option. Instead, at the time of the phobia's onset Hans was still touching his penis regularly and doing so seemingly without any indications of conflict such as anxiety or shame, despite repeated parental warnings. (What happened at later times is considered in relation to Freud's third prediction, below.)

For example, Hans tells his mother on January 8, the day he first reported the phobic symptoms and just *after* he reported them, that he touches himself every night in bed ("[H]is mother asked: 'Do you put your hand to your widdler?' and he answered: 'Yes. Every evening, when I'm in bed'" [p. 24]). Even more revealing is his parents' fresh warning on the day after phobia onset, which was still not effective, with Hans not only continuing to touch himself but manifesting a defiant disregard of his parents' warnings ("The next day, January 9th, he was warned, before his afternoon sleep, not to put his hand to his widdler. When he woke up he was asked about it, and said he had put it there for a short while all the same" [p. 24]).

So, immediately prior to and at the time of phobia onset, Hans's sexuality as revealed in his masturbatory activity appears unhobbled by conflicts or repressive forces that began prior to phobia onset. I conclude that this test clearly falsifies Freud's crucial second prediction.

Freud's Ad Hoc Maneuver to Save His Masturbation Repression Prediction from Apparent Disconfirmation

We have seen that the reports by Hans regarding masturbation both on the day of symptom onset and the next day are incompatible with Freud's hypothesis that Hans had just undergone a successful if painful struggle to repress his sexuality. The problems for Freud do not stop there. In addition, the case record clearly indicates that, while the parents had always cautioned Hans about masturbation, the recent fresh parental prohibitions against masturbation did not occur until just *after* the outbreak of the phobia, when the parents became worried that masturbation might be the cause of Hans's problems. But Freud's hypothesis implies that the parental warnings as the trigger for repression must have occurred *before* the phobia's onset. These facts would seem to make Freud's account chronologically impossible.

Freud realized that the case record's description of the phobia's onset contradicted his repression hypothesis. His response to this disconfirmation was to engage in an astoundingly ad hoc maneuver. He suggested that the case record might be incorrect on this critical point, and that perhaps the mother's warning somehow occurred before the phobia's onset after all:

> Some interfering influence, emanating from his parents perhaps, had made itself felt. I am not certain whether the reports upon Hans were at that time drawn up with sufficient care to enable us to decide whether he expressed his anxiety in this form *before* or not until *after* his mother had taken him to task on the subject of masturbating. I should be inclined to suspect that it was not until afterwards, though this would contradict the account given in the case history.
>
> (p. 137)

This speculation has no prima facie credibility. The parents were keeping a careful diary of Hans's development, often recorded by the father as events occurred. Nor would they have been inattentive to the details of matters concerning masturbation and sexuality, knowing the importance Freud placed on them. Their fresh prohibitions seem to have been set off by the appearance of the phobia. There is no reason to think that the case record should be distrusted in this matter. If we reject Freud's blatant reshuffling of the data, then his prediction regarding conflict over and cessation of masturbation prior to symptom formation remains falsified.

Does Longing for the Mother Undergo Repression at the Time of Symptom Formation?

We have seen that during the two days that the phobia's symptoms emerge in Hans's walks with his nanny and his mother and in the following evenings, and thus during or shortly after the time that repression is supposed to occur, Hans continues to express strong desire to "coax" with his mother (see Chapter 6). So, at the outset of the phobia there are intense symptoms *and* manifest intense desire for cuddling with the mother, and no hint of conflict about this. Moreover, within days of phobia onset, there is the "thingummy" incident in which Hans reports to his mother, with seeming pride and without apparent anxiety, that his aunt admired his penis. Freud's description of this incident as an attempt at seduction may be disputed, but it is surely a free expression of sexuality to Hans's mother, not betraying any internal conflict or repression. The facts of the case record thus again fail to confirm Freud's prediction regarding Hans's relationship to his mother.

Freud's Analysis of Hans's Anxiety Dream as an Indicator of Repression

Freud offers a further argument to support his prediction of sexual conflict preceding the phobia. For this argument, he cites the anxiety dream Hans had a few days before the phobia's onset about his mother being unavailable for cuddling, that we also had occasion to consider in Freud's argument for Hans's intensified sexual desire prior to the phobia's outbreak. Freud uses the same dream as evidence for sexual repression prior to the phobia. The case record does not indicate the exact date in early January that this anxiety dream occurred, but most plausibly it was January 2 or 3 (if on New Year's Day or the same day as the "thingummy" incident, this likely would have been mentioned), so for ease of exposition I will assume January 2. (Given Olga's social anxieties, one might speculate that the family's New Year's socializing caused some turmoil in the family related to Hans's dream.) We saw that Freud defines Hans's disorder as encompassing this dream in his "undirected anxiety" argument against the fright theory (see Chapter 6), and I have already examined this move with a critical eye and leave such issues aside here.

Recall that Freud says of the dream report: "The disorder set in with thoughts that were at the same time fearful and tender, and then followed an anxiety dream on the subject of losing his mother and so not being able to coax with her any more" (1909, pp. 24–25). What does Freud mean when he says that the disorder set in with fearful and tender thoughts that were *followed by* an anxiety dream? The case record describes the occurrence of fearful thoughts *during* the dream ("When I was asleep I thought you were gone and I had no Mummy to coax with"), but reports no thoughts occurring prior to the dream. Freud later clarifies that he is speculating about the latent thoughts that might have preceded the manifest content:

> The first thing we learn is that the outbreak of the anxiety state was by no means so sudden as appeared at first sight. A few days earlier the child had woken from an anxiety-dream to the effect that his mother had gone away, and that now he had no mother to coax with. This dream alone points to the presence of a repressive process of ominous intensity. We cannot explain it, as we can so many other anxiety-dreams, by supposing that the child had in his dream felt anxiety arising from some somatic cause and had made use of the anxiety for the purpose of fulfilling an unconscious wish which would otherwise have been deeply repressed. We must regard it rather as a genuine punishment and repression dream, and, moreover, as a dream which failed in its function, since the child woke from his sleep in a state of anxiety. We can easily reconstruct what actually occurred in the unconscious. The child dreamt of exchanging endearments with his mother and of sleeping with her; but all the pleasure was transformed into anxiety, and all the ideational content into its opposite. Repression had defeated the purpose of the mechanism of dreaming.
>
> (p. 119)

Freud's explanation reveals that his claim that "this dream alone points to the presence of a repressive process of ominous intensity" is based entirely on his interpretation that the dream's painful manifest content represents a repressive transformation of the latent content which, Freud claims, consists of tender thoughts of exchanging sexual endearments with the mother. An attachment-theoretic view might hold that, with Hans's father actively preventing Hans from coaxing with his mother, the dream simply reproduces a real anxiety in Hans's life and, if anything, shows that Hans's desire to cuddle with his mother is *not* repressed in everyday life, but leave that aside. Even if Freud were correct that the manifest content of the dream hides a latent fantasy of pleasurable cuddling, that, according to Freud, is simply how dreams routinely work. There is no obvious implication that in Hans's waking life his desire to coax with his mother has been repressed (the evidence, we saw, is that it is not), yet that actual desire, not what occurs in a dream, is what is at issue in evaluating Freud's second prediction. Freud's dream argument begs the question of whether his prediction of repression is confirmed.

Conclusion Regarding Freud's Second Prediction

Regarding Freud's prediction that we would see evidence of Hans's state of conflict and process of repression immediately prior to or simultaneous with the phobia's onset, there is no supportive evidence and much contrary evidence in the case record. The contrary evidence encompasses Freud's two primary operationalized measures, Hans's continued masturbatory activity and expressions of longing for his mother. Freud's second claim is simply contradicted by the facts.

Note that the hypothesis that the phobia was preceded by repression of sexuality is independent of Freud's broader observation that the phobia depended on many earlier repressions that formed the groundwork for the ultimate disorder. Indeed, Freud suggests that the most crucial repressed desires relative to phobic symptom formation are likely not the ones that were repressed at the time of the phobia but Oedipal desires repressed earlier:

> But these were not the components which were stirred up by the precipitating cause of the illness (his seeing the horse fall down) or which provided the material for the symptoms, that is, the content of the phobia ... These other components were tendencies in Hans which had already been suppressed and which, so far as we can tell, had never been able to find uninhibited expression: hostile and jealous feelings towards his father, and sadistic impulses (premonitions, as it were, of copulation) towards his mother. These early suppressions may perhaps have gone to form the predisposition for his subsequent illness. These aggressive propensities of Hans's found no outlet, and as soon as there came a time of privation and of intensified sexual excitement, they tried to break their way out with reinforced strength. It was then that the battle which we call his "phobia" burst out.
>
> (pp. 138–139)

According to Freud, these earlier repressions formed the basis for a disposition to disorder. However, I have been concerned with the predictions regarding the outbreak of the phobia itself and not with the formation of the disposition to form such a phobia. Whether or not the earlier repressions occurred does not alter the three primary predictions Freud derives from his theory that are evaluated here. I have focused on the evidence regarding those aspects of Hans's desires that Freud claims or implies were repressed at the time of the phobia, not earlier. The postulated earlier repressions enter into Freud's argument in a more subtle way by shaping unconscious meanings, to be explored in the next two chapters.

Prediction 3: Is There Evidence That Hans's Sexual Desire Markedly Diminished After the Onset of Phobic Symptoms, Supporting Freud's Repression Hypothesis?

The repression argument's third prediction, that the development of Hans's phobia was accompanied by a marked diminution in Hans's sexual desire, is both most crucial to Freud's argument and the most easily testable. Whereas there were data limitations in assessing the first two predictions, in this case we have the entire analysis to plumb for evidence, while remaining aware that the suggestion objection increasingly becomes an issue as the case progresses.

Does Hans Markedly Decrease His Masturbatory Activity After Phobia Onset?

Regarding Freud's claim that Hans's masturbatory activity ceased when the phobia began, we have seen that the text does not support such a claim specifically at the time of phobia onset when Hans was predicted to be in a state of conflict. Instead, Hans reports masturbating the day after he reports his phobia despite a stern warning from his mother. But, focusing on Freud's third prediction, a separate (if continuous) question is: once the phobic symptoms formed, was there then a clear diminution in masturbation? For, if Hans successfully substituted neurotic symptoms for his sexual longing for his mother, we would expect to see not only a conflict accompanied by an abrupt repression of that desire manifested by a cessation in masturbation simultaneous with emergence of phobic symptoms, but in addition a *persistent* diminution of masturbation associated with symptoms over time.

The overwhelming evidence is that Hans did not substitute neurotic symptoms for his sexuality, but that his masturbatory activity persisted deep into the case report. This is revealed in an exchange between Hans and his father about *two months* after the start of the phobia:

> On March 2nd, as he again showed signs of being afraid, I said to him: "Do you know what? This nonsense of yours" (that is how he speaks of his phobia) "will get better if you go for more walks. It's so bad now because you haven't been able to go out because you were ill."
>
> HE: "Oh no, it's so bad because I still put my hand to my widdler every night." (p. 30)

The fact that Hans was engaging in masturbation "every night" two months after the phobia began is as conclusive disconfirmation of Freud's prediction as one is likely to get.

Under pressure from his parents, who used harsh Victorian methods such as placing Hans in a sack at night, Hans did finally claim to have stopped masturbating on March 13:

> On March 13th in the morning I said to Hans: "You know, if you don't put your hand to your widdler any more, this nonsense of yours'll soon get better."
>
> HANS: "But I don't put my hand to my widdler any more."
> I: "But you still want to."
> HANS: "Yes, I do. But wanting's not doing, and doing's not wanting." (!)
>   (pp. 30–31)

Having touched himself every night until mid-March halfway through the treatment, Hans finally claimed to have succumbed to his parents' repeated warnings and restraints. However, it is not entirely clear that Hans actually had given up masturbation even at that point. On March 17, with the phobia still clearly present, "he woke up in a fright" and explained: "I put my finger to my widdler just a very little" (p. 32). Freud's claim that Hans's "struggle with masturbation" and his consequent relinquishing of this activity are what triggered the phobia is strongly falsified by the case record.

Does Hans's Longing to Cuddle with his Mother Markedly Decrease After Phobia Onset?

Freud claims that, as a result of the postulated sexual repression that caused the phobia, Hans's attempts at physical intimacy with his mother dramatically decreased or ceased. According to Freud, Hans suffered a "general reversal of pleasure into unpleasure which had come over the whole of his sexual researches" (p. 34). Freud continued to maintain this position as a crucial datum in his later writing:

> In point of fact we know that after "Hans's" phobia had been formed, his tender attachment to his mother seemed to disappear, having been completely disposed of by repression, while the formation of the symptom (the substitutive formation) took place in relation to his aggressive impulses.
>
> (Freud, 1926, p. 124)

Yet the evidence contradicts this claim. There is no evidence in the case report of any diminution of Hans's strivings to be cuddled by his mother, and overwhelming evidence of his continued uninhibited pursuit of such physical intimacy. The evidence occurs throughout the case and thus supports not cessation but rather a continued and unremitting level of intensity of desire and pleasure in such contact. For example, two-and-a-half months after the phobia began, Hans's father reports Hans's giraffe fantasy, and interprets it as a reproduction of a struggle that has been occurring with regularity every morning in which Hans attempts to get in bed with his mother and he (the father) tries to keep Hans out of his mother's bed:

> The whole thing is a reproduction of a scene which has been gone through almost every morning for the last few days. Hans always comes in to us in the early morning, and my wife cannot resist taking him into bed with her for a few minutes.
>
> (p. 39)

Again, three months after the phobia began, the father notes that Hans insists that he will continue to seek out his mother's cuddling despite his father's interpretations aimed at dissuading him:

> On April 5th Hans came in to our bedroom again, and was sent back to his own bed. I said to him: "As long as you come into our room in the mornings, your fear of horses won't get better." He was defiant, however, and replied: "I shall come in all the same, even if I *am* afraid." So he will not let himself be forbidden to visit his mother.
>
> (p. 47)

As late as April 11, just a few weeks before the end of treatment, the father reports that Hans still seeks out his mother in bed daily, just as he always did: "April 11th. This morning Hans came into our room again and was sent away, as he always has been for the last few days" (p. 65). Even Neu (1995), a staunch defender of Freud's account of the Hans case, observes regarding Hans that

> The evidence for his attachment to his mother seems clear and overwhelming, but the evidence for the "repression" of those feelings is not … Hans' desire for his mother is, after all, open and remains open throughout the period under consideration.
>
> (p. 139)

Did Hans Repress His Interest in the Excretory Function?

It is worth briefly considering in passing Freud's additional claim that Hans also repressed and ceased taking any pleasure in his excretory functions, which are interpreted by Freud as components of sexuality, and his pleasure in observing the excretory functions of others: He "made efforts to give up masturbating, and showed disgust at 'lumf' and 'widdle' and everything that reminded him of them"; "He gave up masturbation and turned away in disgust from everything that reminded him of excrement and of looking on at other people performing their natural functions" (pp. 108, 138).

Freud's claim that Hans repressed his excretory, and specifically excretory voyeuristic, interests around the time of phobia onset, like his claims about Hans's masturbation and cuddling, is simply inconsistent with the case record. It is true that in a discussion with his father on April 9, more than three months after the phobia began and just a few weeks before the end of the treatment, Hans did express disgust towards his mother's undergarments and some excretory associations to them. Freud appears to rely heavily on this incident in making his claim. However, at the end of that discussion, it becomes clear, as Freud himself notes, that Hans is trying to hide the truth of his pleasures and desires. That truth emerges when the mother is consulted, with the following result: "I asked my wife whether Hans was often with her when she went to the W.C. 'Yes', she said, 'often. He goes on pestering me till I let him. Children are all like that'" (pp. 56–57). Clearly, whatever Hans said to his father about being disgusted—his remarks may have been influenced by reference in that conversation to enforced times he had in the bathroom accompanied by regular enemas that were justified by his constipated condition—the notion that Hans "showed disgust at 'lumf' and 'widdle' and everything that reminded him of them" is not correct.

As well, somewhat earlier but long after the phobia's onset, Hans had jokingly referred to excretory matters in a conversation with his father:

> I: "But why did you come in in the night?"
> HE: "I don't know."
> I: "Just tell me quickly what you're thinking of."
> HE: (jokingly) "Of raspberry syrup."
> I: "What else?"
> HE: "A gun for shooting people dead with."
>
> (p. 38)

Max explains to Freud: "As regards 'raspberry syrup' and 'a gun for shooting with', Hans is given raspberry syrup when he is constipated. He also frequently confuses the words 'shooting' and 'shitting'" (p. 99). A footnote explains that the German is very close as well: "In German 'schiessen' and 'scheissen'" (p. 99, n. 1). Hans's scatalogical joking suggests that Hans is quite comfortable bringing up excrement-related thoughts and topics.

Conclusion Regarding Freud's Prediction of Cessation of Sexual Striving After Phobia Onset

Freud's third and most crucial prediction in the repression argument is overwhelmingly disconfirmed by the case evidence. Freud's firmly stated assertions about the cessation of Hans's various sexual pleasures due to repression— statements made at the time as well as in his rethinking of the case seventeen years later—are clearly contradicted by multiple entries in the case report.

Does Freud's Shift from the Toxicity Theory to the Signal Theory of Anxiety Change the Evaluation of his Sexual-Repression Argument?

As his thinking evolved, Freud (1926) altered elements of his theory of anxiety and the structure of the Oedipus complex. He replaced his early "toxicity" theory of anxiety as a transformation of repressed sexuality by an understanding of anxiety as a signal of danger, a biologically and psychologically more plausible account. In justifying these revisions, Freud returned to the

Hans case to illustrate the implications of his changing views for under-standing phobias, which he considered the psychoanalytically best understood disorders ("Let us go back again to infantile phobias of animals; for, when all is said and done, we understand them better than any other cases" [p. 124]). Thus, we have two versions of Freud's account of the etiology of Hans's phobia.

These theoretical revisions raise the question of whether the problems I identified with Freud's sexual-repression argument depend on idiosyncrasies of the anxiety theory Freud embraced at the time he wrote the Hans case study and whether his later theory might evade those problems. Fortunately, the differences between the earlier and later accounts are subtle enough that I was able to avoid relying on the idiosyncratic details of Freud's "toxicity" theory in my analysis. Instead, I considered only predictions that are neutral in the sense that they are derivable from both versions of Freud's theory. The divergences between the two theories are at a theoretically deep level, but at the observational level I consider they generally converge. So, in effect I follow other commentators (e.g., Neu, 1995) in seeing the toxicity theory as a theoretical misstep unsupported by the case evidence, and nothing in my analysis depends on the idiosyncratic doctrines of that theory.

Both accounts claim that Hans sexually desires his mother and thus wants to get rid of his father, and that he fears vengeance from his father in the form of castration. Both theories postulate that both the sexual desire and the fear of castration are eventually repressed, and that the horse phobia consists at least in part of displaced fear of the father. So, both theories claim that sexual desire and castration anxiety both have roles in generating the phobia.

However, the roles are different. Freud's early account places more emphasis on the potentially overwhelming nature of Hans's unfulfillable Oedipal sexual desires. The precise dynamic sequence by which repression occurs is not entirely clear even to Freud ("It is hard to say what the influence was which ... led to the sudden change in Hans and to the transformation of his libidinal longing into anxiety" [1909, p. 136]). However, it is clear that some vicissitude to the sexual desire itself triggers repression of both the incestuous desire and the linked fear of castration. The repression of the incestuous desires then directly brings about undirected anxiety (see Chapter 6). Symptoms of anxiety, such as palpitations and breathlessness, are seen as a dissociated form of sexual arousal ("The dyspnoea and palpitations that occur in hysteria and anxiety neurosis are only detached fragments of the act of copulation" [1905, p. 80]). The free-floating anxiety joins with the displaced repressed fear of the father to become directed at horses and form the phobia.

In contrast, Freud's later theory abandons the notion of sexual desire transforming directly into anxiety ("we may legitimately ... give up our ear-lier view that the cathectic energy of the repressed impulse is automatically turned into anxiety" [1926, p. 93]). It places more emphasis on castration anxiety itself as an overwhelming signal of danger that is the trigger for repression of the linked incestuous desire and castration fear. The horse phobia is now generated entirely by the displacement of the repressed fear of the father onto horses as a defense because one can stay at home and escape horses but one cannot escape one's father: "the castration anxiety is directed to a different object and expressed in a distorted form, so that the patient is afraid, not of being castrated by his father, but of being bitten by a horse ... " (p. 125).

Freud explains his earlier error as a result of confusing correlation with causality due to the misleading example of the actual neuroses:

> I found that outbreaks of anxiety and a general state of preparedness for anxiety were produced by certain sexual practices such as coitus interruptus, undischarged sexual excitation or enforced abstinence—that is, whenever sexual excitation was inhibited, arrested or deflected in its progress towards satisfaction. Since sexual excitation was an expression of libidinal instinctual impulses it did not seem too rash to assume that the libido was turned into anxiety through the agency of these disturbances.
>
> (Freud, 1926, p. 110)

To his credit, Freud acknowledges that his new theory leaves actual neuroses entirely unexplained: "We might attempt to do so by supposing that, when coitus is disturbed or sexual excitation interrupted or abstinence enforced, the ego scents certain dangers to which it reacts with anxiety. But this takes us nowhere" (p. 110).

In the later theory, no mysterious transformation of one type of experience (sexual desire) into another (fear) is necessary. The "stuff" of the phobic fear is now the fear attached to the repressed castration anxiety:

> the *affect* of anxiety, which was the essence of the phobia, came, not from the process of repression, not from the libidinal cathexes of the repressed impulses, but from the repressing agency itself. The anxiety belonging to the animal phobias was an untransformed fear of castration.
>
> (Freud, 1926, p. 108)

It is the displacement that makes it pathological: "What made it a neurosis was one thing alone: the replacement of his father by a horse. It is this displacement, then, which has a claim to be called a symptom" (p. 103).

What is important for our purposes is that Freud still embraces the repression argument and that the test I presented of the repression argument remains legitimate under the shift to the later theory. It is true that the precise dynamic causal processes among incestuous desire, castration anxiety, the triggering of repression, and phobic anxiety is left vague and open to question on both accounts, as Freud readily admits: "It is almost humiliating that, after working so long, we should still be having difficulty in understanding the most fundamental facts" (1926, p. 124). However, the repression argument is one point on which Freud insists across theories because it is essential to his sexual theory of the neuroses. In his later work, Freud reasserts his claim that the act of repression was exerted against Hans's increasing incestuous desire for his mother and this led to symptoms accompanied by a decrease in Hans's sexual desire:

> [A] full appreciation of "Little Hans's" case shows that the formation of his phobia had had the effect of abolishing his affectionate object-cathexis of his mother as well, though the actual content of his phobia betrayed no sign of this. The process of repression had attacked ... his tender impulses towards his mother.
>
> (p. 106)

> [T]here still remains a doubtful point to clear up. In "Little Hans's" case —that is, in the case of a positive Oedipus complex—was it his fondness for his mother or was it his aggressiveness towards his father which called out the defence by the ego? In practice it seems to make no difference, especially as each set of feelings implies the other; but the question has a theoretical interest, since it is only the feeling of affection for the mother which can count as a purely erotic one ... [W]e have always believed that in a neurosis it is against the demands of the libido and not against those of any other instinct that the ego is defending itself. In point of fact we know that after "Hans's" phobia had been formed, his tender attachment to his mother seemed to disappear, having been completely disposed of by repression, while the formation of the symptom (the substitutive formation) took place in relation to his aggressive impulses.
>
> (p. 124)

I conclude that the critique I have offered of Freud's repression argument is not affected by the change from Freud's early to late theory of anxiety.

Overall Conclusions Regarding Freud's Sexual Repression Predictions

Freud derived three predictions from his sexual-repression theory of Hans's phobia: Hans had heightened sexual desire (as operationalized primarily by frequency of masturbation and of expressed longing for contact with his mother) in the period leading up to the phobia's outbreak; he experienced conflict over sexuality and repressed this desire just prior to the phobia; and subsequent to the phobia's onset, manifestations of sexual desire decreased markedly.

Examination of the Hans case record reveals that the first prediction (the upsurge of sexual desire prior to the phobia) is, if one extrapolates from minimal data, weakly confirmed by some variables. This outcome is equally predicted by attachment theory. The second and third predictions (the occurrence of conflict over and repression of sexuality, and the subsequent simultaneous increase in symptoms and decrease in sexual desire) are strongly disconfirmed. Regarding repression, Freud cited parental intervention prohibiting masturbation to explain the triggering of repression in Hans, but the case record indicates that the parents, who had in any event been prohibiting masturbation for over a year, did not intervene at this time until a day after the phobia began. Nor did signs of conflict and repression in Hans appear in the case record at this time. To the contrary, Hans seemed unconflicted and imperturbable in his pursuit of masturbatory and cuddling pleasure.

Using the same observational variables that Freud used to indicate Hans's sexual desire, including especially masturbation and longing for contact with the mother, examination of the case data revealed no marked diminution let alone cessation of Hans's sexual strivings subsequent to the phobia's appearance. Freud's pivotal claims that at the onset of the phobia Hans "gave up masturbation" and that Hans's "tender attachment to his mother seemed to disappear" are simply and markedly false, disconfirming his theory that symptoms are a substitute for repressed sexual desires. The case evidence instead reveals Hans's charmingly defiant enjoyment of his self-touching and his continued urgent seeking of cuddling with his mother long after the phobia's onset. This evidence is directly contrary to Freud's repressive hypothesis. The prediction of the pattern of behavior over time is what makes Freud's case history-based test a scientifically serious one. The strong disconfirmation of the second and third predictions means that Freud's repression argument is as falsified as it can be in one case study.

Finally, I want comment on the methodological and conceptual standing of Freud's argument. In light of philosophical critiques of Freud's theory, it is surprising how empirically grounded and scientifically cogent the argument is. Freud's hypotheses are directly linked to observable behaviors on Hans's part, and specific predictions derivable therefrom. There is no in-principle conceptual or methodological obstacle to the confirmation or disconfirmation of these hypotheses. Moreover, the hypotheses have probative relevance. If they had been strongly confirmed, they would, I believe, have impacted the weight we would give to Freud's Oedipal theory, for there is no other available theory that would predict the same pattern. Moreover, these are highly risky predictions that have no commonsense anchoring, unlike the fright and attachment theories. The reconstruction of the logic of Freud's sexual-repression argument should help to dispel the myth that single case studies cannot be used to explore psychoanalytic causal claims. Freud's approach in the Hans case evades the standard philosophical objections to the testability of Freudian theory.

How, then, are we to understand the sharp contrast between the high quality of Freud's formulation of predictions to test his theories versus the gross incompetence he displays in comparing the predictions to the case evidence and evaluating the success or failure of the predictions? The puzzle here is not the falsity of Freud's theory, but the remarkable disconnect between what Freud says about the case record and what the case record actually shows. The analysis reveals Freud as a brilliant theoretician and simultaneously an incompetent and biased reader unable to correctly state the evidence, even when comparing the results of a test he himself constructed to the evidence that is in front of him in a manuscript he edited and partly wrote.

I will return to the issue of Freud's remarkable incompetence as a scientific observer in a later chapter. For now, I note only that the easy explanation that Freud is a liar (Cioffi, 1998) is insufficient as an explanation of this anomaly. Freud knew that the evidence upon which he relied, Hans's father's notes, would be published with his Discussion. The evidence would be there for everyone to see, including Hans's father and mother. This is unlike the situation with the early seduction theory papers in which he has been accused of lying about his claimed successes. There, Freud was reporting on cases that he treated in private and about which nobody else could say very much. Lying would at least make a certain amount of sense there as a pragmatic strategy, but it makes no sense in the Hans case. Greatly compounding the mystery of Freud's gross mischaracterization of the published case results is the troubling fact that subsequent generations of psychoanalysts failed to recognize and state the obvious failure of Freud's predictions.

References

Bowlby, J. (1973). *Attachment and loss (Vol. 2): Separation: Anxiety and anger.* New York: Basic Books.

Cioffi, F. (1998). Was Freud a liar? In *Freud and the question of pseudoscience* (pp. 199–204). Chicago, IL: Open Court Publishing. Reprinted from Cioffi, F. (1976). *Was Freud a liar? Orthomolecular Psychiatry, 5(4)*, 275–280.

Erdelyi, M. H. (2006). The unified theory of repression. *Behavioral and Brain Sciences, 29*, 499–551.

Freud, S. (1905). Fragment of an analysis of a case of hysteria. *SE* 7, 1–122.

Freud, S. (1909). Analysis of a phobia in a five-year-old boy. *SE* 10, 1–150.

Freud, S. (1926). Inhibitions, symptoms and anxiety. *SE* 20, 75–176.

Grunbaum, A. (1984). *The foundations of psychoanalysis: A philosophical critique.* Berkeley, CA: University of California Press.

Jupp, V. L. (1977). *Freud and pseudo-science.* Philosophy, *52(202)*, 441–453.

Lear, J. (1990). *Love and its place in nature: A philosophical interpretation of Freudian psychoanalysis.* New York: Farrar, Straus & Giroux.

Neu, J. (1995). "Does the Professor talk to God?" Learning from Little Hans. *Philosophy, Psychiatry & Psychology, 2*, 137–158.

Popper, K. R. (1963). *Conjectures and refutations: The growth of scientific knowledge.* London: Routledge.

Popper, K. R. (1974). Replies to my critics. In P. A. Schilpp (Ed.), *The philosophy of Karl Popper* (Vol. *2*) (pp. 961–1197). LaSalle, IL: Open Court.

Wakefield, J. C. (2022). *Attachment, sexuality, power: Oedipal theory as regulator of family affection in Freud's case of Little Hans.* New York: Routledge.

Wakefield, J. C. (forthcoming). *Freud's interpretation of dream and fantasy evidence: A hypothesis testing approach to the case of Little Hans.* New York: Routledge.

Wolpe, J., & Rachman, S. (1960). Psychoanalytic "evidence": A critique based on Freud's case of Little Hans. *Journal of Nervous and Mental Disease, 131*, 135–148.

Chapter 9

Methodological Interlude

The Suitability Argument as Freud's
Foundational Methodology and His Reply
to the Suggestion Objection

Freud's Suitability Argument

In addition to the repression argument reconstructed in the last chapter, there is a second major positive argument implicit in Freud's commentary on the Hans case. Whereas the repression argument depends on unusual aspects of the Hans case that allow Hans's sexual behaviors to be traced in an N=1 manner from before the development of his phobia, this second positive argument is Freud's characteristic approach throughout his clinical analyses. In fact, it might be considered Freud's epistemically foundational argument. This second argument concerns what Freud claims is the unique (or, more plausibly, the optimal or distinctive) power of Oedipal theory to explain some of the otherwise perplexing details of Hans's psychoneurotic symptoms.

From the beginning of his writing on hysteria with Josef Breuer, Freud claimed that the singular causal connection between a precipitating trauma, whether physical or psychical, and a resulting symptom is often self-evident. (One might say that he imparted as much obvious clarity to the singular causal connection between trauma and symptom as Cioffi observes in the Miss Havisham case; see below.) Freud defends the evident nature of such causal links by extending the prototypical explanation of a traumatic neurosis to apparently nontraumatic hysterias. This is initially explained at the very beginning of the "Preliminary Communication" that Freud coauthored with Breuer (1893), later republished in *Studies on Hysteria* (Breuer & Freud, 1895). The prototype is the explanation of traumatic hysteria triggered by wartime experiences or by horrific accidents such as train wrecks:

> It is of course obvious that in cases of "traumatic" hysteria what provokes the symptoms is the accident. The causal connection is equally evident in hysterical attacks when it is possible to gather from the patient's utterances that in each attack he is hallucinating the same event which provoked the first one.
>
> (Breuer & Freud, 1893, p. 4)

DOI: 10.4324/9781003272472-9

One might think here of a flashback in PTSD, where, say, a loud noise in a shopping mall triggers a stress reaction and perhaps even a delusion in a veteran of being under fire, so that there is little doubt of a causally relevant link of some sort between the memory of the earlier events and the current pathological response.

Freud was not alone in endorsing such singular causal judgments based on history and the obvious congruence between the flashback-like delusional experiences and hysterical symptoms of the patient. The causal relevance seems obvious, even if other "constitutional" factors predispose some individuals to react to the same experience in different ways. To this day, posttraumatic stress disorder is one of the few disorders in the DSM that incorporates the assumed cause, a specific trauma, into the very definition of the disorder.

By claiming that specific details of an unconscious memory can be linked to specific details of a symptom, analogously to the way the details of a recalled physical trauma are congruent with symptoms in traumatic hysterias, Freud and Breuer transported the legitimacy of such singular causal explanations from the traumatic hysterias, originally conceived as involving hysterical symptomatic responses to physical traumas, to the nontraumatic hysterias reinterpreted as involving psychological traumas:

> The experiences which released the original affect, the excitation of which was then converted into a somatic phenomenon, are described by us as psychical traumas, and the pathological manifestation arising in this way, as hysterical symptoms of traumatic origin. (The term "traumatic hysteria" has already been applied to phenomena which, as being consequences of physical injuries—traumas in the narrowest sense of the word—form part of the class of 'traumatic neuroses'.)
>
> (Breuer, 1895, p. 209)

To Breuer and Freud (1895), and to Freud thereafter, the causal link between uncovered psychic trauma and symptom seemed as securely inferrable as the link between physical trauma and symptoms:

> *Our experiences have shown us, however, that the most various symptoms, which are ostensibly spontaneous and, as one might say, idiopathic products of hysteria, are just as strictly related to the precipitating trauma as the phenomena to which we have just alluded and which exhibit the connection quite clearly.*
>
> (1893, p. 4)

Indeed:

> The connection is often so clear that it is quite evident how it was that the precipitating event produced this particular phenomenon rather than

any other. In that case the symptom has quite obviously been determined
by the precipitating cause.

(p. 4)

However, in the nontraumatic domain, instead of an evident physical trauma
and a spontaneous memory, Freud through psychoanalysis uncovered hidden
psychic traumas located in unconscious memories, leaving an opening for the
suggestion objection.

In an important early paper, Freud set out requirements for an adequate
explanation of a symptom by a postulated repressed memory based on such
links: "Tracing a hysterical symptom back to a traumatic scene assists our
understanding only if the scene satisfies two conditions; if it possesses the
relevant *suitability to serve as a determinant* and if it recognizably possesses
the necessary *traumatic force*" (1896c, p. 193). Grunbaum (1984) refers to
these as Freud's conditions of "explanatory adequacy" (p. 150) or "etiologic
adequacy" (p. 152). I will refer to the singular causal argument from such
linkages between the details of memories and symptoms as the "Suitability
Argument."

Freud's suitability and force criteria are not a theoretical aside but his fundamental epistemic guidelines. In the same paper, Freud presents his theory that it
is not the postpubertal emotional traumas that he and Breuer had identified that
are the ultimate etiology of hysteria, but rather it is childhood (prepubescent)
sexual experiences that are at the root of every psychoneurosis. Freud describes
laboriously tracing associations from the postpubertal traumatic scenes "to the
chains of memories behind them. In doing so, to be sure, we arrive at the period
of earliest childhood" (1896, p. 202). Freud then presents his theory and its evidential grounds:

[I]t is this line alone which, after so many delays, will lead us to our goal.
For now we are really at the end of our wearisome and laborious analytic
work, and here we find the fulfilment of all the claims and expectations
upon which we have so far insisted. If we have the perseverance to press
on with the analysis into early childhood, as far back as a human
memory is capable of reaching, we invariably bring the patient to reproduce experiences which, on account both of their peculiar features and of
their relations to the symptoms of his later illness, must be regarded as
the aetiology of his neurosis for which we have been looking. These
infantile experiences are once more *sexual* in content ... of *sexual intercourse* (in the wider sense). You will admit that the *importance* of such
scenes needs no further proof; to this may now be added that, in every
instance, you will be able to discover in the details of the scenes the
determining factors which you may have found lacking in the other
scenes—the scenes which occurred later and were reproduced earlier. I
therefore put forward the thesis that at the bottom of every case of

hysteria there are *one or more occurrences of premature sexual experience*, occurrences which belong to the earliest years of childhood but which can be reproduced through the work of psycho-analysis in spite of the intervening decades. I believe that this is an important finding, the discovery of a *caput Nili* in neuropathology.

(pp. 202–203)

In italicizing "importance" and "determining" factors, Freud is referencing his criteria of force and suitability of a determinant, respectively. He is explicit that it is suitability in particular that warrants his conclusion on the grounds that the childhood events are "experiences which, on account both of their peculiar features and of their relations to the symptoms of his later illness, must be regarded as the aetiology of his neurosis for which we have been looking." It is immediately after repeating that he was "able to discover in the details of the scenes the *determining* factors" that he considers himself justified in moving to his conclusion ("I therefore put forward the thesis..."). Suitability defines the criteria on which Freud claims etiological validity.

These criteria emerge from Freud's fundamental assumption, again going back to *Studies on Hysteria* and held throughout his life, that the symptoms of a psychoneurosis symbolically express a repressed traumatic mental content. Freud often refers to the causally relevant features of the repressed memory in producing the features of the symptoms as the "determinants" of the symptom's features. Although Freud set out the explanatory adequacy criteria as necessary conditions ("only if"), in clinical investigation they are often used as sufficient conditions for provisional claims of causal relevance and the validity of an interpretation. Freud claims (see below) that the associative link between hypothesized content and symptom is sufficiently distinctive and specific to support the plausibility of a singular causal inference.

The Suitability Argument presupposes some substantive theoretical assumptions at the foundation of Freud's theory. The theory asserts that unconscious memories and symptoms are linked in meaningful ways because symptoms are indirect mnemic expressions of repressed mental contents. Freud starts on the path to the Suitability Argument from the thesis he had developed with Breuer, that hysterical symptoms are a symbolic expression of unconscious memories:

[W]e must take our start from Josef Breuer's momentous discovery: *the symptoms of hysteria ... are determined by certain experiences of the patient's which have operated in a traumatic fashion and which are being reproduced in his psychical life in the form of mnemic symbols.*

(1896c, pp. 192–193)

This "mnemic symbol" account of symptom features is particularly supportive of the possibility of an effective and compelling Suitability Argument approach due to meaning connections. However, throughout my discussion here, I assume that whether or not one holds the mnemic symbol account in any strong sense, Freud's argument can be taken in a broader sense to be the empirical claim that, when unconscious contents lead to neurotic symptoms, the specific nature of the symptoms is an expression of the nature of the contents, so that in some discernible ways the nature and features of the symptoms will express the nature of the etiological contents. This is a major assumption, but it is one of the assumptions that underlies psychoanalysis.

However, sometimes there are lengthy associative pathways from memory to symptom. The meanings have been transformed several times by successive traumas or other associative mediators that may each have a causal role in symptom features. Thus, the relationship can become very indirect between the original memory and the symptom, with many intermediate steps needed to be decoded in order to reveal the ultimate link between original sources and symptom, yielding the challenge of "laboriously" working through the patients' "debris" "layer by layer," as Freud put in the introduction to the Hans case (see Chapter 3). That problem is exactly what the Hans case is designed to avoid with its "more direct" evidence so as to test the theory more cleanly. However, in principle, the symptom always retains, directly or indirectly after various transformations, the stamp of its origin in the form of distinctive and otherwise puzzling features.

The Suitability Argument is an instance of the commonsense understanding evident in science, in the courtroom, and in everyday life, that the explanation of perplexing anomalous details often leads to larger explanations and understanding. This is why the frequent comparisons of Freud to a detective are apt. The solving of a crime is often based on coming to understand a revealing detail that on first glance looks distant from the point of the investigation but in the end reveals a larger causal picture and leads to a conclusion as to who did it, as in the O. J. Simpson trial's refrain, "If the glove don't fit, you must acquit." If you are wondering whether your host used a cookie cutter or shaped the cookies he baked by hand, noticing the detail of an imperfection in his cookie cutter that is reproduced in the cookies' shape is enough to persuade you of an answer.

Given its concern with singular relationships of meaning, the Suitability Argument has affinities to "narrativist" and "hermeneutic" approaches, but it is a causal argument without any of the philosophical fellow travelers of relativism, constructivism, and so on that afflict the usual versions of such approaches, and so I will leave such terms aside to avoid confusion. The causal insights may often depend on similarities that are commonly labeled "thematic affinity," but not in the shallow sense that renders affinity wholly inadequate as a grounds for causal attributions (see below). The Suitability Argument is about singular causal explanation and has nothing to do with therapeutic success, but I will wait until I address Grunbaum's rival "Tally Argument" analysis of Freud's response to the suggestion objection to address the therapeutic success alternative head on (see Chapter 11).

In usual clinical practice, the analyst will assume the Oedipal theory and look for features of the patient's symptoms that are plausibly determined or illuminated by assuming Oedipal meanings. However, in an evidential test of Oedipal theory as in the Hans case, the logic of the argument is more demanding. The claim is that specific features of the patient's symptoms can only be explained or can best be explained by their being derived from Oedipal meanings. Thus, in an evidential context, it is not just that the invocation of the Oedipus complex can yield some explanatory insight into a patient's symptoms, for that is not a difficult target to hit if one simply applies the theory to the case and points to various confirmatory explanatory insights that seem illuminating, as would be routine in a clinical analysis. Rather, it is that there are details of the patient's neurotic symptoms that seem inexplicable based on the precipitating trauma and other known considerations but that find compelling and persuasive explanation in the Oedipal theory that is lacking from any other source. If such an argument can work anywhere it should be able to work in the Hans case, given its unique context of a "more direct" relationship between mental cause and symptomatic effect. Even if it succeeds, such an argument will not confer proof but only a degree of plausibility and probative weight to Oedipal theory. One can acknowledge that Freud's rhetoric about the uniqueness of his suitability solutions is inflated while still accepting that, in the circumstance of the failure of the seduction theory and the seemingly ad hoc proposal of the Oedipal theory (see Chapter 1), a successful novel prediction of this kind can regain Freud's theory its scientific status and allow it to be taken seriously.

As far as I can see, the Suitability Argument involves no rule or method that could be formulated without counterexamples, other than the demand for a manifestly persuasive singular causal explanation (see below). Freud's extremely demanding rhetoric about the criteria for accepting such an explanation make sense if obvious objections are to be avoided. My position will be that slippery and problematic though the suitability test may be, it is not without some basis in our singular causal explanatory practices and it is Freud's ultimate redoubt in addressing the suggestion objection, and so deserves to be taken seriously.

There are three levels that might be distinguished in Freud's overall Suitability Argument. One level is the suitability claim itself that the explanation of neurotic symptoms lies in repressed determinants to be found in earlier traumas. Another background level is Freud's insistence that the results of a thorough suitability analysis based on a complete psychoanalysis will generally yield one uniquely compelling solution. The third level is the Hans case's "more direct" evidence as an epistemological guarantor of the superstructure of the argument. Before documenting Freud's endorsement of the Suitability Argument and exploring its epistemological foundations in singular causal explanation, I start by briefly documenting the background level, that Freud claims that there is a unique suitability solution to the etiological puzzle given all the facts that emerge during a psychoanalysis.

Comprehensive and Distinctive Explanatory Coherence as Determining a Unique Solution to the Etiological Puzzle

The effectiveness of the Suitability Argument rests in part on the assumption that the link between the patient's unconscious memories and the detailed features of the patient's symptoms yields an explanation that is unique in its degree of overall coherence, comprehensiveness, and explanatory power relative to various false stories one might concoct. Thus, the backbone of Freud's response to the suggestion objection is his claim that there is indeed a unique comprehensive explanation of the patient's symptoms. One can read Freud's statements as rhetorical exaggerations of a somewhat more modest claim, but he is basically clear that he thinks the overall evidence in a psychoanalysis eventually allows one to focus in on one explanation as uniquely adequate and compelling, implying just one solution to the etiological puzzle. This is why he repeatedly argues that errors of interpretation—whether they result from suggestions that influence the patient or from the interpretive confirmatory biases of the analyst—inevitably will be corrected as the analytic process continues and further evidence is amassed. One might think of Freud's argument as being analogous to confidence that a good, sustained cross-examination in a legal case will reveal if a witness is lying simply because the truth is inevitably more coherent with other truths than any falsehood can be. Freud believes that a mistaken construction will inevitably be revealed by newly emerging details of an analysis. Comprehensive explanatory coherence is enough to ensure correspondence with reality once all the evidence is in.

Throughout his career, using similar words and arguments, Freud cited this consideration as the ultimate grounds for rejecting the suggestion objection, as in the following four passages:

> We learn with astonishment ... that *we are not in a position to force anything on the patient ... or to influence the products of the analysis by arousing an expectation.* I have never once succeeded, by foretelling something, in altering or falsifying the reproduction of memories or the connection of events; for if I had, it would inevitably have been betrayed in the end by some contradiction in the material. If something turned out as I had foretold, it was invariably proved by a great number of unimpeachable reminiscences that I had done no more than guess right. We need not be afraid, therefore, of telling the patient what we think his next connection of thought is going to be. It will do no harm.
>
> (1895, p. 295)

> But you will now tell me that ... there is a risk that the influencing of our patient may make the objective certainty of our findings doubtful ... This is the objection that is most often raised against psycho-analysis ... that

we have "talked" the patients into everything relating to the importance of sexual experiences—or even into those experiences themselves—after such notions have grown up in our own depraved imagination ... Anyone who has himself carried out psycho-analyses will have been able to convince himself on countless occasions that it is impossible to make suggestions to a patient in that way. The doctor has no difficulty, of course, in making him a supporter of some particular theory ... but this only affects his intelligence, not his illness. After all, his conflicts will only be successfully solved and his resistances overcome if the anticipatory ideas he is given tally with what is real in him. Whatever in the doctor's conjectures is inaccurate drops out in the course of the analysis; it has to be withdrawn and replaced by something more correct. We endeavour by a careful technique to avoid the occurrence of premature successes due to suggestion; but no harm is done even if they do occur, for we are not satisfied by a first success. We do not regard an analysis as at an end until all the obscurities of the case are cleared up, the gaps in the patient's memory filled in, the precipitating causes of the repressions discovered.

(1917, pp. 452–453)

Is it possible, then, that corroborative dreams are really the result of suggestion, that they are "obliging" dreams? The patients who produce only corroborative dreams are the same patients in whom doubt plays the principal part in resistance. One makes no attempt at shouting down this doubt by means of one's authority or at reducing it by arguments. It must persist until it is brought to an end in the further course of the analysis. The analyst, too, may himself retain a doubt of the same kind in some particular instances. What makes him certain in the end is precisely the complication of the problem before him, which is like the solution of a jig-saw puzzle. A coloured picture, pasted upon a thin sheet of wood and fitting exactly into a wooden frame, is cut into a large number of pieces of the most irregular and crooked shapes. If one succeeds in arranging the confused heap of fragments, each of which bears upon it an unintelligible piece of drawing, so that the picture acquires a meaning, so that there is no gap anywhere in the design and so that the whole fits into the frame— if all these conditions are fulfilled, then one knows that one has solved the puzzle and that there is no alternative solution.

(1923, pp. 115–116)

[T]he question arises of what guarantee we have while we are working on these constructions that we are not making mistakes and risking the success of the treatment by putting forward some construction that is incorrect ... [N]o damage is done if, for once in a way, we make a mistake and offer the patient a wrong construction as the probable historical truth. A waste of time is, of course, involved ... but a single mistake of the sort can do no harm. What in fact occurs in such an event is rather that the patient remains as though he were untouched by what has been said ... [I]f nothing further develops we may conclude that we have made a mistake and we shall admit as much to the patient at some suitable opportunity without sacrificing any of our authority. Such an opportunity will arise when some new material has come to light which allows us to make a better construction and so to correct our error. In this way the false construction drops out, as if it had never been made ... Only the further course of the analysis enables us to decide whether our constructions are correct or unserviceable. We do not pretend that an individual construction is anything more than a conjecture which awaits examination, confirmation or rejection.

(1937, pp. 261–262, 265)

These passages, ranging from Freud's earliest to his latest works, are among Freud's most explicit responses to the suggestion objection. In all of them, the focus is on uniqueness of explanatory adequacy when all the facts are taken into account. Freud reassures us that the psychoanalytic process is resilient and can go forward successfully, without damage, even if there is a false suggestion. This is so because psychoanalysis is by its nature a self-correcting process in which errors due to suggestion are eventually corrected as long as the analyst is attentive to the evolving evidence. In a domain of complexly interwoven facts, the truth is more coherent with other truths than any falsehood can be, so only a correct construction will yield an adequately precise and comprehensive explanation of the detailed nature of the patient's symptoms that encompasses all the facts. A false suggestion is "inevitably ... betrayed in the end by some contradiction in the material"; whatever is inaccurate "has to be withdrawn and replaced by something more correct"; the error is "brought to an end" when "one knows that one has solved the puzzle and that there is no alternative solution"; and "we may conclude that we have made a mistake ... when some new material has come to light which allows us to make a better construction and so to correct our error."

There is a marked consistency in Freud's argument and even to some extent his wording across these statements. False interpretations, even when accepted by the patient, will not harm the search for the etiology of the symptoms because the analysis continues until a comprehensive understanding is reached, and emerging evidence will always reveal that the earlier interpretation was false and determine a unique solution. Note that the second passage is famously cited by Grunbaum to support his Tally Argument analysis, and I discuss it again in Chapter 11, in considering Grunbaum's view.

However, the broad claims in these passages require more substance to be persuasive. The doubts that immediately arise about these abstract claims are fairly straightforward. Freud's argument assumes that the evidence subsequent to an incorrect interpretation is itself veridical and independent of the earlier error, and so can act as a corrective to that error. However, without further details, it is unclear why this should be so. It seems possible that once an incorrect interpretation is put forward, both suggestion to the patient and confirmatory bias by the analyst could tend to cause later "data" to be produced that is consistent with the earlier incorrect interpretation, thus manufacturing an overall coherent account that is nonetheless false. Freud's further comments on the specific type of explanation he seeks, to which I now turn, must be examined for whether they help to address this doubt.

Background to Freud's Suitability Argument

Granting that Freud holds that a comprehensive adequate explanation of the patient's symptoms will be unique, what form does such as explanation take? The answer, discussed above, is that it is aimed at displaying that the hypothesized mental contents possess suitability as a determinant of detailed, otherwise inexplicable features of the patient's symptoms.

The Suitability Argument is a continuation of the pivotal original argument by Breuer and Freud, as Freud later described it: "the particular nature of the symptoms was explained by their relation to the traumatic scenes which were their cause. They were, to use a technical term, 'determined' by the scenes of whose recollection they represented residues" (1910, p. 14). Freud continued to write of such determinants at the time of the Hans case, for example: "these childish theories are still operative and acquire a determining influence upon the form taken by the symptoms" (1908, p. 211). In the Dora case, Freud was induced to look for an earlier etiology because "as so often happens in histories of cases of hysteria, the trauma that we know of as having occurred in the patient's past life is insufficient to explain or to determine the particular character of the symptoms" (1905, p. 26). Freud took suitability as an explanatory criterion so seriously that failure to support suitability was a rationale Freud offered for rejecting Breuer's notion that neuroses occur as a result of hypnosis-like "hypnoid states": "What remains decisive is that the theory of hypnoid states contributes nothing to the solution of the other difficulties, namely that the traumatic scenes so often lack suitability as determinants" (1896c, p. 195).

In his seduction theory papers, Freud asserted that the patient's symptoms have a logical structure that reflects the nature of the causative childhood sexual trauma, and he rejected as clinically irrelevant any memories "unrelated to the character of the hysterical symptom" (Freud, 1896c, p. 194). Instead, he pushed the patient to venture further into the past until some sexual memory proved explanatorily suitable to a degree that offered a compelling link to the patient's symptoms:

> Conviction will follow in the end ... The precocious event has left an indelible imprint on the history of the case; it is represented in it by a host

of symptoms and of special features which could be accounted for in no other way; it is peremptorily called for by the subtle but solid inter-connections of the intrinsic structure of the neurosis.

(1896a, p. 153)

In every case a number of pathological symptoms, habits and phobias are only to be accounted for by going back to these experiences in childhood, and the logical structure of the neurotic manifestations makes it impos-sible to reject these faithfully preserved memories which emerge from childhood life ... The influence of the re-activated pathogenic memory is shown by the fact that the content of the obsessional idea is still in part identical with what has been repressed or follows from it by a logical train of thought.

(1896b, pp. 165, 170)

Freud insists that analysis "leads in every instance to the reproduction of new scenes of the character we expect" and that "in every instance, you will be able to discover in the details of the scenes the *determining* factors which you may have found lacking in the other scenes" (1896c, pp. 196, 203). His etiological claims rest "above all, on the evidence of there being associative and logical ties between those scenes and the hysterical symptoms—evidence which, if you were given the complete history of a case, would be as clear as daylight to you" (1896c, pp. 209–210).

Freud also describes how to recognize a failure of suitability: "the scene to which we are led by analysis and in which the symptom first appeared seems to us unsuited for determining the symptom, in that its content bears no relation to the nature of the symptom" (1896c, p. 194). Such a failure of suitability means that the analyst must probe further:

If the memory which we have uncovered does not answer our expecta-tions, it may be that we ought to pursue the same path a little further; perhaps behind the first traumatic scene there may be concealed the memory of a second, which satisfies our requirements better ... until we finally make our way from the hysterical symptom to the scene which is really operative traumatically and which is satisfactory in every respect, both therapeutically and analytically.

(1896/1962d, p. 195)

For a memory to "answer our expectations," to be one that "satisfies our requirements," and to be "satisfactory ... analytically" is just to be compel-lingly suitable as a determinant of the symptoms.

For example, Freud describes two female patients' reports of "astonishingly trivial" pubertal sexual experiences (e.g., a boy stroking her hand or pressing his knee against hers, or an obscene riddle) that nonetheless triggered neurotic

symptoms, where these triggering events "lack suitability as determinants."
He explains:

> As a result of those experiences the patients had become subject to
> peculiar painful sensations in the genitals which had established them-
> selves as the main symptoms of the neurosis. I was unable to find indi-
> cations that they had been determined either by the scenes at puberty or
> by later scenes; but they were certainly not normal organic sensations nor
> signs of sexual excitement. It seemed an obvious thing, then, to say to
> ourselves that we must look for the determinants of these symptoms in
> yet other experiences, in experiences which went still further back.
>
> (1896c, pp. 200–201)

There are often many layers of meaning with varying degrees of suitability
behind neurotic symptoms. For example, there may be a recent traumatic
trigger of symptoms that is dependent for its pathogenicity on a series of
previous traumas since an initial one shortly after puberty, which in turn may
get its pathogenic power from associative links to much earlier childhood
sexual experiences. To some degree, determining content may be transformed
as such new associations form. In "Aetiology of Hysteria," Freud describes
how challenging it can be to identify the fully satisfactorily determining initial
content due to its being obscured by layers of later memories and associations
that may seem determining on first glance but offer an incomplete causal
picture:

> It may happen that the determining power of the infantile scenes is so
> much concealed that, in a superficial analysis, it is bound to be over-
> looked. In such instances we imagine that we have found the explanation
> of some particular symptom in the content of one of the later scenes—
> until, in the course of our work, we come upon the same content in one
> of the *infantile* scenes, so that in the end we are obliged to recognize that,
> after all, the later scene only owes its power of determining symptoms to
> its agreement with the earlier one.
>
> (1896c, p. 216)

Finding a fully adequate suitable determinant that can be presumed to be a
cause of the patient's symptoms is the goal and expectable culmination of
analysis for Freud: "we invariably bring the patient to reproduce experiences
which, on account of their peculiar features and of their relations to the
symptoms of his later illness, must be regarded as the aetiology of his neurosis" (1896c, pp. 202–203). Freud places particular weight on the precise and
compelling way that the hypothesized meaning fits into the overall symptom
picture in an overdetermined way:

But another and stronger proof of this is furnished by the relationship of the infantile scenes to the content of the whole of the rest of the case history. It is exactly like putting together a child's picture-puzzle: after many attempts, we become absolutely certain in the end which piece belongs in the empty gap; for only that one piece fills out the picture and at the same time allows its irregular edges to be fitted into the edges of the other pieces in such a manner as to leave no free space and to entail no overlapping. In the same way, the contents of the infantile scenes turn out to be indispensable supplements to the associative and logical framework of the neurosis, whose insertion makes its course of development for the first time evident, or even, as we might often say, self-evident.

(1896c, p. 205)

As we saw above, in a later paper Freud again cited the puzzle analogy, likening each seemingly inexplicable feature of a symptom to an "unintelligible piece of drawing" which nonetheless when arranged in one specific way "acquires a meaning" such that "there is no alternative solution" (1923, pp. 115–116).

Freud believed that the discovery of unconscious suitable determinants of hysterical symptoms could resolve the mystery of the seeming disproportionality of hysterics' extreme reactions to emotional stimuli:

The reaction of hysterics is only apparently exaggerated; it is bound to appear exaggerated to us because we only know a small part of the motives from which it arises. In reality, this reaction is proportionate to the exciting stimulus ... [L]et us take the instance of a young girl who blames herself most frightfully for having allowed a boy to stroke her hand in secret, and who from that time on has been overtaken by a neurosis. You can, of course, answer the puzzle by pronouncing her an abnormal, eccentrically disposed and over-sensitive person; but you will think differently when analysis shows you that the touching of her hand reminded her of another, similar touching, which had happened very early in her childhood and which formed part of a less innocent whole, so that her self-reproaches were actually reproaches about that old occasion.

(1896c, pp. 217–218)

Nor did Freud give up the suitability approach when he shifted from the seduction theory. In a paper written well after his shift from the seduction theory to the Oedipal theory, and just three years prior to publication of the Hans case history, Freud (1906) restates the "suitability" criterion:

experiences were eventually reached which belonged to the patient's childhood and related to his sexual life ... Unless these sexual traumas of childhood were taken into account it was impossible either to elucidate the symptoms (to understand the way in which they were determined) or to prevent their recurrence.

(p. 273)

He argues that the postulation of the Oedipus complex was a necessary advance to preserve an understanding of suitability: "It was only after the introduction of this element of hysterical phantasies that the texture of the neurosis and its relation to the patient's life became intelligible" (p. 274).

In the same article, Freud explains that nonsexual apparent triggers of neurosis—for example, the horse accident in the Hans case—can be eliminated as sufficient causes because deeper sexual contents are "invariably" needed to explain the detailed features of the symptoms:

> The question may, however, be raised of where convincing evidence is to be found in favour of the alleged aetiological importance of sexual factors in the psychoneuroses, in view of the fact that the onset of these illnesses may be observed in response to the most commonplace emotions ... [A]nalysis invariably shows that it is the sexual component of the traumatic experience ... which has produced the pathogenic result.

(Freud, 1906, p. 278)

Freud thus laid out a pathway via the Suitability Argument to establish that the apparently nonsexual content of symptoms is in fact caused by unconscious sexual memories or desires. Hans's symptoms are not directly Oedipal on their face; their contents are concerned with horses, not incestuous sex or patricide. However, Oedipal meanings can provide suitable determinants that explain logical and structural features of Hans's symptoms in a way that more immediate nonsexual events and memories cannot.

Freud is quite aware of the dangers of subjective judgment in claiming explanatory suitability, so he sets a high bar for accepting such hypotheses. The explanation is "indispensable"; without it, it is "impossible ... to elucidate the symptoms"; it makes the symptom "intelligible" and even "self-evident" so that it is "impossible to reject"; the linked features are "identical" or related by "a logical train of thought"; the symptom feature "bears no relation" to the precipitating cause and is "only to be accounted for" by the sexual memory, so that "clear as daylight" one becomes "absolutely certain" that only the proposed explanation "fills out the picture" and is "satisfactory in every respect"; thus, "one knows that one has solved the puzzle and that there is no alternative solution." Given the many ways that anything can resemble anything else, this demanding approach is essential if arbitrary associations are not to lead to unscientific interpretive excesses.

Collins (1980) reviews Freud's responses to the suggestion objection and also recognizes that Freud's primary solution is the uniqueness of a comprehensive explanation:

> The solution to the doubt is, essentially, in the self-evident rightness of the interpretive puzzle ... [T]he analyst may have misgivings about the objectivity of what he is perceiving which can only be resolved by the realization that "there is no alternative solution."
>
> (p. 433)

As Freud says in the Dora case commentary, "anyone who sets out to investigate the same region of phenomena and employs the same method will find himself compelled to take up the same position" (1905, p. 113).

The Suitability Argument as an Idiographic Singular Causal Explanatory Argument

In principle, there is nothing mysterious about the nature of Freud's Suitability Argument. Freud is engaged in an idiographic analysis of Hans's intentional system and specifically in the construction of singular causal explanations of symptom features. Because the point is to provide evidential support for the Oedipal theory, Freud cannot assume Oedipal meanings and simply apply them in what seems an illuminating manner, as he would in a clinical context in which the truth of the Oedipal theory was presupposed. As Karl Popper pointed out, with such a confirmation-seeking approach, almost any theory, whether true or false, can find ample confirmation. An evidential test is considerably more demanding. To support his theory, Freud must *hypothesize* (rather than assume) that Hans has Oedipal meanings and demonstrate the explanatory superiority of this hypothesis versus rival accounts. The epistemological ground rules in judging such claims are not explicit and precise, so there is inevitably a degree of subjectivity in judging the validity of Freud's claims. Their compelling nature and surplus explanatory power over what we would have without them will be crucial to judging their plausibility.

There has been much talk by philosophers of science (e.g., Grunbaum, 1984; Erwin, 1996) of the need for *experimental* testing of Freudian hypotheses as an alternative to traditional testing "on the couch" in the course of clinical intervention. Surely such testing is sorely needed. However, given contextual details and consensual background theories, idiographic N=1 singular causal analysis can sometimes establish the plausibility of a causal hypothesis without the need for an experimental test. As many philosophers have argued, we regularly use such singular forms of commonsense psychological causal inference in everyday life when explaining other people's actions in terms of their inferred motives (e.g., Hopkins, 1988; Lacewing, 2012; Nagel, 1994).

Frank Cioffi (1997; 1998; 2001) interprets Freud's arguments as being of this singular causal explanatory type. Although critical of Freud's specific claims, Cioffi argues that the type of argument deployed by Freud is perfectly legitimate in principle, and he offers many apt commonsense examples of valid arguments establishing singular causal relationships between meanings and actions or symptoms. To take one vivid example, in Charles Dickens's novel *Great Expectations*, the spinster Miss Havisham engages in a series of odd behaviors. She leaves a rotting wedding cake in her dining room undisturbed, she wears a tattered wedding dress and only one white shoe, all the clocks in her house are set at the fixed time of twenty minutes to nine, she is raising a pretty little girl to "break men's hearts," and so on. These details seem inexplicable in terms of any coherent response to Miss Havisham's current environment. Cioffi observes that "Readers of *Great Expectations* are initially perplexed" by Miss Havisham's behaviors, but

> When they learn that on her putative wedding day many years earlier at precisely twenty to nine, while preparing to embark for church, and while wearing her wedding dress and only one shoe, she was informed that the groom had absconded, their perplexity is assuaged.
>
> (Cioffi, 2001, pp. 161–162)

He agrees that "It seems perfectly reasonable to impute these to the fact that they were the circumstances which prevailed years earlier on her wedding day when she was abruptly informed that she had been jilted" (1997, p. 440). Cioffi's point—that we often do infer causal connections from isomorphisms of detail plus background theories of human nature, and that there are implicit if vague and difficult-to-state standards by which we judge whether such inferences are plausible—applies to Freud's explanatory suitability judgments as well.

In so imputing the cause of Miss Havisham's symptoms to the earlier events, we first judge that there is nothing in the immediate environment that adequately explains the puzzling details of Miss Havisham's behavior. We then take those otherwise inexplicable details of her current behavior and project a set of meanings and a traumatic impact into a past experience that, together with some background assumptions about how people sometimes react to great disappointments and losses, offers a manifestly plausible causal determinant and explanation of Miss Havisham's current behavior.

Such attempted Freudian explanations based on apparent similarities or other relationships between a purported unconscious cause and symptomatic effects are often called "thematic affinity" arguments because they rest on certain similarities or common themes or meanings that suggest a causal link. Just as similarity itself is an elusive property, thematic affinity and suitability are challenging to evaluate. Here are some of the many examples Freud presents in his early "seduction theory" work that are likely open to dispute.

Freud describes an eleven-year-old boy with an obsessional routine: before going to sleep, he had to tell his mother in detail all the day's experiences, the carpet in his bedroom must be perfectly clean without paper or rubbish, his bed had to be against the wall with three chairs placed in front of it and the pillows arranged in a particular manner, and he needed to kick both his legs a number of times and then lie on his side. Psychoanalysis revealed that years before, the boy had been sexually abused by a servant-girl, and Freud explains the symptoms as follows:

> The meaning of the ceremonial was easy to guess and was established point by point by psycho-analysis. The chairs were placed in front of the bed and the bed pushed against the wall in order that nobody else should be able to get at the bed; the pillows were arranged in a particular way so that they should be differently arranged from how they were on that evening; the movements with his legs were to kick away the person who was lying on him; sleeping on his side was because in the scene he had been lying on his back; his circumstantial confession to his mother was because, in obedience to a prohibition by his seductress, he had been silent to his mother about this and other sexual experiences; and, finally, the reason for his keeping his bedroom floor clean was that neglect to do so had been the chief reproach that he had so far had to hear from his mother.
>
> (1896/1962c, p. 172, n. 1)

Just as in the Miss Havisham example, the detailed characteristics of the symptoms and their structural relationship to the circumstances of the earlier sexual scene can be used to argue that this boy's neurotic symptoms are related to his earlier sexual abuse.

Similarly, one can imagine sufficient details being filled in to the following examples to reach a Miss Havisham-level of evidential persuasion, although in fact they are seduction-period non-Oedipal examples that Freud himself probably later partially rejected:

> Sometimes it is the accidental circumstances of these infantile sexual scenes which in later years acquire a determining power over the symptoms of the neurosis. Thus, in one of my cases the circumstance that the child was required to stimulate the genitals of a grown-up woman with his foot was enough to fixate his neurotic attention for years on to his legs and to their function, and finally to produce a hysterical paraplegia. In another case, a woman patient suffering from anxiety attacks which tended to come on at certain hours of the day could not be calmed unless a particular one of her many sisters stayed by her side all the time. Why this was so would have remained a riddle if analysis had not shown that the man who had committed the assaults on her used to enquire at every visit whether this sister, who he was afraid might interrupt him, was at home.
>
> (1896/1962d, p. 215)

Rather than proliferating examples or trying to explore the logic of such inferences in detail, I will summarily accept the broad moral of Cioffi's "Miss Havisham" argument, namely, that nonexperimental idiographic interpretive methodology can in some circumstances yield perfectly acceptable probatively relevant explanations implying a causal relationship, albeit provisional and defeasible explanations as always. The challenge, Cioffi argues, is for Freudian inferences to achieve the quality of interpretive evidence that persuasively establishes the postulated meanings and causal links. If Freud is to convince us of Oedipal causation of symptoms in the Hans case by an idiographic causal analysis, then it is something approaching the Miss Havisham type and quality of evidence that is required.

However, the most that a Suitability Argument can tell us is that there is prima facie causal relevance of a mental content to the structure of a symptom, not that the content is the ultimate initial cause of a symptom. To return once again to the Miss Havisham analogy, one can be quite confident in inferring that Miss Havisham's aborted wedding *played a causal role in determining the form of her later behavior*, but one is taking more of a chance in inferring in a global sense that the earlier wedding disaster *caused* the later behavior. There were surely many features of Miss Havisham's personality, background, and circumstances that caused the wedding disaster to give rise to her later behavior (Freud calls all these other causal influences preconditions or concurrent causes). Analogously, the fact that a dream's content is derived from and thus partially causally explained by a certain daytime event obviously does not imply that in some global sense the act of dreaming was caused by the daytime event, it only implies that the daytime experience shaped the content of the dream and to that extent was part of a larger causal process. Given that my interest here is in whether Freud provides an adequate argument for the existence of the Oedipus complex, the question of causal relevance is sufficient for my purposes, and the precise nature of the causal relationship and its relationship to other causes is secondary, so this issue can be set aside. Indeed, Freud attributes causal roles in producing symptoms to all of the traumas and associative pathways that form a "network of aetiologically significant impressions" leading to the symptom. Freud is of course most interested in the fact that "at the root of the formation of every symptom there were to be found traumatic experiences from early sexual life." However, this does not deprive the later events in the network of their causal relevance but locates its source: "the latter was seen to owe its aetiological significance to an associative or symbolic connection with the former, which had preceded it" (1923, p. 243).

It is worth emphasizing again that the criteria for the evaluation of such singular causal claims and the degree of evidential support provided by specific affinities remain vague. Certainly, sheer "thematic affinity," as similarity of content is sometimes called, is wholly inadequate for probative relevance. The fact that I saw a house yesterday and dreamt about a house last night does not imply a causal relationship, but if the house I saw had certain unique and salient features on its facade and those specific features were clearly reproduced in my dream, we would be much more likely to suspect some kind of causal relationship. Such inferences depend on background assumptions and theories and other such auxiliary knowledge that supports such an inference but may be difficult to specify. But, even if such singular causal claims are difficult to justify formally, some such claims are better than others.

The most striking point is that all commentators, including influential critics of psychoanalysis such as Edward Erwin and Adolf Grunbaum, agree that singular causal claims can have plausibility under some contextual circumstances. For example, Erwin presents a clinical example of a seven-year-old autistic child who "beat his head when not restrained" to the extent that "his head was covered with scar tissue and his ears were swollen and bleeding" and continued to do so when certain extinction therapeutic procedures were applied ("the boy was allowed to sit in bed with no restraints and with no attention given to his self-destructive behavior ... after seven days ... the boy had engaged in over ten thousand such acts"), but when the therapists tried a "punishment procedure ... in the form of one-second electric shocks," "in a brief time, the shock treatment dramatically decreased the unwanted behavior." In such circumstances, Erwin allows that it is legitimate to infer a causal connection between the shock procedure and the reduction in self-destructive behavior despite lack of experimental controls (Erwin, 1978, pp. 11–12). Grunbaum (1984) agrees, noting that in Erwin's example the background knowledge of the natural history of autistic disorders provides "the probative equivalent of experimental controls" (1984, p. 259). Grunbaum offers his own examples from physics, such as assuming that the impact of one billiard ball is what caused another ball to move. Nor do we need formal studies to draw causal conclusions when an entirely novel causal chain occurs, such as a watermelon hitting and breaking a window, because again our background knowledge allows us to generalize from analogous kinds of cases such as baseballs hitting windows.

Freud no doubt understood all of this at a gut scientific level. It seems reasonable and appropriately charitable to take Freud's attempted Oedipal explanations of Hans's symptoms not as flouting experimental scientific standards but as making singular causal explanatory claims that he thought were warranted by background knowledge. Cioffi was correct that the only reasonable way to evaluate Freud is by evaluating the singular causal explanations by which he supports his etiological claims.

Despite many attempts to formulate a set of rules by which to judge proposed single-causal-chain meaning-based explanations of the "Miss Havisham" variety in psychoanalysis, no such system has gained consensus recognition. The many attempts to formulate proposed criteria (e.g., Lynch, 2014; Michael, 2008; 2012; Rosen, 1969; Rubinstein, 1980; Sargent et al., 1968; Sherwood, 1969) have been persuasively argued to be of limited validity (Eagle, 1973; Fonagy, 1982; Kaplan, 1981; Spence, 1980). As the eminent psychoanalytic theoretician David Rapaport earlier lamented, "as things stand, there is no canon whereby valid interpretation can be distinguished from speculation" (Rapaport, 1960, as quoted in Macmillan, 1997, p. 577). Many intuitive desiderata have some prima facie validity, such as Sherwood's (1969) appropriateness, adequacy, and accuracy, or Michael's (2008; 2012) criteria of explaining features that are striking and unusual, explaining many symptom details, and explaining features directly with a minimal number of postulated links in the associative chain from cause to symptomatic details (the latter is the prime advantage of a child analysis). But no formal criteria have evolved from such lists. Despite lack of formal criteria, I accept that Cioffi is correct that we are able to judge better and worse potential single case explanations with some validity. I shall be exercising such judgment in confronting Freud's explanations based on the details of the Hans case.

How the Suitability Argument Evades the Suggestion Objection, and Other Advantages

The Suitability Argument, if it can be executed in a persuasive way, has many potential advantages. First, in claiming that Hans's phobic symptoms require Oedipal meanings for the adequate explanations of their features, the Suitability Argument makes a bold and novel prediction. If confirmed, this adds probative weight to Freud's theory.

Moreover, the Oedipal prediction clashes with the fright theory's prediction that the phobic symptoms are adequately explained by features of the triggering situation, thus posing a challenge to the fright theory. Note that the thesis that Freud is rejecting is *not* quite the thesis that Hans's phobia can be understood entirely in terms of the horse accident, which is a thesis that all parties to the Hans dispute reject. We saw in Chapter 5 that Wolpe and Rachman (1960) argue that a variety of horse-related events and anxieties—including Hans's anxieties when as a young child he witnessed the merry-go-round horses being whipped, the warning he received the summer before that horses can bite, and the Fritzl injury while playing at horses—as well as Hans's personality are factors that prepared Hans for, and were etiologically relevant to, the triggering of the phobia by the horse accident. However, other than personological variables (which Freud also embraces as Hans's sexual "constitution"), all of these additional explanatory meanings involve horse-related content. In contrast, Freud argues that the explanatory meanings go beyond the narrow orbit of horse-related incidents to encompass Oedipal meanings. Thus, the Suitability Argument for the Oedipal theory is simultaneously an argument against the fright theory. Freud's argument is in effect an instance of eliminative inductivism in which Freud argues that the evidence favors the Oedipal theory over the horse-accident theory.

The Suitability Argument also manages to evade the suggestion objection. This is because, first, as in the repression argument analyzed in Chapter 8, the data to be explained—namely, the detailed nature of Hans's phobic symptoms—are known independently of any plausible suggestive process. This is obviously true of the symptoms that constituted the original pre-analysis reports by Hans of his anxiety. It is also plausibly true of symptoms that were reported by Hans as the analysis progressed, when he attempted to explain his behavior in terms of his fears. Freud makes this assumption explicit, perhaps to preemptively fend off a potential suggestion-objection challenge to the symptom reports:

> [A]lthough during the treatment the phobia appeared to develop further and to extend over new objects and to lay down new conditions, his father ... had sufficient penetration to see that it was merely a question of the emergence of material that was already in existence, and not of fresh productions for which the treatment might be held responsible.
>
> (pp. 137–138)

Freud seems to be on solid ground here. Hans's explanations of his symptoms are plausible and they are later elaborated in ways that suggest veridicality in accordance with Freud's criterion of the production of fresh material. A close reading does not reveal any evidence of suggestion from Hans's father that might have shaped Hans's elaborations of his symptoms. Indeed, Hans's father as well as Freud were quite surprised by some of these symptom reports. Regarding Hans's two central fears of horses biting and falling down, the horse biting fear was reported prior to the analysis, and the falling down fear emerged later but prior to any hint of suggestion by Hans's father. Hans spontaneously brings up this fear ("I asked at the time why he was so much afraid, and he replied: 'I'm afraid the horses will fall down when the cart turns'" [p. 46]), and Hans soon offers additional associations that are contrary to his father's initial thoughts. Regarding the important detail that Hans is more afraid of horses with blinkers and something black around their mouths, we are simply told that Freud became aware of this detail during his one interview with Hans and his father, and both Freud and Hans's father seem quite puzzled by this detail's origin.

So, Freud can be granted the legitimacy of Hans's symptom reports as a basis for evaluation of the Oedipal theory. This allows the Suitability Argument to be based on the presumption that the symptom data is not contaminated by suggestion.

Second, the suitability test concerns the logic and plausibility of proposed explanations and does not depend on explicit avowals by Hans of his repressed contents. Indeed, Freud is explicit that unlike the conscious phallic sexuality including masturbation manifested by Hans, the Oedipal meanings that are at "the very heart of ... our understanding" of Hans's symptoms remain unconscious:

> We have seen how our little patient was overtaken by a great wave of repression and that it caught precisely those of his sexual components that were dominant. He gave up masturbation ... But these were not the components which were stirred up by the precipitating cause of the illness (his seeing the horse fall down) or which provided the material for the

symptoms, that is, the content of the phobia ... We shall probably come to understand the case more deeply if we turn to those other components which do fulfil the two conditions that have just been mentioned. These other components were tendencies in Hans which had already been suppressed and which, so far as we can tell, had never been able to find uninhibited expression: hostile and jealous feelings towards his father, and sadistic impulses (premonitions, as it were, of copulation) towards his mother.

(p. 138)

It is true that these Oedipal themes are suggested to Hans by his father and Freud. However, the content of Hans's hypothesized Oedipus complex is firmly and explicitly established beforehand as a matter of theory. The suitability question at issue is not whether Hans can avow Oedipal meanings but whether Oedipal meanings explain his symptoms. The proposed explanatory relationship between Oedipal meanings and the details of Hans's symptoms transcends any avowals by Hans that might be obtained through suggestion.

A further potential advantage of Freud's suitability methodology is that in explaining detailed features of symptoms it promises to be more explanatorily precise than other accounts. This is why the next chapter's discussion of Freud's argument gets to a level of detail regarding the nuances of Hans's fear that fright theorists and suggestion objectors do not match. Philosophers of science have emphasized that greater precision of prediction is often itself a progressive step in scientific development. Paul Meehl (1990) observes that working scientists understand that "a theory predicting observations 'in detail,' 'very specifically,' or 'very precisely' gains plausibility ... That is just scientific common sense" (p. 110). The question is whether Freud can make good on his promise to explain otherwise ignored and inexplicable detailed features of Hans's symptoms.

Does Freud Beg the Question of Explanatory Force in the Hans Case?

I have been focusing exclusively on Freud's Suitability Argument, ignoring his mention of traumatic force as a criterion for adequate explanation. This is because it seems evident that this criterion is met by the horse accident. However, a comment on this seemingly innocuous assumption is necessary because, surprisingly, Freud asserts that the horse accident did not have the requisite traumatic force: "In itself the impression of the accident which he happened to witness carried no 'traumatic force'" (p. 136).

Taken at face value, Freud's assertion makes no sense. Freud himself reports that Hans was "terrified" by the horse accident (p. 125). Erwin (2002) thus claims that Freud is begging the question of the phobia's cause:

What is the empirical basis for Freud's assumption that witnessing the accident, which the child described as giving him "such a fright," lacked traumatic force—which is just another way of saying that it could not have caused the phobia? He does not say.

(p. 327)

If one takes Freud's assertion literally and in isolation, one must agree with Erwin. If an adult being in a train accident has sufficient traumatic force to cause hysterical symptoms, then it seems that witnessing a horse accident might have sufficient force in a four-year-old child. Lack of traumatic force simply won't work as a defense against the fright theory.

However, a more charitable interpretation than his blatantly begging the question is that Freud's assertion that the horse accident "in itself" lacked traumatic force is simply Freud's way of stating his conclusion that the horse accident derives its etiological force largely from prior events, associations, and unconscious meanings. This charitable interpretation is suggested by the fact that immediately after Freud denies that the horse accident has traumatic force "in itself," he goes on to outline his alternative explanation of the many causes of the accident's phobia-triggering power:

In itself the impression of the accident which he happened to witness carried no "traumatic force"; it acquired its great effectiveness only from the fact that horses had formerly been of importance to him as objects of his predilection and interest, from the fact that he associated the event in his mind with an earlier event at Gmunden which had more claim to be regarded as traumatic, namely, with Fritz's falling down while he was playing at horses, and lastly from the fact that there was an easy path of association from Fritzl to his father. Indeed, even these connections would probably not have been sufficient if it had not been that, thanks to the pliability and ambiguity of associative chains, the same event showed itself capable of stirring the second of the complexes that lurked in Hans's unconscious, the complex of his pregnant mother's confinement.

(pp. 136–137)

This construal is consistent with Freud's assertion a few years earlier that "A single pathogenic influence is scarcely ever sufficient; in the large majority of cases a number of aetiological factors are required, which support one another and must therefore not be regarded as being in mutual opposition" (1906, p. 279). I conclude that Freud's assertion that the horse accident lacks traumatic force is best considered an indirect suitability claim, that Freud's evidence reveals that the force of the accident in causing Hans's symptoms was largely derived from or dependent on other factors.

Some Caveats Regarding Freud's Suitability Argument

The Suitability Argument has many potential pitfalls beyond those mentioned above. In this section, I further explore the argument's limitations, offer some caveats about such inferences, and explain why in the end the problems are not insuperable obstacles to the way I will evaluate Freud's application of the argument in the Hans case. In general, I will tend to be charitable to Freud in order to make my evaluation as meaningful as possible.

A major concern in using the Suitability Argument as an end run around the suggestion objection is the danger of ad hoc suitability constructions— that is, the danger that the analyst can simply associate from symptoms to various hypothetical sexual contents (or other theoretically motivated unconscious contents) in a way that produces spurious thematic affinity, and then on the basis of that constructed affinity claim a likely causal relationship. For example, if fat horses and horses pulling loaded carts trigger Hans's fear, Freud can simply associate to Hans's mother when she was pregnant and judge that as suitable evidence of an Oedipal determinant, despite Hans's quite cogent and elaborated explanation that his fear is based on the increased danger of those types of horses falling down. In standard examples of singular causal explanations such as the Miss Havisham example, both terms in the explanation—the proposed cause, and the proposed effect—are known to have occurred, and the question is whether a causal relationship justifiably can be attributed to them. In Hans's case, the symptom features are established, but the existence of the Oedipus complex is precisely what is at issue. With only one term of the possible relationship known, there seems more opportunity for ad hoc hypotheses.

The minimization of such abuses of suitability is one reason that Freud imposes such high demands on the resulting explanation. The explained symptom features, he suggests, should be otherwise inexplicable and cannot be adequately explained by any rival simpler explanation (e.g., the fright theory). Thus, adding an Oedipal gloss to an adequate explanation that does not predict or explain any new features does not satisfy the requirements for the Suitability Argument as Freud formulates it. The explanation must be plausible to a degree approaching "Miss Havisham" levels, vanquishing available rival hypotheses and having the compelling quality of a unique solution to a puzzle.

As to simply constructing suitable ad hoc scenarios, fortunately in the Hans case the danger of ad hoc backwards association from the patient's symptoms to some proposed unconscious memories constructed to have thematic affinity with the symptoms is minimized by the fact that the case is formulated as a test of a preexisting Oedipal theory. Thus, the potential explanatory unconscious meanings are largely specified beforehand. As in the Miss Havisham example, both terms being evaluated for a causal relationship are known and cannot be manufactured. Consequently, there is no "free rein" for backward association; the terminus of the explanations must lie in known Oedipal meanings.

A further caveat concerns Freud's case studies other than the Hans case history. We saw in Chapter 3 that Freud intends the Hans case to independently verify the credibility of his Oedipal interpretations of his adult cases. However, critics have cast doubt, often quite persuasively, on the plausibility of many of Freud's interpretations in his adult cases. In evaluating the Suitability Argument in the Hans case, I make no assumptions about the legitimacy of Freud's application of the criterion to his many other cases. The focus here is strictly on whether Freud succeeds in conferring some plausibility on his Oedipal theory based on the Hans case.

Of course, even if Freud put forward the Suitability Argument effectively in the Hans case, that does not mean that he applied it in a convincing way in his adult cases. Collins dismisses what amounts to the Suitability Argument's uniqueness requirement by noting the obviously questionable nature of many of Freud's extrapolations:

> A sceptical mind would not have been convinced by the claim of evidence that sometimes led to the construction; as, for example, the "Wolf Man" accepted interpretations which depended on the unlikely carelessness of his parents copulating three times on the same occasion under the interested eye of their infant son, the symbolization two years later of what he had seen into a dream, and the accurate recollection of that dream after more than twenty years.
>
> (p. 433)

Macmillan (1997) seconds the point: "As to the likely truth of the constructions themselves, there is a good deal of psychoanalytic opinion against even the ones Freud suggested to his patients being veridical" (p. 580). Whatever Freud's methodological sins in his adult cases, we saw in Chapter 3 that he relied on the "more direct" evidence of the Hans case to vindicate his Oedipal-theoretic conclusions from the suggestion objection. Any weaknesses of his interpretation of his adult cases do not necessitate that the same problems afflict the simpler analysis of a child, and I shall judge the Hans case independently.

These comments regarding Freud's other cases pose a further question: If Freud genuinely believes that his Suitability Argument yields a virtually unique solution to the etiological puzzle in each case and thus each psychoanalytic investigation inevitably converges on the truth, then why is the Hans case uniquely important or even needed to support the results of the other cases? The answer is that Freud understands that the suggestion objection's challenge is deeper than he sometimes portrays it. Freud does appear to believe that within a certain theoretical and clinical context, suitability yields a locally unique or distinctively most plausible explanation of symptom features. Given an overall puzzle, the last piece must have a particular shape, and only one particular piece will fit. Yet, Freud surely understood the limitations of suitability in ruling out alternative explanations from different perspectives. The problem lies with the prior assumptions about the type of explanation he seeks.

Local maxima within a certain context are not always global maxima across contexts. There are different ways of framing the symptomatic puzzle that would have different perfectly or optimally fitting explanations of a given symptom. The formation of competing schools of psychoanalysis made it painfully obvious to Freud that the theoretical frame for psychoanalytic puzzle-solving might instead consist of Adlerian or Jungian puzzles that might yield equally tight overall explanatory schemas with almost-unique optimal explanations of a patient's symptoms within that overall schema. As Lacewing (2012) observes, to show that a proposed psychoanalytic explanation is better than alternatives, the comparison to alternative theoretical frameworks must include both alternative psychoanalytic theories (e.g., Jungian theory) and nonpsychoanalytic theories (e.g., the fright theory).

This is a point that Freud acknowledged:

> Such a certain conviction of the existence and importance of infantile sexuality can, however, only be obtained by the method of analysis, by pursuing the symptoms ... to their ultimate sources, the discovery of which then explains whatever is explicable in them ... I can understand that one would arrive at different results if, as C. G. Jung has recently done, one first forms a theoretical conception of the nature of the sexual instinct and then seeks to explain the life of children on that basis.
>
> (1914, p. 18–19)

The analyst Judd Marmor famously offered the following skeptical observation of the ability of psychoanalysis to validate divergent frameworks:

> [E]ach theory tends to be self-validating. Freudians elicit material about the Oedipus Complex and castration anxiety, Jungians about archetypes, Rankians about separation anxiety, Adlerians about masculine strivings and feelings of inferiority, Horneyites about idealized images, Sullivanians about disturbed interpersonal relationships, etc.
>
> (Marmor, 1962, p. 289)

Freud's anticipatory interpretations communicate the nature of the expected explanation to the patient, imposing on the patient an overarching framework and defining the theoretical domain in which the explanation will take place, namely, his Oedipal theory. Because Freud defines the nature of the overall puzzle into which the pieces must fit, and suggestion could yield the patient's agreement with the uniquely best fit to that preset framework, that leaves a glaring gap in his overall argument for the Oedipal theory and against the suggestion objection. Thus, there must be some external check on the framework for formulating the suitably determining explanations. The Hans case is that external "more direct" check.

Conclusion: A Concession to Freud

Before I turn in the next chapter to an evaluation of Freud's attempted defense of his Oedipal explanation of Hans's phobia, I want to state a concession in my approach. We saw that Freud's "puzzle" metaphor is problematic because the analyst, by assuming a background theory, not only confronts the missing piece of the explanatory puzzle but also constructs the overall puzzle into which it must fit. I cannot enter here into a global comparison of various frameworks for explaining neurotic symptoms, which would take me far afield from this book's focus. Instead, I adopt the charitable strategy of evaluating whether Freud manages to construct an explanatory account within his framework that is distinctively more plausible and illuminating than readily available non-Oedipal rival accounts such as the fright theory and sheer common sense.

So, I will require only that Freud's explanations satisfy the criteria implied by his own discussions. The postulated explanatory unconscious mental content must offer suitability as a determinant of the feature of the symptom to be explained. It must have local uniqueness and add distinctive explanatory power over and above what is available from other available views such as common sense and the fright theory. In the local theoretical-explanatory context, the proposed content must be a more or less unique missing piece essential to solving the puzzle of the target symptom's nature with regard to otherwise inexplicable features and not a superfluous addition to already understandable features, thus necessary for optimizing explanatory adequacy. If these vague but nevertheless demanding criteria are met, the explanatory power added by Oedipal theory does not prove the Oedipal explanation is true but it does show that the Oedipal background theory is at least worthy of further scientific consideration.

References

Breuer, J. (1895). Theoretical. In J. Breuer & S. Freud, Studies on hysteria. *SE* 2, 183–251.

Breuer, J., & Freud, S. (1893). On the psychical mechanism of hysterical phenomena: Preliminary communication. *SE* 2, 1–17.

Breuer, J., & Freud, S. (1895). Studies on hysteria. *SE* 2.

Cioffi, F. (1997). Critical notice: Freud, philosophical and empirical issues. *Philosophy*, 72(281), 435–448.

Cioffi, F. (1998). *Freud and the question of pseudoscience.* Chicago, IL: Open Court.

Cioffi, F. (2001). The rationale for psychoanalytic interpretation. *Psychological Inquiry*, 12(3), 161–166.

Eagle, M. N. (1973). Sherwood on the logic of explanation in psychoanalysis. *Psychoanalysis and Contemporary Science*, 2, 331–337.

Erwin, E. (1978). *Behavior therapy.* New York: Cambridge University Press.

Erwin, E. (1996). *A final accounting: Philosophical and empirical issues in Freudian psychology.* Cambridge, MA: MIT Press.

Erwin, E. (2002). Little Hans. In E. Erwin (Ed.), *The Freud encyclopedia* (pp. 326–328). New York: Routledge.

Fonagy, P. (1982). The integration of psychoanalysis and experimental science: A review. *International Review of Psycho-Analysis*, 9, 125–145.

Freud, S. (1895). The psychotherapy of hysteria. *SE* 2, 253–305.

Freud, S. (1896a). Heredity and the aetiology of the neuroses. *SE* 3, 141–156.

Freud, S. (1896b). Further remarks on the neuro-psychoses of defence. *SE* 3, 157–185.

Freud, S. (1896c). The aetiology of hysteria. *SE* 3, 187–221.

Freud, S. (1898). Sexuality in the aetiology of the neuroses. *SE* 3, 259–285.

Freud, S. (1905). Fragment of an analysis of a case of hysteria. *SE* 7, 1–122.

Freud, S. (1906). My views on the part played by sexuality in the aetiology of the neuroses. *SE* 7, 269–279.

Freud, S. (1908). On the sexual theories of children. *SE* 9, 205–226.

Freud, S. (1909). Analysis of a phobia in a five-year-old boy. *SE* 10, 1–150.

Freud, S. (1910). Five lectures on psycho-analysis. *SE* 11, 1–56.

Freud, S. (1914). On the history of the psycho-analytic movement. *SE* 14, 6–66.

Freud, S. (1917). Introductory lectures on psycho-analysis, part 3. *SE* 16.

Freud, S. (1923). Remarks on the theory and practice of dream interpretation. *SE* 19, 107–122.

Grunbaum, A. (1984). *The foundations of psychoanalysis: A philosophical critique.* Berkeley, CA: University of California Press.

Hopkins, J. (1988). Epistemology and depth psychology: Critical notes on *The Foundations of Psychoanalysis*. In P. Clark & C. Wright (Eds.), *Mind, psychoanalysis, and science* (pp. 33–60). New York: Blackwell.

Kaplan. A. H. (1981). From discovery to validation: A basic challenge to psychoanalysis. *Journal of the American Psychoanalytic Association*, 29, 3–26.

Lacewing, M. (2012). Inferring motives in psychology and psychoanalysis. *Philosophy, Psychiatry, & Psychology*, 19(3), 197–212.

Lynch, K. (2014). The vagaries of psychoanalytic interpretation: An investigation into the causes of the consensus problem in psychoanalysis. *Philosophia*, 42, 779–799.

Macmillan, M. (1997). *Freud evaluated: The completed arc.* Cambridge, MA: MIT Press.

Marmor, J. (1962). Psychoanalytic therapy as an educational process. In J. Masserman (Ed.), *Psychoanalytic education* (pp. 286–299). New York: Grune and Stratton.

Meehl, P. E. (1990). Appraising and amending theories: The strategy of Lakatosian defense and two principles that warrant it. *Psychological Inquiry*, 1(2), 108–141.

Michael, M. (2008). On the validity of Freud's dream interpretations. *Studies in History and Philosophy of Biological and Biomedical Sciences*, 39, 52–64.

Michael, M. (2012). The puzzle of dreams. In M. A. Holowchak (Ed.), *Radical claims in Freudian psychoanalysis* (pp. 53–81). Lanham, MD: Jason Aronson.

Nagel, T. (1994). Freud's permanent revolution. *The New York Review of Books*, May 12, 1994, pp. 1–17.

Rapaport, D. (1960). *The structure of psychoanalytic theory: A systematizing attempt.* New York: International Universities Press.

Rosen, V. H. (1969). Sign phenomena and their relationship to unconscious meaning. *International Journal of Psycho-Analysis*, 50, 197–207.

Rubinstein, B. B. (1980). The problem of confirmation in clinical psychoanalysis. *Journal of the American Psychoanalytic Association*, 28, 397–417.

Sargent, H. D., Horwitz, L., Wallerstein, R. S. and Sampson, P. S. (1968). Prediction in psychotherapy research: A method for the transformation of clinical judgements into testable hypotheses. *Psychological Issues*, 6, Monograph 2.

Sherwood, M. (1969). *The logic of explanation in psychoanalysis.* New York: Academic Press.

Spence, D. P. (1980). *Narrative truth and historical truth: Meaning and interpretation in psychoanalysis.* New York: Norton.

Wolpe, J., & Rachman, S. (1960). Psychoanalytic "evidence": A critique based on Freud's case of Little Hans. *Journal of Nervous and Mental Disease*, 131(2), 135–148.

Chapter 10

"Acquaintance at Close Quarters"

Evaluating Freud's Suitability Argument for
the Oedipal Theory of Hans's Phobia

Having considered the nature of Freud's "suitability" method of argument in the last chapter, I now turn to an evaluation of Freud's attempt to use that argument to show that Oedipal meanings must lie behind Hans's horse phobia. The primary rival hypothesis is that Hans's phobia was caused by his witnessing a horse accident immediately before the phobia began (see Chapter 5).

Given that Hans's witnessing of the horse accident clearly triggered the phobia, Freud's critics have argued that the phobia was caused simply by the extreme fright that Hans suffered from the horse accident, plus some earlier horse-related preparatory events that emerge in the case history. Freud considers the horse accident to be merely the precipitant of the phobia but not its specific cause, as we saw in the arguments analyzed in Chapters 6 and 7. Relying on his suitability criterion, Freud argues that the detailed characteristics of the feared features comprising Hans's horse phobia's symptoms can't be adequately explained by the horse accident alone but rather reveal that the phobia must have its ultimate source as well in Oedipal meanings. His challenge is to show how one gets from the theoretically postulated Oedipus complex to specific otherwise unexplained features of Han's horse phobia in a way that is explanatorily compelling and adequate.

The Details of Hans's Symptoms as the Target of Freud's Suitability Argument

The occurrence of the horse accident as the event that triggered the phobia emerged only late in Hans's analysis, in the following revealing interchange between Hans and his father on April 5:

I: "Which horses are you actually most afraid of?"
HANS: "All of them."
I: "That's not true."…
HANS: "And I'm most afraid of furniture-vans, too."
I: "Why?"

DOI: 10.4324/9781003272472-10

HANS: "I think when furniture-horses are dragging a heavy van they'll fall down."

I: "So you're not afraid with a small cart?"

HANS: "No. I'm not afraid with a small cart or with a post-office van. I'm most afraid too when a bus comes along."

I: "Why? Because it's so big?"

HANS: "No. Because once a horse in a bus fell down."

I: "When?"

HANS: "Once when I went out with Mummy in spite of my 'nonsense', when I bought the waistcoat."

(This was subsequently confirmed by his mother.)

I: "What did you think when the horse fell down?"

HANS: "Now it'll always be like this. All horses in buses'll fall down."

I: "In all buses?"

HANS: "Yes. And in furniture-vans too. Not often in furniture-vans."

I: "You had your nonsense already at that time?"

HANS: "No. I only got it then. When the horse in the bus fell down, it gave me such a fright, really! That was when I got the nonsense."

I: "But the nonsense was that you thought a horse would bite you. And now you say you were afraid a horse would fall down."

HANS: "Fall down and bite."

I: "Why did it give you such a fright?"

HANS: "Because the horse went like this with its feet." (He lay down on the ground and showed me how it kicked about.) "It gave me a fright because it made a row with its feet..."

(pp. 48–51)

The accuracy of Hans's description of these events was confirmed by his mother, who was with Hans at the time.

In his running commentary on the case record, immediately following the horse-accident revelation, Freud acknowledges the horse accident as a precipitating trigger of Hans's phobia:

> We must specially acknowledge one most important result of the boy's examination by his father. We have learned the immediate precipitating cause after which the phobia broke out. This was when the boy saw a big heavy horse fall down.

(1909, p. 51)

However, Freud suggests that greater clarity about the causation of Hans's phobia may be gained from an examination of the detailed characteristics of the phobia's many "diffuse" objects that Hans reveals here and elsewhere in the analysis:

> [I]t does no harm to make acquaintance at close quarters with a phobia of this sort ... For in this way we get to see how diffuse it really is. It extends on to horses and on to carts, on to the fact that horses fall down and that they bite, on to horses of a particular character, on to carts that are heavily loaded. I will reveal at once that all these characteristics were derived from the circumstance that the anxiety originally had no reference at all to horses but was transposed on to them secondarily and had now become fixed upon those elements of the horse-complex which showed themselves well adapted for certain transferences.
>
> (1909, p. 51)

In this passage, Freud sets up his intended inquiry and argument. Citing the variety of feared objects mentioned by Hans, Freud claims that the detailed objects of Hans's phobia—that is, the specific features of horses that Hans is afraid of—are "diffuse." This suggests that they are not just a focal "fear of horses," as one might imagine they would be if the fear was triggered simply by the horse accident. Rather, they are puzzlingly divergent in nature and not tightly linked together by anything apparent in the nature of the horse accident other than the happenstance that they are concerned with horses. The diffuseness suggests the need for further explanatory illumination beyond that possessed by the horse accident, and here Freud offers an explanatory promissory note. He obligingly reveals "at once"—implying that this claim is evidentially premature but will later be demonstrated—that the explanation for the diffuseness of the phobia's objects is that they were derived from some other, original, and primary source of anxieties that was not horse-related and "transposed" onto horses. He goes so far as to claim that some of the phobia's characteristics cannot find an adequate rationale in relation to actual horse-related incidents alone ("all these characteristics ... *originally had no reference at all to horses*" [emphasis added]). These primary anxieties, Freud avers, were then transferred onto aspects of horses via whatever associative pathways allowed easiest transfer of such feelings ("the anxiety ... had now become fixed upon those elements of the horse-complex which showed themselves well adapted for certain transferences"), yielding "secondarily" the horse-related objects of anxiety. This transposition of divergent material onto horses accounts for the puzzling diffuseness of the phobia's details, Freud suggests.

In his Discussion section, Freud reiterates his claim that the diffuseness of the detailed characteristics of the phobia can be adequately explained only if one postulates that the details are secondary to concerns that go beyond the dangers of horses:

> [I]t is most instructive to plunge in this way into the details of a phobia, and thus arrive at a conviction of the secondary nature of the relation between the anxiety and its objects. It is this that accounts for phobias being at once so curiously diffuse and so strictly conditioned. It is evident that the material for the particular disguises which Hans's fear adopted was collected from the impressions to which he was all day long exposed owing to the Head Customs House being situated on the opposite side of the street.
>
>   It was at this stage of the analysis that he recalled the event, insignificant in itself, which immediately preceded the outbreak of the illness and may no doubt be regarded as the precipitating cause of its outbreak. He went for a walk with his mother, and saw a bus-horse fall down and kick about with its feet. This made a great impression on him. He was terrified, and thought the horse was dead; and from that time on he thought that all horses would fall down ... nor was it yet clear through what chain of associations the horse's falling down had stirred up his unconscious wishes.
>
>   (p. 125)

Freud acknowledges that it is "evident" that the surface details of Hans's phobia are borrowed from immediate horse-related events and circumstances, such as the horse accident and the features of the horses at the depot across the road from Hans's house. However, the details of his fears, Freud argues, show that the symptoms extend in a diffuse way beyond anything linking them to the horse accident. Thus, the accident must be only a "secondary" cause that hides some deeper primary cause that explains the phobia's details. He insists that if one is willing to "plunge ... into the details" of the phobia's objects, one will "arrive at a conviction" that the phobic anxiety cannot be due to horse-related incidents alone. The phobia will betray its origins by the fact that otherwise inexplicable and anomalous features of the phobia's contents will be optimally explainable by some further cause, the nature of which is preserved in the associative chains leading to symptom formation.

   In sum, while acknowledging that the contents of the fears comprising Hans's phobia were accumulated from various horse stimuli, Freud will argue that the specific details of Hans's horse-related fears are determined by their relation not to horse dangers but to further Oedipal concerns that were shifted onto horses by convenient associative pathways. Thus, a fully satisfactory explanation of the phobia's details will require not only the understandable fears arising from the horse accident but also Oedipal meanings. As indicated in Chapter 9's review, this type of argument has several potential advantages in the context of the Hans case. To the extent that symptoms emerge prior to or independent of the analysis, the argument evades the ever-threatening suggestion objection. With the contours of the hypothesized Oedipus complex specified theoretically beforehand, the possibility of covert ad hoc creation of seemingly suitable meanings is minimized. Rather than having the accumulation over years in an adult of many intermediary associations between proposed unconscious content and symptom details, in Hans we can expect a more direct associative pathway. In claiming that the details of some symptoms cannot be adequately explained by the features of the horse accident and other horse-related incidents but must be understood in Oedipal terms, the Suitability Argument makes predictions that cannot be matched by the rival fright account that claims the horse accident alone explains Hans's symptoms. As well, the claimed greater precision of the proposed Oedipal explanations in illuminating details of Hans's symptoms left unexplained by the fright theory challenges the fright theory for explanatory superiority. We saw in Chapter 9 that although a Suitability Argument does not offer controlled experimental data, if the evidence is of the right kind, it can command assent as a valid or at least plausible singular causal inference. Finally, the argument does not require reference to anything like Grunbaum's (1984) "Tally Argument" analysis of Freud's response to the suggestion objection, according to which validity of an etiological interpretation depends on the ability of the interpretation to cure symptoms. Indeed, symptom cure has no role in the premises of an explanatory Suitability Argument, which concern only unexplained symptom content.

The proposed Oedipal meanings of symptom features would be expected to offer compelling surplus explanatory power in understanding otherwise inexplicable details of the phobia's symptoms. In the remainder of this chapter, applying Freud's own demanding requirements detailed in Chapter 9 for a successful explanatory Suitability Argument, I examine and evaluate the most important of Freud's arguments regarding the Oedipal origin of the details of Hans's phobia.

Are the Greatly Varied Contents of Hans's Phobic Fear Evidence that the Explanation Must Go Beyond the Horse Accident to Encompass Oedipal Meanings?

In his initial comment on the detailed objects of Hans's phobia, Freud declares that its objects are "diffuse" and that this diffuseness can only be explained by the fact that the phobia's details are determined by considerations having nothing to do with horses or the horse accident. In that passage, to support the "diffuseness" claim, Freud observes that the phobia "extends on to horses and on to carts, on to the fact that horses fall down and that they bite, on to horses of a particular character, on to carts that are heavily loaded" (p. 51).

The phenomena Freud mentions are indeed all aspects of Hans's spontaneously declared fears (with the possible exception of certain readings of the vague characterization "horses of a particular character"), so Freud is on solid ground here in his reading of the case data. However, this initial list fails to support Freud's point that Hans's fears are diffuse in a way that implies that their explanations must go beyond the horse-accident explanatory sphere. Instead, all of the mentioned fears are easily explainable in terms of the horse-accident fright.

Regarding horses, Freud observes that Hans is afraid "that horses fall down and that they bite." The fear that "horses fall down" is of course understandable as a result of Hans's witnessing of the horse accident in which a horse did actually fall down. A large horse falling down is intrinsically frightening.

Freud notes that the phobia extends not only to horses falling down, which actually occurred in the horse accident, but also to horses biting, which did not occur. However, Hans had been warned the summer before at Gmunden that if he tried to pet a horse, it might bite him. One need not cite Oedipal meanings to explain why a child who had been instructed that even a slightly disturbed horse might bite would be afraid that an extraordinarily agitated and angry horse—one that had just fallen down and was whinnying loudly and kicking about wildly—might bite. Nor is there any salient detail or anomaly of the biting fear that remains inexplicable without adding the Oedipal story to the account of the horse-accident and earlier warning.

As to the "diffuse" nature of the two horse fears, Hans himself, when challenged by his father on this ground ("But … you thought a horse would bite you. And now you say you were afraid a horse would fall down"), explains that he means the same horse will "Fall down and bite." Freud comments: "Hans was right, however improbable this collocation may sound. The train of thought, we shall see, was that the horse (his father) would bite him because of his wish that it (his father) should fall down" (n. 2, p. 50). Yet, the collocation of falling down and biting is not at all improbable given the warnings Hans has received, and can be adequately explained without recourse to the Oedipal interpretation, which adds nothing to the explanation of the fears' nature. For Hans, the inherently frightening nature of these core features of his phobia seems palpable and not in need of additional explanation.

Regarding Freud's assertion that Hans is afraid of carts, it is incorrect to say that Hans is afraid of carts *per se* (e.g., when they are sitting unused), independently of horses that are pulling them. For example, Hans says "I'm not afraid with a small cart or with a post-office van." He is afraid only of horse-drawn carts and, crucially, only of those that have properties that remind him of the horse accident or suggest that the horse pulling the cart might fall down because of the weight, speed, or other properties of the cart. Humans are vigilant creatures, and so any associated features that may portend or make more likely the occurrence of the primarily feared event of a horse falling down will also expectably be feared by Hans. For example, he says, "I'm most afraid too when a bus comes along," and when asked if that is because the bus itself is so big, he says, "No. Because once a horse in a bus fell down." Freud observes that Hans is especially afraid of "carts that are heavily loaded" with much weight, as if that is an independent, "diffuse" fear, but in fact Hans explains that he is afraid only because such heavily loaded carts are likely to cause a horse to fall down. So,

Hans's fears of horses and carts mentioned by Freud in the above passage duplicate the specific situation in the horse accident and need no further reference to Oedipal issues for their explanation. Nor does the fear of horses pulling loaded carts require for its explanation a reference to Hans's feelings about his mother's pregnancy, as Freud suggests. Hans's fear of a horse's falling down due to the weight of the cart it is pulling directly links the fear to specific and salient features of the horse accident (the horse that fell down was pulling a bus) without any additional necessary explanatory value provided by Oedipal meanings.

In another passage that might appear to support Freud's claim of diffuse fears about carts, Hans's father elaborates the content of Hans's fear as they watch cart-pulling horses coming and going at a customs station across the street. The passage reveals Hans's fear of horse-drawn carts driving into and out of a courtyard, starting to move, or moving quickly:

> I have noticed for some days that Hans is specially frightened when carts drive into or out of the yard, a process which involves their taking a corner. He is equally frightened when carts standing at the loading dock start moving in order to drive off … He is also more frightened when a vehicle drives past quickly than when the horses trot up slowly.
>
> (pp. 46–47)

Yet, when Hans explains to his father the source of his fear of these various horse carts' comings and goings, it comes down to his fear that a horse might fall down: "I asked at the time why he was so much afraid, and he replied: 'I'm *afraid the horses will fall down when the cart turns*'" (1909, p. 46). Fear when horses come into or exit a yard or turn a corner initially might seem mysterious and "diffuse." However, as Hans cogently explains, horses pulling fast-moving carts or carts turning corners are in greater danger of falling over than are horses pulling slow- or straight-moving carts. No credible, independently supportable Oedipal association would add significant explanatory power in accounting for these details. The generalization of Hans's fear from horses pulling buses to horses pulling heavy carts that may place them in similar jeopardy of falling down seems straightforward, as evidenced in multiple passages, for example: "Hans: 'I'm most afraid of furniture-vans, too … I think when furniture-horses are dragging a heavy van they'll fall down.' I: 'So you're not afraid with a small cart?' Hans: 'No.'" (p. 49).

> When a coal-cart came along, he said to me. "Daddy, I'm very much afraid of coal-carts, too … because they're so heavily loaded, and the horses have so much to drag and might easily fall down. If a cart's empty, I'm not afraid." It is a fact, as I have already remarked, that only heavy vehicles throw him into a state of anxiety.
>
> (pp. 54–55)

Consider the last passage. Hans says that it is not just the analogous size of furniture carts and coal-carts to bus carts that triggers his fear but the fact that coal-carts are "so heavily loaded, and the horses have so much to drag and might easily fall down." To prove his point, Hans observes that he is not afraid when a coal-cart is empty, and the father confirms that this is true. This explanation is cogent and persuasive. It is unclear in what way an additional claim that loaded coal-carts remind Hans of a pregnant belly or a belly filled with "lumf" (Hans's word for feces) can be independently supported and add to the power of the horse accident as explicated by Hans to explain this detail of his fear.

Hans's fears are in fact quite refined, consistent with his nuanced theory of what is likely to cause horses to fall down:

HANS: "I'm not afraid of carriages and pair or cabs with one horse. I'm afraid of buses and luggage-carts, but only when they're loaded up, not when they're empty. When there's one horse and the cart's loaded full up, then I'm afraid; but when there are two horses and it's loaded full up, then I'm not afraid."

I: "Are you afraid of buses because there are so many people inside?"

HANS: "Because there's so much luggage on the top."

(pp. 90–91)

At one point, Hans's father says that Hans "is more frightened of large dray-horses than of small horses, and of rough farm-horses than of smart horses (such as those in a carriage and pair)" (p. 47). Consider, however, the following passage that reports an exception:

Afternoon, in front of the house. Hans suddenly ran indoors as a carriage with two horses came along. I could see nothing unusual about it, and asked him what was wrong. "The horses are so proud," he said, "that I'm afraid they'll fall down." (The coachman was reining the horses in tight, so that they were trotting with short steps and holding their heads high. In fact their action was "proud").

(p. 82)

This was an atypical phobic stimulus, because Hans was not usually afraid of pairs of horses pulling carriages. Rather than being an otherwise inexplicable displacement from Oedipal content, Hans himself explains why this atypical stimulus makes him afraid: unlike most "smart" horses pulling carriages, these carriage horses were trotting in such a vigorous, prancing way that he was afraid they would fall down. The father confirms that the horses were reined in tight, thus trotting with short steps and head held high in a way that could seem to place them at risk for falling down.

The following interchange indicates that Hans also associates such "proud" behavior of a horse with possible anger, as when his father scolds him for coming into the parents' bedroom: "I asked him who it really was that was so proud. He: 'You are, when I come into bed with Mummy'" (p. 82). This association is likely shaped by suggestion. By this time in the case, Hans has been drilled to equate Hans's father and the horse by both Hans's father and Freud himself, and Hans now "gets it" and produces associations to order. One might argue that this is an Oedipally mediated association; proudness is associated with the father's anger, and proud horses frighten Hans. But this is not the reason Hans gives for being afraid. The reason he does give is plausible enough without Oedipal additions, namely, that proud horses (as he perceives them and their prancing) are more likely to fall down. Proud horses also appear possibly angry to Hans and thus more dangerous in regard to biting. To the degree the association of proudness and anger is genuine, it explains why biting might be more likely if these horses fell down.

Anger emerges at another point as well. In addition to the possibility of a horse falling down and biting, another aspect of the original horse accident that Hans identifies as having particularly terrified him was that the horse kicked about and made a row with its feet:

I: "Why did it give you such a fright?"

HANS: "Because the horse went like this with its feet." (He lay down on the ground and showed me how it kicked about.) "it gave me a fright because it made a row with its feet."

(p. 50)

It would seem natural for this sort of kicking by a horse to be frightening to a child, or to anyone for that matter. For example, here is a passage from a 2007 *New York Times* report titled "A Carriage Horse Dies After Bolting Onto a Sidewalk":

A carriage horse was killed near Central Park yesterday after it became startled by a loud noise and darted onto the sidewalk, where it became stuck between two poles and died as it tried to lunge forward, the police and witnesses said ... "It fell into a panic and then fell on the ground, kicking," said Roger Watkins, who was walking by and tried to help.

(O'Connor & Ma, 2007, p. B2)

To the quoted passerby, the most salient aspect of the horse's behavior once it fell down was its panicked and possibly dangerous kicking.

Despite Hans quite understandably being afraid because the horse loudly kicked its feet to the point of demonstrating the frightening behavior himself, Freud's comment is: "May there not have been yet another meaning concealed behind all this? And what can have been the significance of the making a row with its legs?" (p. 52). Apparently, the fact that Hans "saw a bus-horse fall down and kick about with its feet" (p. 49) is insufficient for Freud as an explanation that Hans found the kicking scary. Hans's father, with Freud's prodding, attempts to find a deeper meaning:

> I told him I knew on what occasions it was that he made a row with his feet. "Oh, yes!" he interrupted me, "when I'm cross, or when I have to do 'lumf' and would rather play."
>
> (He has a habit, it is true, of making a row with his feet, i.e. of stamping, when he is angry.—"Doing lumf" means doing number two ... In very early days, when he had to be put on the chamber, and refused to leave off playing, he used to stamp his feet in a rage, and kick about, and sometimes throw himself on the ground.)
>
> "And you kick about with your feet as well, when you have to widdle and don't want to go, because you'd rather go on playing."
>
> (p. 54)

The most salient theme to emerge in this interchange is not micturation or the leg movement of a boy who urgently has to urinate but kicking about as an indication of anger. Hans kicks "when I'm cross," and his father confirms that "He has a habit, it is true, of making a row with his feet, i.e. of stamping, when he is angry." His kicking in relation to micturation and lumf are instances of his kicking due to his frustration and anger at being stopped from playing, as his father notes ("when he had to be put on the chamber, and refused to leave off playing, he used to stamp his feet in a rage, and kick about, and sometimes throw himself on the ground"). Consequently, the frightening impact of the horse's row with its feet would be sufficiently explainable as an understandable sign to Hans of the horse's rage and the potential danger that entails. Looking for a specific infantile-sexuality meaning seems more like backward associating than identifying a necessary explanatory hypothesis for an otherwise inexplicable feature.

Freud is quite aware of the unifying characteristics of Hans's supposedly diffuse fears, as he notes in his Discussion section:

> It was only then that we learnt what the objects and impressions were of which Hans was afraid. He was not only afraid of horses biting him—he was soon silent upon that point—but also of carts, of furniture-vans, and of buses (their common quality being, as presently became clear, that they were all heavily loaded), of horses that started moving, of horses that looked big and heavy, and of horses that drove quickly. The meaning of these specifications was explained by Hans himself: he was afraid of horses *falling down*, and consequently incorporated in his phobia everything that seemed likely to facilitate their falling down.
>
> (p. 124)

When Freud says that Hans's fear extends to certain kinds of horses ("horses of a particular character"), he is likely referring to the fact that Hans's father reports that Hans is especially afraid of large dray-horses and rough-looking horses: "he is more frightened of large dray-horses than of small horses, and of rough farm-horses than of smart horses (such as those in a carriage and pair)." That is precisely the kind of horse that would be pulling a bus-cart and thus likely the kind of horse that fell down. Hans also mentions a white horse at Gmunden, but he mentions that horse in order to prove to his father that some horses—specifically, in this case, a white horse similar to the one that he was warned not to touch at Gmunden—do bite. However, his phobic fear is not limited to white horses, contrary to what Freud confusedly suggests at one point. In sum, Hans is afraid of "horses of a particular character" when and only when horses of that character are perceived by Hans to be like the one he saw fall down and in circumstances that make them, in his mind, likely to fall down and to bite. It is difficult to see any persuasive increment in explanatory power provided by Oedipal associations to the features of horses that pull buses, like the one in the horse accident.

The evidence surveyed thus far indicates that Hans's fears generalize along the lines one would expect if the horse accident's properties had shaped the fear, and if the fear of a horse falling and biting was the central organizing principle of Hans's fear, just as he explains. Consequently, Freud's initial list of the objects of Hans's fears is not in fact explanatorily diffuse. It is adequately explainable by the horse accident and the features inferred by Hans that might cause a horse to fall down and bite or might otherwise indicate danger.

"The Black Around the Mouth": Do Muzzles and Blinkers Represent the Father's Moustache and Glasses?

There is a further salient detail of the content of Hans's phobia that Freud and other commentators have taken to be strong evidence for Oedipal etiology. This detail constitutes what is probably the most prominent detailed-characteristics explanatory-adequacy argument Freud presents regarding Hans. On March 30, during the father and Hans's one joint visit to Freud during the analysis, Freud reports the following "aha" experience and consequent interpretation offered to Hans:

> We were also forced to confess that the connections between the horses he was afraid of and the affectionate feelings towards his mother which had been revealed were by no means abundant. Certain details which I now learnt—to the effect that he was particularly bothered by what horses wear in front of their eyes and by the black round their mouths—were certainly not to be explained from what we knew. But as I saw the two of them sitting in front of me and at the same time heard Hans's description of his anxiety-horses, a further piece of the solution shot through my

mind, and a piece which I could well understand might escape his father. I asked Hans jokingly whether his horses wore eyeglasses, to which he replied that they did not. I then asked him whether his father wore eyeglasses, to which, against all the evidence, he once more said no. Finally I asked him whether by "the black round the mouth" he meant a moustache; and I then disclosed to him that he was afraid of his father, precisely because he was so fond of his mother. It must be, I told him, that he thought his father was angry with him on that account; but this was not so, his father was fond of him in spite of it, and he might admit everything to him without any fear.

(pp. 41–42)

Freud acknowledges that suitable Oedipal determinants of the phobia's features were "by no means abundant," stymying his analysis. However, Hans reported that he was particularly afraid of horses with something black around their mouths and something they wore on their eyes. Freud assumes that this mysterious detail is "not to be explained" by what was known of the horse accident. He concludes that this detail of Hans's fear could best be explained as a fear displaced from the similarly situated glasses and moustache of the father. This provides Freud with a "suitable determinant" of the phobia's detailed objects that supports Freud's Oedipal etiological interpretation. As this is probably the most cited "suitability" evidence produced by Freud in the Hans case, I consider it in some detail. Indeed, it is often portrayed as one of the prototypical instances of the use of the suitability strategy throughout Freud's works, as in Lynch's (2014) illustration of how Freud uses "internal connections between the interpretation and symptoms" to support his etiological claims:

> More generally, we can say that Freud looks for associations between the thought-content postulated in the interpretation, and the symptoms. An example would be supporting his conjecture that the horses in Little Hans' phobia represented Hans' father (or the unconscious thought of him) by highlighting the fact that the horses wore black muzzles or bridles over their mouths, supposedly reminiscent of the father's black moustache.
>
> (p. 7)

On April 5, the following interchange occurred in which Hans reiterated that he was particularly afraid of horses with the black thing on their mouths and his father attempted to gain further clarity about to what Hans was referring:

I: "Which horses are you actually most afraid of?"
HANS: "All of them."
I: "That's not true."

HANS: "I'm most afraid of horses with a thing on their mouths."

I: "What do you mean? The piece of iron they have in their mouths?"

HANS: "No. They have something black on their mouths." (He covered his mouth with his hand.)

I: "What? A moustache, perhaps?"

HANS: (laughing) "Oh no!"

I: "Have they all got it?"

HANS: "No, only a few of them."

I: "What is it that they've got on their mouths?"

HANS: "A black thing." (I think in reality it must be the thick piece of harness that dray-horses wear over their noses.)

(pp. 48–49)

Hans rejects the suggestion that he is referring to the iron bit that horses commonly have in their mouths. He outright rejects his father's interpretation that the black represents a moustache, and he demonstrates with a gesture that the item in question *covers* the horse's mouth, unlike a moustache. The father's thought that Hans must be referring to the thick leather strap that dray-horses wear above their noses fits the idea of its resembling a moustache but it does not fit Hans's description at all.

Subsequent to this interchange, in acting out the horse scene with his father, Hans again displays that the thing over the horse's mouth was literally covering the horse's mouth like a feeding nose-bag and that it was an integral part of the horse-accident scene he witnessed and is acting out:

> For some time Hans has been playing horses in the room; he trots about, falls down, kicks about with his feet, and neighs. Once he tied a small bag on like a nose-bag. He has repeatedly run up to me and bitten me.
>
> (p. 52)

The father, puzzled, persistently raises the issue of the nature of the black thing around the horses' mouths, and Hans continues to refer to it as well:

> April 6th. Went out with Hans in front of the house in the afternoon. At every horse that passed I asked him if he saw the "black on its mouth"; he said "no" every time. I asked him what the black really looked like; he said it was black iron. My first idea, that he meant the thick leather straps that are part of the harness of dray-horses, is therefore unconfirmed. I asked him if the "black" reminded him of a moustache, and he said: "Only by its colour." So I do not yet know what it really is.
>
> (p. 52)

> April 7th. I asked again to-day what the "black on the horses' mouths" looked like. Hans said: "Like a muzzle." The curious thing is that for the

last three days not a single horse has passed on which he could point out this "muzzle". I myself have seen no such horse on any of my walks, although Hans asseverates that such horses do exist. I suspect that some sort of horses' bridle—the thick piece of harness round their mouths, perhaps—really reminded him of a moustache, and that after I alluded to this this fear disappeared as well.

(p. 53)

There did in fact exist at the time some horse muzzles that were partially metal in the part that fit around the mouth. They were sometimes part of a larger protective harness that was mostly leather straps. Indeed, even muzzles that were largely leather were generally secured with some metal fastenings.

Hans is a quick study who is highly suggestible. Having had the link between the father's moustache and the black around the horse's mouth suggested multiple times, he soon shows his father that he finally "gets it" and can anticipate the obvious association his father is likely to offer.

April 9th. This morning Hans came in to me while I was washing and bare to the waist.

HANS: "Daddy, you are lovely. You're so white."
I: "Yes. Like a white horse."
HANS: "The only black thing's your moustache." (Continuing) "Or perhaps it's a black muzzle?"

(pp. 53–54)

Hans's question is not a persuasive confirmation of Freud's interpretation, by Freud's own criteria. It is not a fresh association nor is it accompanied or immediately followed by fresh associations, but rather it is an exact reiteration of the father's and Freud's interpretations. Thus, this comment is most plausibly considered to be the result of the repeated suggestions about the moustache over the previous several days.

The father eventually verifies that there is a black thing of the kind described by Hans around some horses' mouths, and that this must the thing to which Hans is referring:

There is again great progress to be reported. Even drays cause him less alarm. Once he called out, almost with joy: "Here comes a horse with something black on its mouth." And I was at last able to establish the fact that it was a horse with a leather muzzle. But Hans was not in the least afraid of this horse.

(p. 69)

Hans is thus most plausibly referring to a horse wearing both eye blinkers and a black muzzle, the latter primarily leather but perhaps partly metal around the mouth. Even after this confirmation, Hans continues to bring up the issue to be sure his father finally accepts his claim: "Hans: 'Daddy, have you noticed now and then that horses have something black on their mouths?' I: 'I've noticed it now and then in the street at Gmunden'" (p. 90). Freud later comments in a note: "The train of thought is as follows. For a long time his father had refused to believe what he said about there being something black on horses' mouths, but finally it had been verified" (p. 90).

As an aside with regard to Hans's fear of being bitten, one might wonder if there is a conflict between being afraid of being bitten and the horse in the accident being muzzled to prevent biting. However, horse muzzles in the nineteenth century were often made of leather strips and wire and generally left lots of room between the pieces to see the horse's mouth and even to access feed. The muzzle would not necessarily have obscured Hans's view of the horse's teeth. Having been told some time before that horses bite when disturbed, Hans was alerted to this possibility, and he likely had no experience with the constraining effectiveness of muzzles. Moreover, even a muzzled animal can be frightening if it is angry and known to be capable of biting if it should manage to get into a position to do so, as anyone who has dealt with a muzzled aggressive dog will know. For a young boy who has recently been cautioned about horses biting, there is no conflict between a horse being muzzled and fear that if the horse is angry it might somehow nonetheless bite. In any event, although Hans retained a special fear of horses that had on a muzzle and blinkers (see the discussion of this below), the lengthy search for such a horse shows that muzzles were very infrequent and that the horses of which Hans was subsequently afraid generally were not muzzled and thus not so constrained.

Freud construes these unusual details of Hans's fears as an interpretive "smoking gun" that reveals that the feared horse unconsciously symbolizes Hans's father. In his discussion of the case, Freud heavily relies on the moustache and glasses interpretation to support his claim that Hans's fear of horses is in fact fear of his father:

> I thought the right moment had now arrived for informing him that he was afraid of his father because he himself nourished jealous and hostile wishes against him—for it was essential to postulate this much with regard to his unconscious impulses. In telling him this, I had partly interpreted his fear of horses for him: the horse must be his father— whom he had good internal reasons for fearing. Certain details of which Hans had shown he was afraid, the black on horses' mouths and the things in front of their eyes (the moustaches and eyeglasses which are the privilege of a grown-up man), seemed to me to have been directly transposed from his father on to the horses.
>
> (p. 123)

Freud's moustache-and-glasses interpretation and his use of it for understanding Hans's phobia has been a topic of dispute. Wolpe and Rachman (1960) argue that what were initially mysterious features of the phobia turned out to be understandable as the muzzle and blinkers actually worn by some horses:

> The mysterious black around the horses' mouths and the things on their eyes were later discovered by the father to be the horses' muzzles and blinkers. This discovery undermines the suggestion (made by Freud) that they were transposed moustaches and eyeglasses. There is no other evidence that the horse represented Hans's father.
>
> (1960, pp. 143–144)

Wolpe and Rachman point out that the paraphernalia described by Hans as frightening were eventually found to refer to some kind of horse muzzle and blinkers, providing a real, nonsymbolic object of fear. Wolpe and Rachman seem here to inadequately address Freud's point, which is that these features of the phobia's contents are inexplicable by the horse-accident account of Hans's fear alone. Freud agrees that the details of the phobia are features taken from horses (e.g., the horse in the accident, the horses at the Customs House, the horse at Gmunden). However, he claims that the specific features that Hans fears make no sense as objects of horse fear but bear the stamp instead of being shaped by other meanings and require additional explanation, which the Oedipal theory optimally provides.

Is Hans's fear of horses wearing the described paraphernalia as prima facie inexplicable as Freud would have it? An obvious reply is that, although it is not explicitly stated, it makes sense that the horse that fell down while pulling a bus had such paraphernalia on its face. Remarkably, neither Freud nor the father ever directly ask Hans whether such a muzzle-and-blinkers outfit was worn by the horse that Hans saw fall down, although it is likely that this is the fear's origin, as it is for all the other features examined above. A large horse pulling a bus through the downtown area of a major city is one that might well be wearing such protection, including blinkers to keep the horse from becoming frightened by the distractions of the city traffic all around it, and a muzzle to keep it from biting anyone or anything. If the feature described by Hans was a feature of the horse in the accident, as it plausibly was, then Hans's fear is understandable either as a direct generalization from a feature of the actual horse accident, or perhaps via an inference on Hans's part such as that the blinkers might have contributed to the tendency to fall down.

Jerome Neu (1995) defends Freud's Oedipal displacement argument. He accepts that the described features might have been part of the original horse-accident stimulus but argues that this still would not explain why this particular feature of the stimulus would be selected as a route of generalization of Hans's fear given that there is no obvious danger associated with these particular features. Thus, resemblance to the father is explanatorily plausible: "The horses that Hans feared most had black things about their faces, which corresponded with his father's moustache and glasses, making them resemble him more closely, a point first noted during the visit with Freud" (Neu, 1995, p. 142). Neu argues that this resemblance is particularly supportive of the Oedipal account given that the salience to Hans of the muzzle and blinkers among all the possible horse stimuli cannot be explained otherwise:

> [T]he "discovery" that they say "undermines" Freud's suggestion in fact confirms it. It specifies more clearly those particular features which make particular horses more fearful than others for Hans; and they are precisely those features which make them resemble Hans's father more closely (by correspondence with his moustache and glasses). What better evidence for unconscious identification or symbolization could one have? If the muzzles and blinkers show something else, what is it? Why should muzzles and blinkers otherwise be significant? (Why should they be picked out as significant features in the total "stimulus" situation?)
>
> (Neu, 1977, pp. 127–128)

Neu thus argues that the explanatory value of the Oedipal account as a suitable determinant of why these particular features should be so frightening to Hans goes beyond anything that can be provided by the horse-accident account, even though the features themselves were in fact features of the horse in the witnessed horse accident.

Neu's riposte is surely correct to the extent that the fact that the "black around the mouth" corresponds to something real about horses or the horse accident does not imply that it does not have symbolic meaning as well. However, given the demanding level of evidence that we saw is necessary for a valid suitable determination argument, Neu is incorrect in arguing that because the feared horse feature has a resemblance to a feature of the father, that provides evidence for the Oedipal interpretation. The problem here is that perceived resemblances and similarity are all too easy to come by accidentally. Neu's own critique of the behavioral explanation of generalization of fear via similarity has a bearing here. In that critique, he notes that anything is similar to and different from anything else in myriad ways, so just citing similarities is not by itself substantial evidence for a causal relationship:

> Stimulus generalization rests on claims of similarity. The problem with this is that similarity is all pervasive. For any two items in the universe, it always will be the case that there are *some* respects in which they are similar (and, one should immediately add, some respects in which they are dissimilar) ... But if stimulus generalization based on similarity can explain all possible objects, then it can explain no particular actual object. By explaining everything it explains nothing.
>
> (Neu, 1995, p. 148)

Freud, too, is hoist on Neu's petard. It is similarity, and similarity alone, that leads Freud (and Neu) to be so convinced that the meaning of the black around the horse's mouth represents the father's moustache. Freud's immediate "aha" experience when he noted the resemblance of Hans's description of the feared horses' mouth-and-eyes paraphernalia to the father's moustache and glasses was based entirely on his perception of a similarity. By parity of reasoning with his critique of behaviorism, Neu ought to disparage such arbitrary cherry picking of similarities by Freud. Inevitably, the father and the horses most feared by Hans will be similar in some ways.

How, then, should we judge these opposed positions on the evidential value and implications of the moustache-and-glasses interpretation? The interchange makes clear that the interpretation of the "black around the mouth" is a matter neither of sheer similarity to the father nor simply of whether it is based on some reality about horses. Neu's riposte leaves us instead with the challenge of comparing the explanatory power of rival hypotheses about the fear and the claimed resemblance. We are thus confronted with the following two more refined questions. (1) To what degree can Hans's increased fear of horses wearing a muzzle and blinkers be explained by his experience of the horse accident? (2) To what degree is distinctive additional explanatory power (i.e., surplus power over and above that provided by the horse accident) for understanding Hans's fear of horses with those specific features provided by adding the moustache-and-glasses interpretation? That is, what we basically want to know is whether or not it is possible to explain Hans's *heightened fear of those specific features* without the additional Oedipal interpretation.

There are several considerations that argue against the Freud-Neu position that the additional Oedipal interpretation is warranted by an explanatory gap. First, the foundation of their position lies in the initially perceived similarity of the feared features and the father's moustache and glasses. Freud came up with the association to Hans's father's glasses and moustache in the one session they all had together, in which it is reported that Hans said only that he was afraid of horses that had black around their mouths, and Freud looked at Max and drew his conclusion that Hans was symbolizing his father. However, as we saw, that resemblance eroded as it became clear what Hans meant. A muzzle that goes over and around the entire snout of a horse is simply not similar to a gentleman's moustache above his upper lip, as Hans asserts. Nor, for that matter, are a horse's blinkers all that much similar to glasses, but this is perhaps more debatable. Hans placed his hand over his mouth, and a bag over his face, to show his father what he meant and try to correct his father's misimpression. It was with a degree of relief and joy that Hans finally was able to demonstrate to his father the error he had been making. Once it became clear that Hans was referring to a muzzle, the Freudian interpretation was considerably weakened simply because a muzzle does not resemble a moustache in the way that a leather strap does, which is what Hans's father initially thought Hans was referring to when he went along with Freud's similarity judgment. As Hans says, the resemblance is only in the color, not in the form. Freud's hypothesis was based on incomplete information, and when the meaning of Hans's fear became clear, the resemblance to a moustache became moot. To the degree that the claimed similarity is itself questionable, the explanatory power of the Oedipal hypothesis is greatly eroded and we are faced with the point, emphasized by Neu, that similarities can of course be found anywhere if one looks for them.

The more basic consideration is that the phenomenon that is the target of explanation—namely, Hans's increment of fear in reaction to horses having the specified features—is easily explained on the basis of the horse accident alone without the addition of Oedipal hypotheses. Note that focusing on the incremental fear as the explanandum is different from Wolpe and Rachman's simple reliance on a link to horses and responsive to Neu's argument.

There are two obvious reasons why the muzzle and blinkers could be particularly frightening to Hans based on the horse accident. First, the muzzle by its very nature represents the potential for biting. Who is not more frightened by a dog encountered on the street that has a muzzle on its snout than by one that does not, especially if the dog acts aggressively? One immediately infers that a muzzled animal may bite and is dangerous. Generalized fear or cautiousness in the presence of similar animals may easily follow.

Second, the wearing of such a leather face covering is naturally frightening. It covers the horse's face and presents a visage that hides information about emotions and intentions and increases the snout's size and aggressive salience. Warrior headgear and horror movie masks, designed to be frightening, attest to this. Additionally, regarding Neu's puzzlement over why this feature would be salient, in general fear is more likely to attach to features that are unusual or unfamiliar, thus of unknown implication. The case material describes how Hans and his father watched for a horse with the feared type of harness, yet failed to catch sight of one amidst the many horses they saw over a period of several days. Thus, the feature was a rare one in Hans's usual environment, and this would dispose Hans to perceive it as salient.

I conclude that under the conditions of fear induced by the accident, it is readily understandable why a child might fix on such salient paraphernalia as the horse's muzzle and blinders as a particularly frightening feature. There is no unique and compelling surplus explanatory power added to the explanation of Hans's fear by bringing the Oedipal hypothesis and the father's eyeglasses and moustache into the explanation of Hans's fear of horses with blinkers and muzzle. This central "suitable determinant" attempt by Freud to justify the Oedipal theory of Han's phobia based on the details of Hans's fear thus fails, especially when considered in the context of the demanding explanatory guidelines that Freud put forward to avoid obvious methodological fallacies.

Are Hans's Fears of Horses Falling Down and Biting an "Improbable Collocation" that Supports an Oedipal Interpretation of a Death Wish Combined with a Fear of Revenge?

Recall that Hans's father reported to Freud at the phobia's onset that Hans "is afraid *a horse will bite him in the street*" (p. 22). When the father later probes the details of the fear, Hans says that he is most afraid of horse-drawn buses "because once a horse in a bus fell down" and this triggered Hans's fear. Hans's father tries to clarify the precise nature of the fear and rectify Hans's earlier and later statements:

HANS: "When the horse in the bus fell down, it gave me such a fright, really!
    That was when I got the nonsense."
I: "But the nonsense was that you thought a horse would bite you. And now
    you say you were afraid a horse would fall down."
HANS: "Fall down and bite."

(p. 50)

In a footnote, Freud comments: "Hans was right, *however improbable this collocation may sound*. The train of thought, we shall see, was that the horse (his father) would bite him because of his wish that it (his father) should fall down" (p. 50, emphasis added).

Freud's "improbable collocation" characterization is an implicit argument designed to provide evidence for an Oedipal account. The Oedipal theory also requires a compounding of two seemingly incompatible scenarios: the father falling down dead, and the father vengefully castrating Hans. To construct a "suitable determinant" argument, Freud interprets Hans's combined fear ("fall down and bite") as requiring an explanation as to how they could go together because, Freud implies, a horse simultaneously falling down and biting would be difficult to accomplish. If the combination of Hans's two fears is indeed paradoxical, this could be explained by the equally paradoxical structure of the combination of Oedipal contents of Hans's father both falling down dead and castrating Hans, Freud implies.

However, Freud creates a bogus problem in order to take credit for solving it. The presumption of a paradox in Hans's assertion is unwarranted, so there is nothing for Freud's Suitability Argument to explain. A horse that is falling can possibly bite if one gets too close, or it can do so sequentially, first falling and, subsequently agitated, coming over and biting. It is not paradoxical that a horse that has fallen down should be feared as a horse that, if one were to get too close, might bite. Indeed, this coherent meaning of the collocation is demonstrated when Hans plays out the scene with his father:

For some time Hans has been playing horses in the room; he trots about, falls down, kicks about with his feet, and neighs. Once he tied a small bag on like a nose-bag. He has repeatedly run up to me and bitten me.

(p. 52)

Hans's play-acting of the scene may well have been an attempt not only at mastery but also of explanation, illustrating how a falling down horse might run over and bite in answer to his father's skeptical response. There is thus no support for the conceit that Hans's combination of two fears of horses falling and biting are so paradoxical and bewildering that they must be a symbolic representation of an indissoluble combined Oedipal death wish and consequent fear of castration.

Does the Lizzi "Biting Horse" Incident Link Oedipal Meanings to Hans's Fear of Being Bitten by a Horse?

In order to explain why Hans's Oedipal fears were precipitated by the horse accident, Freud must link features of the accident to Oedipal meanings that offer needed explanatory power in understanding otherwise inexplicable symptoms. To forge such links, Freud relies on two incidents. In one, Hans was present when a neighbor's child, Lizzi, was warned that a horse might bite. In the other, a playmate, Fritzl, was hurt while playing horses with Hans. Freud argues that these earlier incidents united Oedipal meanings with horse-related anxieties and thus prepared the way for the triggering of Hans's horse phobia. According to Freud, the Lizzi incident accounted for Hans's fear of being bitten by a horse, and the Fritzl incident accounted for Hans's fear of horses falling down. The Fritzl and Lizzi incidents are thus crucial bridges between Oedipal meanings and horse-accident meanings; they are "memories which, unimportant in themselves, are nevertheless indispensable as a bridge, in the sense that the association between two important memories can only be made through them" (Freud, 1895, pp. 295–296).

I first consider the Lizzi incident, which is initially reported by Hans to his father as follows:

On Sunday, March 1st, the following conversation took place on the way to the station. I was once more trying to explain to him that horses do not bite.

HE: "But white horses bite. There's a white horse at Gmunden that bites. If you hold your finger to it it bites."

(I was struck by his saying "finger" instead of "hand".) He then told me the following story, which I give here in a connected form:

HE: "When Lizzi had to go away, there was a cart with a white horse in front of her house, to take her luggage to the station."

(Lizzi, he tells me, was a little girl who lived in a neighbouring house.)
"Her father was standing near the horse, and the horse turned its head round (to touch him), and he said to Lizzi: 'Don't put your finger to the white horse or it'll bite you.'"
Upon this I said: "I say, it strikes me that it isn't a horse you mean, but a widdler, that one mustn't put one's hand to."

HE: "But a widdler doesn't bite."
I: "Perhaps it does, though." He then went on eagerly to try and prove to me that it really was a white horse.

(pp. 29–30)

In response to his father's insistence that horses do not bite, Hans attempts to persuade his father that horses do sometimes bite and thus that his fear is not groundless. As evidence, Hans says that he overheard a neighbor warning his daughter, Lizzi, that a horse bites. (The father's rather forced attempt to link Hans's form of words to masturbation does not lead anywhere, and I put that aside.)

Common sense dictates that this incident could have contributed to Hans's later fear that a horse that falls down and is kicking may bite. However, the fact that Hans overheard such a warning and that it influenced his later reaction to an agitated horse has no implications for Oedipal explanation. Indeed, even the behaviorists Wolpe and Rachman (1960) accept that the Lizzi incident played a role in sensitizing Hans and preparing the way for his phobic reaction to the horse accident. If the Lizzi incident merely instilled in Hans the fear of being bitten by a horse, then it offers no explanation of how Oedipal meanings entered into Hans's phobia.

Freud summarizes the incident as follows:

Soon afterwards he traced back his fear of being bitten by a horse to an impression he had received at Gmunden. A father had addressed his child on her departure with these words of warning: 'Don't put your finger to the horse; if you do, it'll bite you.'

(p. 119)

This perfectly coherent explanation of Han's fear of being bitten offers no distinctive Oedipal hypothesis whatever.

Freud's strategy is to import an Oedipal meaning into the Lizzi incident so that the Oedipal meaning would then carry over with the biting fear into Hans's horse-accident reaction. Freud and Hans's father see that the Lizzi incident unites a moment at which Lizzi is about to depart from Gmunden with a warning that horses bite. They suggest that via associative pathways it thus links together in Hans's mind two crucial Oedipal features, namely, Hans's desire for his father to depart from Gmunden so he can be alone with his mother (which eventually becomes a death wish) and Hans's fear of his father taking revenge on him (biting him) for these desires. It is the combination of departure with biting that is claimed to be the Oedipal-activating feature of the Lizzi incident.

For example, in trying to explain why Hans becomes anxious when horse-drawn wagons depart from the Customs House across the street from their flat, Hans's father notes both the symbolic link to Hans wanting the father to depart and the consequent fear attached to that wish by the warning about biting:

> In the summer I used to be constantly leaving Gmunden for Vienna on business, and he was then the father. You will remember that his fear of horses is connected with the episode at Gmunden when a horse was to take Lizzi's luggage to the station. The repressed wish that I should drive to the station, for then he would be alone with his mother (the wish that "the horse should drive off"), is turned into fear of the horse's driving off; and in fact nothing throws him into greater alarm than when a cart drives off from the courtyard of the Head Customs House (which is just opposite our flat) and the horses start moving.
>
> (pp. 45–46)

Freud explains the sequence of events yielding the combined desire and fear as follows:

> Hans really was a little Oedipus who wanted to have his father "out of the way" ... [A]t a later stage it became possible for his fear of being bitten ... to attach itself directly on to this form of the wish, owing to a chance impression which he received at the moment of someone else's departure.
>
> (p. 111)

The problem with Freud's and the father's Oedipal interpretation of the Lizzi incident is that the symbolic meanings attributed to the incident are not supported by any further evidence and have no distinctive suitability as determinants of any details of the incident or of Hans's later phobic reactions. There is no such detail that, to achieve an adequate explanation, requires the hypothesis that Hans associates Lizzi's departure with his wish for his father to depart or that Hans associates the possibility of being bitten by a horse with a fear of being harmed or castrated by his father. This is explanatory sleight-of-hand. These Oedipal interpretations are simply imposed on the Lizzi incident in order to justify imposing them on the horse accident, without contributing additional explanatory power.

Indeed, the evidence cited above by the father challenges the father's own assertions. To show that fear of departure is a salient detail of Hans's phobia, he claims that Hans is anxious when horse-wagons depart from the Customs House across from their home. This is an entirely tendentious and misleading reading of his own report:

> I have noticed for some days that Hans is specially frightened when carts drive into or out of the yard, a process which involves their taking a corner. I asked at the time why he was so much afraid, and he replied: *"I'm afraid the horses will fall down when the cart turns."* He is equally frightened when carts standing at the loading dock start moving in order to drive off ... He is also more frightened when a vehicle drives past quickly than when the horses trot up slowly.
>
> (p. 46)

Hans is apparently as afraid of arrivals and of speed as he is of departures. The fear has to do with the increased chance of a horse falling down, not with departure. In terms of evidence and explanation, departure as such does not arise as a salient variable.

There is thus no independent evidential or explanatory case for the imputation of Oedipal meanings to the Lizzi incident. The Lizzi incident may well play a role in the nature of Hans's later phobia, and may offer some "suitability as a determinant" for the specific fear of being bitten, but this is wholly independent of Oedipal hypotheses. This is a case of "backward association" from the features of the phobia to preferred hypotheses that are not in fact required for explanatory adequacy.

Does Fritzl's Injury While Playing Horses with Hans Link Oedipal Meanings with Hans's Fear of Horses Falling Down?

The Fritzl incident is the most pivotal incident prior to the horse accident cited in Freud's account. Freud claims that the Fritzl incident united Oedipal and horse themes, forming the basis for Hans's later horse phobia and specifically his fear of horses falling down. Like the Lizzi incident, the Fritzl incident is generally acknowledged to be relevant to Hans's later phobic reaction, with, again, even behaviorists agreeing that the incident may have prepared the way for Hans's extreme reaction to the horse accident. The issue is whether the addition of Oedipal hypotheses regarding this incident are required to achieve explanatory adequacy.

The Fritzl incident emerges in the following interchange between Hans and his father:

> As we were going upstairs I asked him almost without thinking: "Used you to play at horses with the children at Gmunden?"

HE: "Yes" ...

I: "Who was the horse?"

HE: "I was; and Berta was the coachman."

I: "Did you fall down by any chance, when you were a horse?"

HANS: "No. When Berta said 'Gee-up', I ran ever so quick; I just raced along." ...

I: "Used you often to play at horses?"

HANS: "Very often. Fritzl was the horse once, too, and Franzl the coachman; and Fritzl ran ever so fast and all at once he hit his foot on a stone and bled."

I: "Perhaps he fell down?"

HANS: "No. He put his foot in some water and then wrapped it up."

(pp. 58–59)

Freud argues that this incident in which Hans's friend Fritzl hurt himself while playing horses with Hans was a crucial link between unconscious Oedipal themes and Hans's reaction to the horse accident. Freud identifies the initial line of association between the Fritzl incident and the horse accident as follows:

[T]he accident which he happened to witness ... acquired its great effectiveness ... from the fact that he associated the event in his mind with an earlier event at Gmunden which had more claim to be regarded as traumatic, namely, with Fritzl's falling down while he was playing at horses, and lastly from the fact that there was an easy path of association from Fritzl to his father.

(pp. 136–137)

That is, the Fritzl incident in which Fritzl-as-horse fell down associated in Hans's mind to his father falling down due to associations from Fritzl to his father, and the memory of this incident was activated when Hans witnessed the horse fall down. Thus far, distinctive Oedipal meanings have not been introduced.

Freud claims that for Hans "there was an easy path of association from Fritzl" to his father for several reasons. Fritzl was Hans's favorite playmate at Gmunden and an object of his affection ("Hans's favourite was Fritzl; he often hugged him and made protestations of his love" [p. 16]), and, Freud speculates, perhaps "his rival with his many girl friends" (p. 126). Moreover, Hans played horses with Fritzl ("playing at horses was his favourite game with the other children" [p. 126]), and Hans had first played horses with his father:

I had a suspicion—and this was confirmed by Hans's father when I asked him—that the first person who had served Hans as a horse must have been his father; and it was this that had enabled him to regard Fritzl as a substitute for his father when the accident happened at Gmunden.

(pp. 126–127)

These are not very specific features and could apply to other playmates. Note also that these are all backward associations by Freud from Fritzl to Hans's father, none of which offer any distinctive explanatory power regarding the incident.

The three key non-Oedipal features of the Fritzl incident on which Freud relies in formulating his Oedipal hypothesis are, first, that Hans associates Fritzl with his father; second, that, like the later horse that fell down, Fritzl fell down; and third, that Fritzl fell down specifically while playing a horse, thus the memory of this incident would be activated in Hans when he saw a real horse fall down. (Whether Fritzl in fact fell down is questionable and will be explored separately below; for now, I go along with Freud's claim that he did.)

We now come to the introduction of specific Oedipal meanings into the understanding of the Fritzl incident. In order to account for why Hans develops a phobia, Freud adds an Oedipal hypothesis to the three associative linkages. He claims that Hans's death wish against his father is symbolically realized when Fritzl—whom Hans associates with his father—falls down, which is like being dead. This symbolic realization of his hostile wish activates his fear of his father's revenge, hence, when these associations are activated along with the added weight of seeing the horse accident, his phobia.

The question is whether the proposed Oedipal hypothesis of the activation of death wish and castration fear by the Fritzl incident is required to achieve explanatory adequacy in accounting either for Hans's phobic symptoms or his reaction to the Fritzl incident. If the point is to explain why Hans is so afraid of horses falling down when he saw one actually fall down and was terrified, then the need for additional explanatory power is questionable. Adding the Fritzl incident taken at face value (without the Oedipal gloss) is arguably additionally explanatory because it may have sensitized Hans to horse-falling-down scenarios, underscored by Fritzl's bleeding toe and his need for bandages, and resulting in Hans's poignant thought at the horse accident that "Now it'll always be like this. All horses in buses'll fall down" (p. 49). The question is whether Freud's addition of the Oedipal overlay of death wish and fear of punishment is warranted by an explanatory payoff.

The problem with the Oedipal hypothesis that Hans fears horses falling down because it represents his father falling down due to the Fritzl incident is that it does not appear to explain anything further about Hans's symptoms that is not already potentially explainable by the facts of the horse accident and the Fritzl incident. In the Fritzl incident, Freud claims, a father-associated figure playing at being a horse fell down and, Freud claims, this would naturally come to mind when Hans saw a real horse fall down. If we go along with Freud to this point, we still have no distinctive and essential Oedipal explanatory power used to explain either Hans's reaction to the Fritzl incident or Hans's pathogenic reaction to the horse accident. For example, there is no observable detail of the Fritzl incident that is distinctively explained by any association Hans may have had to his father and the desires and fears he entertained towards him along the lines Freud specifies. The only "evidence" for the hypothesis that Hans reacted to Fritzl falling down with an activation of his wish that his father fall down dead and fear of castration is that it then "explains" the claimed activation of the father schema when the horse falls down. So, one unsupported Oedipal hypothesis about the Fritzl incident is used to buttress another unsupported Oedipal hypothesis about the horse phobia with no inexplicable symptom features being newly explained. Nor do aspects of the Fritzl incident itself appear inexplicably in Hans's reaction to the horse accident. For example, there is no fear of the horse bleeding or hitting its foot on a stone in the account of Hans's fears that might need explanation. Although Freud never speculates in this direction, it seems possible that the horse's kicking wildly that so frightened Hans might resemble Fritzl's pained motions of his foot after it hit the stone. But even if so, this and the other mentioned fears would only help to explain Hans's emotional reaction in terms of his memory of the Fritzl incident, not why that reaction should be related to Oedipal themes.

Did Fritzl Really Fall Down?

An even more fundamental question about Freud's use of the Fritzl incident as an associative pathway between Oedipal desires and horse-accident reactions is whether Fritzl in fact fell down when he hit his foot and bled. Freud not only insists he did but asserts that Fritzl falling down is the crucial feature linking the incident to the horse accident: "this was the event which formed the connection between the two scenes" (p. 82). Freud acknowledges that Hans initially denied that Fritzl fell down ("I: 'Perhaps he fell down?' Hans: 'No.'"), but claims that Hans later changed his account. Freud suggests that Hans's initial denial must have been due to distraction: "Hans, who was at the moment concerned with other things began by denying that Fritzl had fallen down" (p. 82). If Fritzl did not fall down, Freud loses the core of his account of how Oedipal desires explain the horse phobia, so scrutiny is warranted. I will argue that the issue of whether Fritzl fell down is a good example of suggestion providing a persuasive alternative to Freud's account.

Hans's initial "no" regarding whether Fritzl fell down seems quite believable. The whole notion is brought up by Hans's father, whereas if Fritzl had fallen down this would be a salient detail that one might expect Hans to report. The discussion is lucid and focused, and there is no hint in the text that Hans "was at the moment concerned with other things" and so may have denied that Fritzl had fallen down due to being distracted. Freud's rationalization simply has no basis. More impressively, after dismissing the father's suggestion that Fritzl fell down, Hans elaborates with fresh specific details explaining what did happen instead to Fritzl ("No. He put his foot in some water and then wrapped it up"). Such spontaneous associations, Freud holds, are a sign of likely verisimilitude.

Looking at the evidence from April 25, we find that in response to the direct suggestion from his father that "you want me to fall down," Hans offers a fantasied scenario in which his father suffers an injury like Fritzl's:

I asked him who it really was that was so proud.

HANS: "*You* are, when I come into bed with Mummy."

I: "So you want me to fall down?"

HANS: "Yes. You've got to be naked" (meaning "barefoot", as Fritzl had been) "and knock up against a stone and bleed, and then I'll be able to be alone with Mummy for a little bit at all events. When you come up into our flat I'll be able to run away quick so that you don't see."

I: "Can you remember who it was that knocked up against the stone?"

HANS: "Yes, Fritzl."

I: "When Fritzl fell down, what did you think?"

HE: "That you should hit the stone and tumble down."

(p. 82)

Based on this interchange, Freud concludes in a note: "So that in fact Fritzl *did* fall down—which he at one time denied" (n.1, p. 82). Yet the fact is that Hans never directly agrees that Fritzl fell down. Rather, in the best "have you stopped beating your wife" tradition, the father presents Hans with a question that presupposes what Hans has denied, that Fritzl fell down ("When Fritzl fell down..."), a clear case of pressure and suggestion. Having already told his father quite clearly just a few days before that Fritzl did not fall down, Hans goes along with the absurd premise and offers the answer his father obviously wants to hear.

An additional reason to suspect suggestion as a possible explanation is that in a discussion on April 5, the father—not Hans— introduced the idea of an equivalence between the horse falling down and the father falling down, with Hans semi-acquiescing in an unpersuasive way: "'When the horse fell down, did you think of your daddy?' Hans: 'Perhaps. Yes. It's possible'" (pp. 50–51). (Hans's own spontaneous explanation of what he thought when the horse fell down has the ring of truth and reflects neurotic overgeneralization: "Now it'll always be like this. All horses in buses'll fall down.") Then, on April 9, the father—not Hans—introduced the additional idea (denied by Hans) that Fritzl, too, had fallen down ("Perhaps he [Fritzl] fell down?"). Thus, the father set up a "falling down" equivalence between himself, Fritzl, and the horse. When on April 25 the father asks, "When Fritzl fell down, what did you think?" Hans understands what his father expects and his answer simply follows out the father's schema. Suggestion is thus a viable alternative hypothesis to explain Hans's response, and Freud's confident assertion that Fritzl did fall down is tendentious and must be dismissed. It would seem that the easy path of association from Fritzl's injury to the horse accident exists in Freud's mind but not, the evidence suggests, in Hans's.

However, if Fritzl did not fall down, then the crucial link Freud claims to exist between the Fritzl incident and the horse accident no longer exists. Without the link between Fritzl-as-father-falling-down and the falling-down horse, Freud has no clear explanation for how or why Oedipal contents enter into Hans's reaction to the horse accident or are needed to explain Hans's phobia.

Is There Case Evidence for Hans's Oedipal Death Wish Toward His Father?

Freud claims as one of his central Oedipal hypotheses that Hans experienced hostile impulses towards his father that became more extreme over time. When Freud reconsidered the Hans case in 1926, he continued to claim that the Hans case clearly demonstrated the aggressive component of the Oedipus complex:

> Meanwhile we have been able to establish another point with certainty. The instinctual impulse which underwent repression in "Little Hans" was a hostile one against his father. Proof of this was obtained in his analysis ... Analysis justified the inference that he had a wishful impulse that his father should fall down and hurt himself as his playmate and the horse had done ... his wish that his father should be out of the way ... is tantamount to an intention of putting one's father out of the way oneself—is tantamount, that is, to the murderous impulse of the Oedipus complex.
>
> (1926, p. 102)

In considering Freud's claim that Hans experienced Oedipal hostility toward his father, two caveats should be kept in mind. First, Freud acknowledges that the evidence is sparse because the hostile feelings "had already been suppressed and ... had never been able to find uninhibited expression" (pp. 138–139). Second, Freud properly observes that contrary emotions can exist side by side, so evidence of Hans's love for his father is not evidence against Hans's hostility. Hans can have both "fear of his father and fear for his father," yielding a "conflict between his affection ... and his hostility" (p. 45).

The primary evidence for Hans's patricidal wish is supposed to be Hans's thought that he wished his father would fall down dead, which is the association he is inferred to have had to the horse falling down. Examining the case record and previous commentaries, four passages appear most relevant to assessing Hans's hostility towards his father. The first concerns Hans's reactions to the horse accident:

I: "Was the horse dead when it fell down?"
HANS: "Yes!"
I: "How do you know that?"

HANS: "Because I saw it." (He laughed.) "No, it wasn't a bit dead."

I: "Perhaps you thought it was dead?"

HANS: "No. Certainly not. I only said it as a joke." (His expression at the moment, however, had been serious.)

(pp. 49–50)

In a follow-up discussion on the train, Hans's father further attempted to forge a link between the falling horse and the father: "I: 'When the horse fell down, did you think of your daddy?' Hans: 'Perhaps. Yes. It's possible'" (p. 51). Given this weak affirmation, Freud can only bring himself to say that "Hans did not dispute this interpretation" (p. 126).

Based on these passages, Freud argues that in watching the horse fall down, Hans imagined and wished for his father's falling down dead:

> This was when the boy saw a big heavy horse fall down; and ... Hans at that moment perceived a wish that his father might fall down in the same way—and be dead. His serious expression as he was telling the story no doubt referred to this unconscious meaning.

(pp. 51–52)

However, this evidence is less than compelling. Hans's father, not Hans, initially links the horse falling down to the father and to the horse being dead. Hans's responses do not display the flow of additional confirming associations that Freud insists are the mark of a correct interpretation rather than a response to suggestion. Although in this instance Hans initially goes along verbally with the father, Hans knew that his father already knew that Hans had known that the horse was not dead because, just moments before the above interchange, Hans had demonstrated to his father that the horse was kicking wildly as it lay on the ground ("He lay down on the ground and showed me how it kicked about" [p. 50]). Consequently, the father's question, "Was the horse dead when it fell down?" made no sense. When Hans's father takes his initial absurd answer seriously, Hans emphatically backtracks from his initial acquiescent response ("No, it wasn't a bit dead").

The rationale Freud offers for nonetheless taking Hans's initial "yes" seriously is that Hans's expression had been serious, which Freud assumes "no doubt" reflects Hans's unconscious death wish towards his father. However, aside from the possibility that Hans is disturbed by having to make false statements as part of the psychoanalytic game his father is playing, there is a more plausible explanation for Hans's seriousness when asked whether the horse was dead. Hans had witnessed his first funeral at Gmunden the summer before and had remained disturbed by the topic of death since then, as the father notes elsewhere in the case record.

A second piece of evidence cited by Freud for Hans's death wish toward his father is an incident in which a toy horse falls down:

Another symptomatic act, happening as though by accident, involved a confession that he had wished his father dead; for, just at the moment his father was talking of this death-wish, Hans let a horse that he was playing with fall down—knocked it over in fact.

(p. 131)

The passage in question is the following:

I: "Are you fond of Daddy?"
HANS: "Oh yes."
I: "Or perhaps not."

Hans was playing with a little toy horse. At that moment the horse fell down, and Hans shouted out "The horse has fallen down! Look what a row it's making!"

I: "You're a little vexed with Daddy because Mummy's fond of him."
HANS: "No."

(p. 88)

However, Hans's father was not "talking of this death-wish" but saying, "Or perhaps not," an opening for Hans to express any feelings other than fondness for his father. The father says the horse fell down, not that Hans purposely dropped it, and he was in the best position to judge. However the toy fell, Hans's reaction is the best evidence of his thoughts and feelings. Hans responded with anxious comments about how the horse is kicking its feet. In the safety of his father's presence, Hans took advantage of the incident to work through the trauma that inaugurated his horse phobia, the horse falling down and kicking and making a row with its feet. The hypothesis of a death wish offers no additional explanatory power over that provided by the fright theory for any of the details of this incident.

Neu (1995) cites as evidence of hostility a similar instance in which Hans butts his father like a ram during play ("On April 25th Hans butted me in the stomach with his head, as he has already done once before. I asked him if he was a goat. 'Yes,' he said, 'a ram'" [p. 88]). However, Hans had experienced a ram attempting to butt him the previous summer:

HANS: "If you went up to it it used to butt, because it had horns".
I: "Did the lamb butt you?"
HANS: "It jumped up at me; Fritzl took me up to it once ... I went up to it once and didn't know, and all at once it jumped up at me."

(p. 88)

The fact that a boy of four plays a ram and bumps into his father thus turning a passive frightening experience into an actively mastered one is not evidence supporting Oedipal patricidal desires.

The third passage often cited as revealing Hans's Oedipal death wish toward his father occurs in the context of Hans having just accused his father of being angry with him when he tries to come into bed with his mother. Hans's father avoids answering and instead shifts topics to Hans's hypothesized hostility, which triggers Hans to spell out a revealing fantasy modeled on the description in a previous conversation of the Fritzl incident:

I: "So you want me to fall down?"

HANS: "Yes. You've got to be naked" (meaning "barefoot", as Fritzl had been) "and knock up against a stone and bleed, and then I'll be able to be alone with Mummy for a little bit at all events. When you come up into our flat I'll be able to run away quick so that you don't see."

I: "Can you remember who it was that knocked up against the stone?"

HANS: "Yes, Fritzl."

I: "When Fritzl fell down, what did you think?"

HANS: "That you should hit the stone and tumble down."

I: "So you'd like to go to Mummy?"

HANS: "Yes."

(p. 82)

Hans does not actually include his father falling down in his fantasy. Hans instead fantasizes his father hitting his foot and bleeding and having to go away, presumably to get his foot washed and bandaged like Fritzl did, thus allowing Hans to be alone with his mother. Hans's fantasy is not one of being permanently rid of his father, of his father falling down dead, or of Hans permanently possessing his mother. Rather, the fantasy is strictly one of the father being absent long enough to allow Hans some time to cuddle with his mother, after which his father returns, much like the father's return from trips to Vienna during the summer. Hans's fantasied triumph lasts for only a short time ("I'll be able to be alone with Mummy for a little bit") and its culmination is hardly Oedipal fulfilment; the father returns and Hans sneaks away to avoid his wrath ("When you come up into our flat I'll be able to run away quick so that you don't see"). Rather than a desire for the father's death or permanently being away, the fantasy suggests that Hans simply wants to regain access to his mother to satisfy his frustrated attachment needs, as indicated in the last sentence of the passage. (For a fuller defense of this interpretation, see my *Attachment, Sexuality, Power*.) As to Hans's reply portraying his father as tumbling down like, supposedly, Fritzl did, it is Hans's father who first suggested both the idea that Fritzl fell down (which Hans denied) and the idea that Hans thinks of his father as falling down, and there are no confirming elaborations by Hans, so this is best understood as likely suggestion.

Finally, a fourth passage late in the case history returns to the death wish issue and is also relevant to the question of whether Hans is afraid of his father, as the Oedipal "castration anxiety" hypothesis would predict. In this passage, Hans's father questions Hans about his time with his mother at their summer house at Gmunden when his father was away in Vienna and before the phobia developed:

I: "Did you often get into bed with Mummy at Gmunden?"
HANS: "Yes."
I: "And you used to think to yourself that you were Daddy?"
HANS: "Yes."
I: "And then you felt afraid of Daddy?"
HANS: *"You know everything; I didn't know anything."*

I: "When Fritzl fell down you thought: 'If only Daddy would fall down like that!' And when the lamb butted you you thought: 'If only it would butt Daddy!' Can you remember the funeral at Gmunden?"

(The first funeral that Hans had seen. He often recalls it, and it is no doubt a screen memory.)

HANS: "Yes. What about it?"
I: "You thought then that if only Daddy were to die you'd be Daddy."
HANS: "Yes."

(p. 90)

It is not Hans but his father who first puts forward the ideas that Hans is afraid of him and that Hans wants him to die, and Hans's response is consistent with suggestion according to Freud's guidelines. Rather than following the "yes" with confirmatory elaboration, Hans instead offers a vague and evasive general statement, "You know everything, I didn't know anything," which declares ignorance and thus avoids agreement, but also avoids disagreement by recognizing the father's privileged epistemological position. As Garrison (1978) says, "Hans here seems to be placating his father much more than expressing resentment toward him" (p. 528).

A major problem with construing the above passage as evidence for Oedipal fear is that Hans's father had repeatedly expressed his disapproval of Hans spending time in bed with his mother at Gmunden and had actively prevented Hans from doing so (for documentation, see my *Attachment, Sexuality, Power*). Thus, if Hans has some fear, it can be adequately explained as a non-Oedipal realistic fear of his father being angry over Hans seeking attachment soothing from his mother. As a result of his father's prohibitions, Hans is convinced that his father is angry at him and says so, in one of the most moving interchanges in the case history: "Hans: 'you're cross.' I: 'But that's not true.' Hans: 'Yes, it is true. You're cross. I know you are. It must be true'" (pp. 82–83). Hans's fear may also be a result of being humiliated over his attachment needs. The father observes: "Evidently, therefore, my explanation that only *little* boys come into bed with their Mummies and that *big* ones sleep in their own beds had not impressed him very much" (pp. 82–83). Yet, at the time the father's prohibitions started, this "big boy" was turning four years old and newly sleeping in his own bed in his own room and simply wanted some attachment soothing.

There is another argument for Hans's castration anxiety that Freud puts forward based on Hans's comments about his sister Hanna's widdler, but that argument fails the Suitability Argument test for conceptual reasons I have explained elsewhere (Wakefield, 2017). Overall, this brief survey reveals the surprising weakness of the evidence for Hans's Oedipal rage at his father or fear that might be interpreted as castration anxiety. The evidence certainly fails to satisfy the demanding methodological criteria for a Suitability Argument analysis put forward by Freud to justify the scientific legitimacy of hypotheses about unconscious motives.

Does Freud's Later Servant/Master Analogy Justify an Inference to Hans's Fear of His Father?

Acknowledging that direct evidence for Oedipal fear is lacking in the Hans case, in a later reanalysis in which he made Hans's castration fear even more central to his account, Freud (1926) took a different approach to supporting the fear hypothesis. He argued that, if one accepts the broader Oedipal sexual narrative, then a commonsense analogy allows one to infer the existence of Hans's Oedipal fear, even if direct evidence is lacking:

> Let us imagine that he is a young servant who is in love with the mistress of the house and who received some tokens of her favour. He hates his master, who is more powerful than he is, and he would like to have him out of the way. It would then be eminently natural for him to dread his master's vengeance and to develop a fear of him—just as "Little Hans" developed a phobia of horses … If "Little Hans", being in love with his mother, had shown fear of his father, we should have no right to say that he had a neurosis or a phobia.
>
> (1926, p. 103)

The analogy is superficially appealing. An attempt to overthrow an authority figure and to take his wife may indeed engender fear of retribution. Freud implicitly acknowledges there is no direct case evidence for such fear ("If 'Little Hans' … had shown fear of his father…"), but that it follows by analogy. The problem is that the analogy rests on the prior assumption of Oedipal sexual and aggressive desires. In the context of evaluating evidential support for the Oedipus complex, Freud's later argument by analogy blatantly begs the question.

Conclusion: The Failure of Freud's Suitability Argument for the Oedipal Theory in the Hans Case

If the Oedipus complex was already established as a universal psychosexual developmental stage that is essential to neurosogenesis, then it would be justifiable to search for Oedipal resonances in Hans's neurotic symptoms on the assumption that such Oedipal influences likely exist and simply need to be ferreted out with some minimal evidential justification. However, in the Hans case, Freud is not merely engaging in an interpretive exercise of applying Oedipal theory to the case data. He defines the case as a theory-testing context in which he is attempting to establish the existence and neurosogenic role of the Oedipus complex. In this context, one cannot assume beforehand that Oedipal meanings are lurking behind the patient's symptoms awaiting facile interpretive excavation. Instead, one must demonstrate that those meanings are scientifically worthy of postulation based on the evidence. To meet this evidential challenge, Freud suggests that we examine the detailed features of Hans's symptoms for features that remain unexplained by the fright theory.

To obtain the evidential support for the Oedipal theory he is seeking, Freud attempts to show that postulating Oedipal contents provides distinctive explanatory power in understanding otherwise inexplicable details of Hans's phobic symptoms. Freud's writings reviewed in Chapter 9 indicate that he fully understood the ample methodological pitfalls in formulating Oedipal etiological hypotheses to explain Hans's symptoms, and he consequently set the evidential bar appropriately high. He insists on compelling and demanding Miss Havisham or jigsaw-puzzle type levels of fit between etiological hypothesis and symptomatic facts so as to yield presumptive—although by no means infallible— explanatory illumination.

In this chapter, I have surveyed Freud's main attempts to justify Oedipal hypotheses based on the explanatory Suitability Argument regarding the details of Hans's symptoms. These ranged from the claimed diffuseness of Hans's symptoms and the claimed symbolic transfer onto the feared horses of Hans's father's moustache and glasses to the claimed hostile and fearful Oedipal meanings that became united with horse-related memories in the Lizzi and Fritzl incidents. In every instance, I found that Freud failed to satisfy the appropriate validity requirements that he himself properly set out in his methodological prescriptions for justifying such an argument, as reviewed in Chapter 9. He failed to show that there is anything in the details of Hans's phobia or in the incidents preceding the phobia that requires the postulation of Oedipal meanings to achieve explanatory adequacy.

The problem with Freud's arguments for Oedipal explanations of Hans's symptoms is that they violate the demanding methodological rules suggested by Freud himself to avoid creating spurious explanations by associating backwards from the symptoms of a neurosis. Freud specified that there should be features of the patient's symptoms that cannot be explained in terms of the features of the precipitating cause and that uniquely or most plausibly can be explained by the proposed specific cause. Freud's hypotheses about the meanings of the details of Hans's fears do not begin to satisfy these methodological requirements. Freud's signature explanatory Suitability Argument based on the details of Hans's phobia thus fails to support Freud's Oedipal account of Hans's fears.

Instead, the details of the phobia reveal a pattern of fears that are adequately explained by the features of the horse accident itself and earlier sensitizing incidents, and Hans's understandable reactions to those events. Moreover, it emerges that the various details of Hans's fears are not independent of each other in a way that requires specific additional individualized explanations but rather are linked in Hans's mind by his *theory* of horses and their dangers; for example, a falling-down horse is likely to be an angry horse and thus is likely to bite if it gets a chance, and heavily laden horses are more likely to fall down. Contrary to Freud's dismissal of the horse accident as suitably explanatory of the features of Hans's fear, the accident plus earlier experiences are quite adequate as triggers for intense fear in a young child specifically of the sort that afflict Hans.

Applying Freud's own demanding requirements for a successful "suitability" argument, I have argued that a careful examination of the Hans case data reveals the absence of any such persuasive Oedipal-related features of Hans's symptoms. Every salient feature of the phobia's contents cited by Freud can plausibly be explained by horse-related events without the necessary involvement of Oedipal meanings. There is no hermeneutic "smoking gun" in the phobia's contents that reveals its Oedipal genesis or any other genesis outside of the horse accident and other horse-related experiences. I thus conclude that Freud's own signature methodology yields the conclusion that the Hans case does not support his Oedipal hypothesis.

We saw in Chapter 9 that Frank Cioffi defended Freud's "suitability" style of argument as a potentially legitimate form of argument of the type he illustrated with the "Miss Havisham" example. I will allow Cioffi to have the almost-last word on whether Freud's use of this form of argument succeeds in establishing Freud's claims. Cioffi offers the challenge: "But do Freud's etiological explanations meet the Miss Havisham standard?" (Cioffi, 2001, p. 162). He concludes that they clearly do not:

> The right objection to Freud's etiological claims is not that "jigsaw-solving" of the Miss Havisham kind falls short of demonstration but that Freud's explanations regularly fall woefully short of the Miss Havisham standard in spite of a tendentious insistence that they meet it.
>
> (Cioffi, 1998, p. 281)

I agree with Cioffi that Freud cannot be dismissed just because his method was the challenging but in-principle potentially valid one of constructing persuasive singular causal explanations of anomalous features of neurotic symptoms. But sadly I also have to agree with him in concluding that Freud's lack of explanatory discipline—the very thing feared by critics of such explanations—means that his attempt becomes an object lesson in what can go wrong with the use of singular causal explanation, and thus what can go wrong with psychoanalysis as the reconstruction of an individual's intentional system.

Freud's failure has broader implications for psychology. His failure does not of course change the fact that in everyday life and in clinical psychoanalysis or psychotherapy there are myriad valid singular causal inferences that yield correct conclusions. The problem is at the more systemic level of how to translate this into something usable by science in a formal way. The failure of Freud's attempt to solve the problem of the scientific use of singular causal explanation via his "solution-to-a-puzzle" uniqueness hypothesis underscores the difficulty of the problem for theory construction in psychology. It also opens the door to more relativistic approaches to interpretation. One must agree with Grunbaum that subsequent attempts to evade this problem by adopting various anti-scientific twists on hermeneutics must be dismissed because they do not resolve the veridical explanatory challenge but just change the topic. So, here is a form of legitimate causal inference that we each successfully and validly engage in perhaps thousands of times a day in coordinating socially with others, and yet philosophy of science has little to say about how this form of explanation can be regimented by an explicit explanatory methodology to be successfully incorporated into an idiographic science of mind, other than as a generator of hypotheses for other methodologies to examine.

References

Bowlby, J. (1973). *Attachment and loss (Vol. 2): Separation: Anxiety and anger.* New York: Basic Books.

Cioffi, F. (1998). *Freud and the question of pseudoscience.* Chicago, IL: Open Court.

Cioffi, F. (2001). The rationale for psychoanalytic interpretation. *Psychological Inquiry*, 12(3), 161–166.

Freud, S. (1895). The psychotherapy of hysteria. *SE* 2, 253–305.

Freud, S. (1909). Analysis of a phobia in a five-year-old boy. *SE* 10, 1–150.

Freud, S. (1926). Inhibitions, symptoms and anxiety. *SE* 20, 75–176.

Garrison, M. (1978). A new look at Little Hans. *Psychoanalytic Review*, 65, 523–532.

Grunbaum, A. (1984). *The foundations of psychoanalysis: A philosophical critique.* Berkeley, CA: University of California Press.

Lynch, K. (2014). The vagaries of psychoanalytic interpretation: An investigation into the causes of the consensus problem in psychoanalysis. *Philosophia*, 42, 779–799.

Neu, J. (1977). *Emotion, thought & therapy: A study of Hume and Spinoza and the relationship of philosophical theories of the emotions to psychological theories of therapy.* Berkeley, CA: University of California Press.

Neu, J. (1995). "Does the Professor talk to God?" Learning from Little Hans. *Philosophy, Psychiatry & Psychology*, 2, 137–158.

O'Connor, A., & Ma, K. (2007). A carriage horse dies after bolting onto a sidewalk. *New York Times*, September 15, 2007, p. B2.

Wakefield, J. C. (2017). Concept representation in the child: What did Little Hans mean by "widdler"? *Psychoanalytic Psychology*, 34(3), 352–360.

Wakefield, J. C. (2022). *Attachment, sexuality, power: Oedipal theory as regulator of family affection in Freud's case of Little Hans.* New York: Routledge.

Wolpe, J., & Rachman, S. (1960). Psychoanalytic "evidence": A critique based on Freud's case of Little Hans. *Journal of Nervous and Mental Disease*, 131(2), 135–148.

Chapter 11

Critical Examination of Grunbaum's "Tally Argument" Analysis of Freud's Response to the Suggestion Objection

The "Suitability Argument" Versus Grunbaum's "Tally Argument" as Freud's Reply to the Suggestion Objection

In Chapter 9, I argued that Freud's foundational strategy for defending his Oedipal theory of the psychoneuroses against the suggestion objection consists of the Suitability Argument. That is, he argues that hypothesized unconscious Oedipal mental contents offer compelling singular causal explanations of otherwise inexplicable features of the patient's symptoms (i.e., they offer "suitability as determinants" of the symptoms, as he describes it), and that the overall evidence of a clinical case inevitably converges to the Oedipal account as the uniquely suitable basis for such an explanation. I argued in Chapters 3 and 9 that Freud further anchored his overall Suitability Argument in the "more direct" evidence of the Hans case that, he thought, largely evaded the suggestion objection and confirmed the results of his adult analyses and thus vindicated his psychoanalytic methodology.

In a highly influential analysis, Adolf Grunbaum (1984) takes a radically different approach to explaining Freud's argument in response to the suggestion objection. Grunbaum argues that, at least during the early and middle period of Freud's theorizing, Freud relied not on any "suitability" interpretive strategy but rather on therapeutic success in eliminating symptoms as the ultimate evidence for the correctness of his etiological insights. This defense on the basis of therapeutic cure finds expression in a formal argument that Grunbaum attributes to Freud, which Grunbaum labels the "Tally Argument" for reasons explained below.

I agree with Grunbaum that the suggestion objection is the greatest threat to Freud's sexual theory of the neuroses and to psychoanalytic claims based on clinical evidence more generally. I also agree that Freud fully understood this threat. I thus agree that identifying how Freud attempted to respond to the suggestion objection is central to understanding and assessing Freud's argument. Grunbaum makes an enormous contribution to Freud scholarship by clarifying and underscoring this situation. However, it is also true that one must tread carefully in attributing too much importance to claims of

DOI: 10.4324/9781003272472-11

therapeutic efficacy. Freud, like all medical researchers in his time and ours, touted his therapeutic success, apparently with exaggerated rhetoric, as evidence that he was on to a theoretical breakthrough. Such claims based on anecdotal clinical evidence appear throughout the medical literature of Freud's day, including Victorian tracts on how masturbation is the source, and stopping masturbation the cure, of myriad diseases (see my forthcoming *Foucault Versus Freud*). However, such claims were not generally taken as sufficient for scientifically demonstrating one theory of etiology over others for reasons, such as suggestion and spontaneous remission, that were as obvious to Victorians as they are to us. My dispute, then, is with Grunbaum's central thesis that Freud for some major period of time during the early to middle prime of his career elevated therapeutic success into the fundamental epistemological guarantor of the correctness of his sexual etiological theory.

To be clear, if Grunbaum's rival analysis of Freud's argument is correct, then my analysis of Freud's methodology, of his intentions in presenting the Hans case, and of his response to the suggestion objection would all be incorrect. Moreover, my negative evaluation in Chapter 10 of Freud's Oedipal explanations of the details of Hans's symptoms, in which I used the Suitability Argument as the measure of Freud's success or failure, would be misguided and fail to address Freud's argument. Fortunately for me, and contrary to Grunbaum's claims and his surprisingly tendentious reading of Freud, it is quite clear from Freud's writings that he never seriously relied on therapeutic success in the fundamental ways proposed by Grunbaum. Freud relied on therapeutic success neither as the guarantor of the truth of his etiological conclusions nor as the basis of his response to the suggestion objection, as I shall show.

In Chapter 3, we saw that Freud sharply distinguished two aspects of psychoanalysis, science versus therapy—or, equivalently, etiological insight versus symptom cure. Psychoanalysis, as Freud said over and over, is simultaneously a method of research for revealing the patient's unconscious mental contents and a method of therapeutic cure of psychoneurotic symptoms that often dissipate once unconscious conflicts are resolved. We saw that Freud embraces the research aspect of psychoanalysis in uncovering unconscious contents as the more fundamental goal of the analyst, and sees symptom remission as a fortunate and beneficial effect of the scientific investigation:

> It may be laid down that the aim of the treatment is to remove the patient's resistances and to pass his repressions in review and thus to bring about the most far-reaching unification and strengthening of his ego, to enable him to save the mental energy which he is expending upon internal conflicts, to make the best of him that his inherited capacities will allow and so to make him as efficient and as capable of enjoyment as is possible. The removal of the symptoms of the illness is not specifically aimed at, but is achieved, as it were, as a by-product if the analysis is properly carried through.
>
> (1923a, p. 251)

Grunbaum argues that for *epistemic* purposes of evidentially supporting his theoretical conclusions, Freud reversed the causal ordering. He took the therapeutic successes of psychoanalysis to demonstrate that the insights yielded by psychoanalytic research are valid discoveries of the etiology of psychoneuroses. In the next section, I review Grunbaum's reconstruction of Freud's basic argument. There is a vast literature on Grunbaum's Tally Argument analysis (for just a few of the many excellent commentaries, see, for example, Esterson, 1996; Forrester, 1986; Grant & Harari, 1990; Hopkins, 1988; Levy, 1988; Richardson, 1990; Robinson, 1993; and Sachs, 1989). However, rather than reviewing this literature, I follow my own critical and interpretive path here in comparing Grunbaum's "Tally Argument" analysis of Freud's response to the suggestion objection to my own "Suitability Argument" analysis.

Before proceeding, a comment on terminology is needed. Given the close relationship in Freudian doctrine between psychoneurotic symptoms and repressed Oedipal conflicts, the term "neurosis" may be used to refer to either or both. Complicating matters, Freud considered an internal conflict a neurosis in the pathology sense only when it was accompanied by symptoms, and he considers suppressed internal conflict without symptoms to be ubiquitous and not inherently pathological. However, in discussing Grunbaum's thesis, it is often necessary to distinguish the symptoms of a neurosis or their cure from the repressed internal conflict that is assumed to be causing them and its possible resolution. Grunbaum's and other commentators' writings sometimes become confusing because "neuroses" or "cure of a neurosis" are used ambiguously for either one. To avoid such ambiguities, I attempt to carefully distinguish "therapeutic cure" of symptoms from "insight" into and resolution of internal conflict.

Grunbaum's "Tally Argument" Analysis of Freud's Reply to the Suggestion Objection

According to Grunbaum, Freud's "Master Argument" against the suggestion objection, which he calls the "Tally Argument," is based on the therapeutic success of psychoanalysis in curing the symptoms of psychoneuroses: "Let us now articulate systematically the *argument* he [Freud] uses to counter the charge of epistemic contamination of clinical data by suggestion ... His counterargument does invoke *therapeutic* success" (1984, p. 139). Freud does not explicitly state anything like the argument Grunbaum attributes to him. However, Grunbaum claims to find the premises of the argument in a close reading of a passage in Freud's *Introductory Lectures*—let's call it the "tally passage." Prior to the tally passage, Freud, having explained how the analyst uses the patient's transference as leverage to get the patient to accept the analyst's interpretations, confronts the inevitable suggestion objection:

> But you will now tell me that, no matter whether we call the motive force of our analysis transference or suggestion, there is a risk that the influencing of our patient may make the objective certainty of our findings doubtful. What is advantageous to our therapy is damaging to our researches. This is the objection that is most often raised against psychoanalysis.
>
> (1917, p. 452)

Freud then offers the following replies in part (his reply is considered in more detail below):

> Anyone who has himself carried out psycho-analyses will have been able to convince himself on countless occasions that it is impossible to make suggestions to a patient in that way ... After all, his conflicts will only be successfully solved and his resistances overcome if the anticipatory ideas he is given tally with what is real in him. Whatever in the doctor's conjectures is inaccurate drops out in the course of the analysis; it has to be withdrawn and replaced by something more correct.
>
> (p. 452)

The critical sentence in this passage for Grunbaum is Freud's assertion: "After all, his conflicts will only be successfully solved and his resistances overcome if the anticipatory ideas he is given tally with what is real in him." Grunbaum interprets Freud as saying that therapeutic cure of symptoms will occur only if the psychoanalytic interpretations are correct and thus resolve the underlying conflict. Grunbaum thus claims that the sentence is a "bold assertion of the *causal indispensability* of psychoanalytic insight for the conquest of the patient's psychoneurosis" (1984, p. 139).

In more detail, Grunbaum claims to find implicit in the tally passage two "necessity" claims that together Grunbaum labels the "necessary condition thesis," or "NCT." According to Grunbaum, Freud claims, first, that "only the psychoanalytic method of interpretation and treatment can yield ... correct insight into the unconscious pathogens" (1984, p. 139) that are causing the patient's symptoms—that is, only psychoanalysis can reveal the true cause of the symptoms. And, second, "the analysand's correct insight into the etiology of his affliction ... is, in turn, *causally necessary* for the therapeutic conquest of his neurosis" (1984, pp. 139–140)—that is, only insight into the truth about the cause of the symptoms can set the patient free of the symptoms.

From NCT, one can deduce two rather dramatic conclusions. The first—which is the primary payoff for Freud, in Grunbaum's reconstruction—is the conclusion that, for any patient successfully relieved of psychoneurotic symptoms in psychoanalysis, it *must* be because the analysis got at the true etiology: "Conclusion 1. The psychoanalytic interpretations of the hidden causes of P's behavior given to him by his analyst are indeed correct" (1984, p. 140).

However, the cost of this reassuring conclusion is another less welcome conclusion that follows just as logically and inevitably from the same extremely strong premises, namely, that psychoneurotic symptoms can never be enduringly relieved by any method or circumstance other than psychoanalysis: "Conclusion 2. Only analytic treatment could have wrought the conquest of P's psychoneurosis" (1984, p. 140).

In other words, to allow Freud to use therapeutic success to infer that psychoanalysis identifies true causes and does not work by suggestion, Grunbaum attributes to Freud a rejection of any possibility that nonveridical suggestive or other placebo processes ever work to bring about therapeutic success under any circumstances. Veridical insight in psychoanalysis has a *unique* power to enduringly relieve psychoneurotic symptoms, according to this view; psychoanalysis is *necessary* for therapeutic cure and there is *no other way* to achieve enduring relief of psychoneurotic symptoms, so cure implies veridical insight:

> Freud is at pains to employ the Tally Argument in order to justify the following epistemological claim: actual *durable* therapeutic success guarantees *not only* that the pertinent analytic interpretations *ring* true or credible to the analysand but also that they *are* indeed veridical, or quite close to the mark.
>
> (1984, p. 140)

According to Grunbaum, via the Tally Argument, Freud defends himself from both the substantive and methodological attacks on psychoanalysis by the suggestion objection:

> In short, psychoanalytic treatment successes as a whole vouch for the truth of the Freudian theory of personality, including its specific etiologies of the psychoneuroses and even its general theory of psychosexual development. As a further corollary, the psychoanalytic probing of the unconscious is vindicated as a method of etiologic investigation by its therapeutic achievements.
>
> (1984, pp. 140–141)

This is a remarkable claim to attribute to Freud because it rejects the possibility of spontaneous remission, placebo cures, and cures by suggestion that saturated medical discussion in Freud's time. Nonetheless, for Grunbaum's analysis of Freud's argument to work, Freud must deny any such possibilities and embrace this extreme premise. Grunbaum is quite explicit about this bold claim: "Clearly, NCT entails not only that there is no spontaneous remission of psychoneuroses but also that, if there are any cures at all, psychoanalysis is *uniquely* therapeutic for such disorders as compared to any *rival* therapies" (Grunbaum 1984, p. 139).

There are two questions that need to be answered in evaluating Grunbaum's Tally Argument analysis. The first is whether Grunbaum's interpretation of the tally passage—and of another passage he cites in the Hans case as supporting his reading—is a plausible reading so that the Tally Argument analysis has the grounding in Freud's text that Grunbaum claims it does. The second and more substantive question is, tally passage aside, does the overall textual evidence support Grunbaum's claim that Freud believed the doctrines, such as the nonexistence of spontaneous remission or placebo cure of the psychoneuroses, that Grunbaum's analysis necessarily attributes to him? I will consider these questions in turn and argue that the answer to each of them is a clear "no."

One comment before proceeding: Grunbaum takes the entire period of Freud's theoretical development from *Studies on Hysteria* through the seduction theory and on to the Oedipal theory as the period during which Freud embraced the Tally Argument. However, technically, all of Freud's successful cases before he started applying the Oedipal theory must be considered, from Freud's later perspective, to have involved incorrect interpretations and thus to that extent to violate the NCT. It would seem, then, that Grunbaum must hold that Freud believed he had no therapeutic successes throughout those earlier periods. However, with regard to the seduction theory period, it seems charitable to take Grunbaum's phrase above, that the insight must be "veridical, or quite close to the mark," in a broad enough sense that fantasies of seduction that were transformations of Oedipal desires can fall under that category. So, I will follow Grunbaum in allowing that Freud's therapeutic successes during the seduction theory period do not falsify the Tally Argument analysis. However, Grunbaum does draw the conclusion that in the earlier period of *Studies*, before Freud began to trace symptoms back to determinants in sexual experiences in early childhood, the Tally Argument analysis implies that Freud believed he had had no *enduring* therapeutic successes. This claim will be evaluated below.

Is There Persuasive Textual Evidence of Freud Embracing the Tally Argument?

The textual evidence Grunbaum presents for Freud's explicitly embracing the Tally Argument consists of two passages, one from the third part of his *Introductory Lectures* in 1917 and one from the Hans case. I consider them in turn.

Does the Tally Passage Assert the Tally Argument?

In assessing Grunbaum's Tally Argument reading of the tally passage, I am going to compare the plausibility of his interpretation to the plausibility of an interpretation based on my Suitability Analysis of Freud's response to the suggestion objection. I will examine not only the text of the tally passage, but also evidence from other passages from the same work and a few passages from elsewhere in Freud's work.

Looking at the passage and the preceding text, it is clear that, as Grunbaum recognizes, this passage is Freud's primary response to the suggestion objection, considered at the end of his series of lectures. The suggestion objection was raised late in the previous lecture, and the chapter in which the "tally passage" occurs starts with an acknowledgment that the suggestion objection will be the day's topic:

> You know what we are going to talk about to-day. You asked me why we do not make use of direct suggestion in psycho-analytic therapy, when we admit that our influence rests essentially on transference—that is, on suggestion; and you added a doubt whether, in view of this predominance of suggestion, we are still able to claim that our psychological discoveries are objective. I promised I would give you a detailed reply.
>
> (1917, p. 448)

Note that Freud identifies two questions to be addressed. The first concerns therapy. It is the question why, if, as Freud has acknowledged, suggestion still plays a role in psychoanalysis via the use of transference to persuade patients to accept certain interpretations, psychoanalysts don't just return to using hypnotic direct suggestion. The first part of the lecture is taken up with Freud's answer, which consists of the usual historical explanation of how he started by being influenced by Bernheim but soon encountered various problems and disadvantages with the use of direct suggestion, and also found the technique tiresome and of limited effectiveness, whereas transference analysis utilizes suggestion in a more effective way.

The second topic concerns insight and psychoanalytic theory's claims to etiological knowledge. It is the question of how, once any intrusion of suggestion is admitted, one can still claim to achieve veridical insight and knowledge. When Freud turns to this second question, he restates the suggestion objection as he is considering it here:

> But you will now tell me that, no matter whether we call the motive force of our analysis transference or suggestion, there is a risk that the influencing of our patient may make the objective certainty of our findings doubtful. What is advantageous to our therapy is damaging to our researches. This is the objection that is most often raised against psychoanalysis ... If it were justified, psycho-analysis would be nothing more than a particularly well-disguised and particularly effective form of suggestive treatment and we should have to attach little weight to all that it tells us about what influences our lives, the dynamics of the mind or the unconscious.
>
> (p. 452)

This restatement of the suggestion objection is clearly aimed not at anything having to do with therapeutic cure but rather at whether psychoanalysis's theoretical claims are justified given the intrusion of suggestion. Freud observes that suggesting an Oedipal interpretation to the patient could be "advantageous to our therapy" and make psychoanalysis a "particularly effective form of suggestive treatment." The objection thus takes for granted that false suggestions may be therapeutically effective. The concern is that such suggestions might "make the objective certainty of our findings doubtful" and be "damaging to our researches," placing in doubt "all that it tells us about what influences our lives, the dynamics of the mind or the unconscious." The answer to this conundrum is provided in the remainder of Freud's passage, which Grunbaum regards as "epistemologically perhaps the most pregnant single passage in his writings" (1984, p. 138):

> Anyone who has himself carried out psycho-analyses will have been able to convince himself on countless occasions that it is impossible to make suggestions to a patient in that way. The doctor has no difficulty, of course, in making him a supporter of some particular theory and in thus making him share some possible error of his own. In this respect the patient is behaving like anyone else—like a pupil—but this only affects his intelligence, not his illness. After all, his conflicts will only be successfully solved and his resistances overcome if the anticipatory ideas he is given tally with what is real in him. Whatever in the doctor's conjectures is inaccurate drops out in the course of the analysis; it has to be withdrawn and replaced by something more correct. We endeavour by a careful technique to avoid the occurrence of premature successes due to suggestion; but no harm is done even if they do occur, for we are not satisfied by a first success. We do not regard an analysis as at an end until all the obscurities of the case are cleared up, the gaps in the patient's memory filled in, the precipitating causes of the repressions discovered.
>
> (Freud, 1917, pp. 452–453)

In this passage explaining why psychoanalysis can be presumed to yield genuine knowledge despite elements of suggestion, the therapeutic cure of symptoms is not mentioned even once (as others have observed, e.g., Sachs, 1989). Instead, Freud mentions the resolution of conflicts and overcoming of resistances—the internal psychological consequences of insight—and asserts that these internal processes will only occur "if the anticipatory ideas he is given tally with what is real in him." But how do we know that it "tallies with what is real"? Instead of citing symptom elimination, Freud cites the classic rationale for believing that a full suitability analysis yields truth, namely, there is one correct answer to the puzzle of the meaning of the patient's symptoms and eventually all competing answers are disconfirmed by the clinical data as the analysis proceeds: "Whatever in the doctor's conjectures is inaccurate drops out in the course of the analysis; it has to be withdrawn and replaced by something more correct." Indeed, to get to that full unique final explanation, one must be vigilant not to be distracted by premature success at the insight or symptom level, as Freud indicates, for it is the full analysis that yields a unique solution. If Grunbaum's analysis were correct, the last sentence would read, "We do not regard an analysis as at an end until therapeutic cure occurs, guaranteeing the validity of our insights." Instead, it offers a suitability-type rationale of the compelling uniqueness of the explanation that eventually is arrived at of the specific features of the symptoms: the obscurities of the case are cleared up, the gaps in the patient's memory filled in, the precipitating causes of the repressions discovered. The fullness and compelling quality of the explanation supports its truth.

Looked at from this perspective, the tally passage comes into focus not as a unique statement in Freud's work of the Tally Argument but as one more of the many statements of Freud's commitment to the uniqueness claim and the suitability approach. The tally passage's assertions bear a striking resemblance to portions of the passages we identified in Chapter 9 as expressing these methodological commitments, for example:

> We learn with astonishment ... that *we are not in a position to force anything on the patient ... or to influence the products of the analysis by arousing an expectation* ... [I]f I had, it would inevitably have been betrayed in the end by some contradiction in the material.
>
> (1895b, p. 295)

> What makes him certain in the end is precisely the complication of the problem before him ... [I]f all these conditions are fulfilled, then one knows that one has solved the puzzle and that there is no alternative solution.
>
> (1923b, pp. 115–116)

> [I]f nothing further develops we may conclude that we have made a mistake and we shall admit as much to the patient ... Such an opportunity will arise when some new material has come to light which allows us to make a better construction and so to correct our error. In this way the false construction drops out, as if it had never been made ... Only the further course of the analysis enables us to decide whether our constructions are correct or unserviceable.
>
> (1937, pp. 261–262, 265)

Freud's focus on insight and the corresponding alteration of intrapsychic contents and conflicts rather than symptom cure per se as the basic task and epistemological warrant of psychoanalysis is indicated in passages scattered throughout *Introductory Lectures*, for example:

254 Grunbaum's "Tally Argument"

By carrying what is unconscious on into what is conscious, we lift the repressions, we remove the preconditions for the formation of symptoms, we transform the pathogenic conflict into a normal one for which it must be possible somehow to find a solution. All that we bring about in a patient is this single psychical change: the length to which it is carried is the measure of the help we provide.

(1917, p. 435)

The repression must be got rid of—after which the substitution of the conscious material for the unconscious can proceed smoothly. How, then, do we lift a repression of this kind? Here our task enters a second phase. First, the search for the repression ... By searching for the repression in this way, by uncovering the resistances, by pointing out what is repressed, we really succeed in accomplishing our task—that is, in overcoming the resistances, lifting the repression and transforming the unconscious material into conscious.

(p. 438)

An Unworthy Interpretation of Freud

As various commentators, including Grunbaum himself, have pointed out, in the same book as the tally passage on which Grunbaum places so much weight, there is another passage that clearly contradicts Grunbaum's interpretation of the tally passage. Both passages are part of the same semester's lectures in spring 1917 at the University of Vienna, so we can presume that Freud thought they were consistent. This additional passage also sheds light on the "Tally Argument" versus "Suitability Analysis" question.

The passage in question occurs near the beginning of the semester, framing Freud's overall approach. It follows a discussion in which Freud provides some insights into a case of delusional jealousy, to which I will return. Freud then takes up the question of whether psychoanalysis's claims about etiology must be justified by reference to therapeutic outcome:

Perhaps, however, the much-abused psycho-analysis has friends among you who will be pleased if it can be justified from another direction—from the therapeutic side. As you know, our psychiatric therapy is not hitherto able to influence delusions. Is it possible, perhaps, that psycho-analysis can do so, thanks to its insight into the mechanism of these symptoms? No, Gentlemen, it cannot. It is as powerless (for the time being at least) against these ailments as any other form of therapy. We can understand, indeed, what has happened in the patient, but we have no means of making the patient himself understand it. You have heard how I was unable to pursue the analysis of this delusion beyond a first beginning. Will you be inclined to maintain on that account that an analysis of such cases is to be rejected because it is fruitless? I think not. We have a right, or rather a duty, to carry on our research without consideration of any immediate beneficial effect.

(1917, p. 255)

Freud comes close here to explicitly rejecting Grunbaum's Tally Argument analysis. He asks whether psychoanalytic insights can be "justified" by therapeutic cure—"from the therapeutic side." Referencing his delusion example, he asks whether the "insight into the mechanism of these symptoms" that he reached in his earlier discussion makes cure possible, and he answers unequivocally that it does not and that no therapeutic progress has yet been made with this sort of case. Yet, via psychoanalytic exploration, "we can understand, indeed, what has happened in the patient." Freud insists that rather than abandoning analysis because it is fruitless therapeutically, "We have a right, or rather a duty, to carry on our research without consideration of any immediate beneficial effect"—implying that psychoanalytic research has some basis for evaluating validity of insight that is independent of therapeutic benefit.

We now come to the final portion of the above passage, which is where Freud clearly rejects any argument that places the burden for the validity of psychoanalytic insight on therapeutic cure:

Even if psycho-analysis showed itself as unsuccessful in every other form of nervous and psychical disease as it does in delusions, it would still remain completely justified as an irreplaceable instrument of scientific research.

(1917, p. 255)

The Tally Argument claims that the only justification for psychoanalytic claims is therapeutic success, so Freud here in effect rejects the Tally Argument analysis.

Before addressing Grunbaum's response to this textual contradiction to his analysis, there are two further points to be plumbed from the passages preceding the above text that describe the delusional jealousy case, because these passages reveal the Suitability Argument at work. First, Freud identifies details of the symptoms and their genesis that seem puzzling or arbitrary and require explanation, for example: "Must we be content to suppose that it is a matter of indifference or caprice or is inexplicable whether a delusion of jealousy arises rather than any other sort?"; and, "I would draw your attention to the inconspicuous detail that the patient herself positively provoked the anonymous letter, which now gave support to her delusion" (p. 251). Second, Freud claims that the overall facts make certain singular causal explanations virtually necessary, for example: "she let fall a few remarks which allowed of, and indeed necessitated, a particular interpretation; and this interpretation threw a clear light on the genesis of her delusion of jealousy"; and, "the fact that the delusion turned out to be precisely a jealous one and not one of another kind was unambiguously determined by the experience that lay behind the illness" (p. 252). Consequently, "the delusion has ceased to be absurd or unintelligible; ... the delusion was necessary, as a reaction to an unconscious mental process which we have inferred" (p. 253). Freud's example of delusional jealousy is intended to illustrate the foundational point that etiological investigation using a Suitability Argument framework in which one constructs singular causal explanations of otherwise unexplained features of symptoms can proceed without any reference to treatment or cure.

So, what is Grunbaum's reply to this seeming knock-down falsification of his reconstruction of Freud's argument? Grunbaum to his credit acknowledges that there is a conflicting passage ("Yet in an earlier lecture of the same series, he simply ignored the pivotal role that therapeutic success was to play in his Tally Argument" [1984, p. 141]) and cites the critical passage. But then, instead of pondering how to reconcile the two passages or otherwise grappling with the problem posed by the passage for his view, Grunbaum simply marvels at the fact that Freud would say something that contradicts the Tally Argument and accuses Freud of what in effect comes to intellectual dishonesty: "But in the face of the suggestibility challenge, this statement is a gratuitous piece of salesmanship, unworthy of the Freud who gave us the Tally Argument" (1984, p. 141). In failing to take seriously the conflict between the earlier passage and the Tally Argument analysis of the later passage, and in assuming that the problem lies with the earlier passage because, after all, Freud "gave us the Tally Argument," Grunbaum blatantly begs the substantive question raised by the passage.

How can Grunbaum be so uncharitable regarding counterevidence to his thesis, here and (we shall see) elsewhere? Ironically, I think this reaction has an affinity to Freud's "unique solution" methodology. Grunbaum seems to assume that the Tally Argument is the only possible response Freud could have to the suggestion objection and, not seeing another plausible solution (such as the Suitability Argument), that it has a compelling, unique singular causal explanatory quality for understanding Freud's position. So, he thinks, it *must* be right as an analysis of Freud's intentions. Any seeming counterevidence in Freud's text must be misleading and just awaits explaining away.

Explaining the Narcissistic Neuroses

Grunbaum draws attention to some additional passages in *Introductory Lectures* that also seem to challenge the Tally Argument analysis. These passages concern the class of serious mental disturbances, of which the earlier-discussed delusional jealousy is one, that Freud called the "narcissistic neuroses" and we tend to classify as psychotic disorders. As in his comments on delusional jealousy. Freud acknowledges that psychoanalysis cannot provide therapeutic cure for any of the narcissistic neuroses. Yet, he claims to understand their causes. This poses a prima facie problem for the Tally Argument reading.

Here are the relevant passages on the narcissistic neuroses in *Introductory Lectures*:

> There are, however, other forms of illness in which, in spite of the conditions being the same, our therapeutic procedure is never successful. In them, too, it had been a question of an original conflict between the ego and the libido which led to repression ... [I]n them, too, it is possible to trace the points in the patient's life at which the repressions occurred; we make use of the same procedure, are ready to make the same promises and give the same help by the offer of anticipatory ideas ... And yet we do not succeed in lifting a single resistance or getting rid of a single repression. These patients, para-noics, melancholics, sufferers from dementia praecox, remain on the whole unaffected and proof against psycho-analytic therapy.
>
> (1917, pp. 438–439)

> Nor must we fail to point out that a large number of the individual findings of analysis, which might otherwise be suspected of being pro-ducts of suggestion, are confirmed from another and irreproachable source. Our guarantors in this case are the sufferers from dementia prae-cox and paranoia, who are of course far above any suspicion of being influenced by suggestion. The translations of symbols and the phantasies, which these patients produce for us and which in them have forced their way into consciousness, coincide faithfully with the results of our investi-gations into the unconscious of transference neurotics and thus confirm the objective correctness of our interpretations, on which doubt is so often thrown.
>
> (1917, p. 453)

Grunbaum notes that Freud holds that the narcissistic neuroses are refrac-tory to psychoanalytic treatment, and that therefore in that subclass "the Tally Argument is, of course, unavailable to authenticate his clinically inferred etiologies by means of therapeutic success." He then confronts and tries to resolve the puzzle Freud's comments present for his analysis:

> Yet, in another lecture, he explicitly gave the same epistemic sanction to the clinical etiologies of the two subclasses of psychoneuroses. And pre-sumably he did so by extrapolating the therapeutic vindication of the psychoanalytic method of etiologic investigation from the transference neuroses to the narcissistic ones.
>
> (1984, p. 141)

Thus, Grunbaum's solution to the puzzle is that Freud supports his theory of the etiology of the narcissistic neuroses by extrapolating from the psycho-neuroses. This does not fit the textual evidence. Rather than extrapolating, in the passages about the narcissistic neuroses Freud seems to be applying suitability logic to the narcissistic neuroses, and *discovering* that they have the same causes as the psychoneuroses. This fits Freud's description of the procedure as the same as in the psychoneuroses—of tracing back symptoms to the points in the patient's life at which repressions occurred, of offering the same help to the patient by way of anticipatory ideas, of interpreting fantasies, and so on. In fact, Freud suggests that the evidential relationship goes in the opposite direction; he uses the results of his investigations of the narcissistic neuroses as evidence for the valid understanding of the psychoneuroses. He can do this because uncontrolled expression of fantasy in narcissistic neuroses can provide uniquely spontaneous forms of evidence that in other patients would remain unconscious and that are not plausibly subject to suggestion, allowing the results to be above suspicion and thus guarantors of the results in the suggestion-vulnerable transference neuroses.

I conclude that the texts Grunbaum cites from *Introductory Lectures*, including the tally passage, do not support his Tally Argument analysis and point decidedly in the direction of the Suitability Argument as Freud's fundamental answer to the suggestion objection. However, there is another passage, this one from the Hans case, that Grunbaum cites in support of his analysis and that I now briefly address.

Does the Hans Case History Support the Tally Argument?

In the course of presenting the NCT based on the tally passage from *Introductory Lectures*, Grunbaum claims that additional support for his analysis is provided by a further passage from the Hans case history. He claims that the NCT's assertion of the necessity of psychoanalytic insight for therapeutic cure is in fact "a terse enunciation of the thesis that Freud had previously formulated more explicitly in his 1909 case history of Little Hans" (1984, p. 139), and he quotes the following Hans passage:

> In a psycho-analysis the physician always gives his patient (sometimes to a greater and sometimes to a less extent) the conscious anticipatory ideas by the help of which he is put in a position to recognize and to grasp the unconscious material. For there are some patients who need more of such assistance and some who need less; but there are none who get through without some of it. Slight disorders may perhaps be brought to an end by the subject's unaided efforts, but never a neurosis—a thing which has set itself up against the ego as an element alien to it. To get the better of such an element another person must be brought in, and in so far as that other person can be of assistance the neurosis will be curable.
>
> (1909, p. 104)

Grunbaum offers no gloss to explain his claim, but his reading of this passage as asserting that veridical insight is necessary for therapeutic cure is without textual foundation. The above passage is preceded by the following passage:

> It is true that during the analysis Hans had to be told many things that he could not say himself, that he had to be presented with thoughts which he had so far shown no signs of possessing, and that his attention had to be turned in the direction from which his father was expecting something to come. This detracts from the evidential value of the analysis; but the procedure is the same in every case.
>
> (Freud, 1909, p. 104)

The passage Grunbaum cites is thus an answer to suggestion-related doubts raised by the use of anticipatory interpretations. The passage explains why suggestion-like interventions by another person are necessary to bring the patient to accept a proposed etiological interpretation, namely, because it is the only way to overcome the forces of resistance. This remains true even in the Hans case, in which Freud is presenting his best argument against the suggestion objection. Indeed, such anticipatory statements may be more frequent when dealing with a child than with an adult (Freud subsequently says that "It is true that a child, on account of the small development of his intellectual systems, requires especially energetic assistance" [p. 104]). However, the passage does not offer any argument specifically that these anticipatory suggestions must be veridical to be therapeutically effective. Of course, Freud *assumes* that his etiological interpretations are veridical, and he takes evidential comfort if they yield therapeutic success. However, he does not assert let alone argue for the extreme "indispensability" premises of the Tally Argument in the cited passage. The suggestion objector might even agree that bringing in an outside person to provide anticipatory interpretations is generally necessary because that is how suggestion works. The claimed necessity for bringing in an outside therapist is neutral with respect to whether the help is veridical or a matter of suggestion.

Of more interest is a passage following the cited passage in which Freud explains how he can be confident of his etiological conclusions despite the use of suggestion-like anticipatory interpretations:

> But, after all, the information which the physician gives his patient is itself derived in its turn from analytical experience; and indeed it is sufficiently convincing if, at the cost of this intervention by the physician, we are enabled to discover the structure of the pathogenic material and simultaneously to dissipate it.
>
> (Freud, 1909, pp.104–105)

Freud here notes the important link of the Hans case's interpretations to the results of adult analyses. Freud's crucial point, however, is that despite the admitted erosion of the analysis's evidential value by the analyst's antici-patory statements, an etiological insight "is sufficiently convincing" if it trig-gers the patient to produce further material so that "we are enabled to discover the structure of the pathogenic material and simultaneously to dis-sipate it." Note that Freud does not specifically mention therapeutic cure of the symptoms. The "it" in "dissipate it" refers to the pathogenic material that has been discovered due to further material provoked by the analyst's antici-patory statement. We saw in Chapter 3 and above that Freud repeatedly identifies the process of identifying unconscious contents, overcoming the patient's resistance, bringing the repressed material into consciousness, and thus resolving internal conflicts as the primary goal of psychoanalysis, and he distinguishes this process from the additional therapeutic goal of cure of the patient's symptoms. Read this way, Freud's statement reflects the Suitability Argument, that one can have confidence in one's interpretation because of the pathological material that emerges that provides a uniquely persuasive expla-nation of the patient's symptoms. Dissipation of the repressed internal conflict should be accompanied by dissipation of symptoms as well, but the relation-ship is not one-to-one:

> In a treatment which is incomplete or in which success is not perfect, one may at any rate achieve a considerable improvement in the gen-eral mental condition, while the symptoms (though now of smaller importance to the patient) may continue to exist without stamping him a sick man.
>
> (1904, p. 253)

There is one further point about Freud's use of the Hans case that is worth mentioning because it is at odds with the Tally Argument analysis. We saw in Chapter 3 that throughout the rest of his life, Freud cited the Hans case as evidence that he was correct in his etiological claims about adults. This makes no sense if, as Grunbaum claims, Freud held that therapeutic success is in and of itself proof of correct etiological insight. If Freud believed that therapeutic success is the test of correct interpretation, then each successful adult case would stand equally on its own as a conclusive demonstration of correct insight and thus of Oedipal theory. Even if Freud should choose to defend his etiological insight in one case by citing another, the Hans case would have no more weight than others under such circumstances because any successful case is equally assured of having reached veridical etiological insight. Freud's consistent reliance on the Hans case as a demonstration of the validity of the insights in his adult cases, which was extensively documented in Chapter 3, implies a different epistemological structure of his overall argument than Grunbaum's Tally Argument.

A Further Passage Supporting Suitability Over Tally

Beyond Freud's comments about establishing the etiology of narcissistic neuroses despite lack of any therapeutic success using interpretive methods, there are many other indicators that he assumes something more like the Suitability Argument than the Tally Argument as his foundational approach to establishing etiological validity. For example, in his pivotal paper on the etiology of hysteria (1896) in which he introduces the sexual theory, Freud makes several statements that imply that his claims to veridical insight ultimately derive from something other than therapeutic success. Freud describes regularly tracing hysterical symptoms to traumas at puberty or later and puts forward his theory that correct etiological understanding must always start much earlier: "We have learned that *no hysterical symptom can arise from a real experience alone, but that in every case the memory of earlier experiences awakened in association to it plays a part in causing the symptom*" (p. 197). Freud then says:

> You might suppose that the rare instances in which analysis is able to trace the symptom back direct to a [post-pubertal—JW] traumatic scene that is thoroughly suitable as a determinant and possesses traumatic force, and is able, by thus tracing it back, at the same time to remove it (in the way described in Breuer's case history of Anna O.)—you might suppose that such instances must, after all, constitute powerful objections to the general validity of the proposition I have just put forward. It certainly looks so. But I must assure you that I have the best grounds for assuming that even in such instances there exists a chain of operative memories which stretches far back behind the first traumatic scene, *even though* the reproduction of the latter alone may have the result of removing the symptom.
>
> (1896, p. 197)

This passage demonstrates that Freud was quite aware that symptoms sometimes could be removed without first establishing correct and full etiological understanding. It is also clear by implication that he relied on some further process, other than cure, for demonstrating the correctness of his further interpretations of deeper etiological sources despite cure already having been achieved. Indeed, he asserts that "I have the best grounds for assuming that even in such instances there exists a chain of operative memories which stretches far back behind the first traumatic scene." Those "best grounds" transcend cure as etiological evidence. I submit that they must be none other than the Suitability Argument based on the content of the earlier memories.

Ironically, in an aside when considering these texts, Grunbaum seems to have a glimmering of the correct interpretation of this and related passages. He acknowledges that Freud "seems to take it for granted here that the concrete features of a repressed trauma can collectively vouch for its pathogenic potency, independently of any therapeutic benefit engendered by its mnemic restoration to the patient's consciousness" (1984, p. 152)—that is, that Freud takes suitability rather than cure for granted as his criterion for establishing etiological validity. Grunbaum then says, "As Edward Erwin has remarked to me, if such direct etiologic identifiability were indeed granted, then Freud could have spared himself the circuitous detour of trying to vindicate it via NCT" (1984, p. 152). If only Grunbaum had taken Erwin's comment more seriously! Instead, Grunbaum immediately moves on to convoluted attempts to defend his analysis, and leaves this alternative textually apparent possibility unexplored. Yet this is precisely the correct line for understanding Freud's argument and his reply to the suggestion objection. It is the path I have taken in this book.

This completes my review of the Freudian texts in which Grunbaum claims to find Freud's statement of the Tally Argument, and other passages that Grunbaum cites in this context. I find, to the contrary, that these and related texts do not support Grunbaum's reading and support instead a reading along the lines of my Suitability Argument analysis. I now turn to an examination of whether Freud did or did not in fact believe the NCT that Grunbaum attributes to him.

Did Freud Reject the Possibility of Spontaneous Remission?

Even if Grunbaum cannot identify a "smoking gun" text wherein Freud states the Tally Argument as such, there remains the question of whether Freud in fact did hold any of the beliefs attributed to him by Grunbaum. Key among those attributions is Grunbaum's dramatic claim, essential to his analysis, that Freud believed that veridical etiological insight via psychoanalysis—which for Freud would mean insight into Oedipal etiology—is the only way that psychoneurotic symptoms ever remit, and that Freud thus rejected the existence of any instances of spontaneous remission, placebo cure, or suggestion cure of psychoneurotic symptoms. We saw above that Grunbaum was quite explicit that this must be Freud's claim for the Tally Argument interpretation to work: "Clearly, NCT entails not only that there is no spontaneous remission of psychoneuroses but also that, if there are any cures at all, psychoanalysis is *uniquely* therapeutic for such disorders as compared to any *rival* therapies" (Grunbaum, 1984, p. 139).

I now consider whether this central claim of Grunbaum's is correct. Grunbaum's claim has the virtue of being testable by examination of Freud's voluminous writings. Grunbaum makes an enormous effort of textual review to support his thesis—nonetheless missing determinative passages, as I will show. For convenience, I use "spontaneous remission" here as a general term for any way other than Oedipal etiological insight during psychoanalysis that psychoneurotic symptoms are cured, and I use "cured" for any enduring psychoneurotic symptom relief from any cause.

As discussed earlier, I grant Grunbaum that the seduction period analyses are close enough to Oedipal meanings that they are not placebo analyses for Freud despite not reaching specifically Oedipal conclusions. However, with Grunbaum, I classify all of Freud's cases before the seduction theory era as cases clearly lacking relevant veridical insight. Consequently, Grunbaum's thesis, as he agrees, implies that Freud saw none of those earlier cases, including those during the *Studies on Hysteria* period, as enduring cures.

It should be said at the outset that Grunbaum's thesis is dubious on its face. Grunbaum attempts to make it seem as though the Tally Argument might have made sense in Freud's day and that it is only subsequently that it has become obvious that psychoanalysis has no unique absolute claim to therapeutic success. It is true that Freud's was the first prominent psychotherapy and thus did have claims to unique possibilities for success. Nonetheless, in Freud's time, with its history of Mesmerism, hypnosis, Charcot, Bernheim, and its range of placebo treatments from electrophysical to baths to sanitaria, each of which had some placebo successes, it would have been clear that successful treatment is no guarantor of theoretical correctness or etiological insight. Surely the early commentators who put forward the suggestion objection, including Freud's close confidant Wilhelm Fliess, were well aware of Freud's claimed therapeutic successes of psychoanalytic treatment, but posed the suggestion objection anyway, knowing that suggestion and related placebo interventions are capable of yielding some successful outcomes. And surely Freud's dismissal of electrophysiological treatment as a matter of suggestion (see Chapter 2) and enthusiastic embrace instead of Bernheim's direct hypnotic suggestion was based on the belief that the latter had some successes.

I now turn to the various pieces of evidence bearing on this crucial prediction of Grunbaum's. I start with some evidence in the form of incidental comments from early Freud, and then identify central explicit statements by Freud during his prime theoretical years that were missed by Grunbaum, and finally consider Grunbaum's claim that Freud abandoned the Tally Argument only later in life.

Of Lourdes and Miraculous Cures

Turning first to some early textual evidence, Freud and Breuer certainly reported enduring therapeutic successes: "For we found, to our great surprise at first, that *each individual hysterical symptom immediately and permanently disappeared when we had succeeded in bringing clearly to light the memory of the event by which it was provoked and in arousing its accompanying affect*" (1893, p. 6); "[O]nce this acute stage is past, any residues which may be left in the form of chronic symptoms or attacks are often removed, and permanently so, by our method" (1893, p. 17). Although later scholarship casts doubt on the outcome of the "Anna O." case, Freud still believed it was a success when in 1904 he referred to Breuer's "successful treatment of a hysterical woman patient" (1904, p. 249). Moreover, there seems little doubt that Freud thought that some of Bernheim's patients were cured. In reporting on his visit to Nancy, he says that Bernheim "frankly admitted to me that his great therapeutic successes by means of suggestion were only achieved in his hospital practice and not with his private patients" (Freud, 1925, pp. 17–18). And, as early as his January 1895 paper on obsessions and phobias, well before he proposed his sexual theory of the etiology of the psychoneuroses, Freud had claimed that some psychoneuroses were cured by this pre-Oedipal treatment: "we even succeed in curing them" (1895c, p. 74).

Indeed, Freud was so aware—and knew everyone else was so aware—of spontaneous remission without the necessity of Oedipal insight that he joked about it, at one point later in his life acknowledging the obviousness of alternative pathways to symptom cure by saying: "I do not think our cures can compete with those of Lourdes. There are so many more people who believe in the miracles of the Blessed Virgin than in the existence of the unconscious" (1933, p. 152). However, Grunbaum would dismiss this particular statement as evidence against his Tally Argument analysis because it occurred after 1926, when, Grunbaum claims, Freud gave up the Tally Argument (I will examine this claim below)—as if Freud did not know about Lourdes before that time!

So, instead of the Lourdes comment, consider Freud's more serious 1905 essay on psychical treatment, where he makes clear that he accepts the occurrence of "miraculous" cures of both mental and physical conditions:

> It would be convenient, but quite wrong, simply to refuse all credence to these miraculous cures and to seek to explain the accounts of them as a combination of pious fraud and inaccurate observation ... They do really occur and have occurred at every period of history. And they concern not merely illnesses of mental origin.
>
> (Freud, 1905b, p. 290)

Freud holds that such cures occur in both religious and nonreligious social contexts and are largely based on the arousal of psychological expectations, that is, suggestion: "Our interest is most particularly engaged by the mental state of *expectation*, which puts in motion a number of mental forces." As to religious intimations, "There is no need, however, to bring forward anything other than mental forces in order to explain miraculous cures" (1905b, pp. 289–290).

Elisabeth von R's Enduring Cure

During the seduction theory period, in a seeming direct contradiction to Grunbaum's Tally Argument analysis, Freud says that "There are cases in which a complete or partial cure can be obtained without our having to go as deep as the infantile experiences" (1896, p. 206). Grunbaum replies that in such cases, Freud holds that the cure is not enduring, and it is only enduring cures that require true "Tally Argument" type insight according to Freud. Indeed, Freud does say: "In the former cases we are not, I believe, secure against relapses; and my expectation is that a complete psycho-analysis implies a radical cure of the hysteria." Grunbaum ends his quotation of the passage there, and argues that *enduring* cure is an essential part of Freud's NCT criterion—that is, that the NCT only says that correct etiological insight is necessary for *enduring* cure of symptoms. However, Grunbaum fails to quote the last sentence in Freud's passage: "We must not, however, be led into forestalling the lessons of observation." That is, although Freud has a "belief" and "expectation" regarding the potential for relapse, it is portrayed as a contingent hypothesis open to empirical evidence. He does not imply that enduring cure not open to relapse is essential to establishing veridical etiology.

On similar grounds, Grunbaum rejects as relevant evidence against his analysis Freud's early paper, "A Case of Successful Treatment by Hypnotism" (1893), in which Freud reports on the case of a woman who was successfully treated for hysterical symptoms that prevented her from breastfeeding her baby. Freud used only hypnotic suggestion in this case, so there was no etiological insight. Despite Freud labeling the case a success, Grunbaum objects that the cure was not entirely enduring because in a pregnancy some years later the woman's symptoms reoccurred.

However, there is no pathway via the "lack of enduring cure" argument for Grunbaum to escape the clear counterexample of the case of "Elisabeth von R" (Freud, 1895a) reported in *Studies on Hysteria*. Freud interpreted her hysterical symptoms as a reaction to her being in love with her brother-in-law and, when her sister died, to having the unacceptable thought that now he would be free to marry her. There was no etiological understanding of childhood sexual experiences or of Oedipal derivatives at this point in Freud's development. Elisabeth's symptoms were eliminated, and Freud followed the case for some time afterward precisely to be assured that the cure was enduring:

> As my colleague assures me, she is to be regarded as cured. Her brother-in-law's connection with the family has remained unaltered. In the spring of 1894 I heard that she was going to a private ball for which I was able to get an invitation, and I did not allow the opportunity to escape me of seeing my former patient whirl past in a lively dance. Since then, by her own inclination, she has married someone unknown to me.
>
> (1895a, p. 160)

Many years later, Elisabeth's daughter reported that, although Elisabeth denied to her that she had in fact been in love with her brother-in-law, Elisabeth's marriage remained an enduringly happy one. As Peter Gay observes, "In any event, here was one of his former patients—a hysteric who had often suffered severe pains in her legs when she was standing or walking—dancing the night away. Freud ... could take satisfaction in her restored vitality" (1988, p. 72). Thus, this is a clear case known to Freud of enduring cure without accurate etiological insight. Oddly enough, Grunbaum hardly mentions this salient case and does not address its implications for his Tally Argument thesis.

Erwin's Attempt to Defend Grunbaum Based on Freud's Statements About Direct Hypnotic Suggestion

Erwin (1993) attempts to defend Grunbaum by citing two early statements by Freud that, Erwin claims, reject cure by suggestion:

> I gave up the suggestive technique, and with that hypnosis, so early in my practice because I despaired of making suggestion powerful and enduring enough to effect permanent cures. In every severe case I saw the suggestions which had been applied crumble away again; after which the disease or some substitute for it was back once more
>
> (1905a, p. 261)

> It is true that suggestion can bring about a cessation of the symptoms of an illness—but only for a short time. At the end of this time they return and have to be repelled once again by renewed hypnosis and suggestion.
>
> (1905b, p. 301)

The problem is that both of Erwin's passages concern not suggestion or spontaneous remission in general but only the limitations Freud encountered with the specific Bernheim-inspired procedure of using *hypnotic* suggestion to directly eliminate symptoms. Freud used this technique early in his career and we know that he came to greatly dislike it. Even if this particular technique did not confer enduring therapeutic cure of symptoms, that does not bear on the claim Grunbaum attributes to Freud, that spontaneous remissions and placebo cures do not occur under any circumstances or in response to any intervention other than veridical psychoanalysis.

However, the two passages cited by Erwin do not even demonstrate that Freud rejected the occurrence of placebo cures with that early direct suggestion technique. Freud's statements about the lack of permanency of symptom removal by hypnotic suggestive therapy are stated as generalizations but were likely rhetorical overgeneralizations aimed at justifying his rejection of this approach. The quote above about Bernheim's successes is one piece of evidence. Another indicator is in one of the papers cited by Erwin. Although Freud asserts that symptom removal by direct hypnotic suggestion is not permanent, he seems to indicate that he is referring to the effects of a single treatment series, for he also says: "A succession of hypnoses may eventually bring about by degrees the influence over the illness which was lacking at first, till in the end a satisfactory result is achieved" (1905b, p. 301).

An instance of more manifest and revealing backsliding occurs in a passage in the *Introductory Lectures* just a few pages before the tally passage. Freud presents his usual litany of the many limitations of direct hypnotic treatment of symptoms—including symptom recurrence—in very broad statements to explain why he gave up that method. However, he then steps back and admits that he is overgeneralizing and that such problems sometimes might be overcome with repeated efforts: "Admittedly sometimes things went entirely as one would wish: after a few efforts, success was complete and permanent" (1917, p. 449). So, even with regard to his early direct suggestion technique, and despite Erwin's two quotes about that particular method, the textual evidence tilts towards Freud's belief that there were indeed some cases that were complete and permanent therapeutic successes.

As a last early example, in his 1898 article on the sexual etiology of the neuroses, Freud acknowledges that some psychoneuroses can be cured by curing an accompanying actual neurosis:

> For such cases it has quite correctly come to be the therapeutic practice to disregard the psychoneurotic components in the clinical picture and to treat the 'actual neurosis' exclusively. In very many cases it is possible to overcome the [psycho-] neurosis as well which it has brought along with it, provided that the neurasthenia is effectively dealt with.
>
> (1898, p. 279)

This is a case of cure without insight put forward by Freud himself.

Freud's Explicit Statements Recognizing Spontaneous Remission During His Theoretical Prime

Despite his careful reading of Freud, Grunbaum somehow managed to miss three statements from Freud's prime period of theorizing that explicitly assert the occurrence of spontaneous remission, thus cleanly falsifying Grunbaum's Tally Argument account. The first, previously pointed out by Sachs (1989) and others, occurs in a comment in which Freud is writing specifically about the very psychoneurotic conditions he treats. Freud reiterates the obvious, that the kinds of hysterical symptoms that may yield to psychoanalytic treatment may also spontaneously remit:

> We may give as instances of disorders that are accessible to psycho-analytic treatment hysterical convulsions and paralyses as well as the various symptoms of obsessional neurosis (obsessive ideas and actions). All of these are conditions which are occasionally subject to spontaneous recovery.
>
> (1913, p. 165)

Recall that Grunbaum cites a passage from the Hans case as the most explicit endorsement of the Tally Argument. We found above that this is not so. Indeed, it turns out that there are two passages in the Hans case that unambiguously show that at that time Freud understood that neuroses sometimes resolve spontaneously without psychoanalytic treatment, and thus Freud could not have adhered to the Tally Argument. One of the passages occurs in the context of Freud arguing that despite his phobia, Hans is a sufficiently normal child overall that the case's developmental findings can be generalized to children in general:

> [Hans] is not the only child who has been overtaken by a phobia at some time or other in his childhood. Troubles of that kind are well known to be quite extraordinarily frequent, even in children the strictness of whose upbringing has left nothing to be desired. In later life these children either become neurotic or remain healthy. In the course of months or years [the phobias] diminish, and the child seems to recover; but no one can tell what psychological changes are necessitated by such a recovery, or what alterations in character are involved in it ... I think, therefore, that Hans's illness may perhaps have been no more serious than that of many other children who are not branded as "degenerates".
>
> (1909, pp. 142–143)

In this passage, Freud attributes phobias to many children, some of whom simply become and remain healthy insofar as their symptoms go. They spontaneously recover from the symptoms and are symptom-free for decades, perhaps in part due to the nature of their circumstances. Freud speculates that they may still harbor unresolved underlying conflicts from earlier life. Note that one cannot evade this passage's implications by claiming that Freud thinks that animal phobias are not truly neuroses or are only slight disorders because, as we saw, he presumes the opposite when explaining why suggestion in the form of guiding the patient's insights using anticipatory interpretations is necessary in Hans's case, which Freud clearly labels a neurosis. In sum, as Pierre-Henri Castel succinctly puts it in his recent history of child psychoanalysis, "Freud knew all about 'spontaneous cures' of phobias in children" (2021, p. 108, translation provided by the author).

A second Hans passage concerns Freud's explanation of the complexity of the distinction between normal and neurotic people:

> That no sharp line can be drawn between "neurotic" and "normal" people—whether children or adults—that our conception of "disease" is a purely practical one and a question of summation, that disposition and the eventualities of life must combine before the threshold of this summation is overstepped, and that consequently a number of individuals are constantly passing from the class of healthy people into that of neurotic

patients, while a far smaller number also make the journey in the opposite direction,—all of these are things which have been said so often and
have met with so much agreement that I am certainly not alone in
maintaining their truth.

(1909, p. 146)

Freud is arguing against the hereditary taint theory of neurosis that labels
some individuals as inherently neurotic, and arguing instead that neuroses are
conditions that can come and go in otherwise normal individuals based on
multiple quantitative factors including both the "disposition and the
eventualities of life." Freud observes, as he did in the passage about the
spontaneous remission of phobias, that the eventualities of life can change in
ways that bring about or spontaneously remit a neurotic condition: "consequently a number of individuals are constantly passing from the class of
healthy people into that of neurotic patients, while a far smaller number also
make the journey in the opposite direction." Freud indicates that this is both
something he believes and common knowledge.

However, the most definitive textual evidence against Grunbaum's Tally
Argument analysis during this period occurs in Freud's famous five lectures
summarizing psychoanalysis that he delivered at Clark University during his
visit to America in the same year that he published the Hans case, and published the following year. In his first lecture, Freud describes the diverse neu-
rological-type symptoms of hysteria as illustrated by Breuer's case of Anna
O., including, for example, partial paralyses and loss of sensation, disturbed
vision and speech, nervous cough, and loss of ability to drink. He then
describes the standard prognosis of such hysterical patients:

When you hear such an enumeration of symptoms, you will be inclined to
think it safe to assume, even though you are not doctors, that what we
have before us is a severe illness, probably affecting the brain, that it
offers small prospect of recovery and will probably lead to the patient's
early decease. You must be prepared to learn from the doctors, however,
that, in a number of cases which display severe symptoms such as these, it
is justifiable to take a different and a far more favourable view. If a picture of this kind is presented by a young patient of the female sex, whose
vital internal organs (heart, kidneys, etc.) are shown on objective examination to be normal, but who has been subjected to violent emotional
shocks—if, moreover, her various symptoms differ in certain matters of
detail from what would have been expected—then doctors are not
inclined to take the case too seriously. They decide that what they have
before them is not an organic disease of the brain, but the enigmatic
condition which, from the time of ancient Greek medicine, has been
known as "hysteria" and which has the power of producing illusory pic-
tures of a whole number of serious diseases. They consider that there is

then no risk to life but that a return to health—even a complete one—is probable.

(1910, pp. 10–11)

Freud is explicit here that hysterical disorders were standardly considered by medicine—and Freud does not dispute this standard belief—to be likely to remit so that "a return to health—even a complete one—is probable." But is this spontaneous or due to effective medical treatment? Freud hastens to explain that he is of course referring here historically to the time before the advent of psychoanalytic treatment, when no effective treatment of such a hysterical case was available. Thus, the "optimistic prognosis" of a probable complete return to health must be due to an expectation of spontaneous remission:

> For you must not suppose that a patient's prospects of medical assistance are improved in essentials by the fact that a diagnosis of hysteria has been substituted for one of severe organic disease of the brain. Medical skill is in most cases powerless against severe diseases of the brain; but neither can the doctor do anything against hysterical disorders. He must leave it to kindly Nature to decide when and how his optimistic prognosis shall be fulfilled.

(1910, p. 11)

This passage is a clear acknowledgment of spontaneous remission of hysterical symptoms during Freud's theoretical prime and a direct repudiation of Grunbaum's "Tally Argument" analysis. Oddly enough, it is not cited by Grunbaum in his generally exhaustive examination of Freud's work.

Grunbaum's Claim that Freud Gave Up the Tally Argument in 1926

Grunbaum notices that Freud explicitly acknowledges spontaneous remission in a late text. In the cited passage, Freud states that spontaneous remission from psychoneuroses is possible as the ego works to overcome its own repressions or circumstances change to be experienced as less dangerous:

> The ego may occasionally manage to break down the barriers of repression which it has itself put up and to recover its influence over the instinctual impulse and direct the course of the new impulse in accordance with the changed danger-situation.

(1926a, p. 153)

Moreover, analogizing psychoanalysis to treatments in other fields of medicine that facilitate and accelerate the natural recuperative properties of the human body, Freud explains that:

When, in analysis, we have given the ego assistance which is able to put it in a position to lift its repressions ... as a rule our therapy must be content with bringing about more quickly, more reliably and with less expenditure of energy than would otherwise be the case the good result which in favourable circumstances would have occurred of itself.

(1926a, p. 154)

Consistent with his analysis, Grunbaum claims that once Freud in 1926 acknowledged spontaneous remission, he no longer could rely on the Tally Argument to support his etiological claims against the suggestion objection, and thus no longer had an epistemological foundation for his theoretical claims, sending psychoanalysis into an epistemological tailspin:

> Freud grants that neuroses yielding to analytic therapy would, in due course, remit spontaneously anyway ... Hence, even Freud's own evidence placed his NCT premise in serious jeopardy. And once that proposition became defunct, even spectacular therapeutic triumphs became probatively unavailing for the validation of his hypotheses by means of the Tally Argument ... [O]nce intraclinical validation is bereft of the legitimation that he drew from therapeutic success via the Tally Argument, the menacing suggestibility problem, which he had held at bay by means of this argument, comes back to haunt data from the couch with a vengeance.
>
> (1984, pp. 160, 172)

In other words, Grunbaum claims that this belated acceptance of spontaneous remission left Freud with no argument for his etiological claims. Yet, as Grunbaum observes, instead of lamenting the death of his etiological theory, Freud doubles down on the independence of the explanatory power derived from psychoanalysis from the therapeutic power of psychoanalysis, sharply separating the two, insisting on "the inherent [scientific] value of psychoanalysis and of its independence of its application to medicine" and saying, "I only want to feel assured that the therapy will not destroy the science" (Freud, 1926b, p. 254). This implies that at that time Freud had some idea about the grounds for the validity of his etiological theories independent of their curative effects—namely, the same grounds he had proclaimed since his announcement of the seduction theory in 1896, the Suitability Argument. Instead of drawing this obvious conclusion, Grunbaum accuses Freud of incoherence.

There are two immediate concerns one might have about the face plausibility of Grunbaum's narrative. First, it is implausible to claim that the acknowledgment that psychoneurotic symptoms spontaneously remit in the passage cited by Grunbaum represented a dramatic new discovery that overturned Freud's etiological argument. Indeed, Freud himself prefaces the passage with a disclaimer as to any novelty: "What I have to say in this connection has long been familiar and I have nothing new to add" (1926a, p. 153). Are we to believe that Freud had been dealing with the very same condition, hysterical neurosis, for over thirty years and had just lately noticed spontaneous remissions? The ample evidence provided above shows that this is not the case.

Second, Freud, whatever his weaknesses, pays explicit and careful rhetorical attention to potential objections to his theoretical positions. According to Grunbaum, Freud relied on the Tally Argument as his central foundational argument for the validity of his etiological theories and his rejection of the suggestion objection, then arrived at a new view of the possibility of spontaneous remission that directly contradicts the Tally Argument, and never says a word about this theoretical disaster or explains how he would address it. This is not consistent with what we know of Freud. Recall the attribution of unworthy salesmanship to Freud that, we saw earlier, Grunbaum used to evade a straight-out textual contradiction to his analysis. Grunbaum's reaction to the 1926 text in which Freud clearly embraces spontaneous remission smacks of similar uncharitable dismissal in the service of maintaining his implausible position come what may.

In any event, based on the passages discussed above, we now know that the 1926 text is *not* a change of Freud's position. The passages from his *Five Lectures* delivered in 1909, when Grunbaum claims Freud held to the Tally Argument, express the same point, that hysterical symptoms can be expected to eventually remit on their own. By parity of reasoning, no matter how devoutly he desires it, Grunbaum cannot attribute the Tally Argument to Freud at that time.

Conclusion: Tally Versus Suitability on the Status of Psychoanalytic Interpretation

It should be made clear that Grunbaum's book contains many analyses and arguments other than his Tally Argument analysis, such as critiques of certain hermeneutic positions and of the repression theory, and I agree with some of those other positions he develops. However, regarding the nature of Freud's defense against the suggestion objection and thus the nature of Freud's foundational defense of Oedipal etiological theory, Grunbaum's Tally Argument analysis is, I have argued, clearly and repeatedly falsified by both the texts that he, in a remarkably tendentious way, cites in support of his case, as well as those he spuriously omits.

My critique of Grunbaum's Tally Argument analysis also had the helpful side effect of repeatedly pointing in the direction of the Suitability Argument as a better explanation of Freud's foundational argument. In this regard, an important difference between the two analyses is worth noting. As Grunbaum makes clear, if he is correct that the Tally Argument based on the unique ability for therapeutic cure was Freud's basic defense against the suggestion objection, then, given that since Freud's time it has been established that many other forms of treatment sometimes successfully cure psychoneuroses and that there is indeed spontaneous remission, it follows that Freud's one defense of his interpretations collapses, and neither Freud nor psychoanalysis has any argument whatever for the validity of any of his interpretations.

The results of my analysis are not quite as pessimistic. It is true that I have shown that, even in the Hans case in which Freud thought things were clearer than in his usual adult cases, Freud's explanations fail to support his Oedipal interpretations by the criteria put forward by Freud himself. However, as I argued in Chapter 9, there is general agreement among philosophers of science that singular causal explanations, however challenging methodologically, can be valid and that their validity is sometimes plausible or even manifest. Thus, in principle, although my analysis casts extreme doubt on Freud's Oedipal theory, it does leave room for some psychoanalytic interpretations to be valid and even to be plausibly or manifestly so without appeal to further controlled evidence. The epistemological grounding of psychoanalytic interpretations is destroyed en masse by Grunbaum's analysis, whereas my analysis allows an admittedly blurry epistemological grounding that must be assessed singly, interpretation by interpretation.

References

Breuer, J., & Freud, S. (1893). On the psychical mechanism of hysterical phenomena: Preliminary communication. *SE* 2, 1–17.

Castel, P-H. (2021). *Mais pourquoi psychanalyser les enfants?* (But why psychoanalyze children?). Paris: CERF.

Erwin, E. (1993). Philosophers on Freudianism: An examination of replies to Grünbaum's *Foundations*. In J. Earman, A. Janis, G. Massey, & N. Rescher (Eds.), *Philosophical problems of the internal and external worlds: Essays on the philosophy of Adolf Grünbaum* (pp. 409–460). Pittsburgh, PA: University of Pittsburgh Press.

Esterson, A. (1996). Grünbaum's Tally Argument. *History of the Human Sciences*, 9 (1), 43–57.

Forrester, J. (1986). Review of *The foundations of psychoanalysis: A philosophical critique*, by Adolf Griinbaum. *Isis*, 77, 670–674.

Freud, S. (1893). A case of successful treatment by hypnotism. *SE* 1, 115–128.

Freud, S. (1895a). Fraulein Elisabeth von R. *SE* 2, 135–181.

Freud, S. (1895b). The psychotherapy of hysteria. *SE* 2, 253–305.

Freud, S. (1895c). Obsessions and phobias. *SE* 3, 69–82.

Freud, S. (1896). The aetiology of hysteria. *SE* 3, 187–221.

Freud, S. (1898). Sexuality in the aetiology of the neuroses. *SE* 3, 259–285.

Freud, S. (1904). Freud's psychoanalytic procedure. *SE* 7, 249–254.

Freud, S. (1905a). On psychotherapy. *SE* 7, 257–268.

Freud, S. (1905b). Psychical (or mental) treatment. *SE* 7, 283–302.

Freud, S. (1909). Analysis of a phobia in a five-year-old boy. *SE* 10, 1–150.

Freud, S. (1910). Five lectures on psycho-analysis. *SE* 11, 1–56.

Freud, S. (1913). The claims of psycho-analysis to scientific interest. *SE* 13, 165–175.

Freud, S. (1917). Introductory lectures on psycho-analysis, part 3. *SE* 16.

Freud, S. (1923a). Two encyclopaedia articles. *SE* 18, 233–260.

Freud, S. (1923b). Remarks on the theory and practice of dream interpretation. *SE* 19, 107–122.

Freud, S. (1925). An autobiographical study. *SE* 20, 1–74.

Freud, S. (1926a). Inhibitions, symptoms and anxiety. *SE* 20, 75–176.

Freud, S. (1926b). The question of lay analysis. *SE* 20, 177–258.

Freud, S. (1933). New introductory lectures on psycho-analysis. *SE* 22, 1–182.

Freud, S. (1937). Constructions in analysis. *SE* 23, 255–270.

Gay, P. (1988). *Freud: A life for our time.* New York: W. W. Norton & Co.

Grant, D., & Harari, E. (1990). Misreading Freud: Some thoughts on Adolf Grünbaum's "Tally Argument." *Psychoanalysis and Contemporary Thought,* 13, 311–319.

Grunbaum, A. (1984). *The foundations of psychoanalysis: A philosophical critique.* Berkeley, CA: University of California Press.

Hopkins, J. (1988). Epistemology and depth psychology: Critical notes on *The Foundations of Psychoanalysis.* In P. Clark & C. Wright (Eds.), *Mind, psychoanalysis and science* (pp. 33–60). New York: Blackwell.

Levy, D. (1988). Grunbaum's Freud. *Inquiry,* 31, 193–215.

Richardson, R. (1990). The "Tally Argument" and the validation of psychoanalysis. *Philosophy of Science,* 57, 668–676.

Robinson, P. (1993). *Freud and his critics.* Berkeley, CA: University of California Press.

Sachs, D. (1989). In fairness to Freud: A critical notice of *The Foundations of Psychoanalysis,* by Adolf Grunbaum. *The Philosophical Review,* 98, 349–378.

Wakefield, J. C. (forthcoming). *Foucault Versus Freud: Oedipal Theory and the Deployment of Sexuality.* New York: Routledge.

Chapter 12

Conclusion

The Little Hans Case, Philosophy of Science, and the Fate of Psychoanalysis

I end with a brief recapitulation of the findings of my rethinking of Freud's arguments for the Oedipal theory of psychoneuroses from a philosophy of science perspective. This perspective involved reconstructing Freud's arguments and comparing their overall explanatory power and evidential support—taking into account both confirmatory and disconfirmatory data— to that of rival accounts. The rival accounts primarily included the fright theory and the suggestion objection, as well as Bowlby's attachment theory in some instances. This perspective led me to identify, logically reconstruct, and evaluate the specific arguments by which Freud defends his Oedipal theory in the Hans case (Freud, 1909).

The Hans case study was intended by Freud as a unique attempt to provide "more direct" evidence for his Oedipal theory than could be obtained in the complex, long-after-the-fact reconstructions of childhood events in his adult cases. I argued that there are two reasons why the Hans case history is the most important clinical theory paper Freud wrote, at least from a philosophy of science perspective. First, placing Freud's theoretical development within the framework provided by the philosopher of science Imre Lakatos (1970), I argued that when Freud's early seduction theory was falsified, Freud proposed the Oedipal theory as a way to preserve his core thesis of the sexual theory of the neuroses while evading falsification and still explaining everything the seduction theory had explained. However, the Oedipal theory was at that point a purely ad hoc hypothesis, and for it to be taken seriously rather than dismissed as vacuous, Freud needed to show that the new theory predicted something bold and novel. Freud attempted to do this by putting forward Oedipal and sexual predictions in the Hans case (Chapters 8 and 10). If these predictions were confirmed, the ad hoc accusation would be put to rest, making Oedipal theory a scientifically progressive revision of the sexual theory worthy of being taken seriously.

The Hans case was also Freud's ultimate answer to the suggestion objection, the objection that Freud's clinical evidence of the supposed insights and memories of his patients in fact resulted from Freud's suggestions to his patients. The suggestion objection had been strengthened by the failure of

DOI: 10.4324/9781003272472-12

Freud's early seduction theory. Suggestion was an all-too-plausible explanation for how Freud had managed to "discover" the childhood seductions in his patients that his earlier theory had predicted but that in some cases turned out never to have occurred. As I documented in Chapter 2, from Freud's early work to his last publications he recognized the suggestion objection as the single greatest challenge to his psychoanalytic project. This is because it cast doubt on the credibility of not only his substantive psychoanalytic findings on which his theoretical claims rested but also on the psychoanalytic method by which he generated those findings, so that generating additional evidence in the same way would not address the objection.

I argued in Chapters 3 and 9 that Freud's response to the suggestion objection is three-pronged. First, the specific explanatory strategy Freud adopts is the Suitability Argument in which he argues that Oedipal mental contents have a unique suitability as a determinant in explaining otherwise inexplicable features of the patient's symptoms, resulting in distinctive and compelling singular causal explanations of puzzling phenomena. Although the methodology and validity criteria for singular causal explanation remains challenging, plausibly valid singular causal explanations are clearly possible.

Second, Freud claims that a psychoanalysis of a psychoneurotic condition, if pursued until one achieves a complete "suitability" account of the neurotic symptoms' detailed features in terms of hypothesized unconscious mental states, inevitably converges on one unique or clearly optimal and compelling singular causal explanation. Consequently, any false accounts that might be produced in the course of analysis by suggestion or other biasing processes are eventually corrected by further evidence. And, Freud claims, this optimal account always turns out to be the Oedipal account.

Finally, Freud must respond to the objection that the repeated emergence of Oedipal contents in optimal suitability accounts of puzzling symptom features of his adult patients could be due to repeated similar suggestions by, or other biases on the part of, the analyst. Freud seems to recognize that the many layers of interpretation in adult analyses, the analyst's many degrees of freedom in setting the context and deciding on interpretive direction, and the analyst's setting of an overarching explanatory framework offer ample opportunity for the analyst's suggestive manipulation. His reply to this objection, I argued, consisted of his "more direct" analysis of the Hans case. Freud argued that the Hans case lacks the interpretive complexity and the opportunity for unchecked manipulation by suggestion of adult cases, and thus offers some arguments relatively immune to the suggestion objection. Moreover, given the simpler nature of the material, identification and assessment of any suggestions is possible. Yet, Freud argues, the case compellingly converges on the same optimal Oedipal explanation as his adult cases. This, Freud holds, demonstrates that the Oedipal account is unlikely to be an artifact of suggestion and offers independent evidence for both the truth of his Oedipal conclusions in his adult cases and the reliability of the psychoanalytic method that yielded those conclusions.

The suggestion objection holds that Freud's clinical evidence for his theory is contaminated by his suggestions to his patient and other biasing processes. Among other strategies for addressing the suggestion objection in the Hans case, Freud formulated two of his central arguments so as to be largely impervious to the suggestion objection and thus to provide a relevant test of Oedipal theory versus suggestion. One such argument can be formulated as an $N=1$ empirical test based on case data that is independent of possible suggestion. The bold prediction is that the evidence of Hans's changing sexual behaviors over time—including evidence from before the phobia that was recorded in a diary kept by Hans's parents—will reveal a pattern that is derived from Oedipal theory, namely, that Hans experienced an upsurge of sexual desire in the months preceding the phobia; that the symptoms began to occur at the very time that Hans repressed his sexual desires; and that once symptoms began, Hans's sexual desires decreased markedly. This pattern of changing sexual desire is not predicted or explained by the available rival theories. I evaluated the three predictions regarding the trajectory of Hans's sexual desires using criteria of masturbatory self-touching and seeking cuddling with his mother as Freudian indicators of Hans's sexual desires. Examination of the case evidence disconfirmed the predicted trajectory, despite Freud's confident assertions to the contrary. Consequently, this empirical $N=1$ case-study test failed to support the Oedipal theory (see Chapter 8).

Freud's other argument which I labeled the "Suitability Argument," described above, consists of the explanation of otherwise inexplicable detailed features of the patient's symptoms by properties of the hypothesized unconscious traumatic memories. Such connections yield compelling singular causal explanations in terms of meaning connections. In a methodology chapter (Chapter 9), I reviewed the history of this argument and noted its many limitations and weaknesses but also defended its potential viability. I identified it as Freud's central argument in reply to the suggestion objection, and explained why its use in the Hans case largely evades the suggestion objection. In another chapter (Chapter 11), I defended the Suitability Argument as Freud's foundational argument, in opposition to Grunbaum's (1984) rival claim that what Grunbaum famously labeled the "Tally Argument," based on therapeutic efficacy in eliminating symptoms, was Freud's foundational reply to the suggestion objection. In Chapter 10, I carefully assessed the Suitability Argument as Freud applied it to the Hans case, reviewing each of the features of Hans's symptoms that Freud claimed to warrant an Oedipal determinant as an explanation. I found that Freud repeatedly failed to satisfy the demanding criteria that he himself insisted were necessary for the validity of such an interpretation. Freud thus failed to offer cogent evidence in his Hans case history either for his Oedipal interpretation of Hans's phobia or against the suggestion objection or the fright theory. His attempt at offering "more direct" evidence to support his Oedipal theory thus failed.

The arguments Freud presented in support of his Oedipal theory of Hans's horse phobia are also directed against what Freud perceived to be the main rival to his sexual theory of the neuroses, the "fright theory." To this extent, Freud was an "eliminative inductivist" (Edelson, 1984), seeking evidence for his theory that distinguished it from, and disconfirmed, competing theories. Like the suggestion objection, Freud had grappled with the rival fright theory since the very beginning of his theorizing about the neuroses (see Chapter 5). The fright theory focused on immediate traumatic triggers of anxiety as causes of neurosis, and at the outset of the Hans case it did not appear any such traumas were involved, leaving Freud free of this particular objection and offering the opportunity for a clean Oedipal explanatory account. However, late in the case it emerged that a traumatic horse-related event had immediately preceded the onset of Hans's horse phobia. Hans had witnessed a horse pulling a bus-wagon fall down and kick wildly in the streets of Vienna. This unexpectedly brought the fright theory into play as a major alternative to the Oedipal theory in explaining Hans's symptoms. According to this account—later elaborated into a behaviorist critique of Freud's account of the Hans case by Wolpe and Rachman (1960)—the fright from witnessing the horse accident was the full cause of Hans's phobia, and no explanation in terms of deeper Oedipal desires is needed.

Freud dismissed the horse accident as a mere precipitating cause of Hans's phobia but not its ultimate specific cause, which he claimed was Oedipal in nature (see Chapters 5, 6, and 7). He directed two overlapping arguments against the fright theory. First, he claimed that Hans began experiencing undirected anxiety prior to the phobia's onset, so his anxiety condition was broader than what could be explained by reference to the horse accident. Second, Freud disputed the claim that Hans's condition started when he saw the horse fall down, arguing that Hans witnessed the horse accident later in the development of his condition than his opponents claimed. Close examination of the Hans case history revealed that neither of these arguments by Freud is supported by the data reported in the case. Some of the supposed instances of undirected anxiety to which Freud points are likely horse-phobia anxieties that occurred before Hans was willing to admit the source of his fear. Others appear to be Hans's attachment-related anxieties in reaction to his father, who prohibited Hans from cuddling with his mother in the parents' bed. As to the pivotal century-old issue of when the horse fell down, I used previously ignored evidence in the case report to resolve the question. In fact, the horse accident occurred earlier than Freud suggests, so there is no problem with the temporal sequence from the perspective of the fright theory. Freud's arguments thus fail to eliminate the fright theory as a viable account of Hans's phobia.

In the course of this book, I reconstructed and critically examined four central arguments in Freud's commentary on the Hans case materials: the "undirected anxiety" argument (see Chapter 6), the "day the horse fell down" argument (see Chapter 7), the "N=1 sexual repression" argument (see Chapter 8), and the "detailed symptom characteristics" argument (see Chapters 9 and 10). These arguments have not previously been adequately elaborated and evaluated. Interestingly, the arguments are all logically valid (i.e., if their premises about the data observed in the Hans case were true, then their conclusions would follow). To this extent, Freud's arguments are brilliant constructions in scientific rhetoric and evidential logic. However, remarkably, in no case did the claims made by Freud about the Hans case data that formed the premises for these valid arguments turn out to be true—the case record does not support Freud's claims about it. So, in the end, none of the valid arguments were sound.

This result makes assessing Freud's acumen as a scientist and theoretician ambiguous. He appears to be a brilliant, bold, and creative theorist, but one who was totally unable to properly describe the success or failure of his theory's predictions when he looked at the data. It should be kept in mind that Freud, in effect, had two related but separable projects, the clinical project examined here and a philosophy of mind project I have examined elsewhere (Wakefield, 2018). In that examination, I concluded that Freud was indeed a brilliant philosopher and abstract theoretician, whatever his deficiencies were as a clinical scientist. (I thus agree with Adolf Grunbaum's [1984] observation that Freud was a sophisticated methodologist.)

As we saw in Chapter 1, the Oedipal theory either as a universal developmental theory or as a universal theory of neurosogenesis was essentially a long-shot hypothesis to begin with, without independent evidence in its own right. Freud correctly proposed that if the theory was true, it should have some noticeable consequences in child development, in neurosogenesis, and in the nature of the consequent symptoms. All of these processes were closely observed and documented by Hans's parents during Hans's childhood, when they occurred. Freud thus understood that the Hans case was a pivotal test of his theoretical claims. The result was that, in fact, all of the predictions failed and so the Oedipal theory failed. Yet Freud proceeded unperturbed and without acknowledging the true situation.

The Hans case was to stand as the most direct test Freud would ever present for the Oedipal theory. He did not make any subsequent attempts to provide evidence that evaded the acknowledged limitations of his adult psychoanalytic case interpretations or interestingly challenged the suggestion objection. Thus, the implications of Freud's failure in the case are substantial. First, the fright theory is not disconfirmed and remains a plausible account— although I (Wakefield, 2022) have argued that an analysis in terms of attachment theory and the Foucauldian concept of "power/knowledge" illuminates why Hans was disposed to respond to the horse accident as he did. Nor does the case make any dent in the suggestion objection, which remains as potent as ever. Freud's Suitability Argument offers demanding guidelines that go unsatisfied in the Hans case. Freud posed the problem of justifying such singular causal explanations, and we are still without an adequate systematic answer even though this issue lies at the heart of psychoanalytic interpretive constructions.

Most problematically for Freud, the failure of the Hans test leaves him without a reply to the objection that the entire Oedipal theory episode is an instance in which a pseudoscientific ad hoc hypothesis was elevated into a dogma rather than leading to advances in science. Ever since Popper's (1962) initial critique of psychoanalysis as pseudoscientific because it is unfalsifiable—an accusation that, like Grunbaum (1984), I find without merit because in fact the Hans case did provide several potentially falsifying tests—philosophers of science have presented various accounts of when and why the sexual theory became pseudoscientific. The analysis here offers a fresh answer. When Freud used the Hans case to make dramatic predictions based on the ad hoc Oedipal theory, he acted as a scientist who was attempting to turn the falsification of the seduction theory into a scientific advance through a modification of the falsified theory. But, when the test, in fact, falsified the attempted modification, Freud ignored and distorted the nature of the results of the test and embraced the Oedipal theory anyway. In doing so, he departed from acceptable scientific method to a degree that warrants labeling his theory after that point a pseudoscience.

In analyzing and evaluating Freud's specific arguments in the Hans case, I concluded, especially in Chapters 8 and 10, that Freud failed to keep his explanatory promises. Whether or not one agrees with my negative assessment, the reconstruction of Freud's reply to the suggestion objection stands as an independent claim as to how to understand Freud's argument in opposition to the much-discussed "Tally Argument" based on the claim of unique therapeutic success that Grunbaum proposes as Freud's fundamental response to the suggestion objection. I showed in Chapter 11 that Grunbaum's analysis is amply contradicted by Freud's text.

The Oedipal theory must be judged to be exactly what it appears to be: an initially implausible and extraordinarily ad hoc attempt by Freud to save the core thesis, the sexual theory of the neuroses, of his falsified seduction theory at all costs by adjusting auxiliary assumptions in ways that saved the theory but had no independent evidential merit. The Hans case was an attempt to provide the mandatory independent reason to believe the Oedipal theory and thus to overcome the default "pseudoscience" verdict. All of this was perfectly legitimate scientific behavior. When the predictions failed, Freud could have advanced psychoanalysis as science by abandoning his sexual theory of the neuroses and the accompanying sexual nomological hermeneutics that he imposed as a straitjacket on clinical interpretation. He could have repositioned psychoanalysis as a broader idiographic exploration of significant meanings out of focal awareness. When instead Freud ignored the failure, insisted on success, and doubled down by subsequently and repeatedly citing the Hans case as proof that his adult analyses were not hopelessly contaminated by suggestion, he transformed clinical psychoanalysis into what Lakatos calls a degenerating rather than progressive discipline. I would thus argue that at the moment his Hans commentary was published, Freud transformed clinical psychoanalytic theory into a pseudoscience.

The psychoanalytic system of independent training and education institutes meant that the normal corrective mechanisms of scientific criticism did not serve to prevent a century of commitment to an unsupported Oedipal theory as well as the imposition of its mistaken interpretations by well-intentioned analysts on so many trusting patients. Of course, in exploring triangular family dynamics, sometimes the Oedipal theory, used in metaphorical or socially interpreted ways, can be illuminating. But, taken literally as a theory of a universal developmental stage of incestuous sexual desire and patricidal rage, there is no reason to suppose it is true, and the opportunity costs to the discipline of psychoanalysis of a century of fealty to the "shibboleth" has been enormous. Although in the past few decades psychoanalysis has been reconsidering its commitment to the Oedipus complex from a variety of new psychoanalytic perspectives, a solid foundation for progress that does not repeat the mistakes of the past requires a clear acknowledgment and understanding of what went wrong. This book's analysis of Freud's argument in the Hans case will hopefully contribute to such clarity and provide some initial steps toward achieving an improved evidential and epistemological foundation for clinical psychoanalysis.

References

Edelson, M. (1984). *Hypothesis and evidence in psychoanalysis*. Chicago, IL: University of Chicago Press.

Freud, S. (1909). Analysis of a phobia in a five-year-old boy. *SE* 10, 1–150.

Grunbaum, A. (1984). *The foundations of psychoanalysis: A philosophical critique*. Berkeley, CA: University of California Press.

Lakatos, I. (1970). Falsification and the methodology of scientific research programmes. In I. Lakatos & A. Musgrave (Eds.), *Criticism and the growth of knowledge* (pp. 91–196). Cambridge: Cambridge University Press.

Popper, K. R. (1962). *Conjectures and refutations*. New York: Basic Books.

Wakefield, J. C. (2018). *Freud and philosophy of mind, volume 1: Reconstructing the argument for unconscious mental states*. New York: Palgrave Macmillan.

Wakefield, J. C. (2022). *Attachment, sexuality, power: Oedipal theory as regulator of family affection in Freud's case of Little Hans*. New York: Routledge.

Wolpe, J., & Rachman, S. (1960). Psychoanalytic "evidence": A critique based on Freud's case of little Hans. *Journal of Nervous and Mental Disease*, 131(2), 135–148.

Index